# A Journey of Hope

## Oscar Mann

**Hamilton Books**
A member of
The Rowman & Littlefield Publishing Group
*Lanham • Boulder • New York • Toronto • Oxford*

**Copyright © 2005 by**
**Hamilton Books**
4501 Forbes Boulevard
Suite 200
Lanham, Maryland 20706
Hamilton Books Acquisitions Department (301) 459-3366

PO Box 317
Oxford
OX2 9RU, UK

Library of Congress Control Number: 2005930131
ISBN 0-7618-3236-X (paperback : alk. ppr.)

This book is dedicated to the memories of our mother and father. He was a father who devoted his life to his family. She was a mother who was always there for John and me.

This book is also dedicated to the memories of our cousins, Isor Gildenhorn and Oscar Rozansky, who jointly made it possible for mother, John and me to come to America and experience the American dream.

# Contents

# Foreword

There have been times when I believed Oscar Mann, who became my doctor after my heart attack, to be a saint. Now, after reading his book, I know for a fact that he is.

His story, told in his straightforward manner, is that of a man of compassion and accomplishment, who had the courage to have big dreams when even small dreams seemed impossible. Oscar is, in short, a child of France and the Holocaust, who grew to be a saint of America.

I define sainthood not in religious terms but in the language of caring and service. I speak from personal experience.

On two different occasions, he took specific actions as a physician that saved the lives of my wife Kate and me. As my doctor, he detected ominous signs that I was about to have a second heart attack in time to prevent such a thing from happening. With Kate, he answered our daughter's telephoned plea to come to a hospital emergency room, where he quickly saw that Kate was slipping away. Ignoring the hospital staff, he did what needed to be done to save Kate.

And this is only the most dramatic cream of his crop. Time after time, Oscar routinely answered other pleas for help from us and other family members, as well as several of my professional colleagues. Oscar was always there with his comforting words and brilliant assessments and diagnoses. He was also smart enough to know what he didn't know. On numerous occasions I bore witness to his ragging a particular specialist to give him another opinion on an xray, a troublesome cough, a perplexing ache.

Oscar Mann was the single best practicing physician I ever had or ever heard of. Many others with whom I shared his time and star agree with me. I know that for a fact because swapping "Oscar stories" is something we all did —and, with great joy, still do.

My first relationship with Oscar Mann was as his patient. It was quickly on to friendship and finally, now, to worship. We, the Oscar Patients, are truly the fortunate ones—the blessed ones.

On behalf of them all I say: *Thank you, Oscar.*

Washington DC
March 14, 2004
Jim Lehrer

# Preface

*A Journey of Hope* is a personal story. It spans more than seventy years, the latter two-thirds of the 20th and the beginning of the 21st century. It moves from one continent to a new world—from Europe, the "old country," to the United States of America, a young nation. It involves experiences that run the gamut from great sorrow to great joy.

Mother was a young widow with two small children in war-ravaged Europe. Cousins made it possible for us to come from Paris to Washington, where we settled. Once we were here, things began to go right for us. Instead of peddling clothing in the old country, John and I became doctors in America.

It has been said that gratitude is a learned feeling, that few are born with a sense of gratitude. I don't know if I was born with it or not, but my sense of gratitude has been with me for some time—to those who gave me life, helped save my life and helped me improve the quality of my life.

This book is my way of expressing my enormous sense of gratitude. I want to pass along to others what I have learned about the life-sustaining value of hope and the life-enriching expression of gratitude. To say that I have been lucky is true, but wholly inadequate. I have been truly blessed.

I was born Oscar Mankowski on October 13, 1934, at the Rothschild Hospital in Paris, France. My brother was born José Mankowski on November 9, 1936, at the Cochin Hospital, also in Paris. José is not a common name for a first-generation Jewish child, born in Paris of parents from Dombrowitz, Poland. John's given name in Hebrew was Yeshua and in Yiddish, Josi. The French authorities who wrote birth certificates were unfamiliar with these names, so they substituted José, which was a name known to them.

Now we are Oscar Mann, M.D., and John J. Mann, M.D., our names having been anglicized during the naturalization process for U.S. citizenship.[1]

Our parents moved to Paris in the early 1930s from Dombrowitz, which was a village in eastern Poland. They moved in order to seek a better opportunity and to escape the approaching clouds of war. They had a hunch of impending doom.

Our father, Aaron Mankowski, was arrested by the French police on behalf of the Nazis on charges of being Jewish and maintaining a business. The French turned him over to the Nazis for transportation to a "work camp." The French escorted the railway carriage to the German border. Auschwitz was the next stop. Our father was murdered at Auschwitz on June 19, 1942, when he was 40 years old. Our mother was Hinda Biegun Mankowski, her name having been anglicized to Helen Mann, when she became a naturalized U.S. citizen in April, 1962. My mother lived in the *Washington, DC* area and survived to an old age.

Most of this story is from my memory. Friends and relatives have supplied many more facts and details.

In the late 1890s, there were three sisters, the Eisenbergs, in our ancestral Polish village of Dombrowitz. These sisters married and gave birth to many children. My mother, Hinda, and her cousins, Oscar Rozansky and Isor Gildenhorn, were among these children.

In the same era, the elder sister of a Leibel Antel married a Mankowski, but their first names are no longer available for research purposes because the Nazis and the Poles destroyed Jewish birth records. Aaron Mankowski, my father, came from that union, thus making Leibel Antel his uncle.

In the next generation, Aunt Vittle, my mother's sister, married Leibel Antel. Oscar and Shirley, now in Canada, are their offspring. My mother married Aaron Mankowski. John and I are the children of that marriage. My maternal family was one of the town's oldest and most eminent Jewish families. My father also came from one of Dombrowitz's most respected Jewish families. Mother met her future husband through family introductions, as was the custom. Even in that village, there was a social stratification among families, and people were expected to marry only those within their own class.

Many males of my family have been named Asher in Hebrew, which, when anglicized, becomes Oscar. Each is set in his appropriate time and place. Our family tree is reproduced at the beginning of Appendix 1.

## NOTES

1. I was naturalized on February 26, 1954, in Columbia, South Carolina, and John, on January 10, 1961, in the District of Columbia.

# Acknowledgments

This book records the events of my life on the journey from Europe to America. It includes my experiences in Europe and America, and my encounters with the people I met along the way. My brother, John, who has traveled much of the same road, carefully reviewed this work, chapter by chapter, for accuracy. John also contributed two important sections to this book. His quest to find our ancestral roots and his pilgrimage to Auschwitz, where our father was murdered, expanded my own knowledge and enhanced my memories of those years. I am deeply indebted to John.

Mrs. James Fletcher (Fay Fletcher) gave me the idea and impetus for writing this book. She also provided tenacious prodding and great logistical support. Fay Fletcher's bottomless reservoir of enthusiasm nurtured this project to completion.

Mrs. Edmund H. Feldman (Fran Feldman) provided additional ongoing encouragement, as well as assistance in expressing my thoughts and feelings about hope and gratitude in the Preface. She also helped me to draw the distinction between "Oscar" and "Dr. Mann" in chapter 20.

Hedrick Smith sat down with me before I began writing and generously gave me his time and advice. He helped me plan the outline for my book. With him, I decided on a theme and title.

Mary Bennett from Foxhall Internists was always there for me with secretarial support. She was a strong shoulder to cry on whenever I "lost" a chapter in the labyrinth of my computer.

I received editorial guidance from a powerful "editing mill" consisting of family members, friends, medical school classmates, former colleagues and patients. I also called on various people for their help with the "nuts and bolts" of writing the book. My thanks go to many people. My hope is to slight no one.

First, I recognize my wife, Amy, who rigorously edited the text, line by line, page by page. She performed this laborious task nearly every day.

Frank Weiner, Frank Fowler, Frank MacMurray, Ian Spence, Charles Duvall and Caro Luhrs, as well as Barbara Weiner, Bruce MacLaury, Fran Feldman, John Bouchard, William Dabaghi and Oscar Antel carefully proofread, analyzed and edited each chapter.

John Dobrin challenged me to reveal more of myself. He and his late wife, Maryse Pailla, helped me rid the book of extraneous material, and thus, "tighten" the text.

Henry Safrit, Tom Magovern, Joseph Giere and Charles Tartaglia, together with Darby Rove, Karin Safrit, Richard Rivers, Jed Babbin, Barbara Burnett, Julie and Urban Lester, Ginny MacLaury, Mary Tapparo and the late Leo Welt, were particularly constructive in their feedback and commentary during the writing of this book. So was my overseas friend, François Durelle, who added a "French voice" to this effort. They were my Internet and old-fashioned "snail mail" cheerleading support group.

Stefan Pasternack helped me develop the material about the parallel between Europe in the late 1930s and America in the early 2000s. He also assisted me in dealing with the emotional aspects of revisiting the painful events of my life, and he contributed to all the psychiatric passages.

Several of my distinguished peers—John C. Rose, Jack Stapleton, William Gilbert, Raymond Holden, Clifton Gruver and Tom Magovern—scrutinized my chapters relating to medicine. Francis Barnes and the late Zigmond Lebensohn diligently reviewed the section on psychiatry in chapter 15. All of my medical critics, moreover, reviewed selected nonmedical passages.

Additionally, I was privileged to bounce my manuscript off diverse and open-minded readers who gave me a wide spectrum of opinion. Judy Woodruff, Kate Lehrer, Drs. Stephen Green, Marty Allen, Andrew Umhau, Michael Petite and Alexander Chester, as well as Beverly Etter, the late Jane Schwartz (Amy's mother), Harry McPherson, Berl Bernhard, Jeannette Petite, Avis Strader, Corky Vance and Maria Difrancesco, proved to be a balanced and discriminating audience. Barbara Abramowitz, the wife of Rabbi A. Nathan Abramowitz, an authority on the Holocaust, and Professor Joseph Drew, President of the Anglo-American University, Prague, Czech Republic, a scholar of Jewish and World War II history, gave my manuscript an academic boost.

Mariah French, Tom Campbell, Linda Winslow, Annette Miller and Sandi Fox helped me assiduously to establish the names of the physicians on the Vietnam Memorial Wall.

Henry Buchtal, a former patient, who is an experienced and no-nonsense editor, was my chief guru. He made me toe the line. I spent many hours implementing his modifications. He is, more importantly, a gentleman!

I am most appreciative of the efforts made by the genial and talented people at University Press/Hamilton Books to shepherd my manuscript to successful publication in a format that is both pleasingly attractive and superbly produced. I thank them also for their continued goodwill on my behalf: Judith Rothman, Beverly Baum, Michael Marino, Dean Roxanis, and Johanna Dunkel.

And, last but far from least, Jim Lehrer wrote a generous foreword to *A Journey of Hope* and gave me wise guidance. For this, I tender Jim my deep appreciation, in addition to my long-standing admiration and affection.

Others, unidentified, contributed in many ways. To this large group of un-heralded people, I apologize, while extending my gratitude. I certainly have neither forgotten nor ignored their efforts.

I, of course, take full responsibility for whatever flaws may remain.

For supplemental photographs please visit www.journeyofhope.info.

*Part One*

# GOING TO AMERICA

## Chapter One

# Baltimore and Our Family

*A Journey of Hope* opens on a contemporary scene and flashback daydreaming. My reverie includes a sentimental look at the past, a realistic view of the present and a hopeful glimpse at the future.

It is March 24, 2001. Our clan, including relatives from Winnipeg and Montreal, is gathered at the Cross Keys Village Motel in Baltimore. My niece, Gilda, my brother John's eldest daughter, my mother's first grandchild, is getting married. Her husband to be, Brian Zimmet, is bright, pleasant, a great fellow, and a welcome addition to the family. Our mother would have so much wanted to be here to share this moment with us. She would have been joyous and exultant.

The rehearsal dinner is at the Joy America Café, overlooking the Inner Harbor. The morning of the wedding, I have an early breakfast with my wife, Amy, and my twin daughters, Anna and Karen. They and all my relatives seem to have things to do. I decide to take the opportunity for a solo sightseeing tour around Baltimore.

My Ethiopian driver, Eyob, is a lively guide, well acquainted with the city. He is both talkative and discreet, and I sense he will respect my moments of privacy. While touring scenic areas of Baltimore in a comfortable automobile, I become pleasantly relaxed. Soon, I begin to contemplate, reflect and reminisce about our coming to America, about my brother John, and his Baltimore. This American city is of particular resonance for my family because our maternal grandfather, Asher, once had a long love affair with Baltimore.

The pleasant sightseeing tour proceeds without my attention, as I drop off to a tranquil nap. After a while, I sense a sudden change of momentum as my car crawls to a standstill on the grounds of the B&O Railroad Museum. I wake up from my sleep, and from the car I observe a towering display of locomotives and carriages. The scale of these massive machines seems to energize

3

everyone who comes near them, and it also reminds me that Baltimore was a major hub when travel by train was in its heyday.

I begin to envision old Baltimore. Over the years, Baltimore developed vibrant Jewish neighborhoods, neighborhoods which would later be celebrated in films such as *Avalon*, *Diner* and *Liberty Heights* by producer Barry Levinson, himself a Baltimore native. While filming *Liberty Heights*, Barry Levinson became ill. The diagnosis was not clear. The renowned producer appeared to those close to him to be extremely ill. In time, John was called in, a correct diagnosis was established, and patient Levinson made a complete recovery. The premiere of *Liberty Heights*, held in Baltimore, was dedicated to Johns Hopkins Hospital in honor of John.

Our next stop is a majestic edifice with a golden dome, the Billings Building, the old long-time Broadway Street main entrance to Johns Hopkins Hospital, where my driver proudly informs me that Hopkins is the world's top medical center. He also says it is Baltimore's largest employer. I tell my guide about my cardiac bypass surgery episode at Hopkins, a year earlier, and how I was impressed by the excellence of the institution.

We drive to the new Inner Harbor, near Fells Point. This fashionable high-rise residential development, bordering on a stylish state-of-the-art marina, is an idyllic spot. I could happily live there. We then see the Lloyd Street synagogue, a venerable Jewish religious site. This well-established synagogue, built in 1845, is the third oldest in the United States. I am amazed by its grandeur.

I begin to daydream that this may well be the place where my grandfather, Asher Biegun, worshiped nearly a hundred years ago. In the first part of the twentieth century, Baltimore, an aging, cosmopolitan Maryland city, had been home for a time to our maternal grandfather, Asher Biegun.

In the early 1900's, Baltimore was a shelter for many Jewish immigrants as it was unusually attractive to them for several reasons. First, the "Jewishness" of Baltimore was a powerful enticement. Second, Baltimore was a vital railway departure point for Chicago, Cleveland, Denver and many other destinations, thus becoming a major embarkation area for westbound immigrants. Third, Baltimore was a major commercial port, and for both good and bad historical reasons, Jews have long been a significant part of the world of commerce, especially in retailing. Many immigrants stayed in Baltimore, where they established the textile and clothing trades. Their children often continued in these businesses, forming many successful mercantile families. These immigrants and their descendants provided a dynamic center of Jewish life and commerce in Baltimore. The Jewish aspects of Baltimore expanded with the arrival of orthodox Eastern European Jews. Kosher butchers flourished throughout Baltimore, supported by the growing Jewish population.

Ritual slaughtering, my grandfather's trade, became a thriving occupation. Our maternal grandfather recognized the opportunities available for a *shochet*

(Jewish term for a ritual slaughterer) in the early 1900s along the eastern seaboard of America. The city of Baltimore lured Asher Biegun from distant Dombrowitz, and he so liked and appreciated Baltimore that he became a citizen of the United States.

In June 1998, brother John began an Eastern European pilgrimage to our ancestral village. I recollect that John's diary of his trip mentions grandfather:

*My maternal grandfather, Asher Biegun, left Dombrowitz around 1912 and actually came to Baltimore where he worked as a ritual butcher or shochet. He was trapped by World War I in Baltimore until at least 1919. He must have been a very frugal man since he saved $10,000, which he brought back with him to the village. This was an extraordinary sum of money, since $500 was enough to buy a house. He had planned to bring his wife and children to the United States, but his wife, Sarah, thought the United States was too savage a country and refused to leave Dombrowitz.[1]*

Grandfather was never to know that his great granddaughter, Gilda, would some day be married in Baltimore, the city he loved. Inasmuch as my grandfather never returned to America, he was not to be happy again. Mother said he constantly grieved for America, a syndrome well known to immigrants who return to the Old World. I was to experience similar feelings myself after our trip to North America in the summer of 1948. I hope that people fortunate enough to be born in the United States can understand and appreciate this unique form of bereavement. What it says about America, I believe, speaks volumes.

In a state of continued reverie, during a leisurely lunch at Legal Sea Food near the Inner Harbor, I reflect on how Baltimore has been such a part of our family. After a while and two double regular espresso coffees, the trance is over. I am fully awake and ready for a wedding ceremony.

The black-tie wedding is a lavish affair at the venerable but recently restored Belvedere Hotel. Risa and her daughter, Gilda, radiate beauty and happiness. Younger sister Stacie is charming and ebullient. John is beaming. Wonderful people dance to lively music. Gourmet food, fine champagne and wines add festivity to the serious ritual of a Jewish marriage. All the Johns Hopkins medical faculty, it seems, have attended the grand affair. John and I are a long way from the suburban market stalls of Paris. The account of my journey begins below.

## NOTE

1. Personal communication from John J. Mann, October 2002.

## Chapter Two

# Dombrowitz, Our Ancestral Village

Dombrowitz has been home to our people for ages. Before World War II, there were seven thousand people in the village, half of them Jews. Rovno was the nearest large city, with a population of forty-five thousand; it was located about one hundred kilometers and a four hour train ride from Dombrowitz. Warsaw was about five hundred kilometers away; the train trip took almost a day and a half. Trains were slow in that region during the first part of the twentieth century. Depending on weather, rain and mud, there could be substantial delays. In those days, getting to the train station by horse and wagon could add to the travel time.

The Jewish section of Dombrowitz contained religious and secular schools, scholars, rabbis, teachers, merchants, artisans and storekeepers. The Gentile section of Dombrowitz was populated mostly by Ukranian and Polish farmers. The two economies, Jewish and Gentile, complemented each other. The Jewish population purchased food produced by the Ukranian and Polish family farmers; the Gentiles, in turn, bought clothing, shoes and other finished products from the Jewish merchants and shopkeepers. Most people had no electricity until 1935. There was no running water or indoor plumbing. Water was obtained from wells or the river. Few were wealthy enough to have their own horses and traps, so transportation was by rented horse and wagon.

In the first half of the twentieth century, the area changed hands several times. Dombrowitz was at times in Poland, at times in the Ukraine. And from 1917 to 1918 and again in World War II, the town was occupied by Germans. Russia invaded eastern Poland in 1939, capturing the area of which Rovno was the administrative capital. This was part of the deal struck by Hitler and Stalin, their "Non-Aggression Pact" as it was termed by German Ambassador von Ribbentrop. This short-lived agreement was soon broken by Hitler. The

Nazis, during their Russian campaign in 1941, would occupy all of Poland before losing it in 1945 to the Soviet Army. Once again Dombrowitz had to adjust and adapt to a new political reality.

At the turn of the twentieth century, Dombrowitz was a lively, thriving town with a vital Jewish presence. Most of the Jewish community was composed of religious, though not Hasidic, Jews. The Sabbath was strictly kept. All holy days were observed, and all families ate in accordance with kosher dietary laws. There were five synagogues in the town, as well as two Jewish cemeteries.

Gradually, the Polish government made it impossible for Jews, burdened with high taxes and restrictive laws, to thrive. Wisely, our maternal grandfather, Asher Biegun, decided to explore other prospects in America. He lived almost a decade in Baltimore and when he came back to Dombrowitz in 1921, he returned with enough money to provide dowries for several daughters. His money was soon gone. Upon Asher's return to Dombrowitz, his wife, Sarah, distanced herself from him—Europeans who disliked America often were and still are unfriendly toward anyone associated with America. *"Der Amerikaner"* (German for the American) *is no longer one of us; he is no longer from Dombrowitz*, was her chant, according to my mother. He withered away in the old village while longing for America and brooding over a return to Baltimore with his family. He lived only a few years after his return from America, never achieving his dream of going back to Baltimore. He died a broken man and his death profoundly affected my mother and her siblings. They grieved for a long time.

Mother's older brother, Yosel, was the respected head of the Hebrew school, known as the Tarbut School. Mother finished high school before going on to take two additional years of Yiddish and Hebrew studies at Tarbut. She, along with her sisters, trained to become a seamstress. They were all good dressmakers, while their mother ran the family dress shop. In spite of their pooled talent, they only made a modest living.

There were three Mankowski siblings. The eldest was Asher. Next came Borakh. The youngest Aaron, my father. All three brothers served in the Polish Army in the late 1920s. My uncles, both Partisans, fought bravely and helped rescue Jews throughout 1944, before finally helping liberate towns— including Dombrowitz—during early 1945.[1]

Dombrowitz continued to be an active center of Jewish life until the beginning of WWII, although daily existence remained precarious. The older folks stayed on even as many younger people were moving away. Members of my family began to leave our ancestral home. My parents left Dombrowitz in 1931, as did so many others, because they wanted an opportunity to succeed. There was no future in Dombrowitz. The worldwide depression hit

Poland hard in 1929 and again in 1938, with the economy doing poorly between those years. In the early part of the twentieth century, the town was vibrant, but by the 1930s, people barely survived. Additionally, there were the
pogroms of the 1930s, during which Jews were massacred by Polish bigots.
Mother told me about these practices and the extreme terror the pogroms
caused among the Jewish population in Poland.

Uncle Leibel Antel and his wife, Vittle, my mother's sister, decided to
leave Poland along with my parents. They had wished to come to America but
with Asher Biegun deceased, all chances to go were now gone. Emigrating to
the United States in the late 1920s was no longer an option for them as the restrictive Polish quota filled quickly. It could only be bypassed by having a
first degree relative (husbands, wives, fathers, mothers, sons or daughters)
who held U.S. citizenship. These facts precluded my immediate family from
going to America in the 1930s.

As a second choice, their plan was to go to Canada. Uncle Leibel was able
to emigrate to Winnipeg, Canada, in 1929. My aunt Vittle and their children,
Oscar and Shirley, joined him in 1930. My parents were to emigrate to
Canada as soon as visas could be obtained. Historically, Canada had maintained an open but limited immigration policy, notably toward Eastern European Jews, Ukrainians and Russians. Unfortunately, in the early 1930s,
Canada chose to curtail its immigration policy and to close its doors to immigrants.[2]

Unable to emigrate to Canada, my parents decided to relocate to France.
During the 1930s, correspondence between my mother in France and her sister in Canada was maintained but after the French surrender in 1940, the war
cut off all communications.

Some of our relatives, along with many other fortunate Jews, left eastern
Poland for the New World between the early 1900s and the late 1930s. Most
of those who remained in Europe perished. My own family was no exception.
Out of ten siblings, two sisters, my aunt Vittle and my mother Hinda (Helen),
were the only two who survived the war. Yosel, a pillar of the Jewish community, was killed in Dombrowitz. Motel died in France as the war was winding down. My mother's remaining sisters had moved to other towns in
Poland. All were annihilated in the Holocaust. On father's side, only Borakh
outlived the war.

Most Dombrowitz Jews who perished remain nameless. They must not be
forgotten. John's words, from the diary of his 1998 pilgrimage, compellingly
tell of their fate:

*Oscar Antel* [our cousin from Winnipeg, Canada, who, with two of his children,
accompanied my brother John on his pilgrimage] *told me that most of the Jews*

in Dombrowitz were gathered by the Germans, marched to Sarny and executed in a mass grave. Another large group was shot in a mass grave in the cemetery of Dombrowitz. Part of our trip will be to search for these places and say a prayer for our families.

This brings me back to my trip and its purpose. The exact purpose is not entirely clear to me. I want to see where my mother and her family were born and raised. I remember hearing over and over the same stories related by my mother about the village. I do not expect to find much, but I would like to walk on the streets where she played and spent her first twenty-two years. Also, I need to rediscover my father. I think that my only memory of father is seeing him getting dressed on the day that he was arrested, although this may be a learned memory rather than a true memory.

Oscar Antel guided my walk. We seemed, for a while, to be lost . . . .

Finally, Oscar was able to find a bridge which led to the Jewish neighborhood and Oscar's house. That bridge crossed the river which was near Oscar's parents' house. It was a beautiful area with a wide river, lush fields, trees, and many bathers. It was also the bridge over which many of the Dombrowitz Jews were marched to the train for execution in Sarny. Several of the Jews apparently jumped off the bridge or its encampment and were able to hide in the forest. Some were killed by farmers. Some apparently were helped. Survivors probably joined the underground resistance movement or moved into a better area. Several survivors found their way to Winnipeg, Canada.

All of the stones from the old Jewish graves had been removed by the Germans during World War II and used to build roads or fortifications. Mrs. Naiman, one of the few surviving Jewish local residents, had lost two daughters at a very young age, and they had been buried in that old cemetery before World War II. There was a stone monument marking the combination of two mass graves where the eighteen hundred Jews were shot in 1941. Since we had a large entourage, we said Kaddish—a prayer for the dead—in memory of our family. I certainly could not prove that we had ten true Jews but it seemed appropriate. The Kaddish was recited together by Oscar Antel and me. It was a very moving experience for us. In addition to the stone monument which had been built fairly recently, there were two or three stone bases in a field near the monument. They represented the only remaining grave monuments. The cemetery was located on flat land without any sign or marker except for the simple monument. The cemetery was surrounded by no walls or gates. The monument was erected by the Dombrowitz community some time in the last ten years. This is the cemetery where many members of our family, including my grandfather, were buried. It is also most likely that many of my mother's sisters were shot in the grave. The rest were marched and killed in Sarny.

After a sad and emotional visit to the cemetery, we drove to the buildings which were the sites of two of the five Dombrowitz synagogues. Again there was no marking, sign or evidence of their previous use. One building appeared unoccupied, and the other building appeared to serve as a local hairdressing salon. The outside walls had been plastered, and there was no sign of a mezuzah (symbol of a Jewish home adorning a door frame) *slot or other evidence of a Jewish presence. However, the local people were unanimous in telling us that these were two of the synagogues present in Dombrowitz before World War II.*

*I think that this is an appropriate time to relate the history of Borakh Mankowski, my father's brother. My father left the village in 1931 to go to Paris. One of his brothers, Asher, died as a Jewish partisan in the arms of his brother Borakh during World War II. His wife and child emigrated to Toronto, and we did not meet them until several years ago in Toronto. Borakh stayed in the region and became an important part of the underground. Prior to the arrival of the Germans in Dombrowitz, he had tried to warn the Jewish population. At that time, Dombrowitz contained about four thousand Jews. Many of the younger people left, but the older ones did not. Borakh became the head of the local underground and was instrumental in trying to protect the Jews from the local population. His story is related in the* Dombrowitz Yizkor Book.[3]

*Oscar Antel has a copy of this book and I am trying to obtain a copy for myself, although it is written in Yiddish and Hebrew only.*

*Borakh threatened and apparently even killed a couple of the non-Jewish farmers who had attacked the Jews. After the Germans came in, the underground grew eventually to a force of fifty thousand which included Jews and non-Jews. They were very important in attacking the rear lines of the German army as it was moving toward Russia. Borakh distinguished himself sufficiently so that he became a full colonel in the Russian army. After the liberation of this region by the Russians, the local commissar was Khrushchev who eventually became head of the U.S.S.R. Khruschev met with ten important leaders of the underground to congratulate them. He shook hands with everyone except with Borakh. At that point, Borakh understood that there was no place for the Jews in the Russian scheme of things, and he then moved to Israel where he died many years later. Oscar Antel tells me that many of the members of the partisans came to his funeral. I am sorry that I never got to know him, but I am proud to know that he was a member of my family.*

Today Dombrowitz is called Dubrovica and lies in the Ukraine. The population of Dubrovica is approximately eleven thousand, but no more than ten Jews live there now. The Jewish culture that flourished there for centuries is no more. Dombrowitz, as it once was, will never be again. May the spirit of our people, marked by rugged vitality, strength of character, resourcefulness and individualism, survive in us and our children.

## NOTES

1. Partisans were the Underground Russian Forces.

2. *Leaving Poland*, by Oscar Antel, is recommended additional reading. It appears in full at Appendix 4.

3. *Yizkor* means memorial. This particular memorial book was titled the *Sefer* (the Book), in Hebrew. The *Sefer* is the black book issued in Israel by the *Landsmanschaft* from Dombrowitz during December 1964. *Landsmanschaft*, a Yiddish expression, denotes the society or group of people who came from a common area or land.

# Chapter 3

# Idyllic Days In France

We believe that our parents were united in a religious service in Poland. They stepped off the train in Paris in April 1931, seeking a start at a better life. The legal civil marriage of record took place sometime in May at the *Mairie du Quatrième Arrondissement* (City Hall of the Fourth Municipal District of Paris), *Place Baudoyer*.

Their sponsor was Motel Biegun, mother's younger brother. He came to France earlier as a student to do graduate work, and subsequently received a degree in electrical engineering from the University of Grenoble. Motel was proud of his achievement, spoke fluent French with no accent, and was deeply Francophile. He even changed his name to Maurice Bieguin, and became a powerful anchor for my parents in France. My parents learned the French language quickly, but a Polish accent forever colored their speech.

John and I were born in the mid-1930s. We lived then within walking distance of Notre Dame in the *Quartier Saint Paul*, located in the *Marais*, a well-known sector of Paris.[1] Then an old, crowded and dingy area of Paris, today it is a fashionable, high-priced and exceedingly desirable neighborhood with no less than six synagogues within a few blocks of where we lived.[2]

Our apartment was on the *rue de Sévigné*, a street named for the vivacious letter-writing marquise, *Mme de Sévigné*. She had lived in the *Hotel Carnavalet*, on our street, from 1677 to 1696. The *Hotel Carnavalet* today is known as the *Musée Carnavalet*, the museum of the history of the City of Paris. Our street branched off from the *rue de Rivoli* which was a busy artery running east to west on the right bank. The *rue de Rivoli* extended from the *Place de la Concorde* and became the *rue Saint Antoine*, a bustling commercial street leading to the *Place de la Bastille*, just east of our street.

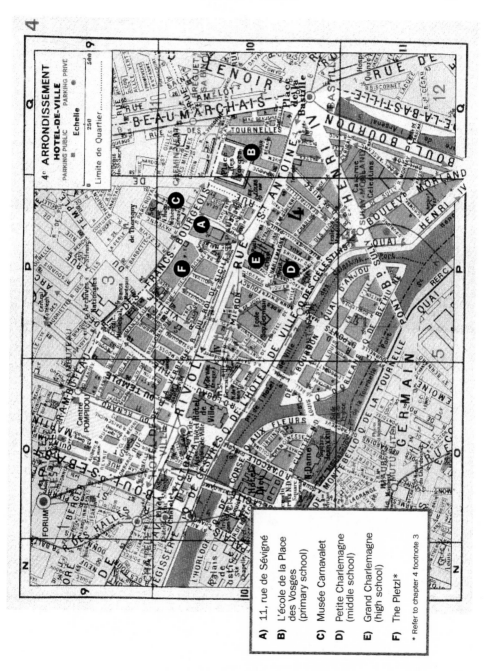

A) 11, rue de Sévigné

B) L'école de la Place des Vosges (primary school)

C) Musée Carnavalet

D) Petite Charlemagne (middle school)

E) Grand Charlemagne (high school)

F) The Pletzl*

\* Refer to chapter 4 footnote 3

The nearest subway station was the *Metro Saint Paul*, between the *Hotel de Ville* and the *Place de la Bastille* metro stations, on a busy subway line running from *Pont de Neuilly* to the *Porte de Vincennes*. *Metro Saint Paul* was about two blocks from the *rue de Sévigné* and one block from the *Pletzl*,[3] a name describing a group of streets converging on the *rue des Rosiers*. This ancient neighborhood became home to a vibrant soul of Yiddish culture. The *Pletzl* has been a focus of ethnic life, dating back to medieval times and, over the centuries, has flourished as a center of Jewish culture in France. The *Pletzl* over time has also been a commercial center, well-patronized by Parisians and tourists, Gentiles and Jews alike.

John and I were too young to have much awareness beyond the scope of our parents' lives. In later years, as I read and attempted to understand twentieth century history, I have often found myself imagining how I would have coped with the challenges presented to our young parents during this period. Aside from making a living and raising a family, what were their worries? I feel certain that as recent immigrants from Poland, they were following public events with great attention and increasing anxiety. Did they feel secure in France? Did they consider emigrating to yet another country? Or were they oblivious, indecisive, and was complacency a result of their illusion? I can only speculate from what I remember.

It was the mid-1930s. Hitler had come to power on January 10, 1933. He was welcomed exuberantly by most Germans and even by many non-Germans living outside Germany. These people, including some from England and France, thought that the political and economic chaos in Germany that had characterized the period of the Weimar Republic had finally come to an end. People believed that order would be restored, communism would soon disappear, trains would run on time, economic growth would be re-established, inflation would be tamed and employment revived, and things would be good for everyone. Bauhaus, that crucible of modernism in Germany, with its utopian dream of a technological society based on simple principles, was gone by October, 1933. Expressionism in the German art world would soon experience a similar fate.

Few people realized that a storm was threatening Western civilization. Impending disaster during this period was not part of the conventional wisdom. The underlying premises of this viewpoint were fundamentally flawed and they can be summarized as follows:

*Hitler was an aberration and his flowering would be short lived. A country as politically, intellectually and scientifically advanced as Germany would not tolerate such a person for long. The Maginot Line would prevent German troops from overrunning France. The line was impregnable and would preserve*

*France's territorial integrity. Britain and France were invincible. Then, too, there was the United States of America to depend on. German Jews and Jews elsewhere throughout Europe felt secure.*

Yet, all of Europe was no match for the little Austrian corporal and wall paper hanger, who defied the conventional wisdom, challenged the order of the world, and came perilously close to triumph.

Life outside the approaching hurricane went on. Father was a dynamic person, an entrepreneur and a workaholic. He soon became adept at outdoor marketing. He mastered the open-air clothing trade in Bezons and Houille, both blue collar zones, and in Argenteuil, a white-collar zone. Bezons and Houille boasted the greatest concentration of *ouvriers d'usine* or factory workers of any towns in France. Argenteuil, on the other hand, had become comparatively upscale as a bedroom community to Paris. It was sustained by artists, poets and painters, who all enhanced its prestige. Renoir and Monet painted some of their most famous works there.[4] These were mostly boat and river scenes as well as paintings of the bridges over the Seine depicting the river as it meandered through Argenteuil. It must have been a very colorful place for our father to work. In addition, Argenteuil was also a town known for its horse racing. Father on occasion took his business to special event markets or fairs in various towns, some far from Paris.

While many traders still operated from push carts and small motor vehicles, Father acquired a big Citroën *camion* (truck) which was absolutely essential for a flourishing open-air trader. He shortly expanded his business by hiring two able young men, Guy Huchon and Benjamin Roditis. Both would later play a significant role in our story. Mother became a full-time homemaker who only rarely went to help at the market stalls. I do not remember any adverse impact of the Great Depression on our life in those days.

Our family rented a spacious apartment in an old, well-structured building at 11 *rue de Sévigné*, located near the Jewish quarter in a middle class neighborhood of the *Marais*. Our building qualified as a historical site because it was linked to the French Revolution of 1789. The lore had it that there had once been an escape tunnel connecting the infamous Bastille with the next apartment building, at 13 *rue de Sévigné*. There was a rumor that our building had been involved in it too.

In our two-story building, the rear section of our apartment was adjacent to a *Caserne des Pompiers* or firehouse and barracks for the famed firefighters of Paris. They were a full-time force and part of both the French Army and the Parisian Police. From our windows, my brother and I were thrilled to watch the *Pompiers* perform their daily exercise routine going through advanced fire-fighting and military training.

Our building at 11 *rue de Sévigné* also featured an attractive compact court-yard and a public bath house called "Les G^ds BAINS-DOUCHES,"[5] which was renowned for its *bains de vapeur* or steam rooms. Best of all, a famous Hungarian delicatessen, *Les Produits Hongrois*, attracted an elite clientele from greater Paris to our building. In the apartment below us lived and worked a skilled craftsman, who was an expert restorer of rare watches and antique clocks. His reputation also brought affluent people to our *rue de Sévigné*. Our address was becoming known. As I remember, several Jewish families lived on our street but surprisingly none of the other tenants at 11 *rue de Sévigné* were Jewish. Our apartment neighbors were genuinely friendly decent people, who were always courteous toward us, and in turn we felt very comfortable with them as our Gentile neighbors.

John and I were enrolled in a well-known public primary school, *l'école de la Place des Vosges*, a mostly Gentile all-boys' school. Our Jewish friends attended a mostly Jewish all-boys' school in the *Marais*. I am not certain why John and I attended a different school from our friends, although our parents may have thought that the standing of the *Place des Vosges* school would facilitate our entering the competitive French secondary education system.

Our parents were ambitious for us. They very much wanted John and me to assimilate into French society. We were taught French and only French from our birth. My parents did not speak Polish at home and would resort to Yiddish only to keep things from us.

After the war, I learned that many French children of the Holocaust, several of whom lived on *rue de Sévigné*, were taken from *l'école de la Place des Hospitalières Saint Gervais* for deportation. In fact, one hundred and eighty boys were deported from that school. Fortunately, the director of the school, Maître Mineret, saved numerous boys from concentration camps by obtaining forged papers for them. With these documents, many boys were able to escape to relative freedom in the *Zone Libre* or Unoccupied France. Two of these lucky boys were my best childhood friends, Georges and Marcel Steinberg, who from unoccupied France fled to Switzerland. They spent the remainder of the war in safety. The name Mineret has been duly inscribed in the Book of Righteous Gentiles in Israel.

The Steinbergs lived across the street at 14 *rue de Sévigné*. Their father, Chaim Steinberg, was a self-employed furrier. He was a devout Jew who prayed daily in *teffilin*[6] and a *tallis* [7]. On Saturday, the Jewish Sabbath, he did not work, but went to synagogue and to the consternation of his wife, worked on Sundays instead. She complained that this work pattern was wrong for Paris; it was ruining their leisure time. Their four children were Georges, Marcel, Lili and Renée. Georges and Marcel became our inseparable friends. Lili, their older sister, would sometimes join us with Renée still in her crib.

John and I were fascinated by the baby. Georges, Marcel, John and I would often play together in our courtyard or in the playgrounds of the *Place des Vosges*, under the watchful eyes of our mothers. John and I also had Gentile friends and playmates, which was the advantage of attending *l'école de la Place des Vosges*.

We loved to visit the *Musée Carnavalet* in the next block. It was exciting, convenient, and best of all free. It was also across from a traditional French *boulangerie* or bakery at the corner of *rue de Sévigné* and *rue des Francs-bourgeois*. This was probably our real motive for frequenting the *Musée Carnavalet*. We craved *les petits pains au chocolat, les brioches et les croissants*. No literal translation can convey the appeal of these treats for us.

Life was fun. We enjoyed the moment as children do. There were no thoughts about the future as we strolled in the marvelous *Bois de Boulogne*. We loved navigating *les petits bateaux* ("the little boats") on the mesmerizing pond. We were particularly fond of the carousels. We rejoiced over ice cream and the flavorful Parisian lemonades. We were taken to the circus and to the movies. The matinee movies often featured Laurel and Hardy, Charlie Chaplin and Fernandel, but these films were commonly preceded by the *Actualités françaises* (newsreels of current events). They regularly featured Hitler and the *victorieuses Armées allemandes* ("victorious German Armies"). These images, laden with subliminal implications, communicated to the French public a favorable view of Germany. This was the post-Spanish Civil War period of 1938–39 during which Hitler played a decisive role on the side of Franco. He was getting famous. British Prime Minister Neville Chamberlain had appeased Hitler at the Munich meeting by agreeing to the German takeover of the *Sudetenland*, the German-speaking region of Czechoslovakia. This expansion and the *Anschluss* or annexation of Austria surely must have sent shivers through the French psyche, although more than a few French citizens were sympathetic to the Third Reich. Things continued to deteriorate. Poland was invaded. The declaration of war against Germany by England and France perversely gave us a false sense of security. *After all, Germany was no match for England and France*, people thought.

A subtle insight into the political mood and strategy of official France toward Nazism may have been revealed by those newsreels. There was a spellbinding quality in these images that seemed to appeal to the masses and we ourselves became enthralled by Hitler. John and I would often beg our parents: *racontez-nous des histoires de Hitler* ( tell us stories about Hitler). Believe it or not, our parents never fretted over our misdirected fascination. They must have felt, as many did, that Hitler's time would pass.

In hindsight, our naivete seems astonishing. I guess a prospering young couple with small boys could easily fall into that kind of denial or even willful

ignorance of a growing threat. It raises one of the fundamental questions of the
Holocaust. How could this have happened? Was the evil so great, so unimaginable, that no one could see it coming? Surely the news of Kristallnacht must have
shaken the Jewish community in Paris.[8] How could it not see the danger?

I suppose that fifty years from now, someone will be writing this of us:
*How did they fail to recognize the danger of terrorism* ? The question, I guess,
is the same.

Gordon W. Prange, a historian, titled his book about America at the time of
the Pearl Harbor attack *At Dawn, We Slept.* It can likewise be said that in the
1930–40 decade, we slept.


Our families attended the celebrated synagogue on the *rue Pavée.*[9] We
joined other children for religious sessions and studied Hebrew under the
tutelage of a dedicated young rabbinical student. The intensity of this religious education did not make us happy. We celebrated the holy days, observed some but not all Jewish traditions and could be classified as emanci-
pated Jews. After our sessions at the *rue Pavée*, our mother would take us for
walks in the confining streets of the *Pletzl*, where senior citizens always made
a fuss over us and regularly treated us to mouth-watering pastries or delectable tidbits. Lavish *charcuteries cachères* (kosher delicatessens), famous
bakeries and enticing food stores were found in abundance in this very ethnic
area. We relished those occasions, delighting in the attention and inhaling the
aromas while savoring Pletzl delicacies.

We lived well, celebrating festive occasions, sharing happy experiences
and continuing to enjoy a carefree, cheerful life. Our father was a true family
man. He would regularly take us for photographs at a fashionable studio on
the *rue de Rivoli* or once in a while the photographer would come to our
apartment where we would pose for portraits. We still treasure many of these
photos in our family album. We loved to visit the markets, where father's
friendly employees would pamper us. Father would usually follow up with a
ride in the family truck along the banks of the Oise River, a tributary of the
Seine, near the market place in Bezons.

We were thrilled at riding the Paris métro to nowhere and back or at sightseeing from the rear platforms of the Parisian open buses. A favorite excursion was to the *Jardin des Plantes* (in spite of its name, the zoo), where our
preferred excitement was riding camels through its lovely gardens. While
camel riding, we fantasized being on exotic adventures in faraway deserts.

As father's business thrived, we began to spend our summer vacations at
Le Corubert, in Normandy, with the Huchons. Guy Huchon, one of father's
helpers, and his family were our frequent companions. *Ils etaient nos amis*
("they were our friends").

A picturesque village, one of many scattered over this charming region of France, Le Corubert was near the little town of *La Nocée*. The big city in the region was *Nogent-Le-Retrou*. The through train from Paris went as far as Le Mans and from Le Mans, a modern bus took us to *Le Corubert* by way of the breathtaking Normandy countryside, where the parents of Guy Huchon had always lived. With them, we often visited the well-kept local cemetery to tend to their family graves. Papa and Mama Huchon were extremely accommodating to our Parisian needs and wishes. Coming from Paris, we were regarded as intellectual and sophisticated, but more persnickety and demanding than plain country folks. We were to learn later about the innate decency of French villagers and farmers; further we were also to discover that big city people did not necessarily harbor virtue.

Our days were spent in the countryside. In the words of the old French ballad, we leisurely sauntered through les *Sentiers tout couverts d'oiseaux et de fleurs* ("paths all covered with birds and flowers"). We bathed in the pristine waters of enchanting streams running through the woods. Inside the forests, the solitude was captivating.

Every day, women gathered around the *lavoir* (washing-shed) built on a stream, near the center of the village. Kneeling down and leaning on washboards, they chatted happily while doing their family laundry. That was a pleasant, refreshing and animated display of country life. I can still easily remember the scene with delight.

Occasionally, father would spend a few days with us in *Le Corubert*. Papa Huchon would take us all fishing or *escargot* (snail) gathering. We cherished these times. Mama Huchon prepared exquisite meals, invariably accompanied by *vin ordinaire* (table wine), even for breakfast. Who could have envisioned John or Oscar as American doctors, recommending red wine to their patients with cholesterol problems? But not at breakfast, I might add. *Plus ça change, plus c'est la même chose.*

Jeanine Huchon, Guy's teenage sister, doted upon us. She referred to us as "mes choux"[10] She would frequently walk us to the hub of Le Corubert to see the bus make its daily stop in the village. The small bus depot was sandwiched between the grocery store and the tiny post office, the three structures composing most of Main Street in this oasis of Normandy. We would linger there, talk to people, pretend to buy tickets and to wait patiently for the bus to take us away on some imaginary trip. It never did, but watching the activities surrounding the bus comings and goings was a high point for me. Now, years later, I still savor my fascination with the Normandy bus.

We existed in an idyllic environment. We lived *La Vie En Rose* popularized by Edith Piaf in this song. Edith Piaf, probably one of the greatest and most celebrated French singers of all time, extolled the virtues of this enchanting world. Even to this day, the words and melody in this song revive memories and emotions within me as do many of her songs.

Le Corubert has a special place in my heart. That spot was revived years later when Jeanine told me on her wedding day after the Liberation:

> *I saw the American troops, our liberators come through Le Corubert. They were wearing combat garb; they were covered with dust, dirt and blood. These were no parade soldiers; these were the genuine American troops.*

Her words still resonate within my body and soul.

In the Spring of 1939, I was five and a half years old. I traveled with my father to Poland so I could be displayed to the entire family in Dombrowitz. I scarcely remember the deluxe train ride or sleeping in the plush *wagons-lits*. I, however, treasure the vague memory of walking the streets of Warsaw, holding hands with my father and wearing a fur coat in a light snow. I often visualize the picture of this scene. It is one of my fondest images. We returned to Paris as light-hearted tourists, bringing back wonderful memories and sundry photographs of our excursion to the ancestral hamlet.

This pleasure trip to Poland as late as 1939 attests to an important fact: we were oblivious to what was happening in Europe. Father talked about France as a haven: *we have America in France*, he was fond of saying, according to what mother related to me in later years. He, indeed, had become genuinely Francophile. In retrospect, things were clearly different. We lived in a fool's paradise.

If we had known better, conceivably we might have fled to Spain or Portugal, and from there to America. However, this was easier said than done. The options were limited and perhaps not practical. We did not know better. Maybe we did not want to know better.

That the good life would continue was our belief. My father's business prospered, and he probably resisted the thought of abandoning it. The aberrant situation will terminate soon, he must have thought. We were totally unprepared for what was to come. We did not act. We did not even react.

The German Army invaded Poland in September 1939. Incredible as it now seems, the Mankowski family read nothing ominous in the Hitlerian invasion of Poland. Feeling confident that the military forces of Britain and France would take care of us, there was never a doubt in our mind that these armies would be anything but successful.

Our wake up call came in May 1940, when, shattering our complacency, French and British troops in northern France failed to hold the line. Defeated, the French forces retreated toward the south of France while the remaining British armies evacuated France from Dunkirk.

Our Paris fell! German troops entered the city of Paris on June 14, parading down the *Champs Elysées* with great fanfare. The formal capitulation, also christened the *Second Armistice*, came a little over a week later.[11] The surrender was ratified at *Rethondes*, a village in northern France, taking place in the same railway carriage in which the Germans had signed their own surrender in November 1918. This decisive event occurred near *Compiègne*, a little town which was to have personal meaning for mother, John and me.

Hitler wanted the occasion staged to reverse and echo the humiliating ceremony the French had staged and imposed on Germany twenty years earlier. He ordered that the railroad car be shipped back to Berlin where, according to William Shirer, it was destroyed in the Allied bombing.

Our days of innocence were behind us as our world came apart. Although we did not know it, the Mankowski family's life would never be the same.

## NOTES

1. See detailed map of the *Marais* which includes the *Quartier St. Paul*.

2. The *Marais* is depicted in an engaging and memorable book by Bernadette Costa, *Je me souviens du Marais* (Paris: Parigramme, 1995).

3. *Pletzl* in Yiddish means small place. An excellent historical survey of the *Pletzl* is Jeanne Brody, *Rue des Rosiers: une manière d'être juif* (Paris: Editions Autrement, 1995).

4. In 1873, Renoir actually painted Monet in the act of painting his garden at Argenteuil.

5. The "Great Baths-Showers."

6. Two black leather boxes worn by men during daytime prayer. *Phylacteries* is a technical term sometimes used to describe *teffilins*.

7. Prayer shawl.

8. The English usage for this German word is "The Night of Broken Glass". On November 9, 1938, Goebbels called for a government sanctioned attack against the Jews. On the night of the same day, synagogues were ravaged and then burned. Jewish shop windows were broken. Jews were beaten, raped, arrested and murdered. The Jewish Virtual Library contains several lengthy articles on this event. See, for example, *http://www.jewishvirtuallibrary.org/jsource/Holocaust/kristallnacht.html* accessed December 20, 2004.

9. This synagogue on *rue Pavée* (often spelled, with equal accuracy, rue "Pavé") was built in 1914. Its architect, Hector Guimard, also designed famous metal entrances for the Paris metro.

10. The word *chou* means "little darling" as well as "cabbage".

11. Shirer, William L., *The Rise and Fall of the Third Reich: A History of Nazi Germany* (New York: Simon and Schuster, 1959), 741.

## Chapter Four

# 1940, Darkness Falls

In Paris in the summer of 1940, I was not yet six years old; my brother John was almost four. We enjoyed our family and friends. However, our parents seemed to be listening to radio broadcasts more and more; they told us little about them. Instead, our parents read to us and told us stories. We loved it. We liked playing, running around in our well-furnished roomy apartment and eating our meals there as a family. Mother was an excellent cook, preparing Jewish or French meals, always served with the delicious French baguettes. Red wine was served with the evening dinner, a visible sign of our eagerness to assimilate.

Of course, as a youngster, I knew and understood little about the catastrophe that already engulfed Europe. My parents were high-school educated, read the newspapers and had many friends who were intelligent and well informed. They must have been somewhat troubled about current events but I never sensed they were. They had fallen into a delusive frame of mind as we all continued to enjoy a state of complacency. I think there must have been subtle changes in our family life that a young child could detect but I can't remember what they were.

It was a happy time for our family. There was sufficient money for a comfortable life. My father was a successful businessman; he and my mother were happy together. They were living with optimism, misled by the apathetic atmosphere of the late 1930s in Europe.

With France's capitulation on June 25, 1940, the France we knew was no more. My parents, as well as their friends and neighbors, were in a state of disbelief. My brother and I sensed their anxiety and our boyhood security began to erode. Fear, greed, anger and panic crept into our lives. Our parents began to quarrel about what was best for us. People began to steal from one another or report on each other. This did not seem real even as German troops approached.

Thousands fled Paris in advance of the German forces entering the city. In early June, we escaped to the south. Our parents did not spend much time in reaching a decision to leave; they did just what almost everyone else was doing. John and I neither needed nor got much of an explanation. We were excited about taking a summer excursion in our truck (*camion*) and packed plenty of mattresses, blankets, pillows, sheets and personal clothing. Father and mother assumed the crucial responsibility of bringing our savings, but everything else was left behind. We had no family pets but did welcome the company of Coco, our friends' dog.

Not everyone left Paris, of course. Many stayed behind because of family members who could not travel or because of businesses they could not easily abandon. The Steinbergs, our friendly neighbors, had no transportation of their own. My father prevailed upon our family friend, Leizer Szerbojn, also an open-air trader with a large truck, to take all the Steinbergs along with his wife and son. We left Paris together as a group. Soon after we were on our way, the two trucks lost sight of each other. We did not make contact again until our return to Paris.

The Huchons—parents, Guy, Jeanine and Coco—all piled into our *camion*, and we headed off towards the Midi (South). It was a fully enclosed truck with a back panel that could be secured in an open position, even while we were riding. The light grey truck, large by any standard, easily accommodated the eight of us, with three passengers in the front cab and five people in the roomy rear van. Papa, Papa Huchon (Mr. Huchon senior) and Guy Huchon sat in the front cab, sharing the driving. Maman, Mama Huchon (Mrs Huchon senior), Jeanine Huchon, John and I would spread out in comfort on mattresses in the rear section of the truck, Coco at our side. We were far from the comfort, decorum and ambience of the *rue de Sévigné*. But, we somehow managed to live in and off the truck with a certain degree of efficiency in a convivial atmosphere.

The *Drole de guerre* ("phony war") bred disorder, confusion, chaos, hysteria and for many, doom. It was an early, bright summer, the weather unseasonably warm, the cloudless sky exquisitely blue. People fled. Many women often cried for no apparent reason. Some people squabbled, while others engaged in noisy arguments or fist fights. I had never before seen such a strange scene. The atmosphere was surreal. So many people with sad or worried expressions carried what they could in all sorts of vehicles. Roads were clogged everywhere with people, bicycles, push-carts and horse drawn wagons. Cruising German aircraft flew low overhead. Motor vehicles puttered along; gasoline was scarce and getting scarcer. Quasi-uniformed French soldiers, many still carrying their weapons, mingled with civilians. Obviously separated from their units, they looked stunned and crestfallen.

The Mankowski and Huchon families slept in the truck, ate on the run and existed mostly on paté de campagne, cheese, loaves of French bread and fruit, all cheap and still available. We left Paris on a main highway and drove toward the Loire Valley. Our parents told us we were headed toward Central France on our way to the South of France. We used the accommodations of Nature, washed out of basins, obtaining water as best we could from wells and fountains. Often we paid dearly for water. Occasionally, we would sleep in a barn, after paying for a meal, provided by a farmer; such meals were usually served on coarse tables while we sat on wooden benches under the cover of a stall.

Meanwhile, my parents seemed to be worrying. My father was surely concerned about the future of his business while my mother must have fretted about losing our comfortable apartment. Desperate as we were, I don't believe anyone fully appreciated the gravity of the situation, even after the Germans first made sport of shooting at us. On a crowded road, between Orléans and Chateauroux, we were strafed by German open-cockpit planes. We ran for cover, jumping into the roadside ditches. We could actually make out the German pilots; the next day in Orléans, we were attacked again. We saw Luftwaffe planes making multiple passes over us. They sprayed us with machine-gun bullets and dropped some sort of bombs. We heard screeching sounds, shrilling noises and the cacophony of terrified human beings. The main purpose of the Germans must have been to induce panic, rather than slaughter people. Had they chosen to annihilate us, we would have been easy targets. I learned afterward that ten refugees were killed and thirty-two wounded. A little later, however, Guy, Jeanine, Papa Huchon, and father were playing ball in a nearby open field with other adults. Mother, Mama Huchon, John, I, some other women and children provided the cheering section from the periphery of the field. We even took photos as if we were tourists on vacation. There was laughter, humor, comedy and clowning around. Reality had not, even then, sunk in; denial was rampant. We lived on eternal hope. I recall that people sang a popular old French refrain to sustain our spirits. It probably was written during World War I and went something like this:

Et hop, On s'en sortira, On s'en tirera comme toujours en France, tout remarchera à brève échéance . . . . ["we will get out of this mess as always in France . . . everything will be fine soon . . . ."]

The song was the French equivalent of *"There'll always be an England."*

I was to learn later from mother that my parents had stashed well over ten thousand dollars in cash on their bodies. Our serious money was in illegal dollars but our spending money was in legal French tender. Safeguarding our precious and hard-earned savings was a constant concern. As a young boy, I sometime witnessed the actions of my parents trying to keep the money hidden. They used books, mattresses, pillows or girdles for that purpose. If we stayed somewhere long enough, they buried our assets with care and trepidation. They would select a landmark, count off a certain number of steps, dig to a given depth, place our money, jewelry and other valuables in the small excavation and then would camouflage the hiding site. This maneuver was duplicated frequently; the format was varied now and then. Later, after my father was gone, I watched my mother go through those same motions. I soon began to be entrusted with assisting in this important task and became an active participant in the process. Father, through hard work and shrewd business practices, had been able to amass a sizeable nest-egg. With this money, we remained financially secure throughout the war.

We were somewhere in south central France. News from the capital was positive; we were told that the situation in Paris was benign, city life had returned to normal, the Germans were tolerant of all Frenchmen, and business prospered. Rumors circulated that the Spanish border was closed and dangerous.

In early July 1940, we returned to Paris. How I wish we had not done so! Other options could have been chosen. For example, after the war, we learned that Felix Rohatyn, destined to become a successful New York financier and still later US Ambassador to France, traveled a nearby road. He and his family fled to the south at the same time we did. They decided to go farther southward and crossed the Spanish border. From Spain, they eventually reached America. It was a bold move. Regretfully, we were not so bold.

The Huchons, minus Guy, went back to Le Corubert while Father and Guy Huchon resumed the market business. They soon were rejoined by father's other dedicated assistant, Benjamin Roditis. We were back, living at 11 *rue de Sévigné*. Things seemed to return to normal. But life in Paris soon changed by degrees and decrees. We accepted these changes passively as adjustments to our new way of life.

During the summer of 1940, Marshal Pétain and his henchmen came to power in France. They immediately adopted a strong stance against foreign Jews, and later against all Jews. Our early expectations of the new French leaders had been favorable. Maréchal Pétain had assured the French people at the beginning of the German occupation that *I make to France the gift of my person* . . . "[1] We naively assumed this assurance applied to us also. The government had relocated to Vichy, a small, sleepy resort town in central France, and had launched a new national motto of *travail, famille, patrie* (work, family, country). Marshal Pétain had founded the "National Revolution," and he

had given us the Vichy regime which, in theory, was to stand between the ordinary French citizen and the Nazi invaders.[2]

Vichy became a household name, and it permeated our daily life. We were
encouraged to sing along with others the song, *Maréchal, nous voilà*, a sort
of promise of allegiance to Marshal Pétain.[3] Every afternoon, all public primary school children were given a national treat of hot chocolate, cookies and
scented pink vitamin pastilles. This was allegedly offered to us by Pétain himself. During those snacks, we were reminded of his concern for us. We were
brainwashed daily into the belief that the old, glorious hero of World War I
was now the savior of France.

The country was divided into the territories of occupied and unoccupied
France.[4] By German intent, Pétain and his minions were given administrative
control of unoccupied France but the reality was that the influence of the
Vichy government reached throughout the whole French bureaucratic apparatus. Thus, the ubiquitous role of Vichy extended over the entire country:

> *In both the occupied and unoccupied zones, the prewar French administration
> continued to operate much as before: a system with prefects and sub-prefects; a
> government-regulated school system, with its rectors and instructors; a national
> post office, with its government employees; and a national judicial system, with
> its appointed judges assigned to different courts throughout the country. The in-
> frastructure, controlled by Vichy, stayed in place throughout the war; even in the
> occupied zone, high-ranking civil servants—prefects, officers and magistrates—
> pledged an oath of loyalty to Pétain.*[5]

The Germans proved to be cunning psychologists. Their leaders announced
restrictions on civil liberties gradually and with astute timing. The collaborating French authorities carried out German commands without hesitation.
The new French government was completely sympathetic to Hitler. Collaboration with, and even anticipation of, German demands, was the order of the
day.

For my family, the rest of 1940 was disagreeable but not calamitous.
Parisian policemen openly saluted German officers. This was a painful re-
minder of their subservient role. It was a preview, of sorts, of their future actions. French state authorities at all levels—French police, French *gendarmes*
(the National Police), French *milice* (the Vichy police force) and, yes, even
some *pompiers* (firemen)—eagerly collaborated. It is now known that these
French authorities, one and all, were instrumental in facilitating the deportation of Jews.

Our family had not witnessed *le grand défilé militaire* ("giant military
parade") by German troops down the *Champs Élysées,* but kept seeing the
event replayed by our old friends, the official newsreels. We went to the

movies several times a week on the nearby *rue de Rivoli*. This recreation was inexpensive, convenient and readily available to us, at least for a while longer.

We were exposed to *petits défilés militaires*—small military parades—by German troops on our own rue de Rivoli. Many French people had tears in their eyes and some wept openly while others seemed not to be disturbed at the sight of this intrusion in our lives. We were most upset by those who even applauded as German troops and military bands went by.

Anti-Jewish propaganda posters and obscene graffiti were now commonplace all over Paris, especially in the *Pletzel*. Our temple on the *rue Pavée* was repeatedly vandalized. Windows were broken, doors were smashed and walls were splashed with paint.

The grade system in French primary schools is in reverse numerical order from seven to one. I look back to an uneventful grade seven. I became more aware of specific events in grade six. I remember a poster which caused me grief at school.[6] It showed a house superimposed on a map of France. The house was being visibly swept by a broom while a large print said: *il faut aussi balayer les Juifs pour que notre maison soit propre* ["Jews must also be swept away to make our house clean"]. A few children, in my mostly gentile school, mockingly simulated sweeping the class-room with a broom. The insult hurt me deeply because I did not understand then how children, my own school-classmates, could be so cruel and insensitive. Years later, after seeing the movie *Lord of The Flies*, I developed a better appreciation for the cruel potential of children.

Rumors were rampant. We learned to trust one clandestine source, known by different names. I will refer to it by calling it the Word. It is unclear to me what the source of the Word was. Was it written by Jewish elders or a device used by the authorities to quell and control the populace? Was it rumor or conventional wisdom? Gossip would come down by word of mouth and travel almost at the speed of light. The Word seemed credible. It provided timely items of news and useful guidelines. We were told that leaks by anonymous individuals, sympathetic policemen, bureaucrats or well-placed sources were carefully evaluated to form the basis of the Word. The information was mostly accurate.

The primary admonition was simple and forceful: do not make waves, offend no one, ruffle no feathers, and, especially, do not antagonize the authorities; in other words, always be deferential. This fundamental advice must have rubbed off on me as I was told later in my life by colleagues and friends that I tried too hard to please people.

We were told to avoid public places as much as possible; not to go to movies, museums or circuses; no more camel rides, no *Bois de Boulogne* or

*Musée Carnavalet*; no more *petits bateaux*, merry-go-rounds, pleasurable metro or bus rides. We saw the open buses used by the French police to transport Jews arrested during the round-ups passing by on the *rue de Rivoli, rue St Antoine*, and *rue des Francs-bourgeois*, loaded with men who were guilty only of being Jews. The heavy presence of French police on these buses was clearly evident. The open buses with rear platforms, once the object of our fancy, now brought a somber reality to our neighborhood.

We were ordered to register as Jews at our local commissariat. In September 1940, the Germans ordered a census of Jews in the Occupied Zone and the stamping of Jew on our identity cards. These cards now displayed the words *Juif* or *Juive*. We did not have to wear any distinctive markers such as armbands or tags. That would come later, in mid-1942, in the form of yellow stars. Our parents tried to minimize the emotional impact of this demeaning practice by telling John and me it was all very routine.

A German chart of the age distribution of Jews in greater Paris, based on a German census taken in October 1940, appeared under the heading of *Alter-stufung der Juden von Gross-Paris*.[7]

> On October 19, the Jewish census is completed in the Seine Department made up mostly of the city of Paris . . . .
>     Begun October 3, under German orders, it was issued by the Préfecture of Police . . . in drawing up lists of Jews for arrest and deportation.[8]

I read later that the French authorities were also consolidating lists of *Juifs étrangers* and *Juifs français* as part of the October census. This was yet another way the Pétain people willingly helped the Germans. How quickly the French hierarchy under Marshal Pétain, Prime Minister Pierre Laval and Commissioner Xavier Vallat supported Hitler's Final Solution.

We were dismayed, bewildered and distressed to see that public playgrounds were now fenced in by light wooden barriers, displaying signs such as *Terrain de Jeux interdit aux Juifs* ["playground forbidden to Jews"]. We became afraid of being harassed or physically attacked. On our way to school, we ceased using the long diagonal alley across the *Place des Vosges*, the most direct and scenic path to class. We furtively walked along and under the outer arcades making up the periphery of this acclaimed majestic place. Our *Pletzel*, where we were usually taken after religious school, became deserted and our synagogue on the *rue Pavée* was boarded up.

We learned a new vocabulary. *Dénonciation* (denunciation), *Compiègne, Pithiviers, Beaune La Rolande, Drancy* (French internment camps), *service du travail obligatoire* ("STO" or "obligatory work service"), *rafles* (round ups), *panier à salade* (paddy wagons), *interdit aux Juifs* (forbidden to Jews), and *étoiles jaunes* (yellow stars), to name a few.

*In September 1940, SS-Haupststurmfuehrer Theodor Dannecker became the Chief of the Gestapo's Jewish Affairs Service in France. A twenty-seven year-old committed diehard underling of Adolf Eichmann, he vigorously set out to implement the application of the Final Solution in France.*[9]

In 1941, under the zealous guidance of Dannecker, the arrest of men and their dispatch to labor camps began on a grand scale.[10] Men were arrested in roundups, on denunciations or by entrapment. Chaim Steinberg, our neighbor, was enticed by letter to come to the Prefecture of Paris on May 14, 1941, to have his status of *Juif étranger* reviewed. He was arrested then and there and was taken to *Beaune La Rolande*, a French internment camp, from which he managed to escape. Spotted in a nearby open field by a peasant who reported him as being suspicious, he was apprehended by French *Gendarmes*, taken back to the camp, and eventually ended up on Convoy V to Auschwitz, never to return.

Jews were systemically being excluded from elite professions and public jobs.[11] At some point in 1941, Jewish men were no longer permitted to conduct business. I recall that father himself stopped going to the markets in mid-1941 but continued to supervise remotely his loyal assistants, who maintained the business for him.

Remembrances of the years 1940–42 are vividly etched in my brain, but their sequence is not always precise. Some memories remain vague, such as being fitted for gas masks some time before May 1940 but learning later that Jews might have been excluded from the issuance of these protective devices. However a crystal-clear picture plays back in minute detail, deep down in the recesses of my mind: the frightening arrest of father.

## NOTES

1. Alice Kaplan, *The Collaborator: The Trial and Execution of Robert Brasillach* (Chicago: University of Chicago Press, 2000), 29.

2. Kaplan, 28–29.

3. *Marshal, we are here for you.* The full text of this song is in Appendix 1.

4. The so called *Zone d'Occupation* and *Zone Libre.*

5. Kaplan, 30.

6. Serge Klarsfeld, *French Children of the Holocaust—A Memorial* (New York: New York University Press, 1996), 16.

7. Klarsfeld, 19.

8. Klarsfeld, 14.

9. Klarsfeld, 9–23.

10. Dannecker would commit suicide in an American prison in 1945.

11. Klarsfeld, 14, 18.

*Chapter Five*

# Convoy One

Denunciations were commonplace. A typical one might be an unfounded allegation of some civil infraction, such as still working in an occupation prohibited to Jews. Most were baseless. In mid-October 1941, we were warned by the Word that an anonymous denunciation against father and Robert Waldman, our tenant, had been filed with our commissariat. We did not know for certain who was behind it and never did find out.

Our apartment at 11 *rue de Sévigné* was in a five-story building, adorned with a massive portal leading into the courtyard. Inside the entrance lived the concierge who had a clear view of who came in and went out. She was Madame Dupont, a woman who meddled in everyone's affairs. Friendly to outward appearances, she turned out to be two-faced and deceitful. This, at least, was our later judgment of her. A more charitable view, perhaps, was that she may have panicked under pressure and that may explain her later behavior.

From the courtyard, there were two stairways, the main one on the right and another on the left; the right stairway led to our apartment, which extended from stairway to stairway over the courtyard. There was a seldom-used heavy back door exiting into the left stairway. It was usually bolted and draped over, so we paid little attention to its existence. The concierge had told father that he could reach the left stairway through that door and then go up to a secret cache on the roof to hide. The right stairway also led to the entrance of a separate suite, connected to our principal dwelling. We were subletting this part to the Waldmans, a recently-married Jewish couple. The front windows of our apartment opened up on the *rue de Sévigné* while the rear-windows gave us an excellent view of the courtyard, the *caserne des pompiers* and the public bathhouse.

In the late fall of 1941, alarmed by the news from the Word and encouraged by the advice of our supposedly friendly concierge, father and Waldman began to practice dry runs of hiding on the roof once or twice a week. One day in early November 1941, we were alerted that father and Waldman might be nabbed that evening. The suspicion was apparently based on a leak from our local *Commissariat*. Father decided not to question the veracity of the information. He and Waldman would stay on the roof in a secret cubbyhole until given a clear signal by the concierge. Later that evening, two French policemen knocked on our door announcing themselves as *Police Francaise* and demanding entrance. Mother let them in. They said they were looking for father and Waldman, charged with being Jews and still doing business.

They did not accept my mother's statement that father and Waldman were not home. They went down to talk with the concierge who told them: "I saw these two people come home earlier this evening." They returned determined, dogged and talking tough. They laughed at my mother's pleas to leave as John and I were terrorized by their presence. I vividly remember that the two policemen were middle-aged, ordinary-looking uniformed Parisian cops, but mean and nasty. They were not the affable *flics de Paris* I once believed the Paris cops to be. Mother tried her best to convince them to go away and even offered them a bribe, all to no avail. They were doing their duty in the name of France, they exclaimed pridefully. They searched the apartment again and went back to the concierge. The concierge this time allegedly said: *They are hiding on the roof.*

More police came after a call for reinforcements. The captain in charge fired a few shots in the air with a revolver from the same window we used to watch our *Pompiers* with such delight. Through the same window, he yelled upwards for my father and Waldman to come down. The police found our back door and opened it. With guns in hand, police officers ran up the left stairway to the roof. Escape was impossible. Father and Waldman came down, hands in the air. They were handcuffed and arrested. That was November 15, 1941. John had just turned five on November 9, and I had turned seven on October 13. John and I watched from our front windows as the two "prisoners" were taken away in a paddy wagon, with sirens blaring, while a crowd gathered in the street, observing the scene. They were taken that very night to Drancy, the notorious French internment camp in the Seine et Marne, a French department, near Paris. *The Camp of Drancy was in a suburb northeast of Paris, guarded by French gendarmes. It was surrounded by barbed wire in an unfinished, low income housing complex. The conditions were squalid.*[1]

We visited father twice at Drancy, bringing him packages of goods and personal items. Father looked tired, haggard and bewildered. He tried to reassure us that he would be fine in a German work camp. He must already have been told where he was going. On our last visit, he had a forlorn look. This is my last memory of him.

We were later informed that father had been turned over to the Germans. In fact, on January 22,1942, father was moved to another French internment camp, Compiègne.

Since Drancy was the principal deportation center in France, I never understood why his transfer to Compiègne had occurred. However, I will always remember that the relocation occurred shortly after father's birthday. He turned 40 on January 13,1942. I will also never forget that father had the ill fortune to be on Convoy One, the first French deportation railroad transport to Auschwitz, "the Heart of the Holocaust," as John later labeled this camp.

*March 27, 1942. The first French deportation train to Auschwitz leaves the suburban Paris station at Le Bourget-Drancy at 5 PM with 565 Jews, half of the planned transport. The rest of the deportees board the train further north, at Compiègne, and it leaves later the same day with its full cargo of 1,112 men plus a separate group of 34 Yugoslav Jews.*

*The convoy is escorted to the German border by French gendarmes under direction of an SS officer, and from there by German military police. This first deportation train is the only one to be made up of standard third-class railway cars.*

*It is accompanied to Auschwitz by Dannecker.[2] On arrival at the camp, the deportees are given Auschwitz tattoos numbered 27533 to 28644. One prisoner, Georges Rueff, manages to jump from the train and escape.*

*Of the prisoners on the train, 1,008 are dead by the end of August, 1942. Twenty-two of the deportees on this first French transport survived the war and returned to France in 1945.[3]*

Father was one of the deportees who boarded Convoy One at Compiègne. Mercifully, he did not ride a cattle or freight train, as later deportees would. His Auschwitz tattoo number was 28042. He was one of the prisoners on Convoy One who would be dead by the end of August 1942. We did not find out until we returned to Paris, after the liberation, that father had been killed at Auschwitz. We spent three long years in blissful ignorance because the unofficial details of what happened came much later.[4]

The list of Deportees of Convoy One is partially reproduced below. My father's correct name was Aaron Mankowski. In the list, he is mentioned as "MANCOWSKI ARON 13.01.02"; the name is misspelled, the date of birth is accurate.[5]

## List of Deportees, Convoy 1

| | DATE | | | | | | |
|---|---|---|---|---|---|---|---|

WOLF 29.12.97 VARSOVIE
JANKIEL 16.10.98
ISRAEL 31.12.24
MORITZ 20.12.07
MARTIN 11.11.22
SZULIM 24.04.21 VARSOVIE
ADOLF 08.02.14 PARIS
ALEXANDRE 18.08.04 STEPANTZKI
ISAAK 17.08.93 LINEZYCA
ALBERT 29.12.10
JOSEPH 15.08.10 VARSOVIE
BRANO 29.12.20
XS ISRAEL 28.01.08
GASTON 19.04.95
DANIA 15.02.15
MARCEL 03.06.23
LEON 17.07.88
AJN NACHMAN 16.09.13
TEJN SIMON 28.06.01
CZ ISRAEL 12.01.22
ITT CHAIM 15.06.19 VARSOVIE
ICEK 15.06.17
AS BORIS 06.09.22 KAUNAS
ISRAEL 15.03.00
IRG JACOB 28.12.11 NOVAALEKSANDRIA
ANAR BORIS 06.09.22
CKI JANKIEL 10.0...
EINIK JACOB
AKOFF

P LEVIAS DAVID 09.02.99 P
LEVIN MOSZEK 20.04.95 LODZ
LEVINE BARUSLAV 11.05.23
LEVINSKY PIERRE 17.04.06
LEVINSON DAVID 27.06.06
P LEVIS PIERRE 16.20.99
R LEVY ALBERT 10.02.07 St-DENIS F
IND LEVY ANDRE 27.05.21 PARIS
LEVY MAYER 01.10.22
P LEVY PETER 05.11.17
LEVY RAYMOND 09.10.22 F
LEVY RENE 21.05.90 PARIS
LEVY ANDRE 18.05.07
LEVY EDMOND 08.03.00
LEVY ISSAC 08.08.88
LEVY JULIAN 13.06.00
LEVY PETER 09.04.98
LEVY SADI 20.02.01
LEVY-LATTES WOLF 07.02.97 IN
LEWEK ISAAK 30.05.94 BRAHO P
LEWIN DANIEL 01.10.94 ZAMOSC A
P LEWKOWICZ ABRAHAM 20.05.99 PILINE F
LEWKOWICZ SIMON 06.03.16
LIBERBAUM MOSEK 12.06.12 PISCIEZNO
LIBESKIND RUBIN 13.03.07
LIBON BENJAMIN 04.10.19 VARSOVIE
LIBRACH JACOB 17.04.01 LAZSWOKA
LICHTENSZTAIN ICEK 27.10.10
LICHTENSZTEIN MAX 14.02.05
LICHTMANN JOSEPH 20.01.11 VARSOVIE
F LIERESANT MORITZ 12.08.19
F LINDENHAYN ARNOLD 02.09.98
LINZEMBERG MOISE 04.08.99 GRABOW
P LIPMAN PAUL 27.11.11
LIPPA SALOMON 11.12.98 VARSOVIE
P LIPSCHITZ JACOB 15.04.96 ZAUNSKA
LIPSZYC JEAN 14.09.91 LECZYCS
LITHUAC JACOB 28.09.97 SIEDLEC
R LITKE MORDKA 05.02.93
P LIWERANT HERZ 23.01.10
P LITWINSKI EDMOND 15.02.20 PARIS
R LOPATA SZAJA 06.07.98 MINSK
LOS ISAAC 21.09.99
LUBETZKI JOSEPH 12.03.96
LUDYM JUNIA 15.03.04 LODZ
LUPKA CHIL 14.04.07 KUTNO
LUSTMAN EDOUARD 25.02.01
LYON WOLF 03.04.95 BREZIN
MACAG GEORGES 18.02.05
MACER CASIMIR 02.08.88 PULAWY
MAIEROVICZ ABRAHAM 18.06.00 UTENE
22.11.97

1

| NAME | DATE AND PLACE OF BIRTH | | NATIONALITY |
|---|---|---|---|

10.10.02 IND
EPH 03.01.89 R
RICE 15.06.04 LUBLIN P
LF 27.09.04 WIENGOW F
HAIM 22.04.96 GORLICE
JANKIEL 10.10.97 VARSOVIE P
SZYJA 08.09.19 TC
NATES 04.09.95 P
SAMUEL 13.12.00 VARSOVIE
SENDER 06.12.04 SATARAJANKELY
HENRI 06.02.02 VARSOVIE IND
CHONIC 31.03.07 VARSOVIE
ABRAHAM 20.08.94 TAINOM IND
HERMAN 29.10.04
SKI SIMUL 15.02.01
MORITZ ...02.98
LUZIAN 06.03.01

JOSEPH 02.07.01 R
HAN CHAIM 13.06.05
R BEREK 05.09.05 PARIS
ANSKI OSIAS 19.06.07 SIMFEROPOL
LICH ANDREAS 07.10.01 F
DER ISAAK 03.08.03
TTON HENRI 17.12.19 PICHAU
LACHER ROGER 20.10.08
LAGODARSKY ARMAND 19.01.18
BLECKMANN LEOPOLD 21.11.88
RLEXMANN MORITZ 02.11.97
RLEIER RAOUL 25.02.07
BLESKIN EDOUARD 03.08.05 SARREGUEMINES F
BLITZ JOHANN 14.12.95
OCH PETER 20.05.22

**MANCOWSKI   ARON   13.01.02**

MANCUPLI ARON 14.05.98
MANCONSKI JACEK
MANDELKORN ELIE 15.01.15 PERPIGNAN
MANTEL JULIEN 25.12.20 FRANCFORT
MARCOVICI ADOLF 01.12.04
MARCOVICI ABRAHAM 13.06287
MARKOVIC HENRI 03.08.97 LOEBAU
MARCUS LOTHAR 28.12.12
 RCUS WALDE 11.01.97 PARIS
COLIWAS MARCUS 11.10.91
RKEWITZ ISAAC 21.11.94
KUS JOSEPH 17.11.07 HANNHEI
COVICI ERNEST 24.01.01
LUCIEN 20.08.98 PRZYAUT
MANDEL 23.08.98 WILKOW
LICK 02.08.04

## NOTES

1. Klarsfeld, "French children," 24.
2. See Chapter 4.
3. Klarsfeld, "French children," 31.
4. It was only in 1998 that we received official word of Father's death from the International Red Cross.
5. Serge Klarsfeld, *Memorial to the Jews Deported from France, 1942–1944* (New York: The Beate Klarsfeld Foundation, 1983), 10–16.

## Chapter Six

# Auschwitz, Evil Incarnate

President Franklin Delano Roosevelt had said that December 7, 1941, the day of the attack on Pearl Harbor, would live forever in infamy. The name of Auschwitz will likewise mean evil incarnate for eternity. The French have used the expression *l'Enfer sur Terre* ["Hell on Earth"] to refer to Auschwitz. John Dobrin, a retired Foreign Service Officer, a former patient and a close friend, has told me:

> *Textile chemists like my maternal uncle were kept alive to work at the Buna rubber installation just adjacent to the camp. Others worked as dye chemists and so forth. While they were a tiny minority, the fact that there was a labor function separated Auschwitz from camps like Sobibor and Treblinka, whose sole purpose was extermination, and is perhaps worth recognizing because it allowed a certain number of Jews to escape death.*

Auschwitz was primarily a death camp and an extermination factory on a grand scale. John Dobrin also gave me a disturbing quote from a plaque at Auschwitz: "Frau Hoess, wife of the Camp commandant, whose backyard overlooked the walkway to the Auschwitz crematoria, wrote a letter to a friend rhapsodizing on the joys of living in Auschwitz. She closed that letter with '*Hier will ich leben und sterben*' ["here I want to live and die"]."

With the permission of the *Baltimore Sun*, I am transcribing the story of what happened to father at Auschwitz.[1] The original account was published by Carl Schoettler on August 6, 1998, under the title *Voyage of the Heart*:

> *His only memory of his father was the day he disappeared. More than 50 years later, Dr. John Mann went to Auschwitz in hopes of learning something more . . . .*

*Dr. John Mann's journey of remembrance brought him at last to the Wall of Death at Auschwitz, a forbidding place, pocked and weathered dead-end between two grim barracks, a place where thousands died . . . .*

*He put on his yarmulke, walked alone to the wall and said the prayer for the dead, El Male Rahamim. 'God full of compassion.' He prayed for his father.*

*Prisoners who had escaped, or broken the kafkaesque—the absurd or the grotesque—regulations of the Auschwitz death camp, or just displeased the guards, were brought naked to this killing place for summary execution. Mann's father, Aaron Mankowski, was shot before this wall sometime in the night hours of June 18 to 19, 1942 . . . .*

*Mann arrived at this haunted place June 11, just about a week before the fifty-sixth anniversary of his father's death. He wept as he recited the prayer that has been offered for the Jewish dead after pogroms and massacres in Eastern Europe since the time of the Crusades. He wept again as he wrote in the diary he kept of this voyage of the heart. He relates what he was told at Auschwitz . . . .*

*The [prisoner] was undressed completely and walked through the iron gate, down three steps into the death courtyard. The courtyard is a rectangular area between the women's Barracks and Barracks eleven. The windows of the women's Barracks were covered so that the women could not watch the execution.*

*At the end of the courtyard there is a stark black wall where a prisoner stood before being shot in the back of the neck at point blank range by a German officer.*

*'I think that's exactly what happened to my father,' Mann says, discussing his trip during a conversation at his handsome home on Springlake Way. He's an associate professor of medicine at Johns Hopkins University and practices internal medicine at the Hopkins Green Spring Station campus.*

*At the start of his journey, Mann had written in his diary: 'I do not know what to expect. The exact purpose is unclear to me.'*

*He hoped at least to bring back some understanding of their heritage to his daughters, Gilda and Stacie. The idea of making sense of the past had grown stronger over the last few years . . .*

*Two years ago, Mann and his wife, Risa, a pathologist who is a professor of oncology at Hopkins, had returned to the small French village where he and his brother, Oscar, their mother, Hinda, and an uncle, aunt and cousins survived the German occupation of France–aided by peasant farmers and protected by the underground resistance movement . . . .*

*This summer, he walked the streets in the town of Dombrowitz, where his mother had lived until she was 22, the town from which a host of his uncles and aunts and cousins were transported to their deaths. They are pictured in a Holocaust memorial book about Dombrowitz, a somber and doomed family of East European Jews . . . .*

*He continued his pilgrimage to the cul de sac where his father was killed. Memorial flowers now bloom at the foot of the shooting wall: beyond the wall, trees grow green in June . . . .*

*'I need to rediscover my father,' Mann's diary reads. 'I think that my only memory of my father is seeing him getting dressed on the day he was arrested.'*

*'I don't think I had ever seen my father in his underwear before,' he says. 'I remember seeing a very pale man getting dressed.'*

*Aaron Mankowski was taken to Drancy, the infamous deportation center for most of the Jews of Paris. Mann learned from the International Tracing Service of the Red Cross that his father arrived in Auschwitz on March 27, 1942. He was shot less than three months later . . . .*

*Mann believes he knows the name of the judge who condemned his father: Rudolf Milner. Milner was arrested after the war. He was judged not guilty of war crimes, Mann learned, because he was a 'legal judge' following the laws of the time . . . .*

*And John wrote in his diary words he recalled from a forgotten author about Jewish life in Eastern Europe: 'It did not die, but it did not survive'.*

John's further comments from his diary give depth to those which appear in the *Sun* story. I give John immense credit for searching out our roots and braving deep-seated emotions to sojourn to Auschwitz. I did not go with him on this trip into our past and I shall never go back to where our family came from. I shall never visit Auschwitz. The reason, candidly, is that I entertain no yearning, even ever so slight, to set foot on European soil ever again. Perhaps that is why I am writing this book.

But John went to Auschwitz. There is nothing more that I can add about Auschwitz. John has said it all. I give my absolute endorsement to his powerful narrative. His eloquent words come from the heart. The facts speak for themselves. Commentary on my part would not be useful. Oscar Antel, our cousin from Winnepeg, Canada, and his sons, Jack and Joel, made the pilgrimage with my brother, John. John's own words follow:

*June 10,1998: After the Jewish part of Krakow, we next visited the Royal Palace on Wawel Hill. On the wall of the Royal Palace embattlement is a huge metal dragon which spouts fire from his mouth from time to time. It is an important part of the legend of Krakow. The courtyard is very large, Italian in style with divided staircases, and quite beautiful. The attached cathedral dates back to the fourteenth century. It is Gothic in style and contains a collection of prehistoric bones. Legends tells us that those are the bones from the famous dragon called Krak and hence the name of the city. The legend states that the cathedral will stand as long as the bones remain in place.*

*The university district is very interesting. Collegium Maius is the second oldest university in Eastern Europe. It has a beautiful courtyard where Copernicus used to gaze at the sky. There is a fountain with magical water which preserves the mind and memory. I used a lot of it. Krakow is indeed a beautiful city, but we are preparing ourselves for the trip to Auschwitz-Birkenau.*

*June 11, 1998 Dombrowitz was the most important part of our trip for Oscar Antel. Today's visit to Auschwitz is my most important quest. Zvi Fein has arranged a very special guide, Wanda Hutny. We had received a fax from Paula Borenstein, the public relations director for the American JDC in Paris, and we had also received a phone call at the hotel[2]. Paula Borenstein had faxed to Wanda Hutny telling her that four important VIPs were coming. I am very grateful to Ellen, Shale and Zvi for making these arrangements. Having a private tour of Auschwitz was extremely meaningful to me. I dreaded the idea of being part of a large group.*

*Auschwitz is seventy kilometers from Krakow, and we had a very pleasant English speaking driver accompanying us in a very comfortable Renault van. The countryside was very peaceful and pleasant. However, from time to time, we saw the railroad tracks which reminded me of the purpose of Auschwitz and my trip. The Germans selected a sleepy Polish town, Oświęcim, as a suitable location for the concentration camp because it contained unused old army barracks, had convenient train connections, and was relatively isolated. Initially, it was to be used as a camp for Polish prisoners. In 1941, Himmler made the decision to use Auschwitz as the main extermination camp mostly for Jews. The exact numbers of murdered people is not available because eighty to ninety percent of arrivees were selected for immediate death and were not counted, registered or given a number. The best estimate for the number murdered at Auschwitz-Birkenau is between one point five and two million; ninety five percent Jews.*

*The tour started at the famous metal gate with the inscription, 'Arbeit Macht Frei.' The gate was smaller than I had expected but gave us a foreboding welcome. The twenty-eight barracks were neatly arranged in rows separated by tree lined streets. These barracks housed the Auschwitz inmates, and a few had special purposes such as the hospital and the death house. After the liberation, these barracks were used to house the refugees. At the entrance near the metal gate was an orchestra made up of talented Jewish performers. The purpose of the music was to make the arrivees walk in cadence more efficiently and presumably to prevent panic. Building four is devoted to documenting the holocaust. A map shows the feeding points from most countries in Europe. Drancy is prominently shown and was the point of departure for my father. A photographic display shows the initial visit to the camp of high German officials such as Himmler. Photos document the arrival of Polish, French, and Russian Jews as well as Gypsies. Selection was made on arrival, with the overwhelming majority of people sent to immediate death without registration. This was the fate of most women, children under twelve years of age and elderly or sick appearing men. A particularly moving photograph shows a group of Jewish children on their way to death.*

*Registration forms were filled out for the survivors of the selection process. They were carefully filled in by hand. The next display graphically illustrated the magnitude of the problem. After surviving the selection process, each prisoner was stripped, his head was shaved, and he was given a uniform. Several large rooms were filled with human hair. This was sent to various factories to make burlap and parts of German soldiers' uniforms. A particularly touching sight is a length of long blond braided hair. The level of killing was so high that at times the capacity of the crematoria was overwhelmed. At such times, they would burn corpses in huge open air fires.*

*Huge supplies of ugly teapot-size cans contained the Zyklon which was such an integral part of the killing machine. Zyklon B is a pesticide which was initially perfected on Russian soldiers. In 1941, the Germans had perfected a method to use it in the gas chambers. In Auschwitz, the gas chamber did not contain any fake shower heads or faucets. It is likely that most people knew their fate on arrival. A large number of children were killed in this fashion. The cans were open, moistened, and inserted through specially constructed holes into the gas chamber. Cyanide would be released quickly and within twenty-thirty minutes it was safe to open the door and bring the corpses out into the crematoria. The Zyklon B was actually dropped by a German soldier. The shoving of prisoners into the chambers and the removal of the corpses was done by selected inmates who had no contacts with the other inmates and who were themselves killed after a short time. It is thought that most of these inmates were non-Jews but some were Jews.*

*Other items collected from the deportees in huge amounts were glasses, brushes, pots, and pans, and shoe polish cans. In one room, there is a collection of a tremendous number of pots and pans and other kitchen utensils. All of these objects attest to the fact that the deportees expected to spend a long time in the camps. All of these items came in a great variety of styles, colors, and sizes with many child size items. The effect of seeing these mountains of personal belongings is overwhelming and testifies graphically to the huge numbers of people who went through the camps.*

*Pictures were not allowed in the camps. However, one German photographer made a series of pictorial records of the events at the camp as a secret present for the commandant. In addition to the previously mentioned personal items was a number of canes, crutches, and artificial limbs. Anyone needing one of the above was murdered immediately to preserve the purity of the race.*

Actually, of course, the Nazis considered all Jews to be members of an inferior race. Those who were disabled or handicapped were murdered only because they were deemed unfit for slave labor. The physically able were worked to death, and if they were somehow strong enough to survive such brutal treatment, they, too, were eventually murdered. Hitler's master plan was to rid the whole world of all Jews.

*One display case contained a number of large talletim [prayer shawls] stolen from religious Jews. One of the most distressing display cases showed baby clothing. A baby could survive only if the mother was not Jewish or the baby was felt to be acceptable for adoption by a German couple—the baby had to have blue eyes and blond hair. Otherwise, the baby would starve to death together with the mother. Certainly anyone with doubts about the events at Auschwitz should be made to study in this building.*

*Building seven was devoted to sanitary condition displays. In some bunkers, prisoners slept on straw. In some, they slept on burlap bags directly on the floor. In others, they were crowded in multiple layer bunks. They had six to eight latrines per thousand people; overcrowding, poor sanitation and lack of mobility were the rule. The* kapo, *a prisoner functionary who oversaw prisoners in their work details, had a private room with a single bed and a table. One picture shows an enormously obese* kapo *in stark contrast with the emaciated appearance of the inmates. In the hallway of building seven were rows and rows of photographs taken of the political prisoners. Essentially all selected individuals were political prisoners. Some famous people could be recognized, such as a well-known Polish Jewish actor. The interval between arrival and death was less than six months, and women did not survive as long as men, often only one or two months. The sanitation was primitive, and a lot of prisoners survived only long enough to work in factories such as Krupp's until they died of disease and malnutrition. Many prisoners, but not from Auschwitz, were sent to the Daimler-Benz factories but were usually returned to the camps to be killed.*

*Shortly after the war, a Jewish sculptor made a miniature representation of the arrival, selection, gas chamber, shooting, and torturing of the prisoners. It is a dramatic and overwhelming depiction of life in Auschwitz-Birkenau. There is a second example of these mini-sculptures at Yad Vashem in Israel and a third one at the U.S. Holocaust Memorial Museum in Washington, DC. Standing at several corners were well-constructed and tall watchtowers, and the entire area was surrounded by high electrified barbed wire. Nevertheless, acts of resistance took place sometimes with the help of outside resistance fighters. Among the most dramatic of such events was the documented history of a very beautiful young Polish girl whose name was Mia Zimetbaum. She was so beautiful that she was spared head shaving and was allowed to work in an office. She fell in love with Edward Galinski, another Jewish inmate. They escaped and managed to get away for a few days. However, she was so hungry that she entered a house searching for food. Unfortunately, Polish policemen were in that house. They realized that she was an escapee because her eyes appeared so hungry that she could not have come from anywhere else. Her fiancé surrendered himself to be with her. She was sentenced to be hanged. Walking up to the gallows, she slapped the face of the German officer and killed herself by slashing her wrist with razor blades provided by the underground.*

*After the liberation, several survivors returned to Paris. We were told by several of them that my father was shot as a hostage. Several weeks prior to our trip, we received from the Red Cross International Tracing Service a copy of the death notice. The name was Mankowski, first name Aaron. The nationality was listed as French. The date of birth was January 13, 1902. Under religion, the entry is not indicated. The document indicates that he was imprisoned in Auschwitz and that his number was 28042. He arrived on the 27th of March 1942 from Drancy. From Serge Klarsfeld's book, we know that he was in the first convoy to* leave France.[3] *His category was 'Jude'* [Jew]. *The notice states the he died in the concentration camp of Auschwitz on the night of 18th or 19th June 1942, cause of death 'not indicated.'*

*When Wanda heard that my father had been shot, she was very interested in this and verified that hostages were often selected for punishment for infractions committed by other prisoners or in retaliation for acts of sabotage done outside the camp by the resistance movement. The entire process took place in bunker eleven and the executions in block eleven.[4] This was the most anguishing part of the visit for me, and I cannot write these lines without crying again. The inmates were taken to the basement for interrogation which usually included a variety of tortures. It is difficult to imagine the cruelty of the Germans in this basement. Some prisoners were placed in specially designed three feet by three feet brick cells and forced to stand in such unbelievable tight spaces that they died of suffocation and shock while standing up. A particularly sadistic German officer would force the prisoners to eat a very salty meal before the process so that thirst would be added to their torture. The prisoners were regularly whipped and kicked.*

*After this interrogation, prisoners were brought up to the first floor to face the judge. I presume that this was what indeed happened to my father. The judge was a doctor, Rudolf Milner, up to 1943, and a doctor, Johannan Thummer, after 1943. The judges came to the camp once a week or so. Between three thousand and forty five hundred people were executed on the order of this court martial. The prisoners were not allowed to enter the room and had to stand at the door facing a table where the judge sat. The prosecutor read the charges. There were no questions, no possible defense and almost always the prisoner was sentenced to death by shooting immediately. The prisoner was then taken down the hall. He or she was undressed completely and walked through an iron gate, down three steps into the death courtyard. In the actual spot, there is an empty prisoner's uniform on the floor before the iron gate. The courtyard is a rectangular area between the women's barracks and barrack eleven. The windows on that side of the women's barracks were covered up so that the women could not watch the execution. At the end of the courtyard, there is a stark black wall where a prisoner stood before being shot in the back of the neck at point blank range by a German officer.*

*This part of the visit, particularly the killing, was absolutely overwhelming. I stood by myself near the wall to read the prayer that Shale gave me. It is the El Malei Rachamim, or the prayer of the departed. I am glad that I practiced reading the prayer daily during the trip because my tears prevented my seeing the words clearly, but I read both the Hebrew and the English versions. As hard as this experience was, and I was prepared carefully by Wanda, I am happy that I was there and able to say the prayer. I felt that I could actually walk the same steps that my father did on that day, June 18, 1942 . . .*

*While in Spain, I watched a program on a French channel. It had to do with holocaust survivors in France. A man who appeared to be in his late 50s, early 60s, was talking about his parents. His father and mother were taken from*

*Drancy and both were murdered in Auschwitz. He made a good point. When a parent dies young, he never ages. Eventually, the child becomes older than the parent. In a way, the child becomes a father to his father.*

*The Antels and Wanda were very supportive, and the rest of the visit was easier. Many barracks are devoted to a specific nationality. We selected the French-Belgian pavilion. There was not much new for me in that exhibit. We saw pictures of Petain's surrender, Hitler dancing a jig after forcing the French to sign an armistice in the same train compartment in Compiegne where the World War I armistice was signed, pictures of Charles De Gaulle, Vichy France, Drancy, Hitler walking down the Champs Elysées, pictures of the liberation, and so on.*

*The next barrack was the hospital. Before the Zyklon B gas was perfected, prisoners were killed by intra-cardiac injections of phenol. This is a rather difficult procedure but I guess practice makes perfect. After the injection, the prisoner had just enough strength to take a few steps and collapse in the room across the hall where his body was then thrown out in the courtyard and then brought to the crematoria. In a few instances, inmates who were sick were brought into the hospital. They were released if they improved in fourteen days. If not, they were killed. In the hospital, we saw some pictures of sterilization surgery on women but were spared the gruesome pictures of the actual medical experimentation carried out by Dr. Mengele.*

*We completed the visit of Auschwitz by walking the peaceful street between the barracks by looking at the forbidding watchtowers and the electrified barbed wire and the railroad tracks which brought the inmates to Auschwitz. We visited the crematoria at Auschwitz. They were located in the basement of one or more of the barracks. They look like large brick ovens such as bakers would use, except for the receiving element, which was clearly designed to receive a human corpse. The crematoria in Auschwitz were relatively small and did not compare to the huge crematoria in Birkenau.*

*We took a very short break during which Wanda tried to find my father's name in the camp records. She did not, at first glance, but she will keep looking. I will send her the documents that we have received from the Red Cross so that their records can be completed, and I will do the same for the Washington Holocaust Memorial.*

*The camp complex consisted of Auschwitz one, Auschwitz two (Birkenau) and Auschwitz three. In addition, to the actual camps, the building project included roads, bridges, the sewage system, the water facility, and heating plants. All of this was built by camp prisoners. In addition, a plant for the I.G. Farben Industrie was constructed nearby to take advantage of the supply of free labor. The camp complex is huge, and it took us five minutes by car to go from Auschwitz to Birkenau. The actual distance is six kilometers.*

*Birkenau was created for the express purpose of killing efficiently. The barracks were built after local villages had been displaced. The barracks were built of wood, between 1940 and 1941, by camp inmates. Birkenau is probably ten times larger than Auschwitz and contains the infamous train platform where the selection was made on arrival. We climbed the main gate tower, and Wanda could explain the setup very effectively from this vantage point. The train came in directly to the camp, and a small forest was used to hide the fact that this was the end of the line. There were three large crematoria at Birkenau, each the size of a football field. One was blown up by the liberating Russian troops. One was blown up by the Germans at the end of the war. Each was capable of high capacity use. Birkenau has been left as is or was at the time of the war.*

*People complain of the physical condition of Auschwitz. I do not agree at all. All barracks have been preserved and used to show the world the working of this effective death camp. I think they have done an outstanding job representing the history of Auschwitz. Wanda, of course, made it an incredible experience. Near the blown-up crematoria of Birkenau is a huge memorial consisting of many flat surfaces leading to a rectangular series of modernistic monuments depicting the various aspects of the camp. At the end, there is a stark wall symbolizing the killing wall. Inscriptions in nineteen languages are displayed in front of the monument. Eighteen of the languages were spoken in the camp, and the last one, English, was added. Oscar read the inscriptions in Yiddish and Hebrew, and I read the one in French.*

*At the very end, there is a Polish monument which contains the Cross of Grunwald which commemorates a Polish victory several centuries ago. Wanda, our guide, who is not Jewish and lives nearby in the town of Oświęcim, made an effort to explain that many of the six million people, among them three million Jews, killed in the concentration camps were Polish citizens and that Poland also suffered a great loss. This explained the placing of this monument which contains a cross which superficially looks like a Christian cross. In fact, it has no religious significance and is just part of the Grunwald commemoration. We all agreed [with Elie Wiesel's famous quote]: 'Not all the victims were Jews but all Jews were victims.'*

*I bought several books at the museum. I gave Oscar Antel a large pictorial essay on Auschwitz. One book contained memoirs of a camp commandant, of one of the many camp doctors and of a German soldier. There were appropriate forewords and warnings about the book itself. Very few diaries of Nazis have been found. If Hitler had won, I guess that many diaries would be available. I left the Auschwitz-Birkenau camp with a heavy heart. My final thought was that I would have rather been a victim than a German murderer.*

*June 12,1998. Yesterday was a heart wrenching yet fulfilling day. The experience was more positive than I expected but not a closure. I hate this word. Everyone uses it in terms of my experiences during this trip. I do not see this trip as a closure. This trip provides better bonding with my parents' early life and a deep understanding of my father's journey from Dombrowitz to Drancy and then to Auschwitz. For me, personally, the visit to Auschwitz was the main reason for the trip. There, I felt closer to my father than I ever had. I felt that I could walk in the steps that he was forced to take, and I was glad that I could recite the El Malei Rachamim in his memory. This visit demonstrated the incredible cruelty of the Nazis and their perverse efficiency in almost achieving their goal of wiping out the Jews from the face of the earth. I cannot forget or forgive them. Dis-*

*cussing my visit with my friends and family will be, for me, the best way to make
sure that they fail to reach the goal.*

John's previous quote, cited in the *Baltimore Sun* from a forgotten author,
is worth repeating: "Jewish life in Eastern Europe did not die, but it did not
survive."

## NOTES

1. Permission granted on October 29, 2001, through Chelsea Newhouse, Sun-
Source, *The Baltimore Sun*.
2. J.DC stands for Joint Distribution Committee, often referred to as "The Joint."
J.DC is an umbrella organization for Jewish charities, the purpose of which is to give
money and aid to Jewish social services worldwide.
3. See chapter 5.
4. "Bunker" refers to the building where inmates were imprisoned. "Block" is a
specific section or cell block in the bunker.

## Chapter Seven

# Life Without Father

We believed that father had gone to a German labor camp to fulfill his obligatory work service, and in our naivete we told ourselves we would be reunited as a family after the war. It was a perfectly credible, reasonable assumption at the time. Hope never dies.

It was April 1942 in Paris. A beautiful spring was all around us. The trees and shrubbery in our courtyard bloomed; green leaves unfurled. Birds sang. The early spring sun began to filter through the clouds, toying with the tree branches and shining into the rear windows of our apartment. On our way to school, we walked through the blossoming *Place des Vosges* Gardens with little awareness of the scenery and no joy in our hearts. Mother tried to hold things together, but she was no longer a young, light-hearted person. She had visibly aged.

We missed father. His absence was constantly on our minds, but at the same time, we always felt his presence. Convoy One had delivered father to Birkenau, from which he was taken to nearby Auschwitz. Father must have seen the infamous affirmation in big metal letters, hanging over the gate of Auschwitz: *Arbeit macht Frei*[1] Was he lulled into a false sense of security by this lie?

Life without our father was grim. The burden on Jews increased. By mid-1942, we were forced to re-register as Jews at our local police station and new national identity cards were issued, with our religion stamped prominently on them. The new yellow identity cards were designed to catch attention. The bright red words *Juif* or *Juive* seemed to jump out at us. As a child, my curiosity was also piqued by the fine print. I remember that mother's card had

45

*sans* ("without") listed for profession. John and I were described as *écoliers* ("schoolchildren"). Then came the yellow stars:

> *May 29,1942. German authorities in France publish regulations adopted the previous day requiring Jews in the occupied Zone to wear a yellow star. The present ordinance will be effective June 7,1942 . . . .*[2]

The *Commissaire*, the civilian head of our local police station, issued two yellow stars per person, made of cotton fabric. These were to be worn in public at all times. To do otherwise would incur grave penalties. A description of the yellow star is on record:

> *The Jewish star is a star with six points having the dimensions of the palm of a hand and black borders. It is of yellow cloth and displays, in black letters, the word 'Juif'. It should be worn very visibly on the left side of the chest, firmly sewn to the garment.*[3]

Mother, an accomplished seamstress, sewed our stars on two outer garments. We realized that the star would always remind us of our status and make us terribly self-conscious. The yellow star proclamation caused uneasiness and revulsion among many French people:

> June 7–8, 1942. *Fearing demonstrations of public sympathy with Jews on the first day the yellow star becomes obligatory, the SS and French police plan to arrest non-Jews who wear the star or a derisory insignia . . .but in a mood of visible disapproval, some French non-Jews display their feelings . . . some end up in internment camps . . . Drancy one of them . . . .*[4]

We were forced to wear the yellow star to school, and we expected our classmates to humiliate us. However, my teacher, a no-nonsense authoritarian and not the friendly type, was genuinely sympathetic to our cause and shielded us from the impact of wearing a yellow star in her class. Furthermore, the director of the school, a decorated World War I veteran, stood before each class, one class at a time, and spoke with emotion about our plight. He said that, *in keeping with the best ideals of France*, he would not allow any hazing and he would tolerate no harassment nor taunting throughout the entire *Place des Vosges* School. There were almost no such incidents in the school.

I shall always be grateful to my teacher and to the director of the *Ecole de la Place des Vosges* for their attitude and kindness at a perilous time in our lives. I do not remember their names.[5] They remain nonetheless a source of inspiration for me.

Notwithstanding, wearing a yellow star in school continued to be psychologically traumatic. Going back and forth to school, we were afraid of being subject to verbal and physical abuse. We began to avoid busy streets and instead, we took a circuitous route to and from school. Fortunately, as things turned out, by the new school year, on October 1, 1942, we would be in the *Zone Libre* (unoccupied France), where the yellow stars were not and never would be required.[6]

Soon after the yellow star rule took effect, the *Word* informed us to ride only the last car of each train on the subway. Serge Klarsfeld touches on this point:

> *June 10, 1942, the prefect of the Seine Department restricts Jews to the last car of all Paris metro trains—no public announcement is to be made or posted; subway personnel will enforce the regulation.*[7]

We stopped using the subway and do not recall ever traveling the subway wearing the yellow star. We were becoming isolated and confined to the *Marais*. It was more a matter of places we did not wish to go rather than a matter of places we could not go. The wearing of yellow stars was the significant factor that kept us close to our neighborhood. A turning point in our lives was heralded by the notorious *rafles* (round ups) *du Vel d'Hiv* (short for *Velodrome d'Hiver*) in July 1942.

> *The* Velodrome d'Hiver *was a large Parisian indoor sports arena in the fifteenth arrondissement. In addition to sporting events, the* Vel d'Hiv *had seen its share of political rallies, including xenophobic and anti-Semitic demonstrations. The objective was to arrest 28,000 Jews in the greater Paris region—what the Germans called 'Das Gross-Paris.' Hennequin, the municipal police chief, drew up the orders of the day, disclosing how the French police were to do the job. They were to concentrate on stateless and foreign Jews, excluding sensitive categories such as British or American Jews.*
>
> *Everyone on the lists, carefully prepared at the prefecture, was to be seized, regardless of the state of his or her health . . . . On the morning of 16 July 1942, 9,000 French police went into action. The force was composed of gendarmes, gardes mobiles [National Guard], bailiffs, detectives, patrolmen, and even students from the police school. Three or four hundred young followers of Doriot also turned out to help, wearing blue cross-straps, and arm-bands bearing the initials 'PPF.'*

Jacques Doriot, a French Politician espousing Fascism, formed his own party, the *Parti Popular Francais* known as the PPF. He used the party paper, *Le Cri du Peuple*, to advocate collaboration with Germany. He later donned a German uniform and was killed as a Wermacht soldier in Germany during 1945.

> *The Germans scarcely appeared on the scene at all. The Jews often were reassured by the French uniform, the instructions in French, and the 'correct' deportment of the arresting officer. For two days the manhunt continued . . . .*

*Most of the victims had no idea of what awaited them. What they found was
administrative chaos, combined with utter neglect. The internment camp of
Drancy received some 6,000 internees, single men and women or families without children. The Vel d'Hiv, which could hold 15,000 spectators, was to receive
the rest of the 28,000. Clearly, if the arrests had reached even close to the intended total, there would not have been room at the stadium. As it was, when
7,000 people, including over 4,000 children, were packed into it, there was
hardly enough space to lie down. Worse still, hardly any physical preparations
had been made. There was neither food nor water, nor sanitary arrangements.
The Germans permitted only two doctors at a time to attend the internees.*

*At first the victims experienced thirst, hunger, the heat of the day, the cold of
the night. Then diarrhea and dysentery. A terrible odor infected the place. Then
came a sense of abandonment as hours stretched into days. The confinement
lasted for five days.*[8]

The name *Vel d'Hiv* will always be part of my being; it is still capable of sending shivers down my spine. These *rafles* marked the first arrest of women and
children. Survival was now the issue. While mother was discussing our options
and considering various plans of action with other Jews, events overtook us.
"The Word" spread the news late one day in mid July that there would be a
roundup of women and children on our street, *rue de Sévigné*, that very evening.[9]
I do not remember the exact date beyond that it was early in my 1942 summer
school vacation. The Word also put out very specific additional advice; we were
not to open the door and were not to generate any noise whatever from inside the
apartment. The police would then leave and not come back for several hours,
giving us a chance to escape. Noise coming from inside a dwelling would cause
the police to break down the doors of the apartment. "The Word" advised using
pillows on children's faces as soon as the police's knock was heard. There were
four of us, Mother, John, Ida Waldman and myself (Ida Waldman was our tenant. She had remained with us after her husband was arrested with father). As
soon as we heard the bang on the door, Mother covered my face and Ida Waldman blanketed John's face with heavy firm pillows. I still have occasional night-
mares that vividly involve this incident.

"The Word" further advised that people leave their apartments without yellow stars and flee to the nearest subway. We were counseled to wait about
thirty minutes to be sure the streets were clear of police presence. At the suggested time, we left our beloved 11 *rue de Sevigné* in a state of confusion,
panic and incredulity. We rushed over to the St. Paul metro station. Ida Waldman went in one direction, while mother, John and I rode the train to the end
of the line, the *Pont de Neuilly*. There we took the number 162 bus, alighted
in Bezon and walked the short distance to the Roditis's home, where Benjamin, my father's devoted assistant, his parents and two sisters lived. We ex-

plained our situation and despite a clear danger to people harboring Jews, the Roditis welcomed us graciously. They were a totally assimilated French family of Turkish extraction. Truly brave and decent folks, they gave us room, board and shelter for a few days. They then helped us obtain forged identity cards under the name of *Manko*. Forgery was expensive and cost Mother a tidy sum. Benjamin went back to our apartment with Guy Huchon, our father's other dedicated assistant, to collect our funds, which had been hidden in a mattress, and valuable personal possessions, as well as additional basic clothing. We believed that we were too close to Paris and the continuing roundup of Jewish women and children. We had to get away. Guy Huchon and his parents were our longtime friends. With peril to themselves, they offered to hide us in *Le Corubert*—about 200 miles to the west. Hiding Jews was becoming a serious offense, punishable by death in some instances.

Our plan was to join Uncle Maurice Bieguin who was now living in Free France with his wife Devra and children, Oscar and Mary. Before the German invasion, he relocated in *Saint Antonin Noble Val*, near *Montauban*. My uncle had become familiar with the area during previous trips, involving his work as an electrical engineering consultant. He had become impressed by the entire region because of its beauty and remoteness.

With Guy Huchon guiding us, we caught the train to Le Mans somewhere well outside Paris. He accompanied us to Le Mans. During the train ride, he drilled into us our new name of Manko. Papa and Janine Huchon, alerted by a telegram from Guy, were waiting for us at the train station at Le Mans. I remember that Papa Huchon was concerned about my mother's Polish accent and advised her to answer questions simply with *oui, non* or *merci*.

Under the close watch of Papa and Janine Huchon, the Normandy bus took us uneventfully to Le Corubert. There was no visible French Police activity or German presence in *Le Corubert* but Papa Huchon advised us to limit our movements and stay close to their home. This time, there was no free roaming in *Le Corubert* or its surroundings. The danger, of course, was an anonymous accusation by a villager. But that did not arise.

We stayed in *Le Corubert* for two weeks while Mother was looking for a *macher* to take us safely to the *Zone Libre*.[10] We soon found out that a special type of *macher* was needed for this purpose, someone recognized as a *passeur*.[11] We were ultimately connected with a qualified *passeur*, paying him a considerable sum of money to take us to Free France.

I don't recall how we traveled from *Le Corubert* to a safe house somewhere in the Paris suburbs, but I do remember we spent two days there under the care of our *passeur*. He was a confident, reassuring, burly individual exuding bravado and we felt greatly heartened. He inspired trust. Even mother was not dubious nor was she suspicious of him. He was Jewish and had to be on our side. We rationalized that he would do his utmost for us. We felt that he could be trusted. We needed both new and additional forged documents and these he would provide. While waiting for things to happen, we became anxious and restless. The *passeur* told us to be patient until he found the ideal time to move us safely to Unoccupied France.

Finally we were on the train with a small group under the *passeur's* protection. We were checked on several occasions by French police and German military police. There was no problem. We got off the train near the border dividing Occupied from Unoccupied France, a spot deep in the Nièvre district. It seemed so easy; our *passeur* knew his business, said mother. We crossed the *ligne de demarcation* at an isolated site without incident. We were finally in the *Zone Libre*. We thought that our *passeur* was taking us to a nearby safe house but instead, he walked us into a French *gendarmerie* in Vichy France (post of the French National Police). Was this part of his scheme?

We were promptly detained. I well remember a large portrait of Marshal Pétain staring at us as we were waiting to be questioned.[12] After this apparent betrayal, our *passeur* vanished. We never heard from him again and I still wonder whether he was working both sides of the street, and profiting from both prey and hunters. No wonder that our trip had been so uneventful. It is possible that he was doing his best and delivered us to a benign Vichy Post. He must have had a magic wand, i.e., bribery, with the French police and the German forces. To this day, I cannot be sure whether he was a hero, a villain, an opportunist or something of each.

The atmosphere in the Vichy France *gendarmerie* was benevolent. The ambience was correct, formal, polite, and very French. We were told that mother would go to jail and John and I, as children below the age covered by the Vichy statutes, would be released in some appropriate fashion. When the questioning by the uniformed gendarmes was finished, we were turned over to an authoritarian older senior civilian, the local Vichy administrator, who was to dispose of our case. In the privacy of his inner office, this dignitary commented on the gravity of our situation, never cracking a smile. He then told us that he had decided to give mother a safe conduct permit to take John and me to our uncle in Southern France. He became friendly and intimate, talking about himself. He spoke of his proud days in Verdun during World War I, about the past glory of France and what was happening to France now. Then in a hushed tone of voice, he bent over and whispered to my mother, *listen to me, do not return here.* He planted the seed. His advice would save mother's life. The safe conduct permit and his warning ensured that she would not be deported.

Opening the door to his office, he advised mother in a loud tone of voice to safeguard the authorization documents that he had signed. He then sternly lectured mother about the penalties of failing to come back within seven days. *We will find you,* he warned, *if you become a fugitive.* The French official had given us a boost. Did our *passeur* plan these events? Many women and children, including very young ones, were subsequently arrested and deported from the *Zone Libre.* We were, indeed, fortunate.

We were soon on our way. The sluggish train chugged along through unoccupied France, ultimately bringing us to Montauban, the Prefectoral seat of the Department of the Tarn et Garonne.[13] This region of Vichy France was to be a moderately safe locale for us.

From Montauban, we traveled by an old bus to Saint Antonin, where Uncle Bieguin was waiting for us at the bus depot. Saint Antonin, which the Romans called Nobilis Vallis, was and is a picturesque little town southwest of the rugged plateaus of the Massif Central. The formal name was Saint Antonin Noble Val. Everyone called it Saint Antonin. The town is situated in the valley, gently nestled between peaks of high points and well protected by natural rocky terrain. Saint Antonin is the home of the oldest city hall in France, its heritage extending back over many centuries. It has been said that each century has left its imprint on Saint Antonin, none greater than the Middle Ages. Many *ruelles* (little streets) of Saint Antonin are medieval in size, appearance, design and character.

This quaint little town welcomed us in early August 1942. The mayor was Dr. Paul Benet, *Chevalier de la Légion d'Honneur.* He drove his own classical black Citroën sedan and had an unlimited allotment of gas.

He was my uncle's doctor; a fine practitioner of medicine and a decent, generous and fair person. He may well have been one of the reasons I went into medicine. My uncle trusted Dr. Benet and he took mother, who was emotionally and physically drained, to see the good doctor. John and I were in tow. Dr. Benet listened with great empathy, stating that mother was in no condition to go back to the *Gendarmerie.* He signed a medical certificate to that effect which the French authorities accepted without question. This occurred because, as the mayor, Dr. Benet officially represented Vichy France in *Saint Antonin.* We were to learn later, from several local people, that Dr. Benet was the leader of the Underground in the region. My uncle, Maurice Bieguin, and his wife, Devra, also apparently worked for the Underground, presumably under Dr Benet's command. Many years later, my cousins told me that Uncle Maurice and Aunt Devra had been arrested briefly for their clandestine involvement before we came to *Saint Antonin.* They had been miraculously released shortly after their capture through the intervention of the mayor, Dr. Benet.

Our uncle, in welcoming us at the bus depot in *Saint Antonin,* announced that he was now living in a small, nearby community, three kilometers from

*Saint Antonin*, known as Le Bosc. Lightly populated, Le Bosc was a pleasant hamlet, about five hundred meters higher in altitude than *Saint Antonin*. Uncle Maurice suffered from severe allergic bronchial asthma. Dr Benet early on had recommended that my uncle move to *Le Bosc*. In those days, the medical treatment of asthma was limited; the move to *Le Bosc* was an advisable decision even by modern medical guidelines. With purer air, less humidity and fewer air-borne allergens, the climate of *Le Bosc* provided a much more favorable environment for our uncle. The move to *Le Bosc* was for our uncle's medical condition but it would later be a life-saving one for all of us.

After telling us about his move to *Le Bosc*, our uncle took us directly to an apartment he had been able to secure for us in *St. Antonin*. Many people were seeking refuge from the war in this quiet, faraway little town with apartments becoming difficult to find. We had to accept an exclusive, expensive and entirely furnished apartment in an older, upper-class section of *St. Antonin*. The owner was an elderly, aristocratic French woman who was compulsive about this special apartment, not relishing the presence of two young boys, and she told us so. She insisted that we keep an ongoing inventory of everything including kitchen utensils, silverware, plates and glassware. Any broken or missing items had to be paid for immediately. We had to pay rent three months in advance. She checked on us daily and mother felt we were living in a museum. The apartment was upscale and more than we needed but it was the only place available at the time. Soon, a more modest apartment became available; this one, on an old *ruelle,* was much better suited to our needs. We felt relieved to be away from that landlady.

As previously noted, the wearing of the yellow star was never required in Unoccupied France, and much to our relief we never had to wear the yellow star again. In early October, 1942, I, age 8, and John, age 6, enrolled in the Primary School of *St. Antonin*, run by a couple, Monsieur et Madame Gagnot, both excellent teachers and decent people. It was a pleasant school with a charming courtyard, and, to our pleasure, a sizable playground. Mother found work as a seamstress and was given the use of a sewing machine, a Singer, at home. We made friends, and we were beginning to enjoy life again. On weekends, we visited our uncle and his family in *Le Bosc*, a great source of pleasure. We became accustomed to a nice new routine in *St. Antonin*.

Everything seemed relatively normal again for us. Without knowing why, we all felt protected by our mayor, Dr. Paul Benet; instinctively, we knew somehow that he was on our side. Police activity was almost nonexistent in this old medieval town.

In November, 1942, the Germans took over the *Zone Libre*. They now occupied all of France. We feared that our idyllic little town was no longer a safe haven. After talking with Dr. Benet and my uncle, we decided to move to *Le*

*Bosc*, where there would be no police or German presence. At least none was anticipated, according to Dr. Benet. He was by now close to my uncle and he was also a good friend of a farmer named Pierre Mercadier. In fact, my uncle was already living on the Mercadier farm.

In late November, 1942, soon after German troops entered *Saint Antonin*, Mother, John and I moved on. The actual move to *Le Bosc* was a short, enjoyable and memorable experience. We traveled in an open wagon drawn by two horses, with Farmer Mercadier in the driver's seat. Mother was seated comfortably next to him while John and I sat on the sides of the wagon with our feet dangling. All our possessions were in the middle of the wagon. It was a clear, beautiful fall day, the sun was high and the air was crisp. Watching the little town of *Saint Antonin* recede from our view, we were treated to a spectacular panorama of hills and elevated landscapes which dotted the entire region above the valley. As we approached the village, we passed the noted neighboring cave, known as *La Grotte du Bosc*, comparable to the beautiful Luray Caverns in northern Virginia, outside *Washington, DC* We were taken in by the peace and quietness of *Le Bosc*, a real departure from hectic Paris.

Our uncle made all the arrangements and we went directly to the Mercadier farm, where he and his family lived. They were four— my uncle, his wife, Devra, their children, Oscar and Mary; now with mother, John and me, we became a total of seven tenants. We were given an old house in which to live, adjoining the main farm. It was modest but adequate; well-maintained, clean, and comfortable. We all helped with the farm chores, i.e. gathering crops, field work, seamstress duties, and the wine-making tasks after the *vendanges* (the gathering of the grapes). This was a big yearly event, a veritable feast. My mother enjoyed caring for the cattle, using the skills developed during her early years in Dombrowitz.

When we first arrived at the farm, we were greeted by the pungent odor of sheep. We became accustomed to this smell as we did to other unique farm scents of animal dung, drying hay, old grapes, pigs and other animals. The diverse sounds of farm life and assorted tastes of this bountiful land were all around us. This was a typical rural French farm. Life here was very different from what we were used to in Paris.

Much has been said about the scarcity of food and resulting nutritional problems in wartime France. On the farm, there was no food shortage. We enjoyed steak, veal, liver, rabbit and lamb. High points of our eating were the *cassoulet*, a superb southern French dish, the *confit de canard*, duck prepared in an inimitable French fashion, and the *bourguignon*, a flavorful French stew cooked in red wine. Savory gravy was dispensed in a special dish, *le saucier*, with two spouts, lean gravy feeding from the bottom and fat gravy from the top. Butter, cream and milk were plentiful. *La miche,* a delectable round

French farm bread, was part of every meal. Wine was never missing from the table. All of this, along with the house, was bartered for our services; and we all worked eagerly and diligently as farm hands. We were well aware of a good situation, not to mention shelter from the war.

It was a great comfort to be together as a family. We felt protected by the closeness of wonderful people, the Mercadiers, Doctor Benet and the other villagers. Everybody in *Le Bosc* knew that there was a Jewish family of seven people living among them, but no one said a thing. No one turned us in. This act was at considerable danger to the local inhabitants. It was common knowledge that French people were being shot for harboring or hiding Jews. Nevertheless, somehow we felt secure among these villagers and the farmers of *Le Bosc*. The war seemed far away. The occasional impromptu round-up of Jews in *Saint Antonin* by the Vichy Government seemed remote to us. It gradually became a happy time and we began to lose fear and regain hope. There seemed to be light at the end of the tunnel. Rumors about an upcoming Allied landing circulated, and news of major German defeats in Russia cheered us as well.

Village life centered around the ancient Catholic church. Next to the church was a one room school opening to a sizable yard. I remember that there was a large stove in the middle of the school room. The school was attached to a small house where the teacher lived with her husband. Opposite the school complex was the village grocery store, home to the only telephone in *Le Bosc*. This telephone protected us from intrusion from the outside and proved to be life saving later. We were notified of anything out of the ordinary in *Saint Antonin* such as a roundup of Jews with the calls coming from city hall. The farms were scattered around the hub of the village. The land was fertile, productive with food products selling easily at handsome profits on the open market. Because of the disparity between the supply and demand of farm goods, a big black market developed with certain foodstuffs such as meats, eggs and butter selling at highly inflated prices. The farmers were happy and flourishing.

The Curé, Père Jean Baptiste, the name I seem to remember, knew we were Jewish[14]. He was a decent, congenial and compassionate man who became obsessed with our welfare. Our blending in with *Le Bosc*'s other villagers was his prime concern. We attended mass, took communion and went to Sunday school along with the children of the village.

To supplement our education, Uncle Maurice tutored us with advanced studies. It began informally but later on, two extra hours of coaching took place everyday. John and I gained much from our uncle who was an intellectual giant and had been dubbed "the Brain" in Dombrowitz (told to me by Uncle Isor years later in Washington). Life was pleasant. We became fast friends with the Mercadier children, playing together all over their farm. Once when we were playing, a German patrol came through the farm, unannounced. A young German officer picked up the blond, curly-haired Jojo—then the nickname of my brother John—lifted him in the air, and said: *I have a boy like him back in Germany.* Mother who happened to be nearby was frozen in fear, but said nothing, just smiled. The episode was brief and without consequences other than to scare us out of our wits.

The German troops occupying the region were said to be jaded, wounded and battle-fatigued soldiers, returning from the Russian front. Rumor had it that these Wehrmacht soldiers, also composed of many older men or young, inexperienced lads, were not elite forces. No crack fighting troops, no S.S. units, no Panzer tank divisions or Gestapo forces were stationed in our area.

One of our favorite pastimes was going with other children from the village to watch these German soldiers work and play. We would ride down to *Saint Antonin* with a farmer, sometimes going by horse and wagon but more frequently by *gasogène* vehicles[15]. These unusual motorcars would coast along all the way from *Le Bosc* to the entrance to *Saint Antonin* with the motor turned off to conserve energy. The privileged few people who owned gasoline-fueled cars did the same. The sweeping scenery was greatly enhanced in our eyes by the added thrill of silently and effortlessly gliding down the mountain in this most adventurous fashion.

There was a German signal corps battalion camp near *Saint Antonin,* and we disembarked there. While the farmer was getting supplies in town, we would watch the German soldiers work on telephone poles or play *fussball* (soccer). It was fun and entertaining. They frequently called each other by names that made us laugh as we soon learned the meaning of the words. Some choice expressions were *Du bist ein Schwein, Du Schwein* or *Du hast Schwein* (you are a pig, you pig and you have luck). These soldiers never threatened or scared us. They were friendly and affable; they gave us chocolate and little cookies. The farmer would pick us up upon his way back to *Le Bosc.* Cheerfully, we rode back to the village excitedly to tell people about our caper. We never told the same tale twice.

Our care-free life in *Le Bosc* was suddenly interrupted in the early spring of 1944. The *Milice*, the dreaded political police force of the Vichy Government, usually supervised by a Gestapo officer, would occasionally come to *Saint Antonin* and arrest a scattering of Jews. In April, 1944, they came with ardor, zeal and vigor. They engaged in a roundup of all the Jews, remaining in *Saint Antonin.* They learned that there was a Jewish family living in *Le Bosc* from records held by the *mairie* (city hall) of Saint-Antonin, where we were registered. They decided to come after us. Dr. Benet himself called the owner of the grocery store in *Le Bosc* on the only existing telephone to alert us that a Gestapo squad car was making its way to us. The grocery owner immediately dispatched his teenage son to the farm by bike to deliver the message. Farmer Mercadier gathered all seven of us together and told us gravely, in his usual unruffled way, that we had to disappear immediately *au fond des bois* ("in the heart of the woods").

He took us to an old family cabin well-hidden in the forest, telling us they'd never find us there. Further, he promised that his children would deliver cooked food and drinks to us on a daily basis until the crisis passed. We stayed in our hideout for five days; we were well taken care of, as promised. After five days, Mercadier himself came to give us the all-clear signal and take us back to the farm. Doctor Paul Benet and farmer Pierre Mercadier saved our lives.

It was a miracle that no one in *Le Bosc* or *Saint Antonin* was arrested, deported or shot over this episode, and I have often wondered why no hostages were taken. This would have been the usual pattern after such an incident. It was, however, close in time to the rumored coming Allied invasion. I read later that Nazi sympathizers, collaborators and diehards were beginning to cover their tracks in fear of future reprisals.

Our lives resumed. Soon April gave way to spring in all its fullness. I was now nine, and John was seven. We all felt something new and undefinable was about to happen. *Les messages personnels* from London began as usual, *Les Francais parlent aux Francais* ("Frenchmen talk to Frenchmen"). These messages accelerated in frequency, increased in volume and became more poetic in nature.[16] The mood of the villagers was becoming distinctly different. People seemed encouraged. It was now May 1944, and suddenly the German troops left the area. The Maquis gradually came out of hiding, becoming highly visible.[17] The allied landings could not be far off. Indeed, D-Day was to come soon.

Living in *Le Bosc* was a happy, carefree and gentle time for John and me. We failed to notice, or did not wish to notice, that Uncle Maurice's health was deteriorating. He was losing weight, developing a swelling in his legs, wheezing constantly and had a continual deep cough. His skin color was ashen and Doctor Benet, looking very worried, visited daily. Our uncle was well liked and respected by the people in *Le Bosc*. Villagers and farmers came by to offer their assistance. John and I did not comprehend the gravity of our uncle's illness but mother did. To further complicate a bad situation, my aunt, who had a history of depression, relapsed. Overwhelmed with anxiety, she began to experience great difficulty in coping with the situation. The brunt of it all fell primarily on our mother. As always, mother was up to the task. In August 1944, our uncle's health took a turn for the worse. He was now gasping for breath. We tried to cheer him up with the news of the impending liberation of

Paris. *Ces bonnes nouvelles ne sont plus pour moi* was his reply with resignation ("this good news is no longer for me"). On August 23, 1944, our dear uncle died at the age of 32. Dr Benet told us that our uncle had succumbed to complications of asthma. Paris was liberated on August 25, 1944.

The few days following his death are somewhat a blur in my mind. John and I were taken in by a fine French family for a few days. The Curé declared a small part of *Le Bosc* cemetery Jewish ground and there Uncle Maurice Bieguin (born Motel Biegun) was buried. In the absence of a Jewish rabbinical or religious presence (no Jewish people remained in *Saint Antonin*), the Curé officiated at the funeral. The Catholic village priest was simply wonderful, conducting a non-denominational service with almost the entire population of *Le Bosc* attending the interment.

My uncle gone, we moved back to *Saint Antonin* in September 1944, primarily to go to a better school. We were sad about leaving the village. However, before long our spirits soared. We began to anticipate our return to Paris where we thought we would go back to find father and everything would be fine again. With joy in our hearts, we effortlessly adapted to quiet and charming *Saint Antonin*, where we had lived briefly in the late summer of 1942, when we first came to the region. This pleasant small French town was unchanged.

In November 1944, mother went to Montauban (the capital city of the Tarn et Garonne) to buy a plot in the Jewish cemetery, a part of the main cemetery there. Soon afterwards, the remains of our uncle were buried in this dedicated Jewish soil. The transfer was greatly facilitated by the assistance of our friend, *le Curé du Bosc*. Subsequently in 1976, the body and the headstone of Maurice Bieguin again were transferred, but this time to Israel by his son, Oscar. Maurice's widow, Devra, died in Israel at the age of 55 and both bodies are buried in the cemetery of the kibbutz where Oscar Bieguin resides.

During our 1944 Christmas school recess, mother went to Paris to reclaim our apartment. She came back hurriedly, saying that the Germans were coming back. She did not know it, but she was referring to the Battle of the Bulge, the Germans' last major thrust in Europe.

In April 1945, we learned of the death of President Franklin Delano Roosevelt. The American President had been a great source of spiritual comfort, inspiration and hope to all of us. The name Roosevelt was music to our souls, magic to our minds and ecstasy to our lips. We never abbreviated the name. He was always President Franklin Delano Roosevelt to us. We seemed to be fascinated by the middle name of Delano and never omitted it. To us, he was the architect of the pending allied victory over the evil of Hitler and German Nazism, the mastermind of the *Débarquement* in Normandy [*Débarquement*, literally meaning landing, was our favored term for D-Day]. To us, President

Franklin Delano Roosevelt was the leader of the Free World. With victory, he gave us freedom. To us, the American President was the giant of the allied war effort—much greater than the other prominent leaders of that period—Churchill, Eisenhower and De Gaulle. At his death, we felt that we had lost our hero and champion. Our consternation was profound, and our grief extraordinary. It was almost as though God had died.

The war ended in Europe on May 8, 1945. French Resistance units paraded in the streets of *Saint Antonin*. Men and women with *FFI* armbands and weapons were a welcome sight.[18] The public responded with enthusiasm and applause. People were joyous, hugging and kissing one another on the streets while many spontaneously sang the *Marseillaise*. We danced, celebrated and watched fireworks until late into the night. The mayor, Dr Paul Benet, gave some stirring speeches. Everyone seemed so happy.

The school year was soon over. Excited and optimistic, our little family returned to Paris in July 1945.

## NOTES

1. "Work leads to freedom".
2. Klarsfeld, "Children," 31.
3. Klarsfeld, "Children," 31.
4. Klarsfeld, "Children," 33, for French reaction to the yellow stars.
5. This event took place over 60 years ago. My attempts to trace their names were not fruitful. The school ceased to exist many years ago.
6. "The wearing of the yellow star was never imposed on Jews in the unoccupied Zone even after the Germans occupied all of France later in 1942." Klarsfeld, "Children," 31.
7. Klarsfeld, "Children," 33.
8. Marrus, Michael R. and Paxton, Robert O.,*Vichy France and the Jews* (New York: Basic Books, 1981), 250.
9. "The Word", as described in chapter 5, was our secret source of information.
10. Yiddish word literally meaning "maker" or "doer." It denotes a broker, facilitator or middleman. According to Weinreich's *Modern English-Yiddish-English Dictionary* (New York: Yvo Institute for Jewish Research, 1990), a *macher* is an influential person.
11. Roughly equivalent to today's coyote— someone who assists others, most typically for a fee, to cross a border.
12. Marshal Pétain and his government had headquarters in the city of Vichy. They freely collaborated with the Germans.
13. The *Préfecture* is the office of the Prefect, a national official charged with duties ranging from infrastructure to political reporting.
14. A *curé* is a Catholic priest, head of a parish.

15. Vehicles refitted with a coal-powered (or *Gasogène*) engine as an alternative to gasoline.

16. Personal messages from Free France in London to the underground. It was forbidden to listen to the radio station broadcasting these coded bulletins. In *Le Bosc* and elsewhere in France, many people disregarded this edict.

17. *Le Maquis*, literally a reference to underbrush, was a popular term for the Underground.

18. F.F.I. stood for *Forces Françaises de l'Intérieur* (French Forces of the Interior).

## Chapter Eight

# Postwar Paris

Paris in 1945 was alive with excitement. Reminiscing about war events was everyone's pastime. Revisionism was rampant, but not debate. Euphoria and patriotism flourished while parading French troops were acclaimed with passion. Although most patriotic displays were heartfelt, some were merely symbolic of popular myths nurtured by delusional national daydreaming. France was not yet ready to face it and certain facts were selectively emphasized:

According to official versions, France came out on top;[1] the Germans didn't take into account the wrath of young Frenchmen;[2] the Vichy government, far from collaborating with the Germans, had done its very best for all during the Occupation; Paris was liberated by French Forces; Parisian police facilitated the liberation of Paris. The French Resistance had played a major role in the liberation of Paris.

Popular lore said all collaborators were dragged through the streets, humiliated and shot. Many collaborators, however, were spared the death penalty, many were given light sentences, many were acquitted and some were never even tried and brought to justice.[3]

There was ample evidence of a rapidly emerging governmental hagiography. Memorial plaques were much in evidence. Testimonials to victims and heroes were heard daily. Newspapers, periodicals, comic sheets, newsreels and documentaries praised the nation and saluted France.

As with all *official* versions of history, inconvenient facts were ignored. The fact that French troops, the Second Armored Division under Brigadier General Leclerc, were the first Allied forces to enter Paris derived from no particular feat of French arms but rather from arrangements carefully negotiated between the Supreme Allied Commander, General Eisenhower, and General De Gaulle. The Paris police had, in fact, gone on strike beginning Tuesday August 15th and had not reported for duty during the days before the liberation of Paris. A prominent part in the liberation of Paris by the French Resistance was discouraged by Eisenhower, who wanted to avoid an armed uprising in the capital. De Gaulle, for his part, was worried about the unruliness of a Resistance leadership, afflicted by in-fighting, rivalry and a lack of central discipline. De Gaulle's primary concern was to prevent his Communist rivals, closely allied to the FFI (French Forces of the Interior) under Colonel Rol Tanguy, from playing a significant role in the liberation of Paris. Not surprisingly, the part of the Resistance in the liberation of Paris remained spotty, limited and ancillary.[4]

France suffered from a collective amnesia. Realities such as the French internment camps, *Drancy, Compiègne* and the many others, the notorious *raffles du Vel d' Hiv;* the noxious Vichy anti-Jewish laws and the outrageous *forbidden to Jews* posters went unmentioned.

Both the national and Parisian city police wanted their shameful role in the deportations to be forgotten and they now began evicting anyone who had stolen Jewish apartments. The French soon eliminated from their memories the role played by the French state toward their Jewish countrymen. Successive governments of the French Fourth Republic encouraged, promoted and disseminated lies about Vichy and the Jews. If the complete story of the Vichy government's persecution of the Jews was disgraceful, it was also suppressed at all levels of the bureaucracy. Years would pass before well-documented evidence demonstrated that Vichy France had done little to protect Jews. To the contrary, the French police had been vigorous in capturing and imprisoning Jews. The dedication of French authorities to rounding up Jewish men, women and children had exceeded the expectations of their German masters. The Germans were surprised by the zeal and efficiency of the Paris police in the pursuit of Jews.[5]

After the war, the mood of the country was ebullient, contagious and pervasive and a popular slogan of the day was *La France aux Francais* ("France for the French"). Mother, John and I embraced this ecstatic atmosphere. We felt very French. Questions would be raised, but not yet. The painful facts would slowly begin to come out over the next decade. It was not, however, until 1969, that Marcel Ophuls's brilliant and lengthy documentary on the subject of the Occupation, *The Sorrow and the Pity*, would clarify the behavior of France and some of the French people during the dark days. Truth was finally told.

We were back at 11 *rue de Sévigné*. It was a miracle! Our apartment, well maintained during the Occupation, was vacant. The furniture was intact. The walls had been freshly repainted. Mother had paid rent throughout the war. The landlady, a wonderful French woman, had protected our home. She had kept her end of the bargain and did not allow anyone to take our place. We were pleasantly surprised by this homecoming and we were certain that father would soon return to us.

It was late July 1945 in Paris, but something was wrong. Father had not returned home. The labor camps were empty and some of the inmates were coming home. They told unbelievable horror stories. We were beginning to hear about extermination camps. Many people thought these accounts were an exaggeration and untrue.

Emotional stories were heard throughout Paris. Their main theme was the same: returnees were wasted, cadaverous and some were not recognized by their families. We did not see any of these people; we only heard about them. We were warned to be on the look-out for father and not miss him. We waited, watched, looked and waited some more. July went by, but father had not come. August came, but father did not.

Late in August, two gaunt, well-dressed strangers came to see us. They told us they were survivors of Convoy One. We did not understand. They gave us the bad news. "Aaron is dead", they said. But we refused to believe them. Father is alive! These men are wrong and he will come home any day now. That is what we wanted to believe. For a while, we denied the possibility that father, in the prime of his life, would not come home from a labor camp. Reality then slowly set in. Mother tried to console us and we, in turn, tried to console mother. We sat *Shiva*, the traditional Jewish period of grief, during September, assisted by members of our synagogue on *rue Pavée*. Our grief was enormous and indescribable for our lives were changed forever. I now worried that something might happen to mother, even though the Nazi threat was over, and that John and I might become orphans.

Adults talked in hushed whispers about father. John and I did not understand everything. We knew certain things were being hidden from us. Nice people were saying that I looked much like my father. I began to believe that I had to replace father, and look after mother and my younger brother.

The two surviving members of Convoy One offered to help us. On their testimony, an official death certificate was issued by the De Gaulle government. I was 11 years old at the time. I remember asking someone what was meant by *le feu* Aaron Mankowski. His matter of fact answer was that the expression meant the *dead* Aaron Mankowski. Mother was declared a *Veuve de Guerre* (war widow) and was told that she was entitled to a pension from the French government. My heart was broken. This episode is so firmly set in my memory, I seem to remember every detail of it. I remember that I did not know what *le feu* meant and learned that it meant "the late". I remember the cold atmosphere of the room and I especially remember the cavalier attitude of the bureaucrats.

Over the years, mother, John and I spoke frequently about father. These conversations were always painful. It was as difficult then as it still is now to understand what happened to our father. The Vichy government betrayed our father simply because he was Jewish. In later years, President Jacques Chirac would admit to the grievous role played by Vichy in World War II. He presented the apologies of the French Nation to all French Jews. This change in the official French attitude, generally well-received, was particularly welcome in the Jewish community. But for mother, John and me, Chirac's words were too late. They were of no comfort to us.

Historically, French enlightenment had occurred in the eighteenth century when the revolution of 1789 proclaimed the principles of *liberté, égalité et fraternité.* Yet, the institutions of Vichy France, in league with the Nazis, caused father's murder and those of thousands of others.

My parents had been accepted as legal immigrants by France; as such they were entitled to protection under French law. John and I were born in France and therefore were French nationals. Father was a loyal permanent resident of France expecting soon to become a naturalized French citizen. His legal status was comparable to that of a resident alien in the U.S., awaiting citizenship eligibility. Under the Vichy government's anti-Jewish edicts, his rights quickly eroded and completely disappeared. Vichy France had no regard for father's status. As far as Vichy France was concerned, this good man was expendable.

France had been brilliant in so many areas. Where was that France? In arts and letters, the quintessential qualities of France had been restraint and balance. Where was that France? France had prided itself on its humanitarian principles. Where was that France? Of course, one might ask the same questions about Nazi Germany, or Stalinist Russia, or Torquemada's Spain. But France, on the other hand, was a nation renowned for its magnanimous ideals and its advanced civilization. The final answer to these troubling questions is still being debated.

Anti-Semitism was a large factor. The roots of anti-Semitism, ever present and growing in pre-war France, blossomed into the official policies and actions of the Vichy government, quite independent of Nazi instigation.[6] Primal anti-Semitism was deeply ingrained and widespread in other influential French circles. In the late 1920s and throughout the 1930s, anti-Semitic journalism grew exponentially. Two well-known columnists were Charles Maurras and Maurice Bardèche. Following in their footsteps, a little-known graduate of the prestigious *Ecole Normale Supérieure,* Robert Brasillach was a prominent French literary editor. He became a prolific writer and a champion of virulent French intellectual anti-Semitism. In early 1945, at the age of 35, he was tried, convicted of treason and executed; his legacy, the "Brasillach myth," has survived. In death, he has become a martyr to extreme political elements, including Jean Marie Le

Pen and his followers in France (Le Pen is the founder of the French National Front party, a notorious extremist organization). Anti-Semitism continues to thrive in France.[7]

History must not ignore the record of Vichy France toward the Jews during the Occupation. It must not be erased, diminished, concealed or denied. I am convinced, contrary to what came out in later official admissions, that the Vichy regime implemented the process of deportation against my father, and was aware of what deportation meant.[8]

The laudable heroism of many gallant French men and women in the Resistance during the war does not mitigate in my mind the Vichy complicity with the Nazis. Even though I fully recognize and acknowledge the heroism of those courageous French individuals who risked their lives to provide assistance to our family and to scores of other Jews, it was the collection of individuals known as the government of Vichy France whom I shall always blame. Perhaps a sense of balance is missing here. Yet, in my heart, I can never forgive *l'Etat français* ("the French state") for actively participating in our father's murder.[9]

For mother, John and me, September 1945 was a poignant time and a point of no return. We dwelt on what Vichy did to Father, but we had to face the future knowing that he would never be with us again. Our former world was gone but life continued and we renewed our daily existence. It was school time again. John, almost nine, and I, almost eleven, were back at the school at the *Place des Vosges*. Our classmates at school asked, "don't you have a father?" and also teased us about our southern provincial accents. We were fortunate that the school director and my sixth grade teacher remained as sympathetic as ever. I thanked them for their help with the yellow stars.

It had been mother's and father's desire that John and I pursue an education. We not only went back to school, but also at mother's urging, we went back with the idea of going on to a university-level education. In those days, most students finished primary school and went to work. A few would go on to enter a *lycée* (high school), thus getting into the competitive national high school system which led to the coveted *baccalauréat* (high school diploma), the gateway to a higher education. Acceptance to a *lycée* was on the basis of merit and an entrance exam. Most students did not pass the exam. Mother arranged for a special tutor to prepare us for that consequential test. John wondered, "where is the money coming from?" Mother answered, "Father left you an education fund."

On our return to Paris, we re-established contact with our family in Winnipeg, Canada. Aunt Vittle began to correspond with mother. As an older sister, she would not allow her only remaining sister, now a widow with two young children, to remain in Europe. My aunt began the process that would allow us to emigrate to Canada. We would not be separated ever again. We were excited. This sisterly advice was welcome. Had we been able to go to Canada immediately after learning of the death of father, we would have been gone as quickly as we could pack our bags. However the immigration papers took time to materialize. Therefore we returned to our daily routine.

Mother was thirty-seven when she sought to resume my father's trade; a task easier said than done. Father's assistants were no longer available. Guy Huchon had taken a position with a private company and Benjamin Roditis had become an open-air trader in our markets, selling socks, underwear and related small clothing items (this was considered a different business). We sold a complete line of primarily larger clothing items to the working class. He would never compete with us, he reassured my mother, and he never did. Born and raised in Bezons, he was well-known there. He became successful.

Mother had little real business experience. She had an old friend from Poland named Eva. Eva was married to Georges Sledz. Their son, Julien, had recently been born. After spending the war years in the port city of Marseille in the south of France, they returned to Paris, adrift and looking for a way to make a living. Eva had a reputation as a *commerçante*, a business lady.

Mother would take Eva in as a partner, and they would revive father's business. Georges, a happy go-lucky, easy going, bon vivant type of Frenchman now would be our trusted assistant. Georges was a native Parisian Jew, well spoken and bright. He was not ambitious, worshiped Eva and was pleased to let her be the boss. He was content simply to be of service. This way he would have ample time in the afternoon to go to a local pub in Bezons, known as *le bistrot du coin*, and engage in political discussions while playing *belote*, a popular French card game. Mother understood that she could not *"faire les marchés"* (manage the open-markets) by herself. Teaming up with Eva and Georges seemed to be a good strategy.

Without a truck, the somewhat distant markets in Argenteuil and special event markets and fairs were out of the question. We concentrated on our old standby locations of Bezons and nearby Houille. Eva and her family moved to Bezons to be close to business, and we used their garage to store our goods. We were given merchandise on a consignment basis by several of the wholesalers who had done business with father. I remember that one firm, *Noveltex*, helped us substantially by not insisting on cash up front. We started on a small scale. Georges would transport mother, Eva and the merchandise to the market stalls in his small old car. Little by little, we made a comfortable living for two families.

Finding father's missing truck would allow us to expand our business. All we had, however, was an official requisition form from the French military.

Our efforts to recover the truck through normal channels were going nowhere. New trucks were not yet available. Needing the help of a middleman, we obtained the services of a reputable broker. "He is the best in this business," we were told. He was a young, pipe smoking, peculiar and eccentric fellow. He was always asking for cash and would meet us only on shadowy streets or in dark alleys. We began to believe that he was playing us for suckers as he inspired no confidence. We started to doubt his integrity and lost faith in him.

One afternoon, however, he casually told us that our truck had been found. We did not believe him. Yet, as he directed, we went to a *caserne de Pompiers* ("firehouse and barracks") in the eighth district of Paris, where much to our surprise, we recognized our truck. It was returned to us right then and there. The officer, after consulting a file, told us that it had been driven as far as the Polish border. It appeared to be in decent condition. Astounded, we had it inspected by a good mechanic in Bezon, who remembered the truck. A new motor was installed, and that vehicle, like a tank, was still running strong a decade later.

With the truck back in our hands, our business grew and expanded. The truck served as our permanent storage place. It stayed in a rented garage between Bezon and Houille with all our merchandise. On business days, Georges, proud as a peacock, drove the truck to the market stalls.

It was now spring 1946. I was 12 years old. We received a letter from an Oscar Rozansky in Washington, DC. I did not recognize the writer of the letter, but mother did. He was a first cousin from Dombrowitz, who was now doing well in America. The letter asked a favor of mother. Oscar's wife, Bertha, had a sister and a brother in-law, Fagel and Avron Sheinbaum who had spent the war years as Russian partisans. They had a teenage daughter, Rosa. Oscar and Bertha were sponsoring them as immigrants to America. The U.S. Immigration Service had assigned them to the U.S. Consulate in Paris, where they would be issued visas "in a matter of weeks." They were coming to Paris from Poland and needed a place to stay. Would we oblige them? Mother immediately sent a letter to Oscar Rozansky stating that she would be glad to help. The prompt action would turn out to be a wise and fruitful decision. Mother's answer to that letter marked the beginning of our link to America and a new era in our life.

On a May afternoon in 1946, John and I were playing in the courtyard when our guests, the Sheinbaums, arrived. John and I immediately took note of the girl. She was 17, beautiful, well endowed by nature, intellectually bright and most charming. They moved in with us the same afternoon and stayed for over two years, waiting for their visas.

It proved to be a long-term relationship and a significant factor in our coming to America. Our families complemented and nurtured each other. The apartment was too big for the three of us and very empty without Father and our former tenants.[10] Avron Sheinbaum became the man of the house, and Fagel, his wife, took over as the lady of the household. Mother, free from routine chores, could concentrate on our business and plans for the future. Rosa fell in love with France, adopting the French name of Rosette (little rose).

Rosette took to Paris in a remarkable way, frequently saying: "I have come from Hell and am now in Heaven." She could not believe the freedom of France. She went to the *Alliance française*, a government-subsidized language school for older students and adults. She learned the language easily and well, in accordance with the common adage that Poles have a facility for foreign languages. Rosette certainly did. She later enrolled in the business program of the school and graduated as a certified secretary, with skills in typing, short-hand and bookkeeping. To this day, she refers to her years in Paris as *les meilleures années de ma vie* ("the best years of my life"). She also became a wonderful big sister to John and me.

An added bonus declared itself shortly. A huge package from Cousin Oscar in Washington arrived. This package contained, among many things, over a hundred Hershey bars. We had not seen chocolate in years. Brother John raided the package, appropriating each and every chocolate bar. He was taken to task, but the reprimand did not deter John. The same thing happened again and again. Our guests gave up. As soon as the chocolate arrived, it was donated to John. John occasionally did share the chocolate bars with me, and our buddies and neighbors, Georges and Marcel.

After intense tutoring, I in 1946 and John in 1948 passed our entrance exams and transferred to the *Lycée Charlemagne*. John and I began to go to the market stalls and help out whenever possible. Our business was doing well now and mother was able to save money. A sense of normalcy and hope was returning to our lives. We were enjoying a new routine. In June, 1948, our Canadian visas for which we had applied in fall 1945 came through.

We were bitter about the Vichy government, yet we loved France. John and I were born and raised in France. We had a mastery of the French language. We had lost our southern accent and were speaking pure Parisian French. We excelled in school. Things were beginning to go right for us. Winnipeg seemed so distant and remote from our sophisticated Paris, and we did not relish upheaval in our lives again. We thought emigrating to Canada would be disruptive. Aunt Vittle was putting a great deal of pressure on mother. All three of us were confused about what to do.

Mother decided to temporize, to buy some time. We would not burn our bridges. We would not give up our apartment. We would not sell our share of the business. We would visit Canada during the summer school recess. We would always have Paris. We did not have to go as immigrants. We could go thinking of ourselves as tourists.

And at the suggestion of the Sheinbaums, we would visit Washington to establish personal contact with our American relatives. "You might benefit some day from this connection" was their reasoning. This advice gave mother the idea to deposit our savings with Oscar Rozansky in Washington. We did not trust French currency or French banks. Our funds consisted of $10,000, most of which had been left to us by Father and had survived the war in makeshift hiding places. The money was in American dollars with a question of its legality in France then. Mother felt burdened by holding illegal cash. This encumbrance would soon be gone.

In the middle of July 1948, we embarked on the *SS Queen Elizabeth* for a trip to the New World. This summer excursion was to play a pivotal role in our lives.

## NOTES

1. *La France a eu le dessus.*

2. *Les Boches comptaient sans Pierre et Jean, la colère et les jeunes gens.* (From a trendy poem of the day).

3. Kaplan, "Collaborator," 79.

4. Stephen E. Ambrose, *The Supreme Commander: The War Years of General Dwight D. Eisenhower* (New York: Doubleday, 1955), 479–492.

5. Marrus and Paxton, "Vichy France," xii, 243, 343–372.

6. Marrus and Paxton, "Vichy France," 25–71, 43.

7. For Brasillach's influence on today's French anti-Semites, see Kaplan, "Collaborator,"143–210 and 230–234. French anti-Semitism today is well profiled in R. Emmett Tyrrell, Jr., *Faithless France*, The American Prowler.org, Published 4-5-02 ["The current Crisis"].

8. See, for example, Tzvetan Todorov, *A French Tragedy, Scenes of Civil War, Summer 1944*: (Hanover and London: University Press of New England, 1996), 96.

9. The "French State" was the name given in 1940 to the government of Vichy under Marshal Petain, as explained in Todorov, "French Tragedy".

10. Robert Waldman had been arrested with father. He was deported and never returned. His wife remarried and left us in late 1945.

## Chapter Nine

# Summer of 1948

The majestic *SS Queen Elizabeth* was making its way toward New York, steaming gracefully, silently and without effort while the powerful Atlantic Ocean appeared to melt into the distant horizon. It seemed that we were on a floating oasis, surrounded by a sea of tranquility and serenity, somewhere in paradise.

Although we were traveling third class, our accommodations were adequate and comfortable. Life in third class was pleasant. Our separate male and female cabins, smaller than most bedrooms, contained bunks and were efficiently furnished. There was enough well-designed storage space for our luggage. I vaguely remember that the bathroom and bathing facilities were communal but gender divided. The sound of the waves hitting the ship and the constant low-grade drone from the engines were always in our ears. The third class dining room was spacious, decorated with chandeliers, fancy tablecloths, shining silverware and fine china. The movie theaters, swimming pools, exercise rooms and steam rooms were always available. English courtesy was everywhere. There were attentive waiters, good food, and several sittings for breakfast, lunch and dinner. Ice cream for dessert was a treat we had not enjoyed since the start of the war. Lounging, playing shuffle board on the top deck and ambling along the side decks were our favorite activities. Time passed quickly.

One sunny, pleasant afternoon, mother was taking a leisurely stroll, watching the scenery of the open sea when she was approached by an officer of the ship, who offered to escort her to the lounge. He spoke to her in flawless Parisian French: *Asseyez-vous, prenez une tasse de thé et des patisseries, je vous prie* ("make yourself comfortable, and have some tea and pastries, please"). Mother was speechless at her introduction to the English tradition of high tea.

During the crossing, mother became friendly with a wonderful middle-aged couple. The wife, Mariette, was of French origin. Her husband was an affable American who owned a lumber company in the state of Washington. They were returning to the United States after visiting the grave of their older son, killed in the Normandy landing on D-day.

They liked mother. She, in turn, shared her concerns about our future with them. Mariette admonished mother to stay in Canada and not to go back to Europe, saying something to the effect that our future in the New World would be better and more secure than in the Old World.

Our passage with this grand couple was fun. We had meals together, walked on deck together, took pictures together and were constant companions.

We wondered what first class looked like. We were invited to take a conducted tour of the ship. Thereafter, we wondered no more. We were awestruck. The first class interiors of this vessel were beyond belief and imagination. John, who was twelve years old, liked first class; he would regularly sneak up into the first class accommodations, returning excited and impressed by the splendor of the dining room, the size of the movie theaters, the majestic stairway and the vast lounges. He enjoyed watching American movies there and was especially fascinated by movies featuring Jerry Lewis.

Luxury and pampering aboard a transatlantic liner must be an ultimate human experience. It could not last forever and did not. Several days later, we entered New York harbor on a splendid summer morning. New York's beautiful skyline was visible through the haze as we slowly passed the Statue of Liberty. Our spirits were high. We had arrived in the New World!

It was soon time to disembark with U.S. citizens being processed first. They were treated speedily and efficiently. I remember telling myself that I hoped to be in that position some day. Our turn came after a long wait. The immigration officer was puzzled. After all, we were supposed to be immigrants to Canada. Trains were readily available in New York to take us to Winnipeg. At first, he was not satisfied with our story. He could not comprehend why we were going to Washington, DC. He could not imagine a young widow and two children becoming tourists in the U.S.A. while emigrating to Canada. We were then interviewed by a senior immigration officer. Mother did not disclose anything about the money that she was carrying. Finally our passports were stamped and we were admitted for a ten-day visit.

At the pier, mother recognized Oscar Rozansky immediately. He looked fit and happy. His lovely daughter, Beverly, was young, charming, friendly and so American. They welcomed us warmly.

Oscar invited us to ride in his new Cadillac. I had never been in such a car. He gave us a grand tour of New York. It was so impressive with its skyscrapers, masses of people and aura of excitement. Was I dreaming? Were we immigrants or tourists on a summer vacation? Were we confused? Yes, we were. In 1948, there was no air service from Paris to Canada for us. Flying was neither as available nor as cheap as it is nowadays.We had taken the time honored way to come to North America by transatlantic steamer to New York which allowed us to detour to Washington, DC to visit family. I was not dreaming. We were in a Cadillac, with Oscar Rozansky and his daughter, Beverly. The thrill of riding in a Cadillac from New York to Washington was real.

We arrived at 3918 Massachusetts Avenue, the Rozansky home. It was such an attractive house. Recessed from the avenue, behind a large well-manicured front lawn, the house had a beautiful open veranda, and the majestic National Cathedral could be seen from the rear of the house. There were so many blooming trees and so much luxuriant greenery everywhere. People here, it seemed, did not live in apartments. It was peaceful and quiet and the pace of life was unhurried. The interior of the Rozansky home was modern, comfortable and pleasant and our quarters were cozy.

We spent a busy and happy week with the Rozansky family. Every morning, we sat in the sunny, bright, contemporary kitchen. Our day began with a large glass of freshly-squeezed orange juice, milk, corn flakes or other cereals and fruit. We were miles away from the French breakfasts of coffee and croissants we knew.

Every day was filled with activities. Beverly Rozansky could not do enough for us. She was—and is to this day—a friendly, unassuming and gracious person. We saw the sights, the campuses of George Washington and Georgetown Universities, the White House, Arlington National Cemetery, Union Station and National Airport with the weather splendidly accommodating.

We visited our cousins. Mother saw cousin Isor several times by herself while John and I were sightseeing. Our cousins seemed to be happy, cheerful and well-established. They had fancy cars. They gave us a good time. They took us to movies and restaurants. One Sunday, we were treated to a restaurant, Fan and Bill's, on lower Connecticut Avenue, where a Duke Zeibert was the manager. Fan and Bill's eventually became Duke Zeibert's Restaurant. There were many places to go, many people to see and we saw almost all of them. They would become part of my life, but I did not know that then.

My Washington family seemed focused on one single topic of conversation that summer of 1948, the upcoming November Presidential election. According to nearly everyone, President Truman was a sure loser. With emotion, I began to secretly root for President Truman as he had been with President Franklin Delano Roosevelt and therefore had to be the better man.

Our visit was a whirlwind of activities with mother being able to place our savings with Oscar. She confided to me that she was relieved and pleased, knowing that Oscar would safeguard and guarantee our nest egg. The money would be safe, and it would earn the then unimaginable sum of 6% annual interest, a new concept for us. Our detour to Washington was a huge success. I loved Washington and I sent postcards to my friends in Paris, expressing my feelings. Washington *m'avait ébloui* ("Washington stunned me").

And Washington is where it happened. One pleasant afternoon, Gerald Rozansky, Oscar's younger son, invited John and me to take a stroll with him. We walked up Massachusetts Avenue, and stopped at the Horace Mann school (I filed the name away in my mind) on Newark Street. This location was to have a significant impact on us for the rest of our lives. The charming, sizable and well-equipped school playground was vacant. We decided to take advantage of the situation. We liked the place so much that we played there every day of our remaining time in Washington. While playing there, I became aware of the Glover Estate across New Mexico Avenue, just opposite the playground. I had already dreamed of becoming a doctor, as many Jewish European children caught up in sadness and hard work secretly wished. Now, I suddenly experienced a vision. In my mind's eye, I fantasized about practicing medicine on the Glover Estate. I vividly saw myself being a well-established physician and working out of an office in that prime location. Little, however, did I realize at the time that the dream would come true some day!

After that glorious week in Washington, we went to Union Station to begin the four day trip to Winnipeg, Canada. We arrived three hours early at the train station with the entire family coming to see us off. I did not want to leave Washington, where I had found my place in the sun. I was brooding and thinking paranoid thoughts:

*No one is here for me. They all eagerly want me to leave Washington. The world is an unfair place. People are against me. Even mother and John are not sympathetic. They do not share my vision. I will show the world not to underestimate me.*

It was a low point of my life. Left to my own devices, soon to be 14, I explored Union Station, plotting my strategy while musing about my plight. I became aware of the presence of multiple water fountains. I sat down on the edge of one, determined to find a solution to my predicament.

A bright idea surfaced and I went into action immediately. I collected pennies from everyone of my relatives who came to see us off to Winnipeg. I threw all my coins in the water fountains, making sure that each fountain received its fair share. With each toss, I wished one day to be back in Washington and one day to become a doctor on the Glover Estate.

Now that I was ready to go to Winnipeg, I cheerfully boarded the Capitol Limited for a spectacular and scenic journey to Chicago. The accommodations of this super train were deluxe, replete with pleasant amenities and relaxing. There was friendly service, fine dining and excellent sleeping car comfort. We loved the top deck of this double-decker railroad car. About twenty hours later, we were in mid-America.

Chicago overwhelmed us by the sheer magnitude of its train station, the exuberance of its activity and the animated atmosphere. We felt lost, bewildered and at sea among the crowd. With difficulty and much help, we finally transferred to a train going to Saint Paul-Minneapolis. The trip was another pleasant train experience. Magnificent views of the landscape of America's heartland, views that can only be appreciated from a train, were our constant heartwarming experience. In Minnesota's twin cities, we caught a Canadian Pacific Railway train for Winnipeg.

The Canadian Pacific Railway station at Winnipeg was also enormous, up-to-date and very active. Aunt Vittle and Uncle Leibel; Cousin Oscar, with wife Bella and three-year old son Jackie; and Cousin Shirley, with husband Nathan, were all there to welcome us effusively, cheerfully and endlessly. Little Jackie waved a musical rattle, giggling and making happy sounds.

It was early August. The weather was delightful. Winnipeg was a friendly, modern and bright city. We were to learn later that it was also a cultural, social, ethnic and family town. Portage Avenue, the main street, was broad and expansive. We swiftly arrived at 504 Manitoba Avenue, the modest, comfortable and warm home where Aunt Vittle and Uncle Leibel lived. We settled in, freshened up and changed clothing. We were given a marvelous welcoming lunch. As we talked, talked and talked, I picked up a disconnect. They assumed that we had come to stay permanently; they did not realize we had only come to explore the opportunities of the New World and that our plans for the future were indefinite.

I was impressed with Aunt Vittle; she reminded me of mother. She was intelligent, down to earth, practical, wise, tough-minded, We felt comfortable in her home. Everyone made us feel welcome. Uncle Leibel was attentive, caring and supportive. Oscar paid great attention to our daily needs, wishes and desires. Shirley, Bella and Nathan were great hosts to us. Little Jackie was adorable. John and I frequently took him for a stroll, without a thought that one day all three of us would become doctors (Jackie is today a prominent Montreal neurologist at McGill University and enjoys an international reputation).

Aunt Vittle told us about her trip on our behalf to Washington. Immediately after the war and as soon as she knew that her sister, my mother, had survived with two young boys, Aunt Vittle had traveled to Washington. She was always aware of her cousins, the Gildenhorns and Rozanskys, and took the trip to re-establish personal contact with them. She felt that the family in Washington could offer us a better opportunity. She wanted to secure this option in case our emigration to Canada was unsuccessful. Cousins Isor and Oscar had advised Vittle that it would be better for us to settle in Winnipeg from whence John and I possibly could emigrate to Washington later. They saw no problem in this sequence of events.

We were now in Winnipeg. This was the first step toward a wonderful re-union of the two sisters. We hoped to stay on this side of the Atlantic ocean. We hoped never to go back to Europe. That this was not to be never entered our minds as we wanted to remain near the rest of the family forever.

With the help of the Winnipeg Jewish Agency, Aunt Vittle arranged for John and me to attend a summer camp. We spent two weeks in a camp at Lake Winnipeg. How wonderful it was! I remember my time at Winnipeg Beach (the name of the campsite) as one of the high points of my youth. We had fun. The camp was far away from the world, on an immense, beautiful and sparkling lake. The weather was perfect. The camp counselors were kind, considerate; and the other campers were friendly. We swam, boated and ca-noed. Our accommodations were comfortable. We were carefree. The entire experience was unforgettable and is a special memory.

Back in Winnipeg, mother was working in a glove factory where Uncle Leibel was the manager. She found it difficult to adjust to her new situation and she was unhappy. It was early September with a nine month winter about to begin. We began to think of returning to France. Our mind-set was not right, forgetting or ignoring Mariette's words which went something like this: "Europe offers no security or opportunities, and little hope for the future."

Unbelievable as it may seem, we chose to return to Paris. On our way back, we stopped over in the buoyant central train station (*gare centrale*) in down-town Montreal to catch a train to New York. The station was abuzz with ex-citement, as big headlines in the newspapers and on the neon public news pro-claimed that Europe was about to be overrun by Russia. We became alarmed and immediately developed second thoughts about returning to France. We called our relatives in Winnipeg and Washington about staying in the New World. We were gently told that such a course was not a realistic option. To this day, I wonder why we did not just settle in Montreal with our command of the French language.

Going back to live in Europe after having seen and enjoyed North Amer-ica was a fundamental blunder and I would spend the next five years regret-ting this decision.

## Chapter Ten

# Paris, 1948–1953

We were back in Paris. It was late September 1948. The cold war had just begun. Headlines were scary: "Russia will take over Western Europe. America and England will not save us from Russia. We are doomed to live with the Russian Bear."

NATO (The North Atlantic Treaty Organization), the West's answer to the feared expansion of the Soviet Union into Western Europe, was created in April 1949. People immediately worried that NATO troops were too few to stop the Russian armies.

Soon after our return to France, Avron, Fagel and Rosette Sheinbaum, having obtained their visas, left for America. Our apartment was empty and lonely again. We never said it aloud, but in our hearts we knew that the New World was far better than the Old World. We had made a dire mistake! During our crossing on the *SS Queen Elizabeth* in the summer of 1948, Mariette had warned us. Mother, John and I were blue, but we tried, nevertheless, to enter life again.

In October 1948, mother and I went to the Canadian Consulate where we learned that immigration to Winnipeg was no longer an option. John snapped out of his doldrums. He was soon his old self, a happy Francophile. Mother and I remained depressed. I began openly to grieve for America. I longed for our family in Washington and Winnipeg. I longed for America. I longed for Canada. I felt isolated in postwar Europe. The Sheinbaums were now in Washington, DC. We missed them. Mother, John and I had no family in Paris, which was one of many things we had not considered when we left Canada. Nonetheless, life continued.

We all loved the American soldiers. They were friendly and their military bearing and uniforms impressed us. One beautiful April day in 1949, John,

Marcel, and I, all in our early teens, decided to make contact with the U.S. troops. We took the subway to the metro station, *Pigalle*, and walked to nearby *Place Pigalle*, a well-known and popular red-light district near the famous Basilica of the Sacred Heart (*Sacré Coeur*) in the *Montmartre* section of Paris. This area was a favorite with American soldiers. It was a place where French ladies of the day and of the night (*Belles de Jour et de Nuit*), who wanted to encounter them, would hang out. This neighborhood, close to *Le Moulin Rouge*,[1] has generated several lasting melodies about Paris, including the lovely song, *Pigalle*, vocalized by, among many others, Georges Ulmer and Marius Coste and his orchestra.

We found our way to a café and ordered Coke in the bottle[2]. Bottled coke was not something every French kid could, in 1948, afford. We had been saving our money for this special occasion. A tall American soldier and his French girlfriend were standing nearby at the counter. Gesturing with his left arm, he knocked over our Cokes, splattering himself and his female friend. Acting out our adolescent immaturity and in a fun-loving mood, we had set him up by placing our drinks critically close to his left elbow. In a wonderfully American way, he was apologetic, paid for the spilled drinks and ordered fresh Cokes for us as well as sandwiches. He gave us Juicy Fruit chewing gum and chocolate bars. When he left, he shook our hands firmly, wished us luck and gave us each a five dollar bill. We were in our glory. We had physically touched *one of them*. We had seen an American uniform *up close*. I shall never forget that American.

The cold war was gaining in intensity, and many Frenchmen began to adopt a new slogan, orchestrated by Moscow and by many if not most French liberals: *Les Américains en Amérique* ("Americans go home"). This catchphrase was displayed on placards, painted everywhere and expressed verbally in public. Some Frenchmen were rebutting by proclaiming *il fallait le dire le 6 Juin 1944* ("it should have been said on June 6, 1944" [the day of the Allied landings in Normandy]). Many French people, however, were openly hostile toward Americans. This sentiment defied both reason and history.

I witnessed an anti-American episode on our own *rue de Sévigné* as I was leaving a small hardware store. Three U.S. Army officers in immaculate dress uniforms with shining black boots slowly walked past the *Caserne des Pompiers* (firehouse) on their way to the *Musée Carnavalet* (museum of the history of the City of Paris) up the street. Several firefighters were outside, hosing down the entrance to the fire station. They turned their hoses on the three officers, by accident they would later claim. There was a brawl. This was followed by belated apologies to the soldiers by senior officers of the fire station. I recall the incident well. In my state of mind, constantly grieving for America, I felt personally affected and disturbed.

The French were ungrateful! They seemed to have forgotten what began on June 6, 1944, with the D-Day landing on the beaches of Normandy, and ended in the liberation of France. They were indifferent to the Marshall Plan, the farsighted strategy that was to promote Western European economic recovery. Animosity by many Frenchmen toward anyone speaking the English language was part of a long standing phobia about Anglo-Saxons. In time, this French attitude would lead to a historical event: De Gaulle withdrew all French forces from NATO'S military commands, including SHAPE (Supreme Headquarters Allied Powers Europe) and in turn demanded the removal of all Allied troops from France, including the NATO military headquarters. With classic French logic, De Gaulle did not withdraw from NATO, and French diplomats sat with their NATO colleagues on the North Atlantic Council, NATO's most senior consultative body. Needless to say, France has remained an important part of the alliance to this day.

It was now the end of the summer of 1949. I was still a bit young at this point, 15 going on 16. However, I was preoccupied beyond my age about the future—perhaps because of my serious nature, I began to believe that I had to replace father, and look after mother and my younger brother. I thought about Washington more and more. I nurtured and cherished the vision, the way many young boys dream of playing professional sports. In November 1948, President Truman—for whom I had secretly been rooting—was re-elected.[3] I felt this event to be a good omen for me: I would go back to America and become a doctor on the Glover Estate in Washington. I saw this clearly in my mind every day, but how this would occur I did not know. I had an ambition, a dream, and I was willing to persevere to achieve my goal. I had hope.

John and I attended the *Lycée Charlemagne*, both the *Petit* and the *Grand Charlemagne*.[4] *Lycée Henri IV* in the Latin Quarter was, of course, the most prestigious one in Paris. Almost as desirable was the *College Sainte-Barbe* followed by *Lycée Janson de Sailly* on the *rue de la Pompe* in Paris's tony 16th District. However, *Lycée Charlemagne* was, in my opinion and the opinion of many, one of the finest secondary schools in Paris.

"Good old Charlemagne," though not glamorous, was a no-nonsense, strongly academic institution.

*Le Lycée Charlemagne a vu passer entre ses murs nombre de célébrités, tant du coté des éléves que des professeurs. Cinquantes anciens de Charlemagne ont donné leur nom à des rues de Paris . . . .* ["The Lycée Charlemagne saw pass within its walls a number of celebrities, students as well as teachers. Fifty Charlemagne alumni have given their names to streets of Paris . . . ."][5]

Professor Barbier, *agrégé de lettres* (a professor qualified to teach by dint of having passed a rigorous examination), a distinguished scholar of French and Latin, took an interest in John and me. He became our academic adviser. He invited us to attend privileged seminars, and offered us extra elective assignments, as well as spending quality time with us.

John paid a courtesy call on Professor Barbier in 1955 before leaving for America. With his typical aplomb, John said something to this effect: we had taken four years of Latin under him; what was the value of Latin?

The savvy professor replied: "The value of Latin is what is left behind when you forget it all."[6]

John still speaks with fondness of this incident. Both John and I can attest to the validity of this truism, that the discipline and the principles of learning do remain.

Professor Barbier encouraged me to join an elite intellectual club, known as "SANLYC" (*Societe des Amis de la Nature du LYcée Charlemagne*). This academic affiliation sponsored many field trips which were designed to foster interest in the pursuit of Natural Sciences. It remains dear to my heart.

John and I owe much to the venerated Professor Barbier and to the *Lycée Charlemagne*. They endowed us with solid learning skills in addition to a hefty grounding in education. John and I would be well prepared for college and medical school in America.

Mother returned to our clothing trade. John and I both worked at the market stalls whenever time permitted. Business was good. John seemed chipper. But I knew mother worried about our future, and I could not dispel my inner longing for the United States. I had fallen in love with America and Washington, DC! I began to talk about my return to Washington and nothing else.

Friends complained about my behavior. They said to me: *Si tu ne veux pas boire l'eau de la fontaine, n'en dégoute pas les autres* ("If you do not want to drink from the fountain, do not spoil the water for others").

English quickly became my favorite *lycée* course and I read newspapers, magazines, novels and detective stories in English. I became an avid viewer of American movies. I communicated my feelings to mother and John. They were sympathetic. They listened, but we had apparently settled into our new life style. Mother and John seemed content. As for me, however I was only going through the motions. I was unhappy. The dream was becoming an obsession. People worried about me. I worried about myself. John was 13 and I was 15.

In early 1949, mother, Eva and Georges Sledz established a retail clothing store, *Chemiserie et Confection de Bezons,* ["shirts and tailoring of Bezons"] on *rue Edouard Vaillant*, the main street of Bezons.[7] This was Eva's brainchild but mother provided the money to open the store. She withdrew the necessary funds from Cousin Oscar Rozansky in America through a Swiss bank. The store, the first such establishment in Bezons, would feature a more expensive line of clothing and would complement our outdoor trade business. This new store would be our future. The time was ripe for such retail. The working class began to favor stores over markets in the purchase of clothing. Eva lived within walking distance of the store. She would manage the store. She told us "I will take care of things when you are in Paris. You don't have to be in the store all the time. Our partnership, both in the markets and in the store, will continue to thrive."

We believed what she told us.

From the beginning, *la boutique* ("the store") was successful and by early 1950 the store had flourished and our future seemed safe. John and I would go on to university studies. Mother and Eva would some day give up the markets. Mother, an accomplished seamstress, began to provide on-site alterations. She loved being a seamstress again. This service, novel in Bezons, became instantly popular, and word of it spread quickly. Mother, John, I, Eva and Georges Sledz were a cohesive business team. We were getting along wonderfully. We socialized together. I began to feel better. France was good to us, I thought, and we would make out well in the long run. Success seemed finally to come our way.

Then little things began to happen. There were subtle clues. Mother felt she was less needed in the store. Well-meaning customers told us that Eva referred to the store as "mine" and to the markets as "theirs." Eva stayed in the store more and more, coming to the market stalls less and less. Georges Sledz was less available, often saying, "Eva needs me in her store." We had to hire a driver. Gradually, we sensed we were no longer welcome in the *Chemiserie et Confection de Bezons*.

One day, Eva and Georges talked with us. The truth finally came out. Despite the "subtle clues," we were surprised and disappointed. The store was in Eva's name only. The store belonged to her. The markets belonged to us.

*You keep the outdoor trade business. Georges and I will continue to help you whenever we can. We will remain friends.*

I don't remember what financial settlement was proposed by Eva and Georges, but this was not the real issue. We felt that we had been betrayed and that our future had been severely compromised. It was a terrible emotional letdown! I was nearly 16. I had just obtained my *brevet* diploma and was on track toward the *baccalaureat*. Sadly, I had to quit school. Mother needed full-time assistance in the business.

As our hired driver was not reliable. I took over the driving of the truck even though I had no driver's license (a commercial trucker's license was not available before the age of eighteen). We obtained the services of an old friend of my father, who now had a high position in the *Préfecture de Paris*. On our behalf, he tried to play the sympathy card for hardship reasons but it was of no avail. I continued to drive carefully without a license the short distances between the rented garage and the market stalls. That proved not to be a problem. However, twice a year we had to take the truck to Paris overnight to stock up on seasonal merchandise. I was uncomfortable driving the truck into Paris and back to Bezons, but brother John felt otherwise. He did it fearlessly many times. John was always more daring than I.

I went through a stage of wanting to emulate what father did with the open-trade business. I tried and failed. My heart was not in the markets. My heart was in Washington. Mother was distraught that our future no longer looked promising in France. We were disheartened with our business and she recognized our frustrations.

In his time, my father had shown a natural bent and a genuine facility for the open-air clothing trade. But by the early 1950s, without my father and his business acumen, mother, John and I found the business a daily grind. The open-air market *schmatta* trade had become an arduous task for us.

On each market day we followed a well-established routine. We would gather our packages, catch a five A.M. subway at our St Paul Metro station, a few steps from our apartment, go to the end of the line and take a bus. A short walk from the bus stop led to our garage. From the garage we drove the truck to the market stalls. In the stalls of Bezons we were under a tin roof, while in the market at Houille we were under a tarp. In Bezons, during the winter months, we had to de-ice the underside of the tin roof. We did it with flaming newspaper, often burning our hands, while the water from the melting ice ran down our inner arms. We had only a make-shift cover for the sides and rear of the stalls. The front was always open. It was often bitter cold and we relied on *pousse-café* [coffee with brandy or cognac] to keep us warm. We were at the mercy of the weather and so was our merchandise. We had to unload our truck and then unpack and display our merchandise carefully on the stands— a slow, tedious and time-consuming process. When closing, we had to pack up our merchandise, another laborious task, load our truck and drive it back to the garage. To return to Paris, we had to take the bus and the subway again, carrying packages of merchandise to be exchanged.

We went to the market stalls four days a week. Wednesday in Houille was a weak business day and we often did not make our expenses, but we had to be there to hold our spot for Saturday. There was a market custom which we observed. We did not allow ourselves to have breakfast before we made our first sale. That was not a problem on the other days, but on Wednesday we often did not make a sale until eleven or twelve o'clock. We thus often combined breakfast with lunch on Wednesday, unaware that we were pioneers in what would become the American tradition of brunch.

On the days between markets, we went shopping for new merchandise from Parisian wholesalers on *rue de Turenne*, *Faubourg Saint Antoine* and various other streets of the *Marais* district. Then we carried this newly purchased merchandise home — we were always carrying packages, it seemed — preparatory to taking it to our stalls on market days.

We began to be encouraged by the Sheinbaums to join our family in Washington. They talked to Isor Gildenhorn and Oscar Rozansky who seemed to understand our plight. We felt good vibrations. The Sheinbaums had stayed with us in Paris. Now, we could stay with them in Washington as long as we needed, they said in their letters.

Mother was discouraged with the open-air *schmatta* business. She had changed her mind and now believed we should emigrate to America. I needed no convincing and John was easily persuaded.

Mother composed a masterful letter in Yiddish. She read it to me. The letter was addressed to Isor, who had lost his wife and child. He would be sympathetic to our request, mother hoped. She did not know how Isor's new wife would react, but she decided to test the adage nothing ventured, nothing gained.

In the letter, mother emphasized several points. We had made a terrible mistake in returning to Europe. She encouraged Isor to discuss the matter with Oscar Rozansky, and she hoped that they would be big enough to overlook the mistake made by a widow with two young children, stating that she had been distraught and did not know what she was doing. We would be good immigrants this time. We would have a place to stay in Washington. She asked forgiveness for her failings, pleaded to get us out of Europe, or at least to get her children to America, since, she said, they have no future here.

We did not dream that Bella, Isor's new wife, would take our side. But from the very beginning, she urged Isor to sponsor us as soon as possible and be there for us after we had arrived. Had we known her feelings, we would have been reassured.

We eventually realized that Eva had actually done us a favor. Her questionable behavior had forced us to make a critical choice. We decided to seek our fortune in America. It was a blessing in disguise, but at the time, it was not obvious. Mother eventually forgave Eva, and they became friends again.

To be fair, it should be noted that Eva was scrupulous about giving mother all that she was due financially. In the end, Eva would also help by forwarding the proceeds of the sale of our apartment, our truck, our market stalls and our share of the store to us in Washington through a Swiss bank. Eva came to visit us in Washington in the summer of 1986, after Georges had died of cancer. We gave her a good time. Mother always said in later years: "She is a lovely person. The incident with the store must have been an isolated blind spot".

In her own way, Eva had played a key role in precipitating our departure for America.


## NOTES

1. *Le Moulin Rouge*, designed as a red windmill, has been a famous Parisian cabaret, a landmark establishment, since 1889. It was revived on a grand scale in the early 1950s.

2. These were the days before canned beverages. Warm Coca Cola in a bottle was appealing to us. It was different from what we were used to drinking and it was connected to the American soldiers.

3. President Truman, the underdog, was my favorite.

4. Middle and Upper High Schools.

5. Costa, "Je me souviens," 54.

6. John recalls these actual words.

7. The Sledz family was introduced in chapter 8.

# Chapter Eleven

# Our Link to America

Mother's letter was sealed. I mailed it via registered airmail with care. The letter would soon be delivered to Cousin Isor in Washington, DC, U.S.A., and we anxiously awaited his response. Would he ever reply? Would he be willing to help mother, John and me emigrate from Europe to America? What we were asking him to do was to sponsor a widow with two young children.

There was ample family precedent for our yearning to emigrate. Several of my mother's cousins had emigrated in the early 1900s from Dombrowitz to the United States. Their foresight and initiative in becoming Americans gave our family a link to Washington. More family followed in the 1920s, as sibling sponsored sibling; nieces, nephews and cousins followed. Sponsoring someone into the United States after World War II was a big responsibility: the sponsoring U.S. citizen had to ensure shelter, food, clothing and a job. The sponsor also had to provide a guarantee that the new immigrant would not become a burden on U.S. public finances and had to provide not only affidavits that the above requirements would be met but also give proof of sufficient funds to fulfill such obligations.

The stories of mother's cousins, Oscar Rozansky and Isor Gildenhorn, who played such a vital role in shaping our lives, deserve to be told.[1] Getting to America from our little village in Eastern Poland was hard for our family. Rural prewar Poland was terrible for the Jewish people![2] Escaping Poland often became a matter of survival.

Born in 1901 in Dombrowitz, Oscar Rozansky was one of nine children.[3] Dombrowitz was then a part of Russia. He attended a *cheder* where he learned Hebrew and religion.[4] He spoke Yiddish at home and learned Polish and Russian on the streets. The Rozansky family lived in a big old four bed-room house, with a living and a sitting room, which was very roomy by Dom-browitz standards. Oscar shared a bedroom with his brother Velvel, sleeping near the stove during the cold winter months. Their father owned a beeswax candle company while their mother operated a yard-goods store. Tragedy struck when Oscar was eight years old. His mother died of mastoiditis. This infection of the mastoid bone in the skull, behind the ear, was a common and often fatal affliction before the development of antibiotics.

From 1901 to 1913, Oscar Rozansky's life in Dombrowitz was simple and comfortable. At the beginning of World War I, however, Polish troops looted the town and began a *pogrom.*[5] (The word "pogrom" came to mean random massacre of Jews). Later, during the Russian revolution, Russian soldiers at-tacked Jewish businesses in Dombrowitz and robbed everyone known to be Jewish. The Cossacks, Russia's elite cavalry, followed with more of the same. Oscar's father's business was closed. The Germans had arrived in 1917 and were relatively tolerant of the town's people, but they imposed a 6:00 P.M. curfew, a throwback to medieval strictures.

Dombrowitz was then home to a group of young Jewish men and boys who wanted to go to Palestine which was then a British colony. They were less interested in political "Zionism," a term which had come into use only after 1898 and the publication of Theodore Herzl's book, *Die Judenstaat* ["The Jewish State"], than in living in a place they believed was safe. These lads merely wanted to get out of Dombrowitz. In 1919, with military conscription imminent, Oscar and his friends left Dombrowitz, and pro-ceeded to Pinsk and then on to Warsaw. Eventually they crossed into Czechoslovakia, which was then a new country that had recently been carved out of the old Austro-Hungarian Empire. Oscar Rozansky often said that on entering Czechoslovakia he felt free for the first time in his life. It was an emotionally and physically challenging journey. The boys hitch-hiked to Austria, where they briefly worked in a carnival before continu-ing on to Italy. They joined the Italian merchant marine in Trieste (I would later be stationed there with the U.S. Army). Their ship stopped at many Mediterranean ports before finally arriving in Egypt. Oscar had managed to save what was then the princely sum of 25 English pounds. He left the life of a seaman in Egypt to go to Palestine.

The Balfour Declaration had been signed in 1917. Zionist Chaim Weiz-mann, in Palestine, headed the group that in time would form Israel's first government. On November 2, 1917, British Foreign Minister Arthur James Balfour had proclaimed that the British government was committed to the idea of establishing a Jewish homeland in Palestine. Weizmann's access to British government officials at high levels had been enhanced by his development of a crucial new process for the production of acetone, an organic solvent used in the production of munitions.[6] Ammunition was vitally needed by the British military during World War I (1914–1918).

Oscar and his friends decided to settle in Palestine. Work was readily available in their newly-adopted country. When Oscar arrived in Haifa, his first job was as a longshoreman loading cargo from larger ships onto smaller ones along the waterfront. He was physically hale and hearty and blessed with a cheerful disposition. Oscar enthusiastically took on every work opportunity. His second job was building houses. His strength enabled him to carry heavy loads of concrete. He later joined a kibbutz near Tel Aviv and worked in the fields as a laborer for the Carmel Winery. While at the kibbutz, Oscar met David Ben Gurion, the future Israeli Prime Minister, who was then simply one young settler among many.

Fierce Arab attacks, which challenged and provoked the Jews, were not uncommon. The Arabs often threw rocks at the new Jewish settlers. Oscar and the other workers used switchblade knives to fight off their attackers (years later I saw Oscar in his store comfortably holding a knife at the ready and even, on occasion, brandishing it). He always considered Israel to be his permanent home, but he was anxious to visit his oldest brother, Joseph, who had moved to America in 1902, when Oscar was only one. Neither brother remembered the other, but their sense of family was keen.

Once in the United States, Oscar decided to settle in Washington, DC, because of his family ties. He and a brother-in law purchased a grocery store on 22nd Street, Northwest, near George Washington University (Oscar would own the business by himself in later years).

When prohibition was repealed, Oscar obtained one of the first liquor licenses granted in the District of Columbia. The license number, 355, was stamped on each bottle of spirits in Oscar's store. I remember getting a sore arm stamping liquor bottles when I worked part-time for Oscar in the mid-1950s. The grocery store had been a success. Now, coupled with a liquor store, the business really flourished.

Oscar had met Bertha Burka (later anglicized to Burke) in Poland during World War I. Bertha, with her brothers and sisters, had come to Washington in the early 1920s. As Oscar told the story, he needed another person to work with him and thus Bertha became his indispensable assistant. In time, they married. They had been married for 57 years at the time of her death in 1981. Oscar Rozansky and Bertha always said that raising their family in Washington was their happiest endeavor. All his children have been successful: Bill became a thriving liquor store owner, Gerald became a well-known physician in California, and Beverly married Bob Rosen, a West Point graduate, who went on to a distinguished military career.

Oscar often expressed fond memories of their home at 3917 Massachusetts Avenue, N.W. He had purchased the house for $16,000, which was considered a fortune in 1937. Oscar and his family moved into this elegant home in 1938. Oscar would say that his hard work had finally paid off: "Life is good, I have arrived."

After World War II, Oscar purchased a new car, a shining blue 1948 Cadillac. This model was the first with tail fins, and he displayed "1948" on the license plate. Oscar rejoiced over this Cadillac, which was to become the first of many for him. He became acquainted with Floyd Akers, the owner of Capital Cadillac, a dealership located across the street from Oscar's liquor store. Many employees and patrons of Capital Cadillac became Oscar's customers and friends.

The other cousin was Isor Gildenhorn, born and raised in Dombrowitz.[7] Isor was one of seven brothers born to a mother who had wanted a girl badly, but after seven boys, she gave up. The eldest boy, William, emigrated to America in 1912, and when he was well established and a citizen, he brought over his brothers Oscar, Harry and Nathan in 1921.

The three remaining Gildenhorn brothers, Herzel, Chaim and Isor had not as yet succumbed to the lure of America. They all worked in Chaim's shoe store in Dombrowitz. When their father died at a young age, Isor went to work with his mother, who was the proprietor of a dry goods store. Isor entertained no desire to join his brothers in Washington, who by now were U.S. citizens. He was too busy courting young non-Jewish girls. His mother, so concerned that Isor would marry a Gentile, asked her sons in Washington to obtain documents for their younger brother to come to America as soon as possible.

Before his papers were finalized, Isor married his first wife, Rosa, in 1937; to his mother's relief, Rosa was Jewish. She came from a village not far from Dombrowitz. In 1938, their son, Joseph, was born. In August 1939, Isor's visa to emigrate to the United States suddenly came through, but he could not obtain timely visas for Rosa and their son. This was a common problem in the sometime capricious processing of U.S. visas. Isor left Poland with just two days to spare before World War II began in Europe.

On September 1, 1939, the Germans invaded Poland. Seventeen days later, the Soviets also invaded Poland from the east and immediately occupied Dombrowitz. After leaving Dombrowitz, Isor traveled to England, where he booked passage to America on the liner *SS Athenia*. While in Liverpool waiting to embark, Isor checked into a hotel. In Isor's words: "During the night they woke me and gave me bad news. The Germans were invading Poland. I was being bumped off the ship, along with twenty other passengers, to make room for American dependents." Isor was upset when he was told that there would be no definite new date of departure.

The *SS Athenia* left Liverpool on September 2, with Isor remaining stranded in England. A day later, September 3, 1939, the *Athenia* was torpedoed and sunk by a German U-boat; 1,103 passengers were on board. Due to quick rescue efforts on the part of the British Royal Navy, only 112 lives were lost.[8] Isor, arrived in New York safe and sound two weeks later aboard the *SS Queen Mary*.

It was this Isor, who received our mother's letter on November 12, 1952. His answer came back to us on November 26. Isor had consulted with Oscar Rozansky. They said "yes" without reservation, perhaps in great part because their character had been forged by their own trials and tribulations. Both had experienced personal adversity.

They initiated the formal process to bring us to America by referring our case to the respected, competent and dedicated Hebrew Immigrant Aid Society, known as the HIAS. Its Paris branch would contact us soon, they wrote. Mother and I were elated. John was ambivalent about the idea. We all three understood, however, that what we did not openly admit: emigrating to America would be a momentous change in our lives.

## NOTES

1. A few other select personal stories are recounted in Appendix 1.

2. See Chapter 2, *Dombrowitz* and Appendix 4, *Leaving Poland*.

3. Amy and I were privileged to view a video in which Oscar is interviewed by one of his granddaughters on the occasion of his 80th birthday. In it, Oscar recounts his life. The video was made available to us by Beverly Rosen, Oscar's daughter, who recapped many of the details.

4. Yiddish word for an early school where Hebrew, Yiddish and religion were taught.

5. *Pogrom* is a Yiddish word, coined in Eastern Europe, which describes the organized massacre and looting of Jews, usually with the connivance, knowledge and encouragement of public officials.

6. Excerpted from Abba Eban, *Heritage: Civilization and the Jews* (New York: Summit Books, 1984), 245–256.

7. Uncle Isor often talked to me about his life in detail.

8. See, for example, http://www.tartans.com/articles/athenia.html.

*Chapter Twelve*

# Coming to Washington

Our decision to emigrate from France was now final and in the process of being implemented. The episode with Eva, the store, and the open-air markets, had been the immediate cause of this decision. I have often reflected on the all-encompassing role which our trade played in our determination to immigrate to America and to come to Washington.

*Marchands forains* ("itinerant merchants") have a long and distinguished history in France, where they became one of the primary forces of urbanization.[1] Medieval balladeers sang about the trade, which was known for being a hard but lucrative life. For centuries, the French blue class, and, to a lesser extent, French white-collar people, distrusted stores and preferred shopping at street markets which had existed in France since the Middle Ages. Although some of these locations were enclosed and called *marchés couverts*, most were a sort of open-air market made up of stalls; initially father, then mother, John and I rented such a stall just a few miles from downtown Paris. In these markets, a vast variety of merchandise was on sale, ranging from clothing to all kinds of household goods. Collectively, *marchands forains* were nothing more or less than traveling department stores.

The marketing of clothing had become known as the *schmatta* trade. *Schmatta* is a Yiddish word meaning rag or cheap clothing.[2] In modern clothing jargon, the word has no derogatory implication, though in my own mind it still does. We were not only *marchands forains*. We were *marchands forains* in the *schmatta* business. In my heart, being a *marchand forain* in the *schmatta* business symbolized a fruitless life, and a daily routine of monotony and insecurity. Many traders were comfortable in this business and some even loved it. Not I.

Most of the clothing merchants of this period were Jewish and would find a springboard in the *schmatta* business to start their children on the road to success. Many French Jewish professionals and corporation executives came from the families of these open-air traders; however economic reality meant that while children did escape from the market stalls, their parents had no escape.

Father and the other old-timers in the open-air *schmatta* business had no option but to remain in this trade. After our 1948 visit to North America, I sensed that John and I had other options. I grew unhappy in the business. It was never much more than a livelihood for me. I had never had any real enthusiasm, passion or inclination to be an open-air merchant. If behavior is determined by motivation, as many psychologists say, my motivation to get out of the market stalls was the prime reason for my wanting to leave France. The contrast between life in the open-air *schmatta* business and what I perceived our lives might become in America began to consume me.

I came to think of America as the opposite of the open-market life of France. I pictured the American dream as freedom and opportunity to realize one's potential. Although I did not know what my potential might be, I knew in my mind that I would not find it in the *schmatta* trade. The kind of personal fulfillment I sought could be found only in America. Mother now felt strongly that our best hope for the future was America. Emigrating to America would be a huge undertaking for our little family. John and I, French-born, could come under the French quota, where there was no waiting period. Mother, Polish-born, was by then a French citizen. However, U.S. immigration quotas only recognized the country of birth. Mother would face a long wait because of the Polish quota.

A long separation for our family seemed inevitable, perhaps eight to ten years, or even longer. It clouded our future, but we were not dismayed and continued to be optimistic.

We agreed on a plan. I would go to America first, before I became obligated to enter the French military service at age 19. John would stay behind with mother in Paris and help her tend the market stalls. Although that meant he would have to quit the *Lycée Charlemagne*, he would attend night school and would follow me to America before he reached military age. Eventually mother would join us. We developed this timetable with the help of the HIAS (Hebrew Immigrant Aid Society). The HIAS was likewise helpful to us with our visa applications and furnished sustained guidance and pertinent advice. As a case in point, I learned from the friendly people at HIAS that there was a solution to our problem. Mother would be able to join us in America without much delay after I became a citizen. Even though it would take five years for me to attain citizenship, mother never wavered.

On May 1, 1953, May Day, the traditional celebration of springtime and Labor Day in Europe, I departed for America. Mother, John, Georges, and

Marcel came to the train station, the Gare Saint Lazare in the 9th *Arrondisse-ment* (municipal district of Paris). We were all wearing a sprig of lily of the valley (*un brin de muguet*) on our lapels as we faced our first separation since father had been taken from us. Everyone tried to be stoic. We failed. We cried.

Even though I had been unable to obtain a third class reservation, mother did not hesitate. She bought me an expensive cabin-class ticket, which let me travel aboard the *SS Queen Mary* in accommodations best described as luxu-rious. The transatlantic trip was such a wonderful experience, and it seemed much too short. There were fine looking women, mostly wealthy American girls looking for adventure and fun. The casino, the pool, the movie theaters and the decks, as well as the sumptuous dining room, were all places where *couples d'occasion* ("couples of the moment") formed. Many transient ro-mances flourished aboard ship. There was never a dull moment during the days and nights of this ocean voyage.

After five days at sea and a train ride from New York to Washington, I ar-rived at Union Station late in the evening on May 6, 1953. Bill, Oscar Rozan-sky's eldest son, greeted me graciously. I was at Union Station, the very place where, five years earlier, I had tossed coins in the fountains and made wishes to return.

Bill took me to 2153 Newport Place, a Northwest Washington house, where Avron and Fagel Sheinbaum, our long-term guests in Paris, also had their grocery store. Their reception was heartwarming, after which they showed me to my own room. I was also welcomed by their daughter, Rosette, married and expecting a baby. The same night, members of my family visited me. Isor Gildenhorn and wife, Bella, Oscar Rozansky and his wife, Bertha, came and we all had a meal together. I felt wonderful about their greeting me so soon after my arrival.

Within a few days, I began to attend the English language night school course for foreigners at George Washington University although by now my English was fairly good. The study of English at the *Lycée Charlemagne*, ex-posure to the language during our trip to North America, and camp time at Winnipeg Beach all had helped me. Just as important was my self-directed immersion into the English language. I tried hard to think in English, and suc-ceeded. It was difficult, but gradually this mind game I played with myself developed into a natural thought pattern. In the daytime, I worked full time at the National Airport Pharmacy as a clerk. Uncle Isor had arranged the job for me through his dear friend, Dr. Albert Michaely. He was the pharmacist and manager of the pharmacy, the news stands and the gift shop at National Airport.[3]

Although I had few difficulties with the language, I ran into some embar-rassing problems with idioms, nuances and colloquialisms in American English. One evening I was by myself behind the counter in the pharmacy when a U.S. naval officer rushed in and asked for "a dozen rubbers." I did not understand and no one was available to help me. The naval officer became restless. I became frustrated. Suddenly, I noticed pull-on rain boots in a corner next to umbrellas, advertised as "indispensable when traveling." Despite my confused state of mind, I decided it was not what he wanted. "No one could possibly need 12 slip-on galoshes at one time," I said to myself. My roving eye caught sight of the packages of rubber bands on a display stand. Each package contained numerous rubber bands. Puzzled and frantic, I opened a package on the counter in front of my customer, counted out 12 rubber bands and proudly gave them to him. He threw up his arms and yelled "I don't believe it, find me the manager" just as the pharmacist walked in. With finesse and diplomacy, Dr. Michaely explained that I was a recent immigrant ("greenhorn off the boat" is the expression he actually used) and saved the day. Afterwards, he took me aside and showed me where the condoms were kept in a special drawer. He proceeded by saying: "I thought you knew all about these things, coming from France." Mortified, I replied that, in France, these things were known as *capotes Anglaises* ("English raincoats"). It seemed there was always something novel to learn in this new country. I am certain that the naval officer would be flabbergasted to learn that I went on to become a physician.

I was 18 years old. I was in the New World. I was in Washington, DC. I was here to stay. The market stalls of Paris were behind me. It was all exhilarating. I often reflected on my mother's courage, her real love, in letting me go, and on John's gallantry in staying behind. I was committed to bringing my family to America quickly. The thought of a long separation was intolerable. I came to this country troubled by my separation from mother and John, but also filled with optimism, faith and a can-do attitude.

My immediate goal was to resolve my mother's immigration problem. I again consulted the obliging staff at HIAS hoping and wanting to expedite my mother's visa application. They referred me to their immigration counsel, one David Mintz as I remember. He was sympathetic, listened attentively and promised to research the matter further. He contacted the Department of State, and discovered the solution to my problem.

In the early 1950s, during the Korean conflict, Congress had passed a law allowing foreign-born members of the Armed Forces to apply for citizenship after a waiting period of only 90 days of service, instead of the traditional five years. This law gave me the means to remove the obstacles holding up mother's immigration. It was an obscure law (which President Bush recently reactivated for the benefit of foreign-born volunteers who have been serving in the military since September, 2001).

I decided to volunteer for the U.S. Army, an idea which frightened my mother. In early August 1955, I received a long letter from Lili Steinberg, the older sister of our friends Georges and Marcel Steinberg, on behalf of mother, who spoke French well but did not feel comfortable writing in French. She often resorted to Yiddish when under pressure or in emotional situations. Mother dictated to Lili in Yiddish and Lily translated into French. In the letter, mother begged me to return to France. Lili, on her own, inserted a French newspaper clipping. Referring to French public opinion, the editorial stated: "The truce in Korea of July 27,1953 signed at Panmunjom is only temporary; it will not hold." Mother feared that I would be cannon fodder in Korea.

I thought of the opportunities my grandfather had given up when he left America and returned to Poland. The story of his unhappy return to Dombrowitz played a role in my thinking. Mother had spoken a lot about how disappointing this had been for him.

My response was prompt, gentle and unequivocal. Grandfather had gone back to Poland in 1921. We had gone back to Paris from the south of France during the 1940 exodus. We had gone back from Canada in 1948. I was not going back to Europe. I was not going back to the market stalls. I was going forward, and I intended to bring my family to America, even if it meant going to Korea. I would handle what came my way. I was here to stay.

I enlisted in the Army (technically, I "volunteered for the draft") and was inducted on October 22, 1953, in Alexandria, Virginia. During infantry training, 127 days later, on February 26, 1954, in Columbia, South Carolina, I became an American citizen. I had been sent for basic training and advanced training to near-by Fort Jackson, South Carolina.[4] Both my company commander and executive officer were my witnesses when I became a citizen.

The judge asked me if I desired to change my name. The name of the Horace Mann school, near the Glover estate in Washington, DC, where I had played and dreamed during the summer of 1948, suddenly popped into my mind. I spontaneously said Mann. Since I was a citizen. Mother could now come to America sooner than we had planned. I was relieved, satisfied and happy.

I graduated from the Fort Jackson infantry leadership school for enlisted men. I became a squad leader and an expert .30 caliber machine gunner. As a privilege of my new position, I proudly carried a side-arm, a .45 caliber Colt pistol.

So much had changed in my life. In addition to what my joining the Army did for mother, my entire Army experience was productive and fruitful. I had fun and traveled. I saved $2,000 in U.S. saving bonds and I earned a high-school equivalency diploma. The Army helped me to become an American and to blend into my new country. The G.I. Bill was an unexpected gift yet to come.

I have often reflected on my Army life. The background of a young market merchant from France, a recent immigrant to the U.S., joining the Army soon after his arrival, certainly was not anything like that of the other men in my unit. Though not an athlete, I survived basic training and rigorous advanced infantry training. This surprised many, including me.

I was selected for infantry leadership school, which I completed as a non-commissioned officer. That was even more remarkable! Frequently, I was called on to demonstrate to new recruits my skill at taking apart and assembling the .30 caliber machine gun and the .45 caliber pistol blindfolded.

That I loved and thrived in the United States Army was amazing to my relatives. I must have been projecting my feelings. After the first time Colonel Bob Rosen (Beverly Rozansky's husband) and I met, he said that he had never seen a happier sergeant in the U.S. Army.

Now a U.S. citizen and a noncommissioned officer in the U.S. Army, my first overseas assignment took me to Trieste. The mission related to a dispute between Italy and Yugoslavia. I soon found Trieste was home to beautiful women and the best pizza in the world. We were called the "TrUST" command; this stood for Trieste U.S. Troops. The military post of Trieste was proclaimed to be the forgotten paradise of the U.S. Army. I can attest readily to that fact.

In October, 1954, the signing of a border agreement between Italy and Yugoslavia meant that U.S. troops would be departing Trieste within six months. My unit was first transferred to Livorno, Italy, near the leaning tower of Pisa, before being sent to Camp McCauley in Linz, Austria (ironically enough, Hitler's birthplace). Linz was also famous for a bridge spanning the Danube River which separated American and Russian troops. One side of the bridge was manned by U.S. Military Police and the other by Russian sentinels. On a bright day, the Cold War enemies could clearly see each other.

In the spring of 1955, while on duty in Austria, I learned that John's U.S. visa had been delayed. He was approaching the age of 19, when French military obligations would arise. Soon he would not be permitted to leave France without first serving two years in the French military. This would be disastrous to our plans.

I consulted the army chaplain, an Episcopal minister, a fine person who proved to be the right man in the right place at the right time. He contacted the Embassy in Paris, which advised that I should travel to Paris and sign a sworn affidavit documenting that John was my younger brother. This simple step was all that was required to get John on his way to America.

Then, a sort of Catch–22 situation arose. At that time, the French considered any male born in France, regardless of citizenship, to be forever eligible for military service. There were no exceptions. The army chaplain helped me obtain permission to go to Paris, but my leave papers explicitly warned that I could be drafted into the French Army, my American uniform notwithstanding.

The problem went beyond my concern about our being drafted into the French army. I was afraid that if John and I were conscripted, we would never leave France. Although people have emigrated from France after completing their military service, it somehow never occurred to me that this could be an option for us. In my mind, being drafted was, in some fashion, equal to being bogged down in the market stalls for eternity.

There was a popular saying among outdoor traders in those days: *Une fois sous les tôles, toujours sous les tôles* ("once under the tin, always under the tin").[5] I wanted no part of that life. I pictured myself as trapped, cold, and gloomy in the market stalls, and I saw no way of escaping them for the rest of my life if I were drafted into the French Army.

All of this meant to me that John's application for a U.S. visa had to be expedited. This was the prime consideration. We needed a plan to deal with our dilemma. Mother and John met me in Rome. This was the first time we had seen each other since I had left Paris two years before. It was an emotional reunion; John and mother could not take their eyes off my American uniform.

The next day, Mother took me aside. John had become a true Francophile. He saw things a bit differently from the way that I did then, maybe because of our age disparity and my U.S. citizenship. Mother was not sure that John wanted to come to America. John and I discussed it and I was relieved to learn that John, for all his feelings for France, was not opposed to joining me in America. I concluded that he was actually eager to come. As a result, we decided that I would take the risk and go to Paris to present myself at the US Embassy.

While still In Rome, we decided that once in Paris, instead of staying at 11 *rue de Sévigné* with mother and John, it would be safer for me to stay at a hotel. Given the prevailing anti-American mood in Paris, we were afraid someone might wish to report me as a French citizen. After checking in, I went directly to the US Embassy, located in a beautiful section of Paris, close to the *Place de la Concorde* and across the street from the Hotel Crillon where Woodrow Wilson stayed during the peace treaty negotiations at the end of World War I. On a sergeant's pay, I did not stay at the Crillon but rather at a very inexpensive hotel near the *Gare de l'Est* ("East train station"). I wore my U.S. Army uniform at all times, even sleeping in it. I was terribly nervous and very cautious. The uniform and my pride in it was a wonderful symbol for freedom from the *schmatta* business and the past.

At the embassy, my declaration in support of John's visa was completed in a matter of minutes. I went back to the hotel, intent on catching an early morning train back to Austria. Toward the late afternoon, content that my mission had been accomplished, I was resting peacefully when I was startled by a phone call from the front desk. The man there informed me that two French military policemen were looking for me. I became paralyzed with fear. Before I could react, there was a loud knock on the door, followed by another louder knock. I finally reluctantly opened the door. There stood John and our friend Marcel, laughing uncontrollably. Shaken and agitated, my game plan changed. I left Paris immediately.

Soon after my return to Austria, in mid-May, 1955, a state treaty signed by the four occupying powers ended Austria's occupation and French, British, American and Russian troops were withdrawn. With less than six months of active duty left, I and others in the same category were advised that we would be shipped back stateside in the near future while soldiers with more active duty remaining were to be relocated to Germany to finish their tours of duty.

In the summer of 1955, my mood was good, my problems seemed resolved and my future appeared promising as I awaited my evacuation orders. I even managed to get a long weekend pass to Salzburg, a week-end I shall always cherish. Every time I watch the Sound of Music, so many pleasant memories flood my mind! The formal gardens with their many colors spoke of an age of grandeur which had long since passed. The people were friendly, the scenery was magnificent and the hills nearby provided a perfect background. The *Wiener schnitzel*, accompanied by fine German wine, was the best I ever savored. Salzburg is a jewel in an enchanting land.

It is difficult to imagine how Austria, such an engaging country, could have produced Hitler. How could Austrians, such an ingratiating people, have played the role they did in World War II? How could the *Anschluss* (the annexation of Austria by Germany) have occurred with such fervor in a nation with so many grand and venerable traditions? Yet, all this happened in beautiful Austria. Nazism found fertile ground in this old central European bed of civilization, intellectual and scientific advancement.

## NOTES

1. Fernand Braudel: *The Wheels of Commerce* (Los Angeles: University of California Press, 1992) [translated by Sian Reynolds from Braudel's *Les Jeux de l'échange* (Paris: Librairie Armand Colin, 1979)], 25–66.

2. The term *schmatta* is used today in the U.S. clothing trade and has lost its meaning of "cheap" clothing. Today, the term can refer to upscale as well as downscale merchandise.

3. In view of subsequent events, the name "Albert Michaely" is fictitious to respect the privacy of living members of his family. Dr. Michaely was an impressive

individual, extremely gifted and talented. He was admired by Uncle Isor and many other people.

4. Fort Jackson, named in honor of Major General Andrew Jackson, the seventh president of the United States, was and still is the largest training center in the United States Army.

5. Most prime locations in the open-air markets had a permanent tin roof. The rest had no shield at all. The *marchands forains* in these spots had to resort to makeshift coverings made of tarpaulins.

*Part Two*

# IN AMERICA

# Chapter Thirteen

# Life Anew

In late July 1955, I boarded the *USNS General Maurice Rose* in Bremer-haven, Germany, for the trip to the U.S. The crossing was a good deal less luxurious than my earlier experience on the two *Queens*. About half the passengers were service dependents, mostly wives and children. My main duty was to command a squad on guard duty in the areas between enlisted soldiers and dependents. The food was so good that members of my squad said that their next enlistment would be in the Navy. The excitement of going back to the New World made each day special. I was going to America for good, and I was going to be an American forever.

The ship stopped in Casablanca, French Morocco, to pick up more American dependents. We were given shore leave for an afternoon. The houses were white, the streets were lined with palm trees, the sun was blinding, and the beaches were wide and sparkling. The restaurants served a delicious lamb and rice dish. The women were casually dressed. All too briefly, I was on holiday.

But heavily armed French Army patrols were everywhere. The soldiers and the city residents seemed to be living in a constant state of confrontation. I neither knew nor wanted to learn about their problems. When it dawned on me that I was on French soil, I became uneasy. I was still susceptible to the French military draft, but I was safe in the company of my military unit. I was relieved to return to our ship.

The ship arrived in New York after another 10 days at sea. After disembarking at the Staten Island Terminal, all soldiers returning from Austria were given an unexpected 30 day leave. Since the Army had no immediate use for us, I traveled to Washington, where I stayed again with our friends, the Shein-baums. I wore civilian clothing and resumed my job as a clerk at the National Airport Pharmacy. I visited relatives and began to dream about civilian life. To me, Washington was more beautiful than ever that summer. I dated several charming girls who appeared completely American to me. I was happy and enjoyed my extended leave time.

John would soon be arriving in America and Mother's visa application had been processed without a snag. She would join us in Washington as soon as she completed the liquidation of our assets in Paris. I had peace of mind. Our new life was rejoined in America, away from the *schmatta* business forever.

In late July 1955, I was reassigned to Fort Devens, 35 miles west of Boston.[1] Fort Devens was a beautifully landscaped old military post. Army routine was strict, and so were the camp assignments; I liked the discipline. Infantry sergeants (and physicians) seem to be always training. I attended classes in map reading, the use of the compass and night orientation.

There was a delightful 18th century New England village nearby, the little town of Ayer. The restaurants served excellent food, and the shops were interesting.

I received word that John had come to the United States on the *SS Castel Felice*, a small Greek ship which took 9 days to cross the Atlantic. He had been in a cabin near the engine room and had difficulty sleeping at night because of the noise. He played bridge with many of the U.S. college students returning from Europe.

It was early August 1955 when John arrived by train at Washington's Union Station. There was a bus and trolley strike. He shared a taxi with several people, riding up and down the streets of Washington and was the last person to be taken to his destination. By the time he arrived at 2153 Newport Place, it was midnight. No one had expected him that night. He stood outside, in the dark and rain, and knocked on the side door for a long time, feeling lonely. Ultimately, the door opened, the Sheinbaums welcomed him with warmth and John began his new life in America.

In late August 1955, my unit was transferred to Camp Drum in northern New York state for eight weeks.[2] Many "weekend warriors" spent their two weeks of annual active duty there.

My squad's duty was to support the training of the civilian reserve troops. We spent long days on the firing range. In the firing pits, we alternately pulled up, scored and pulled down targets. There was muster every morning. Otherwise, all else was familiar Army routine. On weekends, I visited nearby towns, especially Watertown, New York. The area was not as attractive to me as New England. We went to movies or had meals at a cafeteria. I was surprised that most of these small towns had Sunday blue laws but this mattered little to me because I did not drink.

In mid-October, 1955, we returned by truck to Fort Devens. The beautiful fall scenery of western New England was breathtaking. Our convoy spent two days on the road; we slept in tents and ate in the open fields. The magnificent

New England surroundings were enhanced by delightful weather and fall foliage. To this day, I love New England.

In late October 1955, the Army processed my discharge. I was released at Fort Devens. There was no retreat parade. In a few days, I was back in Washington as a civilian. John was there with our friends the Sheinbaums. We stayed with them for several weeks. John seemed in fine form and pleased to be in America. In time, we sublet a double room in a spacious private home at 16th and Crittenden Streets, across from the B'Nai Israel Synagogue. We decided to stop speaking French to each other. Since then, we have rarely spoken in our native language. French is now reserved to impress the Maitre d' and the staff at our favorite French restaurants.

We looked forward to mother's coming to America. In early Spring 1956, we rented a two bedroom garden apartment in the Doreen at 5920 14th Street, N.W., at the corner of Missouri Avenue and 14th Street. In April 1956, John and I went to New York by train, met mother at dockside and returned to Washington on the Eastern Air Shuttle. It was the first time that John, mother, and I had ever been on a plane. It was an extraordinary event for us. The sensations of take-off, occasional air turbulence and landing coupled with the aerial views of various cities and traveling above, below and through clouds were all novel experiences.

We settled in at the Doreen. The bus stop was only two blocks away on 16th Street, at the intersection of Military Road and Missouri Avenue. This location was important because we had no automobile. The sole access to the nearest bus stop from our apartment was through a heavily wooded area, poorly lighted at night. Mother worried about our safety in this area and constantly admonished us to be careful walking to and from the bus.

Mother began to go to an Americanization school in a historic building at 18th Street and Belmont Road, behind the future site of the Hilton Hotel. Soon afterwards, she was employed at Lerner's Clothing Store at 14th Street and Park Road. An able saleslady and seamstress, she quickly adapted to work in America. She enjoyed the nearby Scholl's cafeteria, where she limited herself to one dollar per meal.

From the very beginning, John began to pursue selected studies at George Washington University on a part-time basis, while working with me full-time at the airport pharmacy. In addition to "English B" for foreign students, he took chemistry. Because of his job it was difficult to fit in courses, so that he ended up taking a less demanding course in religion, which he enjoyed. I was not interested at the time in a college education. After all, I had been out of school for several years. I saw myself as a man of the world. I thought my childhood dream of becoming a doctor was not realistic. I decided it was better for me to go into the world of business, where my family had done well.

Enter Uncle Isor. He felt that the family had too many business people. He wanted John and me to become doctors, the time-honored profession for bright Jewish boys. Doctors were held in high esteem. They were healers, wise in head and heart. Helping to bring life and sustain it, physicians traditionally were looked upon with tremendous respect, sometimes awe. Uncle Isor wanted this for us. "You can be doctors," he said. And with a rare sense of purpose, he made it happen. Uncle Isor spent many hours with Mother, John and me trying to convince us that in America it was possible for us to become doctors.

I remember him saying, time and again *All you have to do is to make up your minds to pursue this goal. I will be there for you. If money considerations become an issue, I will see to it that you are taken care of. I would be personally honored if you took my advice. Do not be afraid. You are no longer in Europe. You are legally in America now. All things can happen here.*

John agreed, but mother and I were not sure. We felt that John could become a doctor while she and I earned the daily bread. Uncle Isor and Aunt Bella did not demur. "Both John and Oscar will become doctors," they said. Mother and I reluctantly gave in, but we still had some doubts.

John and I applied to the pre-med program at George Washington University. We were accepted based on our transcripts from the *Lycée Charlemagne* in Paris, John's *baccalauréat* (French high school diploma) and my high school equivalent degree from the Army. There was a technical delay in my case because of the wait for the Army to confirm my scholastic status. One day as I was inquiring about this problem, the registrar, a grouchy middle-aged lady, told me: " Don't build up your hopes of becoming a doctor—only the cream of the crop are accepted in medical school." I was hurt and disappointed but not discouraged.

John and I continued to work as clerks at the National Airport Pharmacy and News Stands. Our boss was the manager-pharmacist, Dr. Michaely, Uncle Isor's old friend, who was gracious and solicitous to us. We had to take the S2 bus down 16th Street to the Federal Triangle, near the Main Post Office. At 12th Street and Pennsylvania Avenue, we caught the bus to the airport. It was a pleasant commute, but it soon interfered with our tight schedule.

On Sundays, mother, John and I were habitually invited by Dr. Michaely to his home for lavish brunches. He and his wife lived in the Margate, a new building, near where we lived.[3] We were impressed by the manned front desk, the lobby, the spacious apartment with a balcony and the appealing open roof garden.

The airport was a different world for us. It was a small city with its own post office and police department. The place was exciting and buzzing with activity. The hustle and bustle of a busy modern airport, the planes, the constant blare of the PA system and hordes of people rushing about all gave it a vibrant atmosphere. We were amazed by the clientele that came through: politicians, media celebrities, foreign dignitaries and uniformed military brass. We could not understand how young college students could waste considerable money on large stuffed animals, but they often did, buying the unique Steiff animals imported from Germany.

That little pharmacy, along with its related news stands, was our window into the daily life of America. John and I learned our "American street smarts" at National Airport.

A company from Buffalo, New York, Air Terminal Services, owned and operated all the concessions. In addition to the pharmacy and the newsstands, Air Terminal Services ran the cafeteria, the main restaurant, the fountain counters, the stores and the barber-shop. John and I were given meal tickets which we could use in all the food facilities, except in the main restaurant. The latter was available to us only on Christmas, Thanksgiving, and sometimes on special holidays. At the airport we first learned about iced tea, banana splits, fudge brownies, chocolate chip cookies and even sweet potatoes (I have never developed a taste for these).

John became the supervisor of the stock rooms. I continued to work mostly in the pharmacy or at the stands. We began to notice strange things. Many salesmen were treated unceremoniously, while others were warmly received. We soon discovered the secret reasons for the difference, namely, bribes and kickbacks. We also became aware of a cozy relationship between the various managers at the airport—fancy prime steaks or family dinners at the expensive restaurant were bartered for Polaroid cameras, small window air conditioners or other extravagant gifts.

Soon, I was "promoted" to inspector of incoming merchandise. My job was to verify the contents of each package shipped to Air Terminal Services at the National Airport. My new assignment called for checking off each item and placing an "OK" on it, followed by my signature at the bottom of the invoices. I was puzzled that there were often two invoices for each package of goods from certain well-known wholesalers. The significance of the two invoices triggered alarm bells in my brain. I began to suspect double billing fraud. My queries were answered by "Don't worry about it, don't ask questions, you boys are lucky to be working in a place like National Airport. "

I became frightened. Dr. Michaely was no longer friendly to me and began to make my job unpleasant. I discussed the situation with Uncle Isor, who was astonished, almost incredulous. After several disagreeable incidents, I rebelled and, to the surprise of everyone, including me, I quit my job. A year later, my hunch was proven right. Doctor Michaely later was fired by Air Terminal Services.

John soon also left his job at the National Airport and went to work for Silberne Souvenirs in Southeast Washington. His new job as a clerk in the stock rooms of a warehouse proved intolerable. It was a hot summer; the warehouse was not air conditioned and John felt stifled. John learned that the Washington souvenir trade was a highly competitive business, permeated with greed.

After I left the airport, I worked part time for a while in Oscar Rozansky's liquor store, near George Washington University, where I was going to school. Uncle Isor provided great support, saying "Don't become discouraged, things will work out for the best." A break came a few weeks later. I was offered a permanent job at another liquor store. Myer Gildenhorn, one of Isor's nephews, owned Circle Liquors at the corner of Livingston Street and upper Connecticut Avenue in Chevy Chase. He was looking for help. I began to work as a clerk at Circle Liquors. This new job offered many advantages over the job at the airport. The location was much better, closer to my classes at George Washington and much easier to get to by bus. Myer Gildenhorn would drive me home after work. Instead of the minimum wage of $1.25 an hour, I started at $2.50 an hour with a promise of bonuses. The job itself was much easier than my work at the airport.

Myer was very accommodating and a good man to work for. The hours were flexible and I could keep up with my school schedule. I worked mostly in the evenings, on weekends and during peak holiday periods. There was no Sunday work. It was an ideal situation for a full time student.

As soon as John turned 21, a prerequisite to working in a liquor store, he too was hired. Between the two of us, one or the other was always available, and often the two of us worked together. Myer was happy and so were we.

Rose Gildenhorn, Myer's wife, was exceptionally nice to us as well. We felt at home with Myer and Rose. They frequently took us out for dinner after work. Eating hard-shell crabs at the Chesapeake Restaurant in Takoma Park was a special treat. They regularly invited us for New Year's Eve and family occasions.

John and I also did odd jobs, putting in spare hours on Sunday at Sparkle Car Wash on Florida Avenue at U Street, near 16th Street. This business was owned by Isor's brother, Nathan. We also did baby sitting in the evening at our apartment complex and ran errands for people who knew of us through our family.

We visited Uncle Isor in his beautiful air-conditioned store, Mayflower Liquors, on Connecticut Avenue, opposite the Mayflower Hotel. He saved night deliveries for us. We made after hours deliveries to the Mayflower Hotel and pocketed nice tips. At other times, Uncle Isor would take us shopping at Louie's on 8th and D Streets. He would buy us suits, shoes and other items.

He always emphasized the need for good quality shoes and would buy us Bally shoes. John still wears only Bally shoes.

One Sunday morning, as a favor to Uncle Isor, I was asked to observe a car wash facility in Northern Virginia and to count the cars entering the enterprise. I was provided with a comfortable chair, a table equipped with a parasol and a hand-counter. I spent the entire morning faithfully clocking the number of cars being washed. I was finally relieved of my assignment by a friend of Uncle Isor, who thanked me profusely and paid me the equivalent of a week's wages. He later informed me that based on my count, he had decided to buy the car wash. Needless to say, I was impressed.

We worked hard, without vacations or days off. Going to school all day and staying up a good bit at night prepared us well for the hard work and crazy hours of medicine. To stay up at night, we began to resort to No-Doz, freely available and then popular. Our studies were constantly encouraged by Uncle Isor, Aunt Bella and a gracious lady, Bess, the wife of Isor's younger brother, Nathan. Between Mother, John and me, we made a comfortable living without touching our nest-egg. Something of a shock was in store for us, however. We had not yet experienced the financial strains of college tuition.

George Washington University (GWU) became the center of our world. As a veteran, I would be entitled to apply to medical school after completing 90 credit hours and obtaining an Associate of Arts; the GI bill would help cover both pre-med and medical school. John would go for the usual 120 credit-hours and obtain a Bachelor of Science degree.

GWU had an excellent evening program to accommodate daytime workers who were furthering their education, many under the G.I. Bill. John took many of his pre-med courses at night. We were so busy with our schooling and our jobs that we had little time to socialize. For that reason, we were not part of the in-groups or cliques which to us seem prevalent. We also felt many of the Jewish students(a typical example of an ingroup) who partied constantly were not prepared to welcome us.

This situation came as a surprise to me. I felt that the Jewish students, coming mostly from well-established Washington Jewish families, acted *plus royaliste que le Roi* ("more royal than the King") as the old French proverb has it or, as it would be in English, "more Catholic than the Pope." In our particular case, these Jewish students did not seem eager to associate themselves with two recent Jewish immigrants. This was my subjective and possibly erroneous assessment.

There was a notable exception. David Steinman, a premed student a year ahead of us, was popular as well as an outstanding student and seemed to have everything going for him. His father, a prominent Washington physician, was a graduate of George Washington University's School of Medicine.

David had already been accepted to the medical school for the following year. He was a very good-hearted young man who proved to be our friend. He knew we didn't have a car, so he generously drove us around in his, regularly picking us up at home or taking us to work after school. He never failed to invite us to his social events and made us feel he enjoyed our company, respected us and valued our friendship.

Our premed advisor was Robert Corbin Vincent, Ph.D. A professor of chemistry who taught both qualitative chemistry, a course that is now obsolete, and quantitative chemistry. He was an excellent teacher and a fine man. He advised generations of pre-medical students with genuine devotion and great expertise. A wonderfully accommodating person, Dr. Vincent gave extra attention to John and me, perhaps because he felt we were somewhat at a disadvantage in an American college setting. Dr. Desmond taught embryology and comparative anatomy, and Dr. Hansen taught histology. They were also truly superb teachers who greatly influenced their students.

In addition to our heavy schedule of required courses in the sciences, we took several elective classes. One in particular stands out. Current Events was given every Friday at noon by the venerable Elmer Louis Kayser, Ph.D., L.L.D., professor of European history and university historian. Dr Kayser was a powerful lecturer. He prepared meticulously and delivered each lecture with the aplomb of an experienced orator, including irony and humor as part of his analytical and intellectual arsenal. He loved to act in front of an audience. He also had a reputation of never having failed anyone, perhaps because no one wanted to miss a lecture. We hung on every word. His course on current events was extremely popular; the large Lisner auditorium always overflowed for his class. John and I still laugh, recalling the excitement in the room when Professor Kayser referred to John Foster Dulles as the "greatest misguided missile of our time."

Frank Weiner recently told me in a telephone conversation from North Carolina, where he retired: *I don't think about organic chemistry much these days, but I do remember that Dr. Sam Wrenn, born and raised in North Carolina, loved watermelon, as, we've discovered, do most true North Carolinians.*

Dr. Wrenn, in whose organic chemistry course we had to do well to get into medical school, was a friendly popular chap who lessened the rigors of his teaching with a great sense of humor and frequent pearls of wisdom. Every day he would write in large letters on his blackboard: *Nothing in this world will earn you a passing grade in my organic chemistry class but yourself.*

Frank Weiner was a little older; a totally self-assured, recently discharged Marine noncommissioned officer, who took all his courses at night with his mustering-out pay from the Marine Corps. He was Jewish and proud to have been in the Marines. He was fond of articulating something which immediately caught my attention: *It was only through the grace of God that I was born in the U.S.A., affording me the opportunity of becoming a Marine in this blessed country of ours. Otherwise, I could have been turned into soap as so many of my people were in WW II Europe.* We have remained close friends to this day.

We soon began to feel the pressure of college tuition and we had to resort to tapping into our savings. This situation became a source of concern to all three of us. About this time, we heard that it might be possible for mother to get a lump financial settlement and a lifetime pension from the German Government for father's death and for all the other trouble the Nazis had caused us. We were put in contact with one Frederic Alberti who practiced law in New York City. He came to visit us after we established a relationship by letter. He was a German Jew, despite his Italian name. He was, indeed, a survivor of the Holocaust. He informed us that mother was entitled to financial compensation under a new reparation law recently adopted by the Bonn federal government. After telling us that he was well-versed in this field and handled many such claims, he offered to represent mother in this matter on a contingency basis. John and I perused the papers in English and French. He then asked mother to read the papers carefully in French before she signed them. We were satisfied, saw no problems and did not think of getting advice from anyone in the family or from another lawyer. In our eagerness to welcome a solution to our future tuition problems, we were rather cavalier in letting mother sign on the dotted line. Alberti remained in close touch with us for about a year, asking mother from time to time to sign or provide additional papers. He emphasized the process would take a long time, but assured us he would work things out for us in the end. We had no doubts that this man was legitimate, and we put the matter out of our minds.

We began to entertain serious thoughts about applying to medical school. Our grades in premed were excellent. John and I tested each other nearly daily, using an old effective method we had learned from our uncle in the French village during World War II. Recitation on a daily basis to each other worked well for us from the very beginning and it was to serve us well throughout our years in pre-med at George Washington. To me, the only disquieting thing were the frequent comments by well-meaning people who questioned my seriousness about becoming a doctor, "considering your circumstances."

By the spring of 1957, John and I were both determined to go to medical school in spite of all obstacles. We grew up in an environment which had glamorized the medical profession. Uncle Isor yearned for us to become doctors. Premed did not seem to be too difficult. The strong desire to become doctors in America, after our days of adversity in Europe, settled in our blood and could not be denied any longer. Oscar Rozansky offered to help us. He asked his son, Gerald, who was in medical school at Georgetown University, to explore the situation for us. An administrative decision by the powers-that-be of Georgetown University, made before John and I were born, was to assume great importance in our lives.

> *In 1927, the University appointed a regent to the medical school. This officer became the official representative of the president and board of directors of the university* [the regent thus carried clout] *and was responsible for efficient maintenance of discipline and scholastic standards. The regent was always a Jesuit.*[4]

Gerald was quite gregarious and had become friendly with Father Thomas J. O'Donnell, the regent of the medical school. Father O'Donnell offered to meet with John and me in early June, 1957, after Gerald told him about us. It was to be a preliminary interview. We were looking for a frank, realistic assessment of our chances of getting into medical school as well as for guidance as on how to gain acceptance. John and I had not yet taken the medical aptitude exam or formally applied to medical school. We expected to be told politely and diplomatically that our chances of being accepted into medical school were slim to none.

Father O'Donnell reviewed our story, transcripts and degrees. He seemed most impressed that John and I had taken four years of Latin. For some reason, he dwelled on this aspect of our background and then left the room with all of our credentials. Half-an hour later, he returned with a big smile and told us: *You are both in. You have just been accepted. Oscar will be in the class of 1962. This means he will begin medical school in August 1958, and John will be in the class of 1963, and will start in August 1959. You will receive official letters of acceptance within a week.*

We did.

The only condition he assigned to these acceptances was our successful completion of all premed courses, 90 credit hours for me as a veteran and 120 for John. John and I looked at each other. We were unprepared for what had happened. It was a moment of pure joy.

This momentous event in our lives happened in the late 1950s; it could not happen today, with the complicated application process, all-powerful admission committees and extensive red tape.

Of course, mother, John and I were overjoyed. But soon all three of us began to wonder how we would pay for our medical educations. We alternated between emotional highs and lows. Uncle Isor and Bella were elated and did not seem to be worried. Oscar Rozansky was pleased that his advice had worked out well. He told us he would be there for us, if need be. Mother, who sought to be as independent as she was industrious, remained worried about our financial picture.

John and I had experienced the usual sibling rivalries and had held differences of opinion on France, immigration and our futures. We pledged to each other that whatever our discords might have been in the past, we would be one for two and two for one, come what may. We came to the conclusion that now, fully united, things would somehow work out. We gradually developed an unshakable self-confidence in ourselves to pursue a common goal, successfully completing medical school. From a financial viewpoint, we would try to do it on our own, but knowing that Uncle Isor and Aunt Bella were firmly committed to our success made all the difference. Oscar Rozansky added to the strength of our resolve. The rest of the family and our friends were incredulous.

John and I were now firmly on the path and getting closer to the gate. What had seemed an impossible dream, admission to medical school, had been realized for both of us. We entered the Georgetown School of Medicine on Father O'Donnell's timetable.

## NOTES

1. Fort Devens was named after Major General Charles Devens, a Civil War hero and later a Massachussets Supreme Court Justice. Opened in 1917, the installation closed in 1996.

2. Camp Drum was named after General Hugh A. Drum who had served under General John J. Pershing in France during World War I as a division and corps commander. It was a major training center for the Army Reserve and the National Guard.

3. "The Margate" is a fictitious name to protect the privacy of living members of Dr. Michaely's family. As mentioned in Chapter 12, "Dr. Michaely" is also a fictitious name.

4. John F. Stapleton, *Upward Journey* (Washington: Georgetown University, 1996), 49.

## Chapter Fourteen

# Medical School—The Basic Years

I began the study of medicine at Georgetown University five years after forsaking the open-air market stalls of the Old World. Much had occurred in a few short years. An incredible transformation had taken place. In short order, I, a Jewish *schmatta* merchant from Paris, had become a soldier in the U.S. Army. I had a most enjoyable and profitable Army career without running afoul of rednecks or master sergeants. I had become a U.S. citizen and had been accepted as a premed student at George Washington University in Washington, DC. This progression had enabled me to become firmly focused with the emotional maturity to attempt the process of becoming a physician. I closed my eyes, and it seemed miraculous that I found myself in the Georgetown University School of Medicine.

My formal high school education had been interrupted in Europe by world events. It resumed during my time in the U.S. Army where I was awarded a U.S. high school equivalency certificate. Two years in the U.S. Army allowed me to adapt to my new country. Many other people, I am certain, can attest to the character building benefits of service in the Armed Forces of the United States. This military seasoning prepared me for the hardships of medical school. I was ready to implement the advice that my drill sergeant used to bark at me during basic training: "Get the lead out of your ass and put a fire in your belly."

My inner voice encouraged me. I had successfully endured advanced infantry discipline and adjusted happily to exacting army life. I knew that I could survive medical school. I would tackle my new challenge with enthusiasm, gusto and perseverance.

John and I soon realized that our background, dissimilar from our classmates as it was, offered us a considerable advantage. The other students seemed to take America for granted and frequently devoted themselves to living it up. We took nothing for granted. We were cautious in each new situation, yet quick to seize an opportunity when it became available. My classmates did not always take full advantage of having been born here. We, the ex-*schmatta* guys, John and I, partook liberally of the zeal of the non-native in this country so we could make it in Medical America.

I vividly remember that warm, almost tropical morning of September 25, 1958, when, with great anticipation, I arrived at Georgetown Medical School. I carefully carried the second-hand Zeiss monocular microscope I had recently purchased from a scientific bookstore downtown. The medical school was housed in a large brick, federal-style edifice, with two end wings running off a wide central hall. The building was three stories, and complete with a tower and cupola covered with green aged copper, much like the ancient spires of Paris. The medical school stood on a knoll in the northeast quadrant of the Georgetown campus, next to the hospital. It overlooked Reservoir Road and the Archbold estate beyond.

My entrance into the world of medicine was through a small back door off the rear parking lot which led to a dimly lit hallway. I had approached the impressive main doorway of the school on Reservoir Road, where a guard stopped me. He directed me to the rear of the building and the student parking lot. My future classmates were parking their cars there. The irony was not lost on me; I was the only one who had arrived by bus. A large sign directed all new students to an orientation seminar in Lecture Hall 102. Room 102 was a massive room, at least two stories high, with ascending rows of combination desk-chairs arranged in circular fashion about a large pit. In the pit was a table, a black board and a sink. It was like nothing that I had ever experienced. At least 200 people could be accommodated. This amphitheater room along with its mirror image, Room 101, is where for the next two years I would endure lecture after lecture, test after test, demonstration after demonstration, until the end of the second year.

A small medical library was located in the south end wing off the lobby of the medical school. The library, opposite the north end wing housing the offices of the dean and other administrators, featured an old fashioned spiral staircase, a cozy quiet atmosphere and a friendly, obliging staff.

Orientation day is well fixed in my mind. Our acquaintance and supporter, Father Thomas J. O'Donnell, who had been instrumental in inviting John and me to medical school, introduced himself as the regent of the institution. His witty and informative talk was well received. He emphasized these philosophical words: "Forget about catching up; from now on, you never will, just do the best you can and do not worry about being caught up."

Later that day and to my dismay, he did not recognize me as the young Jewish refugee whom he had summarily admitted to his school less than two years previously.

This good priest next introduced the dean of the medical school, Hugh Hudson Hussey, M.D., "the man with a hallmark signature". With that, Father O'Donnell paused and wrote on the blackboard in big letters: $H_3$. Dr. Hussey was a tall, thin, laconic man who reminded me of Abe Lincoln. Dean Hussey began his remarks by quoting Will Rogers: "What will get you in trouble is not what you don't know but what you know that ain't so." He gave an eloquent welcoming speech and concluded by saying "From now on, you must think, talk and breathe medicine every minute of your day. Medicine is a jealous mistress."

As the day progressed, the class was introduced to the basic sciences faculty and staff. Later, each clinical department chairman greeted us. Some faculty members showed orientation slides. In the late afternoon of that first day, we were dismissed with instructions to return on September 29th for the start of classes. I had brought my microscope with me unnecessarily; I left with it in hand.

School began on September 29, 1958, with Anatomy. One of my most vivid memories centers on the Anatomy Laboratory, which was a large, clean room situated on the south side of the top floor of the medical school. Many windows allowed a great deal of light into the immense expanse of the Anatomy Lab where gray cadavers, covered with white linen shrouds, were aligned side by side on their metal slabs. The atmosphere was unreal. The stench of formaldehyde permeated the place. Dr. Solnitsky, the Professor and Chairman of the Department of Anatomy, divided us in groups of four with each group assigned a cadaver. After a short introduction by Dr. Solnitsky, we began to dissect under the close supervision of attentive instructors, one to each table. We were all called "embryo doctors" by the gentle Dr. Solnitzky. I was overwhelmed by queasiness, but too proud to admit my feelings. Each evening for the rest of the week, I walked the streets of Georgetown, disturbed by the encounter with my cadaver and wondering whether I really wanted to continue medical school. I was soon to learn that my apprehension was not an unusual reaction among first-year medical students. I finally acclimated to the Anatomy Lab, helped by the repeated admonitions of Josephine King, M.D., an English physician and an excellent anatomy instructor. With characteristic British aplomb, she urged us to "carry on, carry on," as only a Brit can do. My classmate, Frank Weiner, put it this way:

> *My first day in the anatomy lab . . . dissecting the pectoral girdle of an emaci-ated female . . . coming home to a breast of chicken dinner. Needless to say, no appetite.*[1]

There was never enough time for us to keep to the schedule for dissection of our cadavers. I am now convinced that all of this was part of the grand plan for our medical education. Other courses required our time at lecture and lab. The only chance we had to stay current with our dissection was to go up to the Anatomy Lab at an off hour, usually during the evening or on weekends. That worked well for a while, but soon the custodian of the building began to lock up the place in the late afternoon, making it impossible for us to access our cadavers. A story began to circulate, and it was given as the reason why the lab became always accessible to us soon thereafter.

As the story went, the caretaker had to be dealt with, so one bold classmate offered to fix his wagon. This particular medical student sneaked into the Anatomy Lab just before the doors were locked. He then moved an empty gurney next to a window, lay down on the stretcher and covered himself with a white sheet. A little while later, the custodian made his appointed rounds and, in the process, closed each and every window. As the custodian was bolting a nearby window, the classmate, disguised as a cadaver, suddenly propped himself into a full sitting position, lifted the sheet and said clearly and loudly:

*Peter, this is Stiff #11. Please, leave the windows open, it is a little stuffy here, and incidentally make sure that the doors to the lab remain open after hours so that the hassled medical students of today and the future doctors of tomorrow can keep up with their required assignments.*

He then pulled the sheet over himself and lay motionless again. The shaking attendant bolted for the door and made a quick exit.

Was this true or just medical school folklore, someone's vivid imagination or pure fiction ? I suspect it was a little of each, with an ounce of truth.

The class of 1962 entered in the fall of 1958, 125 strong. The pages of the *1962 Georgetown Yearbook* reflect the optimism and vigor of youth. The years have changed us all. Some are gone. Life has been cruel to others. The survivors have replaced their youthful naiveté with the wisdom of age.

A large percentage of our class came from Georgetown University's undergraduate school. I believe that group numbered about 45 to 50. As expected, the remainder of the class came from Catholic colleges, mostly Jesuit schools in the east. Seven were from Notre Dame, which is not a Jesuit school. A few were Ivy League types. Then, there were Frank Weiner and I, Oscar Mann, the two Jewish boys from George Washington University. Frank recently reminded me that we were the only ones from the George Washington University student body who went to Georgetown Medical School in the class of 1962. Frank also told me that prior to his admission, he had met Father Thomas J. O'Donnell, who interceded for him in much the same way he had done for me. There were other

Jewish students in the class, and there were those who wondered if Father O' Donnell was making amends for past, real or imagined, anti-Semitism which had been alleged against the Georgetown University School of Medicine in by-gone years. In his authoritative book, *Upward Journey*, John F. Stapleton touches on the issue of gender and religion:

> *As in its early history, the school continued to accept non-Catholics—10 percent in 1931, 13 percent in 1940. A decided shift took place after World War II when the number of non–Catholic students declined. Only two non-Catholics joined the entering class (120) of 1949! During the 1950's this trend again changed so that 20 percent of the entering class of 115 in1963 was not Catholic. Most non-Catholics were now Jewish rather than Protestant. This ethnic and religious distribution persisted.[2]*

I would be remiss not to share with the reader my opinion on the touchy issue of religion. John and I felt genuinely comfortable at Catholic Georgetown. We never encountered the slightest hint of prejudice, anti-Semitism, or anything even remotely resembling bigotry. To the contrary, pluralism was the theme of the day. The regent, Father O'Donnell, made certain that John and I observed the Jewish High Holy Days.

In those days, an acceptance was no guarantee of graduation with an M.D. degree. There was a devastating dropout rate in the first year. We were told to look and make note of the persons to the right and left of us, while being admonished that some of these people would not be in the sophomore class.

True to that prediction, 17 students were dropped from the class at the end of the first year. Most of the flunk-outs came about as the result of failures in Dr. Walter C. Hess's biochemistry course.

The selection process for the medical school was through an admission committee with some exceptions like Frank and me. Less than five per cent of the applicants for admission were successful. Each accepted student was outstanding academically and otherwise. It always has been a wonder to me that one course, biochemistry, and one teacher, Dr. Hess, could wreak such havoc with such a select group.

Hess had obtained a Ph.D. in chemistry at the University of Pennsylvania. His work was on nutrition. He came to Georgetown soon afterwards. He impressed all as being an unhappy man. He has been accused of "making life difficult for generations of Georgetown medical students." In the late 1950s, in addition to being chairman of biochemistry, he became the associate dean. He wielded inordinate power and control within the school. Upperclassmen warned us: *Biochemistry is a lightning rod for the first-year class. One has to survive biochemistry to become a sophomore medical student. If Hess turns against you, you have no recourse.*

I recall vividly the way Hess would stand in the doorway of the Chemistry Lab, puffing on a big pipe, carefully watching the entrance and exit of apprehensive freshmen. We tried to escape his attention by covering the name plates clearly displayed on our crisply starched white lab coats. He frequently subjected the class to unscheduled ten-minute quizzes, which he said were a significant factor toward a passing or failing grade in his class. Medical school lore had it that the questions on these quizzes were the same as in years past, but that the answers changed every year. The student was forced to guess this year's correct answer. Given the charged atmosphere of this particular course and the gullibility of freshmen medical students, it all seemed plausible to us.

One Friday afternoon before a long weekend and during a biochemistry lecture, he commented on our poor class attendance for that day. He then announced: "There will be a special make-up lecture on the chemistry of nutrition tomorrow, Saturday from 8 A.M. to noon. Attendance will be carefully recorded, and failure to be there will negatively influence your standing in my class."

No one missed the Saturday lecture! People who had gone out of town for the long weekend, frantically contacted by phone or telegrams, returned for the lecture. A beaming Hess began his session by surveying the class and proudly saying: "It is obvious that the word got out; I see no need to take roll-call. I shall dispense with it. "

The senior member of our class, Charlie McCauley, Ph.D., was 48 years old when he started as a freshman medical student. After receiving tenure in organic and physical chemistry at St. Peter's College in Jersey City, he had decided in mid-life to get an M.D. degree to expand further his qualifications to conduct basic medical research. He was always congenial, accommodating and enlightening to us. Charlie tutored our class in biochemistry on the informal premise that Hess was factually antiquated and morally reprehensible. Somehow, Hess and McCauley never openly challenged each other in class or in the laboratory; however, when coaching us, Charlie would often mutter under his breath, just above a whisper: "Hess, hell: this is the right way."

There was another side to Charlie McCauley. At age 48, he seemed, many times, to be younger than the rest of us. Ex-Jesuit, former college professor, one of the boys, flirtatious with the students' girlfriends and wives, he was in spite of this, or because of it, beloved by all.

It was said that the medical students dropped at the end of the first year were guilty only of incurring Hess's displeasure. The majority of my classmates always spoke and still speaks of him in derogatory terms. A select few breezed through biochemistry. Hess did have a handful of favorites. I was in the amorphous group that kept their mouths shut, asked no questions and made no waves. We, a frightened and silent bunch, obtained a passing grade without fanfare, while shaking in our boots for the entire first year. I received a B minus. A big weight had lifted.

If truth be told, the first year was arduous and tense for me. I really fretted over Biochemistry and truly feared Hess. I was trying to cope with the stress of medical school. School life was difficult enough without Hess. At times, he made life impossible.

Hess was born into the Jewish religion. His full name was Walter Cohen Hess. In his youth, he converted to the Catholic faith. Thereafter, he became known as Walter C. Hess. It was amusing to see Hess come to class on Ash Wednesday. To me, he displayed a strikingly Jewish countenance with a long nose. Somehow, the large spot of ash on the forehead of his bald head seemed incongruous.

I am now older and hopefully wiser. And I shall never know for sure if Hess made the proper academic assessments. In my mind, the dismissal of so many select students was unconscionable, and represented a flaw in the medical educational design for first year students. I have questioned frequently the fairness of a system that allowed this to happen. Hess was a complex, autocratic and arbitrary man. His impact went far beyond the chemistry lab. The source of his all-powerful status remains a mystery to me.

This much I do know from my later activities with the Georgetown Alumni Association. Ours was a different era. Hess's capricious authority remains in the memories of countless former Georgetown medical students. Today, medical students are protected from the Hesses of their school. The pendulum may even have swung too far in favor of students. An admission nowadays virtually means a degree in four years in the absence of voluntary withdrawal or bona fide due cause.

To be fair and balanced, no less an authority than the universally esteemed John C. Rose, M.D., recently confirmed what I had long suspected: *Hess did have a positive side. He did many good things for the Georgetown University School of Medicine.*[3]

The mellowing of the passing years allows me to accept this viewpoint. Hess did toughen us psychologically. At times I even wonder if this was a plan designed by the school for such a purpose. He may have been the proverbial bad cop at the behest of the powers-that-be. This would be a more charitable view of Hess's behavior than is espoused by most of his former students. Hess is gone. May he rest in peace.

On the bright and positive side, the medical school generally was blessed with a competent, sincere, devoted and dedicated faculty, enriched by notable ethnic diversity. Many of our teachers were bigger than life. They gave us basic scientific knowledge, clinical skills and a sense of purpose. They also infused us with passion, enthusiasm and idealism to become accomplished physicians. They helped us acquire a deeper understanding of our fellow man, a sense of patient reverence, with appreciation of the individual rather than the case. They repeatedly emphasized the art of *Caritas Medicini* or the practice of compassionate medicine.

Dr. Solnitsky, the Anatomy Department's chairman, was a source of encouragement to my classmates and me while we were still under Hess's dominance. Although I felt Dr. Solnitsky and I had much in common in terms of background, our relationship was quite formal, as befits interaction between a student and his professor. On one occasion, we spoke in French about the diminishing role of gross anatomy in the curriculum of first-year medical students. As one would expect, Solnitsky bemoaned this modern trend.

He was an M.D. with a Ph.D. in anatomy. His gross anatomy lectures and later his neuroanatomy lectures were classic works of beauty and substance, and we invariably looked forward to his lectures. He was a fine, gifted intellectual who dedicated his life to medical education. His most memorable quote remains with me: "Man can't die of nothing, he has to die of something."

Many years later, I would come upon him in a nursing home. He was restrained in a chair and unaware of his surroundings. Alzheimer's disease had rendered him helpless. He was gone when I returned a month later, having passed on in the interim. I walked out of the nursing home, disturbed, thinking of his quote, and wondering about life and the ravages of dementia. He had displayed such brilliance; and yet old age had robbed him of it.

The breath of fresh air in anatomy was a welcome relief from the oppressive ozone layer of biochemistry. This new ambience prevailed in physiology, the other big and important first-year course which was beginning to make ever greater inroads into the time previously allotted to anatomy.

*After only two years as chairman* [of medicine, in 1958], *Hugh Hussey became dean of medicine.*

*One of his first acts as dean was the bold and perceptive decision to appoint John Rose as professor and chairman of physiology . . . . Hussey knew that physiology was floundering at Georgetown . . . . The appointment paid handsome dividends as Rose turned the department around with the help of Lawrence Lilienfield and Estelle Ramey.*[4]

Worthy of fond remembrance and special mention are John C. Rose, M.D., Estelle R. Ramey, Ph.D., and Larry S. Lilienfield, M.D. This brilliant trio of scientific educators had recently reorganized the physiology department and soon became the heroes of the freshman class. From them, we learned much. They taught us a comprehensive, firm and dynamic basis of medicine. I have never forgotten their preaching of a physiological law: "The human body will always strive for homeostasis—a state of harmonious balance."

Their superlative lectures bolstered by elaborate laboratory demonstrations of the *reticular activating system* (part of the brain involved in the maintenance of consciousness), of the "all or none phenomenon," of the mechanisms of the human lung and bowel, and of the animated cardiac cycle, with emphasis on the critical role of hormones in the body, remain unparalleled. These innovations were pioneering giant steps, and represented a creative new type of medical education.

Over the next 25 years, Dr. Rose's name would be synonymous with what was great at Georgetown. In his various positions as a teacher, clinician, researcher, department chairman, dean and humanitarian, he always epitomized the quintessential Georgetown spirit. It was my good fortune to mingle with him during these years. Rose frequently attended and participated in Grand Rounds, Mortality Conferences, Georgetown Medical Alumni functions, Georgetown Faculty events or Memorial lectures. He was always inspiring, upbeat and humorous.

Former Dean of Georgetown University School of Medicine John Rose is now enjoying retirement in the same lovely historic residence which has been his home for many years in the little incorporated town of Somerset, off Little Falls Parkway in Chevy Chase, MD. John Rose, Professor Emeritus of Physiology and Medicine, Mr. Georgetown.

Dr. Estelle Ramey was an engaging person, an assertive lecturer and a superb teacher. She talked with passion about the "reticular activating system," the *endocrine* (glandular) make-up of the body and the sex hormones. Dr. Ramey was also, in her day, an enthusiastic feminist and champion of liberal causes. She was especially distressed about the dominant male role over "the stronger sex." Ramey was a popular, much sought after dinner guest lecturer on this topic. I once heard her say in front of a large predominantly male audience at the Bethesda Naval Hospital Officer's Club:

*Georgetown University Medical School, once a stronghold of male chauvinism* [In 1944, Sarah Stewart became the medical school's first woman student . . .[5]] *and Jewish tokenism, is now crawling with Jewish students and faculty members. I, Estelle, a Jewish gal, am now well accepted as a full professor in that same institution. If such a progressive evolution can take place at Georgetown, one day women will prevail in the professional world and in politics by continuing to outtalk, outshine and outlive men.*

Today, there are more female students than male ones in the law and medical schools. A woman President of the United States has become a distinct possibility in our lifetime. Women survive men. How prophetic she was. Her son, Jim Ramey, a distinguished Washington internist and endocrinologist, has been my physician for several years. We talk about his brilliant mother, who is now getting on in years.

Dr. Larry Lilienfield, a princely person, became chairman of the Department of Physiology and Biophysics, when Dr. John Rose was named dean of the medical school. He served with distinction as the chairman of that department for many years, while ably conducting elegant basic and clinical research in kidney-vascular diseases.[6]

On September 11, 1959, the survivors of the freshman class began their sophomore year. The summer had been a fun time, a time to relax and a time to reflect. I dated Jewish girls, often arranged by the family. My brother and I took advantage of the summer to work extra time at Circle Liquors. We made good money that summer. John was now in the freshman class. I gave him tips about first year life and especially the "to be afraid" course. Biochemistry for me, like my old nemesis, the *schmatta* business, was gone forever. All that was required now was hard work, long hours and perseverance. We felt free from anxiety and stress about survival.

The major teaching players of the second year were colorful characters and renowned in their fields.

Charles F. Geshickter, M.D., professor of pathology, one of the most debonair men I have ever encountered, possessed a prolific mind.[7] He was also among the most interesting characters of my life. A native of Washington, DC, he came from a very affluent family and grew up with many privileges. He was a 1928 honors graduate of the Johns Hopkins Medical School. While a third and fourth year medical student there, he teamed up with another classmate, Murray M. Copeland. They began to study material of gross specimens and microscopic slides of bone pathology, the extensive collection of a distinguished John Hopkins surgeon, Joseph Colt Bloodgood, M.D. He was the grandson of the inventor of the Colt revolver, and is to many the father of surgical pathology.[8]

During the early 20th century, most great surgeons would leave the *sterile field* (the immediate area surrounding the operative site — it is bacteria free, hence the term *sterile field*), and make their own decision on the frozen sections of tumor. Only then would they return to the sterile field to do the necessary surgery. Dr. Bloodgood differed from other surgeons because he saved his many surgical specimens in an index reference library. He had been the protege of Dr. William Stewart Halsted, the legendary Hopkins surgeon and educator at the turn of the century.

With much acclaim, during their senior year Geshickter and Copeland wrote and published articles in the *Annals of Surgery* and in *Surgery, Obstetrics*

& *Gynecology* on the subject of bone tumors.[9] In the year following their graduation from Hopkins, while still interns at Hopkins, they collaborated on and
published a book, *Bone Tumors* (the book can only be obtained nowadays
through private collectors and rare book stores). This was the first attempt ever
to classify bone tumors, a veritable milestone in surgical pathology. *Bone Tumors* sent giant waves into the fields of surgery, orthopedics and pathology. In
the late 1940s, Geshickter and Copeland published a book on the surgical
pathology of the breast, *Tumors of the Breast*. This was the conclusion of work
begun before WWII in Baltimore. Although the book did not have the impact
of the monumental *Bone Tumors*, it went through four editions and was used by
several generations of surgeons and pathologists.[10]

Geshickter spent WWII as a captain in the U.S. Navy and as a pathologist
at the Naval Hospital, Bethesda. Dr. Copeland had a distinguished wartime
career as a surgeon in the U.S. Army, eventually promoted to Brigadier General and Chief Surgeon in the Pacific Theater. In 1947, they both came to
Georgetown. Geshickter was named professor and chairman of Pathology
while Copeland became the professor and chairman of Oncology, a unique
department that included surgical and pathological disciplines as well as
x-ray therapy. The two remained close colleagues and inseparable friends
throughout their long and distinguished careers. Copeland left Georgetown in
the early 1960s to become the medical director at M.D. Anderson Clinic in
Houston, Texas. I well remember some of his scintillating lectures during the
basic years.

Geschickter was a self-assured, talkative, friendly and cordial person. His
lectures were extemporaneous, interesting, entertaining, at times specific and
factual, more frequently dealing with theoretical fundamental questions in
medicine. My brother, John, who eventually specialized in Infectious Diseases at Hopkins after two years at the National Institute of Infectious Diseases and Allergies, still reflects on Dr. Geschickter's brilliant basic concepts
and foresight in the role of immunity in tuberculosis and in both fungal and
bacterial infections.

There was always a quorum during Geschickter's lectures; one seldom
slept through them. Taking notes in class was an exercise in futility as his
style of lecturing forced students to learn pathology from a textbook. However, no one ever failed his course. How much I learned in there is open to
debate, but I remember some of his comments verbatim. He liked to talk
about the normal concomitants of senescence:

> *The aging brain looks like Swiss cheese on the shelves of a delicatessen store. The
> development of obstruction to urinary flow from enlargement of the prostate gland
> in older men is like a beaver building a dam—both are processes of nature.*

His favorite adage, as he walked to and fro in front of the class, bouncing on his heels and toes, was: *For want of the nail, the shoe was lost, for want of the shoe, the horse was lost, for want of the horse, the battle was lost.*

He dramatically attempted to emphasize the importance of paying attention to details in medicine, especially when caring for patients. He philosophized at length and often discussed the differences between the malignant cell and the benign cell. He was fond of repeating: ''The malignant cell is like the man who came for dinner and never left."

He not infrequently popped up in the pathology lab, smoothly run by two able associate professors of Pathology, Drs Tatiana T. Antonovych and Eie B. Chung. The place was normally an area of concentrated learning and hushed diligence. Geschickter's levity would quickly break up the quiet decorum. Students would flock around him, and he would reward them by showing special specimens or slides. He once called me out from a group of students gathered near him and beckoned me to the large demonstration binocular microscope in the center of the lab. In his inimitable manner, he slowly pulled out a slide from his pocket, wiped it off, and put it in the viewing slot with deliberate care; he proceeded to ask me to describe what I was seeing. It was obviously a vessel occluded by a blood clot. That was easy. He prodded me in a friendly way to look for more findings. I drew a blank. He pointed to some blood cells, distal to the clot. I fumbled the ball. He proclaimed loud and clear with good humor: "Your characterization, identification, and recognition of these cells leaves a lot to be desired."

He went on: "These are sickle cells, and they are the cause of the clot which killed a patient with Sickle Cell Anemia. Next time, look harder, my friend." I learned my lesson. This was vintage Geshickter. Despite his full-time professorship at Georgetown, he also maintained an active clinical practice as a cancer specialist on Connecticut Avenue. I do not believe that he was ever taken to task for this out-of-school activity. Everyone at Georgetown accorded him great respect. In his field of pathology, he was a controversial visionary.

In lecturing and in practice, he championed his theory that cancer was a disease of immunity. In his private practice on Connecticut Avenue, he treated cancer patients with desiccated tumor material to stimulate an immune response to their tumor. Nowadays, at the National Institute of Cancer, and in cancer centers throughout the world, cancer research is actively focused along the same promising immunity trail. He was truly a forward thinker.

He was also eccentric with his wealth. He owned a river front farm on the Potomac in Virginia and he was fond of referring to this place "as being down the river from George Washington."[11] He gave new Chryslers as Christmas presents to members of the surgical faculty, and gifted his Georgetown salary to the university. And best of all, every year he paid for the sophomore class annual Christmas holiday party at a downtown hotel. Geshickter was indeed a unique individual.[12]

Dr. Theodore Koppanyi was the renowned professor of pharmacology. He was a colorful old-world professor and, in his earlier years, was among the most sought after lecturers of prewar Central Europe. Theodore Koppanyi received his Ph.D. from the University of Vienna, and came to Georgetown in September 1930 from the University of Chicago. In 1947, about the time Geshickter and Copeland became entrenched at Georgetown, Koppanyi became chairman of pharmacology and Georgetown's most productive basic scientist. He wrote more than 800 papers and remained an active member of the faculty until 1974.

Koppanyi set up residence at the prestigious Cosmos Club; his home address at this bastion of academia merely added to his mystique. He was quite gregarious with his peers and became fast friends with Copeland and his circle. The professor was a permanent Saturday luncheon guest of Copeland, who was also a member of the Cosmos Club. Copeland regularly used the facilities there to entertain visiting men of science at his Saturday luncheons during the winter season. Those were the days of three Gibsons before lunch. Koppanyi was always the first one there, taking part in raucous conversations, relishing the hearty food, and thoroughly enjoying life with his peers.[13]

Koppanyi was by then past his prime in research but still at the top of his game at lectures. He preached that "lecturing is a fine art." His beautiful lectures on digitalis are still with me. Often asked about the ideal dose of digitalis, he was fond of repeating, "Enough, but not too much." His lectures were brilliant, elegant, witty, well organized and delivered in his unique humorous style. He was constantly dispensing many pearls of wisdom in pharmacology and philosophy, punctuated with numerous Old World anecdotes. At the conclusion of these lectures, the students often applauded and tossed coins his way. Thoroughly enjoying the accolades, he would beam a broad smile and bow repeatedly before the cheering class. He is remembered and memorialized by the annual Koppanyi Lecture in Pharmacology at the Georgetown Medical School. Fittingly, this lecture is given by a world renowned scholar. I have supported and attended these proceedings.

Roy Ritts, Ph.D. and M.D., was the professor and chairman of bacteriology and microbiology. When he first came on the scene, he revamped the department. Dr. Ritts resembled and sounded like the late actor Edward G. Robinson. He and the other able members of his group were powerful lecturers who inspired us with a substantial foundation in bacteriology. One of Dr. Ritts's protégés was James A. Curtin, M.D., who arrived in 1959. Curtin, who had completed a two-year fellowship in infectious diseases at Johns Hopkins, accepted the task of reviving the Division of Infectious Diseases. He later would become the Washington Hospital Center Chairman of Medicine. Our paths would cross again in the late 1960s.

Still in the department was the venerable Dr. Mario Mollari, professor emeritus of bacteriology and tropical medicine. He studied at the University of Padua, Italy. After receiving his M.D. degree, he took post-graduate training in Microbiology and was awarded a Ph.D. at his alma mater. At the turn of the 20th century, he began to work with the famed microbe hunters of the time. Dr. Mollari spent over a decade at the Pasteur Institute in Paris, working beside Madame Pasteur and her staff. During this time he became intimate with many of the great European scientists of the early 20th century. Dr. Mollari endeared himself to many generations of Georgetown doctors as a teacher and friend. With a straight face, he would joke at lecture that "I am giving you syphilis the way Noguchi gave it to me" (Dr. Noguchi, was a Japanese world-renowned expert in venereal diseases). Dr. Mario Mollari came to Georgetown in 1922 and never left; like an old soldier, he just faded away.

Following this workaholic first semester, I finally began to examine real people in the physical diagnosis course, which began in the second half of our sophomore year. We were outfitted in short white coats or as Frank Weiner reminisces: "How proud we were going out to the clinical field with our white coats during the second half of our sophomore year. We didn't wear white pants until the third year and then the big decision was buttons or zippers on the pant-flies."

Having received complimentary black medical bags from a drug company and primed by a series of excellent didactic sessions, we were sent to clinics and hospitals all over the District, as well as to Maryland and to Virginia, to begin our clinical training. Everyone had purchased a physical diagnosis textbook and was eager to examine patients.

Going from years of classroom study into the art of examining a live patient is an awkward transition. This new learning experience produced many humorous episodes. Our yearbook recorded some of these moments.

*Joe Zaia heard a 'brewery over the umbilicus.' Frank Weiner listened for S1* [a heart sound] *at the apex* [a point on the anterior chest wall, below the left breast] *by placing his bell* [the listening piece of a stethoscope] *over some woman's left areola. Joe Zaia again asked an ample female to cooperate while he listened to her lungs by 'taking a deep breast.' Don Shutello, with chart in hand, strolled to the hall and called out, 'Mr. Peutz.' He led the man to the examining room, asked him to bare his bottom and touch his toes. After ample palpation of this fellow's prostate, he doffed off his glove and said 'Thank you, Mr. Peutz.' 'But, Doctor,' replied the shocked man, 'my name is Hughes, and I am just here to visit my wife.'"* [14]

Our little family was living at the Doreen, the same garden apartment at 14th Street and Missouri Avenue we had occupied since Mother joined us in Washington, DC We lived there until John and I graduated from medical school. John and I were sharing a bedroom with twin beds. During my first year of medical school, John was a premed college senior at George Washington University. Most every night, before we fell asleep, John coached me to be sure that I was digesting my lecture notes and book assignments. This exercise in almost daily recitation was immensely advantageous to me. I offered to do the same thing for John when the time came. It proved unnecessary.

My second year was less harassing and quite pleasant. I finished the first two years, to my surprise, with a B plus average. I was fulfilled, content, relieved, and looking forward to my next two years of medical school.

John easily succeeded in biochemistry, surviving Dr. Hess with no trouble, and receiving an A in the course. He finished his first year as number two in his class. He resolved to do better in subsequent years. John would prove to be at ease throughout medical school. He was able to maintain an A average, play serious bridge, and work in the liquor store. John possessed a strong and gifted intellect. He was a quick learner. He would place number one in his medical class while simultaneously and successfully defending his title as a champion bridge player.

At the end of his second year, John let his well-developed sense of humor, sometimes bordering on wise-cracking (his own words), get him into an embarrassing situation. He received a call from Bruce Shnider, M.D., the assistant Dean of Georgetown University School of Medicine. Dr. Shnider, who directed medical oncology at DC General, was correct and aboveboard, but on the shy or aloof side.

He informed John: "You have been selected to receive the Roche Award, given yearly to the medical student ranking number one in his class at the end of the sophomore year. You are getting a nice watch."

John replied, "Is it a Mickey Mouse watch?"

Dr. Shnider became very upset and threatened to withdraw the award. However, he complained that he could not because the certificate had already been printed. John still wears the gold watch.

Before turning to my clinical years, it is only right to recall that behind the scenes were some wonderful staff people—librarians, secretaries, janitors and security officers—dedicated to improving the lot of all medical students and encouraging their journey toward the M.D. degree. Additionally in each department there were assistants and associates, research fellows, and Ph.D candidates who were available in labs and seminars, and privately, to help us.

The words of a classmate, whose name escapes me, were most pertinent: "The voluminous didactic material hurled at us from the podium defies immediate assimilation."

The many hours in the laboratories during those grueling days required the support of these persons for overcoming our frustrations. Many of them went on to distinction as teachers and scientists in their fields. These good people were all part and parcel of our lives while we were exposed to the intense and heavy curriculum of the first two years of medical school. As I leave this period, let me pause for a moment to relate a personal experience which left its mark on John and me. In fall 1959, our good friend from premed days at George Washington and now a medical student, David Steinman, was transferred to the service of George E. Schreiner, M.D., Professor of Medicine, Georgetown University School of Medicine, and Chief of Nephrology, the specialty dealing with kidney diseases, at the Georgetown University Medical Center.

A pioneer in the development of the artificial kidney,

*George Schreiner served as president of the National Kidney Foundation, president of the American Federation for Clinical Research, president of the World Nephrology Society, president of the American Society of Nephrology, and president of the American Society for Artificial Internal Organs.*[15]

David Steinman was placed on the artificial kidney machine, then the only one readily available in Washington. He had just sustained cardiac arrest at George Washington Hospital, where he was a patient with acute viral myocarditis. His kidneys had shut down. It was hoped that this was a temporary event. Complications set in. David expired a few days after his transfer. John and I were terribly saddened by these events.

Our friend's heart, preserved in a jar of formaldehyde, labeled with his name and diagnosis, was shown during a demonstration session in gross anatomy; John, then in the first year of medical school, encountered the same jar of formaldehyde with David's heart in Pathology Lab a few weeks later. We were shocked beyond belief and terribly chagrined. John and I have never forgotten the sight of David's heart floating in its formaldehyde bottle. What a distressing event. This incident underscored for us the uncertainty and fragility of human existence: *Life comes with no guarantee.*

I have reflected about what the basic and clinical years meant to me. My personal thoughts about these two contrasting educational periods are still vivid.

I found I was best suited and most comfortable in the clinical arena of medicine. I am not a book worm or a lab creature; I am a people person. This apparently innate skill, nurtured by my years in the *schmatta* trade and the army, began to surface in physical diagnosis during the second semester of my sophomore year. My aptitude for clinical medicine became even more evident in my third and fourth years, which were primarily clinical in nature. Then I had the daily opportunity to deal with real patients. Whereas the rigid disciplines of the basic years of medical school were a natural outlet for my obsessive compulsive personality, the flexibility inherent in the clinical years began to rub off on me. I remained compulsive but I became more and more at ease, both at work and play. My new self was noticed by some of my classmates, and they accorded me the diagnostic label of "compulsive male with a degree of flexibility." The word obsessive was kindly dropped. These future psychiatrists were not far off the mark.

Bridging the gap between the basic years and the clinical years was the regent, Father O'Donnell, in his capacity as the professor of medical ethics. We have never forgotten how Father O'Donnell addressed the complex question of terminal care. He had written *Morals in Medicine*, a book on medical ethics.

Holding up this book with one hand, the good Father said: *This is like holding a life in your hand. You have a right to let the book fall, withdrawing all life support. You do not have the right to push the book over to its other side and commit euthanasia.*

John and I were always impressed by the caliber of Father O'Donnell's moral precepts. He certainly was a powerful teacher. As a non-Catholic, I still value his book. I also treasure the memory of his cherubic smile in class the day after the combined faculty-student St. Patrick's Day party, when he said that everyone had behaved abominably the previous night except the Irish. Father O' Donnell, S. J., a great man!

John and I continued to work at Circle Liquors during these years while pursuing our clinical studies. The atmosphere was pleasant. John and I spent as many hours as we could in the liquor store. Myer Gildenhorn, our boss, obliged the requirements of our medical schedule. From the beginning, we knew it was officially a no-no to work outside medical school. On several occasions, we had to resort to subterfuges, such as going to the doctor or dentist, to explain our early departure from a lab, lecture or assignment. We grew uncomfortable with the secrecy. John and I decided to bring the matter out in the open by talking to Dean Hussey. He listened sympathetically to our dilemma.

He reviewed our files, asked some questions, and announced in an amicable manner that he had reached a decision: "I just made an exception to the rule. Maintain your good scholastic standing. My door is always open to you. Best of luck."

John and I were touched by his comportment.

We remember Dean Hussey with admiration and fondness. Dr. Hugh H. Hussey was a *mensch.* (this Jewish word means a "stand-up guy," a decent man of wisdom and compassion. It is the highest compliment that the language of my ancestors can bestow on someone).

*In 1978, Georgetown made Hugh Hussey Professor of Medicine Emeritus and Dean Emeritus. He died in November 1982, at age 72, of metastatic lung cancer. Dr. Blasingame, Executive Vice President of the AMA, visited Hussey three weeks before his death and remarked on the 'nobility' with which Hussey confronted his diagnosis.[16]*

I was shaken and saddened to learn that Dr. Hussey had died. Yes, this fine man's only vice was to smoke two packs of cigarettes a day. He had been an outstanding dean. Happily for our class, we had recognized Dr. Hussey's sterling qualities and had honored him during his lifetime!

*For the most recent four years, Georgetown [University School of Medicine] has been led by a vigorous personality and renowned organizer who has taken firm strides to develop in his graduates a wealth of knowledge from which to reason, a constant demand for 'how' and 'why' and a conviction that their education is just beginning.*

*The class considers it their honor to underscore their appreciation for this man by dedicating Grand Rounds 1962 [our class yearbook] to Hugh H. Hussey, M.D.[17]*

Hugh Hussey, Dean Emeritus, a life too short.

With the onset of the clinical years, the number of married students increased significantly. Half of my classmates had spouses. Barbara and Frank Weiner were one of the few premed school married couples. I was invited to their home regularly for dinner, often with an amiable Jewish girl, or simply alone to chat while sipping coffee and savoring delicious tidbits. I even began to go to parties for the first time. The whole clinical period of medical school struck a warm, sensitive chord in me. I began to feel a great deal more in my element and my attitude became more light-hearted. The hectic years of basic science had vanished. The wallflower became a sheepish rogue. I discovered the wonderful world of nurses about the same time I realized the extent to which our white coats acted as an aphrodisiac. I stopped dating Jewish girls. I thought that they expected more than I could afford. I did not own a car, and this complicated matters. Nurses were obliging, and there were so many of them, especially in the outlying hospitals. The good times were here. I was having fun. Mother worried about the emancipation of her elder son. These were the early 1960s.

In the 1970s, I learned the labels "JAP" (Jewish American Princess) and "High-maintenance girls." I was reminded of those days of my clinical years. Now older and wiser, I am happy to assert that these terms apply only to some and not all Jewish girls. I also found out later, contrary to my earlier experience, that Jewish nurses did exist.

## NOTES

1. Personal communication from Frank Weiner, M.D., February 2003.
2. Stapleton, *Upward Journey*, 108.
3. Personal communication from Dr. John Rose, January 2003.
4. Stapleton, *Upward Journey*, 138.
5. Stapleton, *Upward Journey*, 107.
6. I was immensely flattered in later years when he brought his wife to me as a patient.
7. Personal communication from Francis D. Fowler, M.D., of the class of 1954, a distinguished retired orthopedic surgeon who specialized in total joint replacements. A National Cancer Institute fellow with Murray M. Copeland, M.D., in 1957–1958, he is especially well-informed on professors Geschickter, Copeland and Koppanyi. He is a wonderful former neighbor and remains a close friend. We often exchange reminiscences about our medical days at Georgetown.
8. Personal communication from Fowler, October 2002.
9. Fowler, October 2002.
10. Fowler, October 2002.
11. Fowler, November 2002.
12. More on Geshickter and Copeland can be found in Appendix 1.
13. Most of the material about Koppanyi and the Cosmos Club was personally communicated by Fowler, October 2002.
14. *Grand Rounds, 1962* (Washington: The Georgetown University School of Medicine, 1962), 5.
15. Stapleton, *Upward Journey*, 158.
16. Stapleton, *Upward Journey, 146.*
17. *Grand Rounds,1962,* 5.

## Chapter Fifteen

# Medical School, The Clinical Years

On completion of the sophomore year at Georgetown, it was mandatory to pass an examination given by the National Board of Medical Examiners (NBME), founded in 1915 by faculty representatives of various U.S. medical schools. The full National Boards, a three-step examination, allowed a medical faculty to assess its curriculum, and enabled licensing bodies to evaluate applicants more fully. Part One was taken after the first two years of medical school, and primarily covered the basic sciences, Part Two, prior to graduation, and part Three usually with the end of internship. These latter two examinations evaluated a student's competence and readiness for clinical medicine. The traditional timing of the various parts of the National Boards was designed to maximize the probability of success. There was a high pass rate and I had no problems passing the entire test series. Later, I found the boards for specialty and sub-specialty certification formidable in comparison to the National Boards.

Between the sophomore and junior years there was a short summer vacation. It was highly welcome and I enjoyed this change of pace as much as the previous year's longer summer vacation. However, much of my time was spent confronting and solving a family problem. Our savings were becoming seriously depleted by school tuition.

At the time, mother received a small pension from the French government. If the compensation from Germany, a much larger amount, came through, she would lose the French pension, but gain considerably in the process. Mother had not heard from Mr. Alberti in over two years, but she did not accord this lack of communication any significance, at least not until this point. Worry about our dwindling finances, however, awakened her concern.

At the beginning, despite her Eastern European background, mother intuitively had decided that Mr. Alberti, who spoke Yiddish to her, was trustworthy. Now, when calls to his office did not bear fruit, she began to entertain suspicions. For some reason, Eastern European Jews did not look favorably upon German Jews ("yekkes"), and her inherent distrust of them overcame her initial enthusiasm for this German-born Jewish lawyer.

In that connection, there was a distinguished customer at the liquor store, a Dr. Anthony Schwartz, a noted Ph.D. in surface chemistry, a gentle man with a powerful intellect. He was a victim of poliomyelitis with lower extremity weakness. He walked with two canes and wore a left leg brace. He came in occasionally for a bottle of bourbon, scotch or wine, and it was my habit to carry out the small order to his car. He soon learned that I was a medical student and told me: "I will double your tip for being a student, and double it again for being a student in a scientific field; this is my practice."

Instead of the going tip of 25 cents, he gave me a dollar. Myer Gildenhorn felt that I could trust this gentleman, who had wisdom and maturity. Dr. Schwartz never seemed to talk about his adversity. To the contrary, he conveyed the notion that his glass was half full rather than half empty. Myer encouraged me to seek his counsel on mother's dilemma.

Before long, I discussed the situation over with Dr. Schwartz. Little did I know then that I was chatting with my future father-in-law. I had noticed that Mr. Alberti's office was on Madison Avenue. "Pretty impressive," I thought. I asked Dr. Schwartz whether or not the Madison Avenue address was any guarantee that Mr. Alberti was on the level. He replied: "You can rent a lavatory on Madison Avenue if you want." Tony (as I later called him) advised me to consult a prominent immigration lawyer, David Carliner. "He is a friend of mine," he said. "I will get in touch with him, facilitate the referral, and ask him to keep down his fee as a favor to me."

David Carliner was gracious and sympathetic. In my presence, he made a call to Mr. Alberti, and told him about our concerns. Mr. Carliner was satisfied with the response and recommended that we adopt a wait-and-see attitude. He charged me a very modest legal fee, $25.00. Soon afterwards, I received a telegram from Mr. Alberti who, not pleased with our distrust, offered to return the entire file, and get off the case. His message concluded with a sharply-worded note: "I am handling many such claims, traveling over the entire globe to settle these reparation cases, and do not have the time to deal with your petty feelings."

Taken aback, I replied by immediate registered mail. With the advice of Mr. Carliner, I apologized, and asked Mr. Alberti to continue with our case and promised not to doubt him in the future.

Mr. Alberti turned out to be an honest person and a few months later, he came through with his promises. He took his cut and no more. His fee was 20% of the lump sum and nothing of the lifetime monthly pension. The net lump sum was $12,500.00 and the pension $800.00 per month, pegged with a cost of living clause. This development allowed my brother and me to finish medical school without asking anyone in the family for financial help. Remember, the year was 1960. Such a financial solution would not be feasible today. The tuition for the academic year 2002–2003 is $31,764.00. Including tuition, the living budget scales from $50,052.00 for the 1st year to $54,470 for the 3rd year, and for some reason, the 4th year levels off to less at $53,540.00.[1] Mother, with the support of her two physician sons, the lifetime German pension and Social Security, was financially secure in old age.

Although John and I did not own a car until well after medical school, I never traveled by public transportation to go to my various clinical assignments. Neither did John. People in the classes of 1962 and 1963 chauffeured us. John and I were fortunate to have such friendly and collegial classmates.

In my case, David Robbins and Sol Snyder supplied most of my transportation requirements to medical school and back home during my first two years. In my last two years, Charlie Tartaglia provided the necessary transportation, and in a pinch, Frank Weiner was my back-up.

On August 8, 1960, my clinical years formally began. Our names would be preceded by a qualifier for the remainder of medical school, $GT_3$ in the junior year and $GT_4$ in the senior year. Each rotation of a clinical service was called a clinical clerkship, and lasted usually from four to eight weeks. The locations varied from "the Mother House," Georgetown University Hospital, to "the General," DC General Hospital, (the new name for what was then the Gallinger Hospital of the District of Columbia). In between these two clinical pillars were rotations at Mount Alto Veterans' Hospital, Bethesda Naval Medical Center, Walter Reed Medical Center, Saint Elizabeths Hospital, Children's Hospital, Arlington Hospital, Andrews Air Force Base and Providence Hospital. We were no longer home-based as we had been in the first two years.

My first clinical clerkship was in junior surgery at the old Mount Alto Veteran's Hospital. Our group included Charlie Tartaglia, Jack Wissinger, Bob Menegaz, Bob Carnathan and myself. We reported, as instructed, at 10 A.M. on a Monday morning in early August, to the office of the Chief of Surgery at Mount Alto, Dr. George Higgins, a distinguished thoracic surgeon and a fine person totally dedicated to the education of medical students, interns and residents. After a warm greeting, he turned us over to his chief resident who proceeded with detailed instructions of this particular clerkship. Our duties would begin at seven A.M. the next day. "Today, your only obligation is to attend the Monthly Professorial Conference scheduled for three P.M."

We were advised not to be late for the conference, "otherwise, you guys are free for the rest of the day."

As an afterthought, the chief resident said: "I mean everyone, except $GT_3$ Oscar Mann." My team mates began to disperse with smiles on their faces, waving at me.

I followed the chief resident to a nursing station, where he handed me a chart and said: *You are to present this case to Dr. Coffey. It is now 11:30, grab a quick lunch and you will have three hours to review the chart, interview and examine the patient. We expect a flawless presentation. Dr. Coffey is like a God to us. Do us proud.*

Then, the chief resident vanished. I was dumbfounded and felt that I was being baptized by fire on the very first day of my maiden clinical clerkship. We had seen Dr. Coffey briefly during orientation day at Georgetown. I distinctly remembered the words of Dean Hussey in his introduction of Dr. Coffey that day: *Dr. Robert J. Coffey is the Professor and Chairman of Surgery. A graduate of the Georgetown University Medical School, class of 1932, he obtained both a master's degree* [in medicine] *and a Ph.D.* [in surgery] *at the Mayo Clinic. Dr. Coffey is a masterful surgeon, and a true giant in his field. He served with distinction in WWII as a Naval Surgeon and attended President Franklin Delano Roosevelt.*[2]

Through the grapevine during the basic years, I had learned about Dr. Coffey's national reputation. His name inspired respect and fright. He was reputed to be a tiger of the old school in the O.R. (operating room), and a correct, austere patrician in public. It was said that even the school dean and the other department chairmen felt awed by Dr. Coffey.

The case was straightforward, the patient cooperative, and my examination was thorough and proceeded without a hitch. I had the time to put my thoughts in order, prepare a sound synopsis of the case and bone up on the patient's ailment. I had a good intellectual grasp of the entire problem and I should have been calm, cool and collected. I was not. I sweated the hour prior to the conference.

At exactly 3 P.M. Dr. Coffey, who seldom arrived anywhere punctually, made a majestic entrance into the conference room. He was warmly greeted by Dr. George Higgins. All the doctors and nurses of Mount Alto Hospital crowded into the room, or so it seemed to me. Dr Coffey looked every bit the distinguished, acclaimed surgeon. He was tall and slender, about six feet, with wide shoulders and white curly hair. There was no question that he was *le pa-*

*tron* ("the boss") as the French refer to the chief of a clinical service. Fit, tanned and relaxed, and sporting a powerful facial expression with a slight smile, Dr. Coffey projected a commanding presence. He wore a brown pin striped double breasted suit. His demeanor was affable and he put me immediately at ease by thanking me for the preparation of the case for presentation. All the butterflies left me.

The presentation went well. He complimented me at the end of the conference. On my way home with Charlie Tartaglia that evening, I was talking eagerly: "*I did not fail in front of the Chairman of Surgery. My successful encounter with the Dr. Coffey is an auspicious beginning. It is a good omen for my clinical years. I cannot believe my lucky star.*"

The day following the conference, I was still basking in the afterglow of my presentation to Dr. Coffey. Early that morning, my team mates and I began our surgical clerkship as phlebotomists, drawing morning bloods. The diagnostic lab supervisor and his staff instructed us in the proper techniques. Further, they advised us that for the time being, we were not allowed to inject anything by vein or start any intravenous fluids. That would come soon enough. We were turned loose to the floors where patients, at the receiving end of our bloodletting, were exposed to the lack of experience of third year students, known as novice $GT_3$s. However, drawing blood proved to be an easy task. Patients in veteran's hospitals, for the most part, are very accommodating with young doctors—yes, they called us doctors—and seemed to enjoy the attention we offered them.

I purged my last patient of that morning of five tubes of blood which I proudly placed in the upper left open pocket of my white coat. On my way to the Nurses' Station, disaster struck as I bent over to straighten one of my shoe laces. All the tubes fell out of my pocket, the cork tops came off, blood spilled all over my white uniform and the tubes shattered upon hitting the floor. I was mortified. I had to go back to redraw the blood. The patient tried his best to comfort me: "Doc, it is only your first day. Don't let it bother you. Accidents will happen."

I came home early that day as Charlie and I did not have night call until later in the week. Mother was at work at Lerner's and John was in his medical school class, where he was beginning his sophomore year. I was not expected at the liquor store that evening. Our friendly janitor saw me in my bloody uniform, sympathized with me and recommended that I "take [my] bloody clothes to the laundry room, put them in the washing machine, and use plenty of Tide. I will take care of everything else. Go up, have a drink, and relax. I will bring up your uniform, clean and dry."

I was not then domesticated in the least; so I took his advice literally and poured the contents of an almost full king size box of Tide into the washing machine to give my uniform the surgical scrub it deserved. About half an hour later, the janitor was at my door, visibly agitated, and murmuring with alarm: "The entire laundry room is flooded with soap suds and water. I unplugged the washing machine—nothing doing. It won't stop overflowing. How much Tide did you use? The box is empty."

I described what I had done and added: "I was so intent on getting a clean uniform that I thought the more, the better."

He threw up his hands and left shaking his head. A little later, an irate neighbor, usually a friendly person, came to berate me: "You ruined my clean laundry; it was in a hamper on the floor, waiting to go into the drier."

She further exclaimed in no uncertain terms: "How can you be smart enough to be in medical school, and at the same time so dumb about laundry?"

It all blew over eventually, but my self-esteem was taken down a few notches. My ego, inflated one day, was deflated the next. I learned that the ups and downs of daily life were further intensified by doctoring. It is interesting to contemplate how these professional jolts affect physicians. Experience has taught me that the cumulative effects of these humbling incidents take their toll. There would be more bumps in my career and I have tried to learn from each one.

Back at Mount Alto the next morning, in a sparkling clean uniform, I had breakfast in the cafeteria with Charlie and his lovely fiancée, Ann Bergquist. Ann, a head floor nurse at Mount Alto, gave us tips about the place, and healthy advice about getting along in the Mount Alto system and other clinical clerkships: "Always get the nurses on your side. Nurses do not get angry, they get even." She said that she would look out for me, "like your big sister."

True to her word, she arranged a date for me with a nurse friend and I knew that I had a personal anchor with Ann.

We began to go to the operating room, but this thrilling sounding activity turned out not to be so glamorous. Our chore was to hold retractors for hours on end and our privilege was to observe. We learned how to scrub in and not contaminate or break the sterile field.[3] All was done with the critical supervision and humiliating scoldings of the O.R. nurse.

This creature, the O.R. nurse, the equivalent of a master sergeant in basic training, was rivaled in her crude manners only by the ob nurse I would later encounter in the delivery room. These types are made of the same mold. They are qualified, competent, self-centered, autocratic and imperious; they serve as a necessary evil. They can best be tolerated by a certain attitude which I had learned from basic training in the U.S. Army and from the *schmatta* trade in France, "letting insults roll along the rails of one's indifference."[4]

Our main function on the Mount Alto surgical service was not in the operating room. Our place was at the bottom of the service chain. We were phlebotomists. We were drawing more and more blood, and beginning to start IVs, change dressings and do other routine procedures. We were assigned patients by the chief surgical resident, worked them up with histories and physicals for the chart and went to the library to study their ailments. We were expected to be able to present details of our patients, formally or informally, at any time. We took night call along with the interns and residents. We were disappointed that we had no real patient responsibility. We were not wise enough to appreciate what Dr. George Higgins. Mount Alto's Chief of Surgery, meant by saying: "Some day, you will worry about too much patient responsibility, and look back fondly to the days when someone else shouldered this burden."

Dr. Higgins paid concentrated attention to the medical students. He was always pleasant. We felt that we had a friend in him. He made our rotation in Junior Surgery a good experience. Our group responded and did well. Each received a grade ranging from B plus to A minus. This first clinical clerkship was constructive and gave members of the group encouragement for success as we faced the rest of the clinical years.

Dr. Higgins and I would meet in subsequent years, usually at Georgetown conferences or Georgetown social events. He became one of my favorite people. We would reminisce about the good old days at Mount Alto. The members of my group left Mount Alto with an enthusiasm that boded well for our remaining clinical years.

I spent my eight weeks of senior surgery at Georgetown Hospital, where Dr. Robert Coffey maintained his office and practice and from which his renown radiated far and wide. I saw him daily in various capacities and was to learn much more about him. He was friendly and gentle to the medical students, harsh with interns and residents. Once he took off his surgical mask and stopped hiding behind his public facade, the private Dr. Coffey was a most gracious and congenial person.[5]

In the O.R., he honored the tradition of the old time teaching surgeons. The brunt of his ire was directed at the chief surgical resident; except for medical students, he spared no one. Surgical residents, interns, nurses and O.R. personnel, all got it big time.

During my senior surgical rotation, I witnessed Dr Coffey's explosive and volcanic temper in the operating room. However, a junior surgical resident, Tony Boglio (I may not have his name right), born in Italy, but raised in New Jersey, swore that Dr. Coffey walked on water. This was a new expression to me, so Tony explained it as follows:

*Uncle Bob's ranting and raving in the O.R. do not amount to a hill of beans; it means zilch. His anger usually blows over with breaking scrub* [finishing the operation]. *What really counts is that his patients get off the table and do well; besides, Uncle Bob breeds ace surgeons like Pete Conrad, Tom Lee and La Salle Lefall. I would send my wife, parents, or any members of my family to Uncle Bob any time, no questions asked. Dr. Coffey looks out for people like you and me.*

What Tony meant by his last sentence was that Dr. Coffey did have a soft spot for immigrants; moreover, Dr. Coffey welcomed foreigners to his training program, some of whom went back to their countries to be academic surgeons. His wife, Mary Catherine Coffey, a gentle gracious lady, always followed suit. I can, indeed, vouch for this side of the Coffeys. So can others. For example, La Salle D. Lefall, Jr. was a surgical resident on Robert Coffey's service at Gallinger Hospital (later DC General).

*Those early Howard residents at Gallinger were trailblazers, carefully selected from the most able trainees; perhaps as a result, Lefall said, they were accepted onto the Georgetown team and experienced no discrimination. 'But first the door had to open and Dr. Coffey played an important role there. He had a major impact on the training program at Howard. What he did for minorities might not seem like so much today. But at the time it was a tremendous thing'.*

*Coffey later followed, with interest and pride, Lefall's spectacular career in surgery and oncology which brought him [Lefall] a succession of honors until, in October 1995, he became the first black president of the American College of Surgeons.*[6]

My introduction to the junior clinical service of obstetrics and gynecology (Ob-Gyn) came early, while I was still on the surgery service at Mount Alto. One Thursday morning, I had to open the liquor store—Myer had a sudden family emergency—and I was given verbal permission to be two hours late at Mount Alto. Charlie Tartaglia had kindly driven me to Circle Liquors and went on to Mount Alto. By 10:30 A.M., Myer was back. I changed into my white uniform, walked up the two blocks to the bus stop at Connecticut Avenue and McKinley Street. Suddenly, and to my surprise, a black sedan stopped. A distinguished middle-aged, white-haired, ruddy, round-faced man with an engaging smile leaned out, pushed open the passenger-side door, and in a cultivated voice said: "Son, you look like one of our boys. Hop in. I'll give you a lift."

I instantly recognized Dr. Andrew A. Marchetti, Professor and Chairman of Obstetrics and Gynecology at the Georgetown University School of Medicine.

*He had been a senior professor at Cornell University School of Medicine where, among other notable achievements, he had helped develop the Pap smear to detect cervical cancer.*[7]

I knew that an operation, the Marshall-Marchetti procedure, carried his name in part. En route, Dr. Marchetti inquired about my background, and I gave a capsule summary of my immigrant story. Dr. Marchetti had a pleasant way about him. He was charming, graceful and sensitive. He could not have been friendlier while he drove me to Mount Alto on his way to Georgetown Hospital. He remarked that he looked forward to seeing me on his service soon—it actually was my upcoming clerkship—and let me off with a pearl of obstetrical wisdom: "Things usually go well in the delivery room nowadays. The thing I always worry about is the occasional healthy young girl who comes in for a routine childbirth, and the case goes sour. Things obstetrical can quickly turn ugly. Remember that, Oscar. Godspeed."

This episode could not have taken place in the Old World, where a strictly formal relationship is maintained between the professor and his students.

Soon, we were on junior Ob-Gyn at Georgetown and again acting as phlebotomists and performing lab work. The main object of our training in gyn was to learn to do pelvic exams in the out-patient clinic. The basic exam was not difficult to absorb; but, the art of mastering the bimanual part of a pelvic exam—appreciating the ovaries and pelvic organs—eluded me. I was not alone. Many medical students and many seasoned practitioners were uneasy with this particular aspect of a pelvic exam for years. Ultimately, I embraced the premise that only Ob-Gyn specialists perform competent bimanual pelvic exams. With the advent of pelvic ultrasounds (non-invasive visualization of the ovaries and the entire pelvic area, with no radiation exposure), the tricky bimanual exam has become less crucial than it once was. Ob—the *pre-partum* and *post-partum* watches, the wisdom of delivery room and, yes, the labor room nurse—all these were our focus.[8] The didactic teaching, together with the closely monitored hands-on instruction during deliveries, was outstanding. Let me quote a personal communication from Tom Magovern, former chief resident in Ob-Gyn at Georgetown:

*We had, I am sure, similar experiences on the ob service. You were referring to Miss V., the head nurse on the delivery suite who ran the place with an iron hand in the manner of the old school of nurses, maintaining a hierarchy of who did what and when. Nurses were instructed that all patients, on admission, were to have their first exam by one of the residents, which sometimes meant that the patient, who moved along quickly in labor, may have delivered before the first exam. In the interest of minimizing infection, only rectal exams, instead of direct vaginal exams, were done. These exams were uncomfortable for the patient and more elusive for the novice examiner as to the degree of childbirth progress. Back in those days, before "natural childbirth," when things got active and noisy, there was always the memory eliminator, scopolamine, and the sure thing sedative, IV Nembutal, that allowed the excitement to come under control. Dr.*

*Marchetti, the southern gentleman who had come from Hopkins and New York Hospital, always had a presence on the scene that conveyed calmness, discretion, elegance, a warm smile and an attention to detail with his obstetrical and surgical technique. This man commanded respect.*[9]

The excellent training we received during Ob-Gyn at Georgetown was wonderful ground work for the delivery rooms of the District of Columbia General Hospital—the pits of the General—where we were to spend our senior rotation in Ob-Gyn.

There, we saw quality and quantity. We became numbers to another labor delivery nursing supervisor and her underling nurses who conveniently forgot that we had names. There was mad confusion, moaning mothers in labor, and cries of *precip, grab your precip kit quick, catch the baby, don't let the baby drop for God's sake;* other shrieks emanating from the pits are best left there. *Precip,* an abbreviation for the word precipitation, refers to a spontaneous rapid delivery and is extremely common among multiparous women (those who have borne multiple pregnancies).

The swinging doors of the delivery suite flew open almost continually to allow racing stretchers to carry in an impending *precip.* In uncomplicated ob, as the routine delivery suite was called, although residents were nearby, it was just us and the nurses. They called us by numbers. We called them by their names, and we called them often out of pure necessity. They were experienced with the pits, and we were not. The problem was that they knew it and expressed this knowledge openly to us. We were at their mercy. Except for fatigue (we were on for long stretches, three days on, one day off), the harassment from the nurses, and the prevailing tension—the actual delivery service was more fun than work. I delivered many babies. After the first awkward delivery, and the next easy 20 deliveries, I stopped keeping track. Dr. Stanley Silverberg, a Chevy Chase cardiologist, preceded me in the pits by several years. He told me once at a party of his unforgettable pit experience: "I had just delivered a baby and was wrapping things up, when the new mother, pointing to her belly, told me: 'There is another one in here.' Sure enough, she was right. I ended up delivering twins."

It was the last night in the pits for my team and me. An interesting little interlude with Frank Bepko, M.D., Georgetown chief of the Ob-Gyn service at DC General Hospital, took place. Charlie Tartaglia and I had been on for almost 72 hours straight with almost no sleep. Don Martindill and Phil Caulfield had been off the night before and were out late, Don painting the town while Phil was making plans for his upcoming wedding. By two A.M. there was no one in labor in the pits, a most unusual situation at DC General Hospital. All four of us, bone tired, retired to the on-call room, and soon had entered a state of deep slumber. As dawn was breaking, Dr. Bepko, full of vim, vigor and vitality, barged in on us and in his customary booming voice began to read from a piece of paper he was holding with his right hand. It was a letter of commendation being sent to Dr. Andrew Marchetti, Chairman of Obstetrics and Gynecology at Georgetown University School of Medicine " . . . for industry shown by GT$_4$s Phil Caulfield, Oscar Mann, Don Martindill and Charles Tartaglia in the delivery suite at DC General Hospital . . . ." We barely managed to murmur our thanks and appreciation before Dr. Bepko left the room. Then, we each turned over in bed and went to sleep without saying a word to one another. Dr. Bepko had played before an unreceptive audience.

In other sections of Ob-Gyn at DC General Hospital, we were closely supervised by experienced physicians. We assisted with the common D&Cs (dilatation & curettage), the Caesarians, induced labor deliveries and other gynecological operations. In another area referred to as *complicated ob*, women with toxemia of pregnancy were our big challenge. Toxemia, a potentially fatal condition characterized by elevation of blood pressure, retention of fluid, kidney failure and premature birth, is a serious complication occurring sometimes even with good prenatal care. It was all too frequent at DC General Hospital. The medical students spent long hours in "tox watches" and "pit drips" (*Pitocin®* infusions), monitoring vital signs, doing their own blood counts and urinalyses.[10] The clinical progress of our patients was regularly reported to a senior resident. During these toxemia watches, ob attending physicians looked in on our patients. However, it was mostly medical students against toxemia. The solution for a toxemia case was a timely delivery and a successful result called for a well-coordinated team effort. On these cases, the medical students and the nurses worked together amicably.

The last two weeks of senior Ob-Gyn saw us back at Georgetown for gynecology. When Charlie Tartaglia and I were in this last stretch at Georgetown, Joan, the wife of our classmate and friend, Mike Lemp, was admitted to the ob wing in labor with their first child. Unlike today when labor rooms are more hospitable and husbands are invited to be with their wives during that sometimes traumatic, painful and possibly prolonged process, the labor rooms of that day were quite different. Husbands were banned and women in uncomplicated labor lay unattended in a room furnished with a metal hospital bed and night stand with only a crucifix (an image of Christ hanging in agony on the Cross) for company, a clock ticking off the seconds, minutes, and, in Joan's case, hours of intermittent pain.

Early in the day, it was clear that it was to be a slow day for us with little that needed our attention. About mid-morning we ran into Mike, who informed us of Joan's situation and his chagrin at being unable to be with her. Since Charlie and I were on service, we had legitimate access to the area from which Mike had been banished. We stopped in to see Joan but the head nurse, our old friend Miss V., threw us out. Undaunted, we returned, first one and then the other. Our visits lasted about a half hour or so before Miss V. detected our presence and summarily evicted us. Between the two of us, however, we were able to keep Joan company and somewhat distracted for most of the day. Thank heaven that rules and attitudes have changed and the people who staff the labor room have become more sensitive and compassionate.

I must not forget my fondest memory of the pits at the General. It was sometimes necessary to have an X-ray of a patient at term. The X-ray Department at DC General was a 30–minute distance by stretcher from the OB suites. Therein lay the challenge. The interminable corridors, the winding tunnels and the poorly working elevators made transporting these women to X-ray a difficult task for students. The student pushed a stretcher, with a term patient nestled next to the precip kit, through an obstacle course every bit as difficult as those I had encountered in Army basic training. The X-ray Department was not a user-friendly place. One had to find a technician. One had to find the developed X-ray. One had to find a radiologist. Then, one had to get the radiologist to give a wet reading. And then, there came the long, lonely trip back to the pits with the X-ray and the hope of a stable patient still in her pregnancy.

Yet, Ob-Gyn, a totally new experience for me, was immensely beneficial to the shaping of my development as a clinician. It was my first truly intimate contact with my patients and was also the first time I undertook a medical act without direct senior supervision.

At this point, I turn now to another pillar of our clinical years, psychiatry and its leadership.

Dr. Richard A. Steinbach became the chairman of psychiatry in 1960 at Georgetown. Born in Atlanta, he graduated from the Medical College of Georgia and received his psychiatric training in Cincinnati, Ohio. He came to the Washington area in 1954, and joined the Georgetown Department of Psychiatry soon thereafter. He had been psychoanalyzed, which was customary at the time, by Dr. Leo Bartemeier, a prominent analyst from Baltimore. Dr. Steinbach was a dedicated educator, a fine chairman and a wonderfully pleasant person. He was a Jewish intellectual in the finest sense of the expression.

For reasons which are totally unclear to me, I began medical school with an anti-psychiatric bias. However, I graduated from medical school with a deep respect for the art and science of this specialty. My respect for the psychiatrist only deepened with my years of practice. Dr. Stefan Pasternack, clinical professor of psychiatry at Georgetown, distinguished Washington psychiatrist and close friend, reminded me recently of the influence of WWII on the emergence of a new, modern Department of Psychiatry at Georgetown.

He rekindled the inescapable reality of my past:

> *The development of the Department of Psychiatry at Georgetown is significant in several ways. WWII made several factors clear. First, the very fact that there was a large number of young Americans who were not fit for military service in the war because of mental health problems indicated the need for a national approach . . . the importance of such a mental health movement was duly appreciated . . . After the war, the National Institute of Mental Diseases, NIMD, was created . . . Second, because of the war we once again saw men and women suffering from 'combat stress.' These patients challenged the existing theory of the mind . . . We could not easily explain nor easily treat these individuals. Third, the serious mental illnesses we observed among Holocaust victims . . . provided the impetus for a great deal of research into the trans-generational effects of the war, its influence on subsequent generations. Fourth, the psychology of the 20th century could not adequately explain the bestiality of Hitler . . . how such a civilized nation could produce Nazism . . . spurred many efforts to expand and extend the theories of Freud regarding human motivation and human destructiveness . . . . The work begun as a result of WWII was given added importance with the Korean war and then the Vietnam war . . . New insights were developed into the post traumatic stress disorder, PTSD, and the complex interplay of both psychological and biological factors in acute trauma situations . . . . At Georgetown today, work in depression and psychic trauma is still our chief opus among the biggest areas of study . . . . And a number of sons and daughters of the men who fought our wars have gone into mental health research—including me.[11]*

Dr. Pasternack's perceptive analysis of modern times and the new direction of psychiatry, integrates well with my personal experiences of WWII, especially my vivid recollection of the arrest of my father. With this book, I seek some personal meaning in what took place in World War II Europe. To John and me, the *Holocaust* is not an abstraction. The *Shoah* is a real-life event which profoundly affected our family.

Germany was a highly educated society, a country that produced a Goethe and a Beethoven. All the world regarded France as an enlightened land. Europeans were supposedly highly civilized and cultured human beings, but this view, at least in my darker moments, now seems superficial. Beneath a veneer of civilization, the 20th century allowed the emergence of man's most primitive animal instincts and the occurrence of the vilest evidence of man's inhumanity to man.

By osmosis, John and I learned an important lesson in psychiatry. A negative emotional reaction to a patient tells more about the doctor than the patient. Dr. Steinbach always emphasized the significance of this truth: "Such a response is not to be ignored. You will learn about yourself by paying attention to your own disapproving inner feelings."

The psychiatry program at Georgetown was reorganized in the late 1950s, and since then it is presented to the students in lectures and practice for all four years. It is the only clinical discipline to extend from day one to the end of medical school. Designed to produce the complete physician, the new psychiatric curriculum begins with didactic teaching in conjunction with the technical courses of the basic years. We became imbued with the classical concepts of *id, ego* and *superego*, while learning new terms such as *Freudian, subliminal, normal and abnormal personality, character flaw* and *character disorder*, not to mention *paranoia, schizophrenia, unipolar* and *bipolar depression,* and *passive aggressive personality disorder.*

Within the first two years, Dr. Steinbach and his able staff equipped us with a solid foundation in basic psychiatry. Beginning in the third year, exposure to clinical psychiatry was gradually phased in, with rotations at DC General Hospital and the VA Hospital. In our fourth year, we became involved with clinical psychiatry under close supervision in the outpatient clinic at Georgetown. Dr. Steinbach warned us not to ask patients leading questions. These patients suffered from ambulatory psychiatric problems. Some were seriously ill and others less so. Dr. Steinbach added something that I did not fully understand initially: "Patients will inundate you with lurid stories to impress you and try to shock you; beware and be careful of your demeanor. If you must get your kicks, do it on your own time and somewhere else."

An example of what Dr. Steinbach meant was the fellow who announced to me, "I am an alcoholic, a petty thief, a homosexual, and Jewish." This seemed to me an odd combination and almost a non sequitur. It reminded me instantly of the truth of Dr. Steinbach's words. Dick Steinbach died of cancer in the prime of his life. I was deeply affected.

Enter Dr. Zigmond Lebensohn, the dean of practicing Washington psychiatrists. The stature of Dr. Lebensohn, clinical professor of psychiatry at Georgetown, is brought to life by the Kober Lecture.[12] On the personal invitation of Dean Hussey, Dr. Lebensohn, long a champion of psychiatric units in general hospitals, delivered the 1962 Kober Lecture at Georgetown, entitled *American Psychiatry: Retrospect and Prospect.*

Dr. Lebensohn bordered on the austere, with an old world countenance. In my mind, he personified the father of modern psychiatry, Sigmund Freud himself. A close teaching colleague of Dr. Lebensohn was the distinguished Dr. Francis F. Barnes, who reminded me of Dean Hussey in appearance and demeanor. Dr. Barnes, a prominent Washington psychiatrist, and clinical professor of psychiatry at Georgetown, served for many years as the director of the Sibley Memorial Hospital psychiatric unit, created by Dr. Lebensohn.

Drs. Lebensohn and Barnes introduced us to the clinical manifestations and classification of psychiatric disorders and diseases. These two men complemented each other. They were a magnetic, powerful and effective teaching duo. They have remained the best of friends in their retirement years.

During the 1950s, the Department of Psychiatry at Georgetown entered a new age under dynamic leadership, with a focus on ambulatory care and pharmacological intervention. A large, brand-new psychiatric building had opened recently at DC General Hospital, and Georgetown Psychiatry provided the professional personnel. It is in this building that I spent my junior psychiatry, treating in-patients and out-patients—a psychiatric inpatient service did not open up at Georgetown until July 1974. I now began to appreciate the important role of psychiatric social workers, clinical psychologists and nurse practitioners and their work with psychiatrists in treating mental illness.

This modern facility was relatively luxurious, with a friendly, professional atmosphere. The old admonition that "one can't tell the staff from the patients" proved to be false here. A superb full-time in-house teaching staff was there for the training of psychiatry residents. We, as senior medical students, benefitted greatly from the presence of this program. We acted as interns in various two-week rotations, and enjoyed a great learning experience.

My first rotation was on the general ward. To my pleasure, I was assigned to interview a patient before the entire group—the students, the professional staff doctors, nurses, social workers and clinical psychologists. A senior resident was my coach. The patient proved cooperative, subdued, polite and deferential. The interview was basically over, and the attending psychiatrist, Dr. James Foy, an erudite scholar, and also the deputy chief of service, began to make some teaching points. Suddenly, the patient interrupted him: "Mister Doctor, I have a comment. This is a wonderful place. You have first-rate facilities. The staff is wonderful; the food is excellent; everyone is helpful. There is only one problem, as I see it. You are running this place ass-backwards."

Pandemonium ensued. The patient's voice had changed and so had his demeanor. He would have continued, but the orderlies immediately began taking him back to the ward. He was laughing out loud, screaming and kicking. Decorum finally returned to the conference room. A straight faced Dr. Foy declared: "You have just witnessed a classical case of mania."

Then, a picture of calmness, Dr. Foy continued as if nothing had ever happened, concluding with an excellent discourse on the subject of manic-depressive disorder.

For my next two weeks, I was assigned to the unit called Mental Observation. Many patients had been sent in by the authorities for short-term observation and opinion. A significant DC police presence gave this unit an official flavor. All White House gate crashers were brought here. One of them, a physical giant, was assigned to me. He was a lawyer or so he claimed. An extremely well-spoken individual in an elegant, dark suit, he had successfully jumped over the main gate of the White House before being wrestled to the ground by Secret Service agents. At well over six feet, he towered over me. I was happy to see him under escort. There was something striking about him. He wore a large, loud, multicolored tie and told me that he always wore his tie untied. I was slow to react, but finally asked him why. In a deliberately cultivated voice, he answered my query in an emphatic way and in slow motion: "I leave my tie untied, because I so choose. Life is too labyrinthine. I am who I am. I do not wish to become involved in the complexities of a knot."

I was baffled, said nothing but the next day, I reviewed the case with my supervising psychiatrist, Dr. Foy. Usually laid back, he was visibly excited by the patient's comments, and told me "this statement is pregnant with Freudian meaning. I will work closely with you on this case until we comprehend the psychodynamics of this patient."

In fact, the patient was not a lawyer as he claimed, although he did attend law school for a few months. We probed deeper. According to Dr. Foy, the patient was a dangerous paranoid psychotic individual. He soon began to unravel, finally to crack and he was committed to Saint Elizabeth Hospital.

It was mid-December 1960. Holiday cheer abounded. Christmas spirit was in the air. There were things to do, people to see, and everyone was busily rushing around. So was I, in my own way. I had just been assigned to the detoxification unit for two weeks, and ironically, every evening I hurried to the liquor store where John and I had promised Myer to work extra hours for the holidays.

On the second day in the "Detox Bin," I admitted a patient in DTs (delirium tremens). He dried out in a few days. As his acting doctor, I gave him the usual admonitions. "You have a big liver; You must give up your daily bottle of vodka, or you are going to die of cirrhosis." And so forth, and so on.

He was discharged on a Tuesday. That same evening, I waited on him at Circle Liquors. Yes, I sold him a bottle of 80 proof Smirnoff vodka. He looked at me. I looked at him. Nothing was said. Two days later, he was back to "Detox" and as per DC General Hospital policy, he was reassigned to his previous "doctor," namely $GT_4$ Oscar Mann. We went through the same routine. On New Year's Eve, I waited on him again at the liquor store, selling him another fifth of vodka. This time, it was a 100 proof of Circle in-house-labeled vodka (for John and me, there was a financial incentive in switching customers to in-house-labeled spirits over brand names). My patient, now customer, looked at me and said: "Aren't you the doctor who takes care of me at the hospital?" I sheepishly answered in the affirmative. He went on: "I simply don't understand how you can be my doctor in the daytime and sell me

vodka at night." Primed in psychiatry, I answered: "I don't understand it myself. That makes two of us."

He walked out, shaking his head. We never saw each other again.

Medicine was next, the big clerkship.

By the early 1960s, Georgetown was a powerhouse of medicine. The 1930s
had ushered in a new era with Wallace Yater, M.D. as the chairman from1930
to 1945. A Georgetown graduate, he had taken his postgraduate training at the
Mayo Clinic. There, he excelled, developed a brilliant academic reputation,
setting the stage for the golden age of medicine at Georgetown.

> *Yater, thirty-five years old, became Georgetown's first full-time chairman of a clin-
> ical department, with a salary of five thousand dollars a year, an office and a sec-
> retary, the promise of research work, and the privilege of holding consultations with
> private patients at the university hospital. Almost everyone admired Yater's ability.
> His special talent was differential diagnosis—telling the difference between similar
> diseases . . . . In 1927, before returning to Georgetown, he had already published
> his famous book,* Symptom Diagnosis, *the first work on the subject . . . .*
>
> *Although Wallace Yater's primary interest lay in diseases of the heart and
> blood vessels, he considered himself an internist rather than a cardiologist . . .
> In 1938, he published* Fundamentals of Internal Medicine, *a concise and well-
> written textbook . . . . In this book, Yater himself wrote the chapters on heart dis-
> ease, kidney disease, diseases of the blood and blood forming organs, diseases
> of the respiratory system, infectious diseases, diseases of the blood vessels, dis-
> eases of metabolism, and diseases of the spleen . . . . He shared authorship of
> the chapters on allergy, intoxications, and diseases of the digestive system. Only
> endocrinology, neurology, eye, and ear diseases, and mental illnesses were de-
> ferred to specialists in these fields . . . and concluded with a thoughtful and prac-
> tical chapter entitled 'The Physician Himself.'*
>
> *Wallace Yater himself exemplified the attributes of which he wrote in 'The
> Physician Himself' . . . He did not jump to conclusions and abhorred 'snap di-
> agnoses.' 'A doctor cannot afford to become angry with patients.'*[13]

In 1945, embittered by political in-fighting, Dr. Yater left Georgetown. He
went on to create a group practice, the Yater Clinic on Massachusetts Avenue,
in downtown Washington, DC.

The medical giants who followed Dr. Yater fortunately were not ivory
tower prima donnas. Like Yater, they walked the wards of Georgetown in
his footsteps, nurturing, strengthening and expanding Georgetown medicine.
Yater was succeeded by a newcomer from Boston.

> *He was Harold Jeghers, Yater's successor to the chair of medicine. Already a
> renowned educator, Jeghers had been professor of medicine at the Boston*

*University School of Medicine and chief of its medical service at Boston City
Hospital, where for years he had worked closely with colleagues from Harvard and Tufts. He thus arrived at Georgetown with a masterly grasp of the
interaction between academics, clinical education, and research in the leading medical schools and teaching hospitals around Boston.* [14]

Jeghers was the prime moving force for "The Boston Influx," a group of
young doctors, trained in the mecca of medicine, the famed medical world of
Boston, to be full-time heads of medical divisions at Georgetown. These peo-
ple were Proctor Harvey, M.D., Charles Rath, M.D., Irving Brick, M.D., and
Laurence Kyle, M.D. A new era began with the talent and tradition of the
Boston academic system.[15]

In 1956, Jeghers departed to be the chairman of medicine at the new Seton
Hall College of Medicine in New Jersey. Georgetown clinical old-timers said
that Jeghers "made the mistake of his life in leaving Georgetown." Others believed he felt that it was his mission to spread the Boston system. Stapleton
offers a somewhat different interpretation:

*Valuable as was his contribution to Georgetown, Jeghers' departure was timely.
He preferred building to sustaining. Day-to-day administration was not his
forte. His job at Georgetown was done. Creating a new department in New Jersey made better use of his skills than continuing to preside over the department
he had developed in Washington.*[16]

Harold Jeghers was an important and pivotal figure for Georgetown in the
20th century. He will never be forgotten because he exhibited

1. aloofness
2. superb organizational skills
3. the "Jeghers method" of clinical teaching, i.e., conferences featuring case
   presentations in preference to didactic lectures; patient in person presence,
   whenever possible; and the carrying of "poop sheets" by house officers.
4. his imposing physical presence.
5. personal rectitude; a clinical giant, he gave more than he took.[17]

"After Yater's departure in 1945, Hugh Hussey supervised the Georgetown
medical division at Gallinger/DC General until he moved to the university
hospital as chairman of medicine in 1956."[18]

Hugh Hussey, first in his class of 1934, was the first Georgetown University medical graduate *summa cum laude*. A protege and former resident of
Yater, Hussey evolved into a towering person among the medical faculty. An

internist and clinician of national reputation, he was also a widely published author. With the advent of the Hussey era, the last of the old Georgetown system came together with the best of the Boston one.[19]

Hussey finally achieved his lifelong ambition when he became dean of his alma mater in 1958, the year I entered Georgetown.

*As Harold Jeghers' principal lieutenant, Kyle involved himself in the full range of departmental activities. When Jeghers left for Seaton Hall, Kyle was similarly supportive of Hussey's chairmanship and developed a close relationship with him. Kyle was the logical choice to succeed Hussey as chairman.*[20]

Dr. W. Proctor Harvey, the Chief of Cardiology, also added a prodigious and monumental dimension to the Department of Medicine. I will devote a later chapter to Dr. Harvey.

Locally trained, Sol Katz, M.D., also a Yater protege, was a famed pulmonary expert. "A chest x-ray was to Dr. Katz as a heart sound was to Dr. Harvey."[21]

Chief of the pulmonary service and of Georgetown medicine at the DC General Hospital for years, then at the Veterans Administration Hospital, Katz superbly taught generations of students, interns, residents and fellows. He became the director of the Pulmonary Division at Georgetown University Medical Center in the late 1960s. Sol Katz was a native of New York City (B.S. from CCNY). His knowledge and insights into diseases of the lungs was nonpareil.

During our junior and senior years, we would return to the campus for weekly diagnostic and therapeutic sessions by some of the clinical Georgetown greats. This was always a high point of our clinical days. The most memorable of these clinical stars, in my mind, were Proctor Harvey and Sol Katz.

Kimara March quotes Harvey: "A good teacher has the ability to take the topic that he is discussing and put it in terms so simple that everyone can understand it; he has the ability to sit in the place of those being taught."[22]

With Katz, three things were consistently true, i.e., never sleep, never smoke, as one could in other lectures, and learn how to read chest radiographs. Frank Weiner says:

*All too well do I remember the x-rays of Hamman-Rich syndrome* [idiopathic pulmonary fibrosis] *that Katz showed. Many years later, I was to make this diagnosis on the x-ray of a favorite uncle . . . a diagnosis that had been missed by his own physician.*[23]

In my subsequent formative clinical years and in practice, the teachings of Dr. Katz served me well on many occasions.

Some of the additional greats of clinical medicine in the Department of Medicine were George Schreiner, Joseph Perloff, Modestino Criscitiello, Thomas Keliher, Robert Donohoe, Frank Marcus, Joseph Canary, Nathan Zvaifler, Donald Knowlan, James Ronan, Paul McCurdy, all full members of the medical faculty. The voluntary faculty provided excellent additional back-up. All, from the top on down, including Hussey, Kyle and in particular, Harvey and Katz, were clinicians in the best sense of the word. Harvey was, in addition, a bedside manner teacher par excellence. Their influence on my formative clinical medical years is incalculable. Georgetown had a national clinical reputation for well-trained medical students. The great Hopkins clinician, Phil Tumulty, M.D., said: "Georgetown graduates are the best clinically trained doctors. John Mann is a prime example."[24]

The Department of Medicine had reached critical mass and was functioning well under the leadership of Dr. Laurence Kyle, notwithstanding his often brusque personality. It is against this background that I served my medicine clerkships.

*When Kyle became chairman in 1958, he withdrew junior students from DC General because he believed that more experienced students adapted better to the city hospital environment. Hussey, as dean, approved this change. All junior students, thenceforth, devoted six weeks to the university hospital and another six weeks to the V.A. Hospital. Walter Reed Army General Hospital became another option for junior students*[25]

My senior rotation was divided between DC General Hospital and Arlington Community Hospital. The closely supervised clinical teaching was superb. My clinical facility with patients, and my identification of them as people rather than cases, grew significantly. I began to appreciate the art of auscultation under Dr. Harvey and his team. Learning this skill became my private joy.

Although I never mastered the art of the bimanual pelvic exam, I badgered the mighty Dr. Thomas Keliher to teach me his examination of the abdomen, something he was known to do adeptly. Under his personal tutelage, I was able to learn to appreciate an enlarged spleen. My clinical self-confidence soared one day when Keliher said to me: "Oscar, you have acquired a medical skill that separates the men from the boys."

Acting as interns under the guidance of such wonderful and inspiring physicians was exciting and challenging. In my graduate and postgraduate medical training, entirely spent in the Georgetown clinical orbit, I came to know and fully appreciate these teachers as professional giants and real people.

*Pediatrics* was our remaining long and important clerkship. *Junior pediatrics* was spent at Georgetown, Walter Reed Army or at Bethesda Naval Medical Centers.

At Georgetown, the tall, all-American, boyish Robert T. Scanlon outshone his peers. Frederic G. Burke had just left his long-time private practice to become the chief of pediatrics at Georgetown. Some called this change a working retirement. An agreeable, congenial but powerful person, Dr. Burke seemed content to let the younger Dr. Scanlon be the rising clinical star. Dr. Scanlon was the pediatrician who cared for the children born to Georgetown students or doctors, including eventually my daughters. I wonder now if he ever had time to see paying patients. Dr. Scanlon was an outstanding teacher and practitioner of pediatrics. He was admired and respected by students, interns, residents, patients and colleagues alike. He believed and taught that the preponderance of pediatric diseases was caused by allergic mechanisms. In time, he specialized in pediatric allergies and ran an active private practice dedicated to asthma. Much in demand in the community as a volunteer, speaker and leader, he still made time for Georgetown, his alma mater. Bob Scanlon was chair of the Medical Alumni Board when he died of lymphoma in the prime of life. I was called on to take over his position. Clifton R. Gruver adds: "Some doctors, teachers and leaders have a special kind of charisma —Bob Scanlon was certainly one of them."[26]

At Walter Reed Army Medical Center, Dr. Ogden Bruton was the chief. A wonderful teacher, scientist and clinician, he had done the basic work on a condition called *agammaglobulinemia;* this was the first primary immunodeficiency disease to be described. He was ably assisted by his chief resident, Captain Billy Andrews, who later became chairman of the Department of Pediatrics of the Louisville Medical Center in Louisville, KY. The pediatric affiliation at the Bethesda Naval Medical Center was under the direction of Dr. Thomas Cone and Dr. Howard Pearson. Dr. Cone, after leaving the Navy, went on to become professor of pediatrics at the Children's Hospital of Boston and the Harvard Medical Center. Walter Reed and Bethesda Naval Medical Centers were powerhouses of pediatrics. Both of these places had a strong influence on Frank Weiner's choice of pediatrics as his practice specialty.

Dr. Cone, along with Dr. Fred Burke from Georgetown, was one of the founding members of the Irish and American Paediatric Society (IAPS). Dr. Pearson, following his stint at the Navy, went to Yale and became a pediatric hematologist and later the chairman of the Department of Pediatrics at

Yale/New Haven Medical Center. "Both Drs. Billy Andrews and Howard Pearson are members of the IAPS. As, too, am I, so not everyone in the group has to be Irish, as you can see."[27]

Senior pediatrics was at the old Children's Hospital down on 13th Street, having recently been placed under the direction of Dr. Robert Parrot, a Georgetown graduate and a clinical and research virologist at the National Institutes of Health. He was a great teacher and a wonderful human being. There were residents and fellows, but no interns at the old Children's Hospital. We were the acting interns, along with George Washington University students, under the supervision of an excellent staff. It was a busy in-patient hospital. We saw many interesting patients, learning much about sick children there and being involved with their care and treatment. We were also exposed to the active out-patient department of Children's, mostly dealing with well-care pediatrics.

Pediatrics was a pleasant, productive and rewarding clinical clerkship. I discovered, however, that pediatrics did not give me the same degree of satisfaction as adult medicine did. Additionally, I did not feel completely comfortable caring for children. Years later, my daughters identified this fact.

It was the end of February 1962. I was a senior, coasting towards the M.D. degree. The junior year had been good to me. I finished it in excellent standing, having elevated my class average to A minus. The senior year was going well. All the big ones, medicine, surgery, Ob-Gyn, pediatrics and psychiatry had been successfully completed. My official class average was not available yet; but, the eternal grapevine delivered good news. My personal vibrations were positive. My own intuition reassured me. Everything indicated that my performance was excellent in my senior year and I felt good about myself.

I had met many other faculty members, not previously mentioned. There was a protege of Dr. Coffey, Dr. Thomas C. Lee; a pioneer of cardiovascular surgery, Charles A. Hufnagel, and his skilled associate, Peter W. Conrad. There was Roger C. Baker, who had a Ph. D. as well as his M.D. He was well-known in urology. William C. Maxted, a rising star, had just joined Dr. Baker in urologic practice. Desmond O' Doherty, the professor of neurology, was a masterful clinician and teacher. Dr. George W. Hyatt, from Bethesda Naval Medical Center, a research pioneer in freeze dried human bone, its new bone-forming potential and tissue transfer techniques, became the first full-time chief of the Orthopedic Division at Georgetown in 1960.[28] There were other interesting original thinkers who would become part of my life at Georgetown.

My faculty advisor during medical school was Margaret M. Kendrick, M.D. She specialized in physical therapy and rehabilitation. A recognized leader in her field, well-thought of by her Georgetown colleagues and in the community at large, she was a wonderful woman. I was blessed to have her as my advisor. She was helpful to me throughout medical school. Toward the end of my senior year, I visited with Dr. Kendrick, talking about my plans. I told her that I probably would go into internal medicine, which best suited my temperament and intellect. I also told her that I wanted to stay in the Washington area for my internship. There were three reasons: I loved it here; mother, a widow, was still working, and, finally, my brother John was in the medical school class of 1963. It was unrealistic for me to leave town for my internship. We discussed my upcoming electives, as well as reminiscences of Dr. Hess. We recalled my worries and trials during my days under Hess. We also talked about a book that I was reading, *The Choice of a Medical Career*. She finally called the Dean's Office, and gave me the good news: "Oscar, if you keep out of trouble, you will graduate with an A minus average."

Years later, Dr. Kendrick called me one day at the office, and asked me to stop in to see her on my way home that evening at her house on Connecticut Avenue in Chevy Chase. We had several patients in common, and I presumed that she wanted to discuss them with me. She greeted me warmly as usual but I was not prepared for her words: "Oscar, I just got hit with a 'shockeroo'. Earlier today, I was diagnosed with a melanoma in my right eye. I am scheduled to have the eye removed tomorrow. I wanted to tell you in person. Pray for me."

I was speechless.

The wonderful Margaret Kendrick died within six months. I was again reminded that life is not fair. Clifton R. Gruver, a prominent retired Washington internist says: "Dr. Kendrick was a good friend and colleague, helped many patients of mine. What a tragic loss. How shocked I was! "[29]

I decided to explore with my electives the other facet of medicine, the civilized 9:00 A.M. to 5 P.M., 5 days-a-week world. I spent two weeks downtown with a prominent ophthalmologist, the venerable Dr. Bernard Gurwin. This was especially arranged for me, as Dr. Gurwin was not on the Georgetown staff. My family had told me about him. I loved the entire experience and began thinking seriously that ophthalmology might be a good field for me. On the last day of this short elective, Dr. Gurwin had a long chat with me. He told me that by all considerations, he had been successful in his practice; but, he added: "I am doing routine refraction day in and day out. It has changed my personality. I am not happy professionally. Unless you are thinking of becoming a hot shot eye surgeon, my advice is to avoid ophthalmology as a career. Take it from this old timer." That was the end of ophthalmology for me.

Dermatology was my other elective. There was no full-time division of dermatology at Georgetown until 1971; but, there was Peter N. Horvath,

M.D., a department in himself. He was a gregarious person, an experienced private dermatologist and a born comedian, dedicated to the teaching of dermatology to Georgetown medical students. The elective was well-designed and appealing. I spent two days in his office, two days at Walter Reed and one day, usually Friday, at Andrews Air Force Base, each week for six weeks. The dermatology elective was easy, fun and instructive. I saw a great deal of interesting dermatology, especially at Walter Reed, where there was a strong academic Department of Dermatology with a worldwide case mix. In Dr. Horvath's office, the cases were mostly of the routine garden variety. He once told me in jest: "My patients don't usually have earth-shattering skin problems, but they complain of itching to death. It makes for wonderful patient-doctor relationship. I use a dose of tender loving care, cortisone cream, and not infrequently a short course, or two, of Prednisone®. The patients get well quickly. They are appreciative and grateful. I am happy. Dermatology is right for me."[30]

His patients loved his bedside manner. I greatly enjoyed my time on this elective. I felt that I was on a working vacation. I recognized soon, however, that I was not a 9:00 to 5:00, five days a week person. The work was too confining for me. As with ophthalmology, dermatology was not for me.

One Friday in April 1962, while on the dermatology elective at Andrews, I was notified that Dr. Kyle, the chairman of medicine, wanted to see me the following Friday at 3:00 P.M. in his office at Georgetown. I panicked, and made some frantic calls. None of my classmates had received such a message. Dr. Kyle's secretary pleaded the fifth amendment. Brother John, who is not the worrier type, felt that there was no cause for alarm. He reassured me, but I still worried.

Initially, I was concerned about Dr. Kyle's temperament. He was mercurial and unpredictable. I had seen him eat interns alive, but like Dr. Coffey, he was always pleasant to medical students. I finally decided that Dr. Kyle wanted to talk about my upcoming internship. With this thought in mind, I was able to function while waiting to meet the chairman.

I gave long thought to internships. There were two kinds, the *rotating internship* and the *straight medicine internship*. There were two schools of thought about their merits. The old school was adamant that the *rotating* one, a little of everything, was the best preparation for any medical career. The new school advocated *straight* medicine. *Straight* medicine was considered more intellectual than the more practical *rotating* internship. In general, medical specialties favored *straight* medicine while surgical specialties preferred the *rotating* one. Dr. Coffey, who obtained a master's degree in medicine before his Ph. D. in surgery, strongly believed that surgeons were *physicians plus*, and liked to see applicants to his training program with a *straight* medical internship under their belts. Today, this has become a moot point with the elimination of the internship year and its replacement by the first year of a given specialty.

I decided on *straight* medicine and had already thought of cardiology as a sub-specialty. The final selection of the hospital for internship was through a national matching program. The applicant lists his choices by numerical preferences, and the hospitals rank the applicants in similar fashion. A big computer apparently does the rest. There is room for the element of chance. However, most will have had an interview and most often an informal agreement.

The time had come. I was sitting in front of Kyle in his well-appointed office, with diplomas, degrees and pictures lining the walls. The office was adjoining the Jeghers Conference Room. This room, named after the former great Georgetown professor and chairman of medicine, was the setting where all departmental conferences and meetings took place. It also had a well-stocked little medical library, as befits the chairman who had a private access to the room. Kyle this day was in a fine mood. I was relieved, and began to relax.

He told me that he thought of himself as an endocrinologist first and as chairman of medicine second. As an endocrinologist, he said: "I am interested to find out something about you. Oscar, are you taking the time to sow your wild oats? You will not be young for ever. Don't let time pass you by. Your glands will not always be there for you . . . . "

What an introduction to such an important meeting. I thought that I was dreaming, and babbled something about nurses. He kept on chuckling, obviously enjoying himself at my expense. After a while, he switched subjects and said: "I have recently reviewed your background, and let me tell you what is on my mind. Believe it or not, Oscar, my own father was prejudiced. He went to his grave with anti-Semitism in his blood. Fortunately, I grew out of his state of mind. I trained with Jewish people. There is only one remnant of 'anti-Semitism' in me. I expect all my Jewish boys to work hard and do well. Incidentally, your brother is a straight A student, and you are not far behind him."

He could not be the same Kyle I had seen destroy one's spirit at conferences or during case presentations. Then he continued: "Oscar, you have earned a 96 in senior medicine. That is a big feather in your cap. I congratulate you on this achievement. I am ready to help you get an internship wherever you wish."

I thanked him, and explained that my personal preference was to get a straight medicine internship at Georgetown. I told him that I did consider, at one time, interning on the West Coast, but that my family situation precluded that option. He answered: "In that case, all you need to do when you apply to the matching program is to list Georgetown as your first and only choice. I guarantee your acceptance. We will be glad to have you intern here. Remember that I tend to be rough on my interns. Don't take it personally. You will do fine, Oscar. Best of luck."

I had just discovered the real Kyle.

In June 1962, I graduated *cum laude* near the top of my class. A year later, John graduated *magna cum laude* and number one in the class of 1963. John was the only *magna cum laude* in his class. We both were elected to Alpha Omega Alpha, the national medical honor society. Our father would have been proud of us. He wanted so much to see us educated. *Schmatta* peddlers we were no more.

## NOTES

1. Current tuition and estimated living budget information is prepared yearly by the Georgetown University School of Medicine for prospective students.

2. Patricia Barry, *Surgeons at Georgetown* (Franklin, Tennessee: Hillsboro Press, 2001), 215, 230.

3. The sterile field is the immediate area surrounding the patient on the operating table. It is bacteria free, hence the term sterile field.

4. Adopted from a French expression, which translated, goes something like this: "The train of your insults rolls along the rails of my indifference".

5. For Dr. Coffey's career, see Barry, "Surgeons,"275–77. John C. Rose M.D., former Dean and Professor Emeritus of Physiology and Medicine at Georgetown, contributed a tribute to Dr. Coffey to Barry's book. Barry (pp. 232–233) describes Dr. Rose's words: '*The new chairman of surgery made an instant impression on the medical students. One was John Rose, the future dean of the medical school, who as a twenty-two-year-old veteran airman had entered Georgetown on the GI Bill in 1946. As soon as we encountered Bob Coffey, he recalled, everybody said: 'That is what a doctor should look like. Tall, handsome, and always impeccably dressed, he was a dashing figure–particularly on those occasions when, called from an evening engagement, he would sweep into the emergency room in white tie and tails. And he wore taps on his shoes. When he came down the corridors of the hospital, you knew the chief of surgery was coming'.*

*But Robert Coffey impressed the students for more reasons than sartorial elegance, Rose said: 'In lectures, often delivered in his scrubs, he was always a good speaker. His level of training was significantly better than most surgeons, and he was academic in the true sense. He'd done research* [experimental and clinical research in pancreatic disease, an especially difficult area of surgical intervention], *knew the literature, and his lectures were substantive. The thing that distinguished him was that, perhaps due to his training at the Mayo Clinic* [M.S. in medicine, Ph.D. in surgery from the University of Minnesota], *he understood and talked about the physiology of illness, not just the pathology and the surgical techniques. In that sense, he was a cut above the other surgeons who could tell you what they did, but it wasn't always clear they knew why they were doing it. Sophomores and juniors are always impressed by clinicians, and especially by people as impressive as he. Many of my classmates went into surgery and they did it because of Bob Coffey.'*

6. Barry, "Surgeons," 275–276.

7. Barry, "Surgeons," 230.

8. *Pre-partum* and *post-partum* are medical terms, which mean pre-delivery and post delivery.

9. Personal communication from Tom Magovern, M.D., January 2003.

10. *Pitocin* is a labor-inducing pharmacological agent.

11. Personal communication from Dr. Pasternack, February 2003.

12. George Kober, M.D. was Dean of Georgetown University Medical School from 1901 to 1929, and a financial benefactor to the school. The prestigious Kober Lecture, established in 1923 as his gift to the school on the 50th anniversary of his graduation, has ever since been delivered on his birthday, March 28th, by a distinguished member of the medical profession. On Kober himself, see Barry, "Surgeons,"148–151 and Stapleton, *Upward Journey*, 37–51. For the origins of the Kober Lecture see Barry, "Surgeons," 186. Robert Coffey's Kober Lecture on hyperparathyroidism is described in Barry, "Surgeons," 291–292.

13. Yater's Georgetown career is well-described in Stapleton, *Upward Journey*, 53–75, and Barry, "Surgeons,"196–199.

14. Barry, "Surgeons," 228.

15. See "The Boston Influx" in Stapleton, *Upward Journey*, 98–100.

16. Stapleton, *Upward Journey*, 117.

17. I am indebted to Frank Fowler, M.D., for having suggested this analytical framework for appreciating Jeghers's achievements.

18. Stapleton, *Upward Journey*, 120.

19. Again, I have built on suggestions offered by Frank Fowler, M.D.

20. Stapleton, *Upward Journey*, 139.

21. Personal communication from Dr. John C. Rose, December, 2002.

22. S. Kimara March, "W. Proctor Harvey: A Master Clinician-Teacher's Influence on the History of Cardiovascular Medicine," *Tex Heart Inst J* 2002; 29:185. March's article was written when its author was a 3rd-year medical student at Georgetown.

23. *Idiopathic pulmonary fibrosis* refers to a disease characterized by progressive replacement of normal lung tissue by scarring of unknown cause. The quote is from a personal communication from Dr. Frank Weiner, December 2002.

24. My brother, John, worked closely with Dr. Tumulty for years. It is interesting to note that John, now retired from practice, is in charge of the continuing Tumulty Weekly Rounds, a long tradition at Hopkins. He remains active as a teaching scholar at Hopkins and has received award after award for excellence in clinical teaching from the Department of Medicine at Hopkins. John's clinical skills and love for clinical medicine originated in the Department of Medicine at Georgetown. In September,

2003, Clifton R. Gruver, M.D., a prominent and now- retired Washington internist commented "I used to go every spring to the Hopkins course on 'Clinical Topics in Medicine,' marvel at the skills and teaching abilities of Dr. Tumulty and refer patients to him on occasion. What an accolade for John!"

25. Stapleton, *Upward Journey*, 123.

26. Personal Communication from Dr. Clifton Gruver, September 2003.

27. Personal communication from Dr. Frank Weiner, November 2002.

28. Barry, "Surgeons," 257.

29. Personal communication, Gruver, September 2003.

30. *Prednisone* is a form of *cortisone*. A short course of *prednisone* is a standard treatment when local measures fail. This treatment works nicely in inflammatory itching cases such as hives, poison ivy or an allergic skin condition.

# Chapter Sixteen

# Postgraduate Medical Training

l began my medical internship at Georgetown University Medical Center on Sunday, July 1, 1962. I had been a big man on campus with my M.D. degree in June. Less than a month later, I was back down at the bottom of the ladder. There is nothing lower than an intern in the medical hierarchy, or at least it seemed so at the time.

Georgetown University Hospital was, in my era, a private hospital owned, run and primarily staffed by the university.[1] Each of the clinical departments had a chairman, who usually was a professor on the medical school faculty. The hospital had several floors with a total of 350 patient beds, extensive office space for each department head and his—there were no female department heads at the time—staff, clinical and research laboratories, and a beautiful chapel. All of these functions were crammed into a 150,000 square foot building.

As befits a large teaching hospital, hundreds of people worked, lived, and were treated within its walls. The halls seemed always to be crowded, the wait for an elevator often appeared interminable. The cafeteria was adequate only for early Sunday morning breakfast.

Each department had its own area and was regarded as its own little kingdom where the chairman reigned like a feudal lord. The chaplains of the department of pastoral counseling were a Jesuit priest, an Episcopal minister and an orthodox Jewish rabbi. These clergymen conducted their respective religious services in the chapel. The hospital administration office was, like the chapel, on the lobby floor. Administration claims to the contrary, this hospital was a very expensive and inefficient organization that served many masters. The only two things that held everything together were a common goal—to help patients—and a unifying strand—the continuous rotation of students through each department. To its credit, the "Crystal Palace," as we interns called the hospital, survived; and we the interns also survived and were trained.

The medical wards consisted of two very plain, well-worn wings on the second floor. These were referred to as 2-East and 2-South. These wards were located not far from the office of the chairman of medicine. "House" or indigent sick patients provided most of the teaching cases for these nursing units, with the occasional acutely ill private patients assigned here also. Many of these men and women were very sick, some posed diagnostic challenges, all had some unusual medical problem. Stable private medical patients were admitted to what we called the "Gold Coast", located on the 6th and 7th floors. As the name suggests, this is where the more affluent were treated.

2-East then was considered to be the most demanding and the busiest unit where the reigning intern was most tested. It was here that the full power and practice of modern medicine was brought to bear on the patient. Diagnosis was king, the predominant task. 2-East was the closest thing to what we today call an intensive care unit. In contrast, 2-South was a "step down unit" for patients who had been diagnosed and were well along in their treatment program. By tradition, 2-East was given to someone who was known to be very familiar with the Georgetown system and who was an intern of outstanding credentials and promise. At least this was the publicized word and I felt fortunate and proud to be assigned to 2-East. However, I suffered acutely in the early weeks of my internship as I felt barely adequate to the task at hand. As time progressed, I became more confident. Dr. James Waters, the chief medical resident, gave this evaluation of me at the end of my internship:

> *Oscar turned out to be our best intern. Yet, at first, he was scared, almost skittish, unsure of himself and too deferential. But he worked hard, was pleasant to everyone and rapidly gained self-confidence. He ended up the year, relaxed and in top form. Those who started their internships too confident, did not end up doing as well as Oscar. They became too cavalier. Oscar is a superb house officer. He is well respected.*

I vividly recall that on my first internship day, seven seriously ill patients were admitted to my service: A *GI bleeder* (patient with gastrointestinal bleeding), an *acute myocardial infarction* (patient with a fresh heart attack), a *convulsive seizure disorder* (patient with convulsion), an *icteric* (patient with jaundice), a *hypertensive crisis* (patient with severe uncontrolled blood pressure and secondary acute symptoms) and two *FUOs* (patients with persisting fever of undetermined origin). This was my baptism by fire and I had to learn on the job. I gave up sleeping but not eating as I needed the energy that food provided.

What did that first day of my internship feel like? Much too much patient responsibility was thrust upon me too quickly. I was overwhelmed. My internship, when compared with my clerkships, was like comparing U.S. Army basic training to summer camp. I suddenly longed for my previous relatively carefree clerkship days.

The medical service had a strict hierarchy that blended tradition with practicality. Monday morning report was conducted by the department chairman, Dr. Laurence Kyle, who often criticized me severely as was his habit with all interns. I found myself slow to answer his pointed questions. Nothing seemed to please him, but Kyle's scorn, however, did not disturb me. The psychiatrist in me had figured him out during my internship interview. I had diagnosed Kyle then as someone hiding a heart of gold beneath a crusty exterior.[2] Therefore, I resolved to work hard, think clearly and independently and give my best care to my patients.

The chain of command on the wards went up (and still does) from the intern to the resident, to the chief resident and then to the attending physician of the month, who was often a physician on the volunteer faculty. The ultimate responsibility for patients, however, rested with the chairman, who really ran the show. The bedside care on the wards was given by the interns, the nursing staff and fate. I owe a major debt of gratitude to nurses on 2-East and 2-South, who in stark contrast to their counterparts in the operating room or in the delivery suite, were courteous and extremely helpful to the interns. I would have failed without their support.

Medical interns worked in pairs. Joe Romeo, who was my partner, came from New Jersey. He and I were on call every other night and covered for each other. We often worked late at night on our days off as there was always something else to do. I lived in Kober-Cogan Hall, a residence building behind the hospital. The nursing school, also located near the hospital, provided in-house recreation, relaxation and companionship during the few free hours that were available. My initial ward assignment had been for two months. I seldom had an opportunity to see mother and John during this period. John understood, but mother never did.

About ten days into my internship, things were slow on my call day. It was a beautiful summer day with no admissions coming into the unit. This streak of good luck cannot happen to a nicer guy, I thought. Finally I did get one lone admission, but what an admission it turned out to be!

It was late afternoon, when the head nurse of 2-East, whose name I remember as Mary, announced a STAT (urgent) admission. Mary, an attractive, middle-aged Irish lady with a pleasant personality, was a hard working nurse who provided essential assistance to many an intern. The call from the emergency room nurse announced "You are getting a patient in 'acute pulmonary edema'. You better come down and look things over."

That was the extent of the call. I rushed down one floor to the emergency room. Before intensive-care units were established at the hospital, everything seemed to revolve around 2-East. The patient in question was a morbidly obese woman in obvious acute respiratory distress, who was struggling with the apparatus covering her face. The ER resident commented:

> *She is in 'acute pulmonary edema'. We have taken care of the initial standard treatment. She is all connected* [this word (see below), with its antonym, "disconnected", would recur time and again in my professional life]. *All you need to do now is to get her upstairs pronto.*

*Acute pulmonary edema* is the flooding of the lungs by fluid backing up from a failing heart. In addition to placing the patient in an upright position, initial management of this dramatic condition required the application of a face mask with positive pressure oxygen, inserting an IV (intravenous) line and extremity tourniquets. The resident's use of the word "connected" meant that all of these measures had been applied in the ER. The patient arrived on 2-East with her chest X-ray beside her on the gurney. I examined the patient as carefully as her condition and corpulence would allow but did not remove the positive pressure oxygen mask to examine her throat area, thinking it was best not to disturb this vital piece of equipment already in place.

Thanks to Dr. Katz's teaching, the x-ray showed me a patchy pneumonia, not the presence of generalized fluid in the lungs. This bothered me since the patient was not improving, not even after a shot of mercurial diuretic, the only diuretic then available. I worried about this case or, in the language of house officers, "I sweated the case." My intuition told me to call for help but I procrastinated. Mary, the head nurse, stayed overtime to help me in caring for this woman, telling me gently but unequivocally:

> *Dr. Mann, this case is not acting like 'acute pulmonary edema'. Something is not right here. The working diagnosis from the ER may be a red herring. You better get some help now, before people go home.*

I suddenly thought of Vincent F. Garagusi, M.D., a Georgetown medical graduate and an outstanding diagnostician. In 1962, Vincent Garagusi was appointed full-time chief of infectious diseases. Garagusi, an unselfish person, was always there to help; this seemed to be his mission in life. As a clerk on the medical wards, I had learned that when the "going gets tough, you call in the Goose" (Garagusi's affectionate nickname). I ran down the one flight of stairs, and was in Garagusi's office in a few seconds and explained my problem. He came right up. I watched him in action. He never skipped the basics and always looked at the sick person carefully, observing her body language, while attentively examining her. He quickly picked up on the finger pointed by the patient at her neck area. I had dismissed this gesture as being nothing more than a sign of respiratory distress.

Garagusi commented: "Oscar, this patient is trying to tell us something." He acted systematically to remove the oxygen mask and illuminate the patient's throat. With the hint of a smile on his face, he asked for tweezers and proceeded to remove a chicken bone from deep inside the patient's throat. She instantly stopped struggling. I was utterly amazed. The correct diagnosis was partial airway obstruction with secondary aspiration pneumonia. My diagnosis and that of the ER resident, acute pulmonary edema, was totally wrong. The patient was treated with intravenous antibiotics, steroids and other supportive measures.[3] She made a complete recovery. A clinical disaster had been barely averted. Years later, what almost happened to my patient became known as a *café coronary*.

My ego plummeted, but my learning curve rose. Never again would I accept someone else's diagnosis at face value nor would I ever skip the basics. Never again would I ignore what a patient was trying to tell me. Never again would I procrastinate about calling for help. I began to respect my clinical intuition and, more and more, I paid attention to my gut reaction. In just a few minutes, Garagusi, a gentle, low-key individual, had taught me some powerful clinical lessons, and he had done this with grace and ease. He became a frequent consultant to my patients, as well as a personal friend. He is now retired, in good health, and lives in Bethesda, Maryland.

Another patient remains firmly in my memory, a patient who benefitted from my previous experience. In mid-August 1962, while I was still the rookie intern on 2-East, a beautiful young secretary was admitted with an overdose of sleeping pills and a major complication, *acute rhabdomyolysis*.[4] She had not been discovered for several hours and was found lying on her left side. Blood and urine tests indicated extensive muscle damage, impending kidney failure and the release of threatening levels of potassium in the blood, a situation which can cause dangerous, even fatal, disturbances in the rhythm of the heart. I needed help as soon as possible. Even an uncomplicated overdose was reason enough for an early kidney consult and this was a complicated one.

I phoned the nephrology (the sub-specialty of kidney diseases) fellow (post-residency trainee in a sub-specialty) on call, who was home, having dinner with his wife and children. He was not very receptive and told me to completely work-up the patient and to call him back. Perhaps he did not realize how urgent the situation was, but I did, and I did not hesitate to get help even if it meant stepping on someone's toes. I went directly to the office of the well-known George Schreiner, M.D., Director of the Georgetown University Division of Nephrology (kidney diseases), who at the time was alone, working on a research paper. George Schreiner was a world class medical specialist, a major player in his field and a very brilliant physician. He listened to me, complimented me for recognizing the gravity of the situation and for calling upon him sooner rather than later. He offered to do the consultation himself and do it immediately.

Schreiner spent two hours with the patient. Everything was taken care of masterfully. As he was finishing the consultation, the fellow called me to check on the progress of the patient. It was about 9:00 P.M., and Schreiner took the phone from me and talked to the fellow. Schreiner never raised his voice. He did not utter an angry word, but rather talked to the fellow at length and asked him to closely monitor the case. Further, Schreiner indicated that he wanted the patient to be placed on the artificial kidney as soon as possible. The fellow came in within minutes; he must have taken a plane, I thought, and while chuckling to myself, I watched him stay with the patient all night, giving her attention galore.

There were many kidney patients at Georgetown and the teaching by Schreiner and his associates was so effective that I learned this field well without ever taking an elective in it. Dr. Schreiner and I became long term colleagues and friends. Years later, he would claim in jest at social or professional gatherings that, "I taught Oscar all he knows, and that's a lot."

Both at Georgetown and elsewhere, the life of a medical intern was complicated in those days. BSP, a dye, was then the time-honored test for liver function. A BSP test was ordered frequently as part of a baseline examination. It was used also as a follow-up test or to monitor the side-effects of medications or chemotherapy. Sometimes it was given to satisfy the whims of clinicians. A normal individual would void most of the intravenously injected BSP dye in 45 minutes. Anything more than a 5% retention meant that the excretion was delayed because of liver damage or dysfunction.

Students were not allowed to inject BSP and residents considered it below their dignity. Administering the BSP test was the agonizing responsibility of the intern and the intern alone. The dye could cause potential allergic reactions and due to leakage from the vein into soft tissues, BSP could cause severe sloughing (loss of normal skin and related structures). This usually required plastic surgery to correct. One therefore had to be very careful while injecting the dye. It was time consuming to do this procedure well and if one did not return to the patient at the right time, the test would not be accurate and all that intense concern about injecting the dye would be for naught, to say nothing of the inconvenience and discomfort to the patient. In recent years, thankfully, the BSP has become an obsolete test. We now have better methods of testing liver function and superior visualization techniques of the liver anatomy.

Another challenge during my medical internship, one which would persist throughout my house officer days at Georgetown,was my assignment to work in the out-patient medical clinic every Friday afternoon. The problem was that, while I was assigned to 2-East, every other Friday was also an admission day for me. I disliked being notified of an admission while in the out-patient clinic because I feared that I would not be able to give adequate attention to either the new admissions or to my existing patients. The most that I could do was to give verbal orders by phone or ask Joe Romeo to tide things over until I could return to the floor. I am not an inherent complainer, but I would have gladly supported some positive action to protest the practice of super-imposing clinic time on admitting days. I once actually asked that this practice be changed. But I was not successful. I was told that "the system cannot be altered, this practice is too embedded in medical tradition."

Other irritants in my internship also come to mind. The glass IV bottles were connected by flexible IV lines to the patient's vein. The IV design and materials used in the tubing was such that it was not always possible to be sure that all the air bubbles had been eliminated. Further, some patients in need of IV fluids had no usable veins and we had to resort to an almost barbaric method, called clysis. The procedure entailed the direct insertion of long two-pronged needles into the subcutaneous tissue of the thighs to allow the administration of 5% dextrose/water. Clysis was commonly done and the cry of certain patients so treated, "get those damn hairpins out of my leg," still resonates in my ears. If intravenous access was critically needed, we called in the surgeons to perform a *cut-down* on a peripheral vein.[5] Today, with sophisticated techniques, multiple access adaptors and specialized, full-time and experienced personnel called "vascular access teams", it is possible to connect a main (central) vein to a wide-caliber line intended to accommodate several intravenous products simultaneously. Nothing similar existed in those days and in the era of my internship, we could only connect one line to a vein at a time. Sometimes we had IVs going in all four extremities.

It was early August 1962. I had been an intern on 2-East for over a month. Having regained my bruised self-confidence, I gradually became aware that I had become, in a way, a new person. My experience on 2-East represented a critical transformation for me, from being a member of the general public to becoming a member of the medical profession. And here again, one thing that cannot be repeated enough is how often interns were given a "leg up" in this professional transformation by extraordinary nurses like Mary.

In 1947, Jeghers had established a regular weekly conference known as Medical Grand Rounds. This conference was suspended during the summer but resumed after Labor Day. During July and August, lectures directed at the interns replaced Grand Rounds. These didactic sessions, primarily concerned with topics such as acute pulmonary edema, acute G.I. bleeding, acute heart attack and other emergencies, were delivered by some of the great full-time clinicians on staff at Georgetown. I looked forward to attending the entire series.

In early August 1962, the scheduled lecturer was an "LMD" or local medical doctor, as we unflatteringly called doctors in outside practice. The announced topic was the overly familiar subject of patient-doctor relations. I considered not going, but word came down from Dr. Kyle that he expected every intern to attend this particular conference. Dr. Kyle had asked Dr. W. Proctor Harvey, director of cardiology, to introduce the guest speaker.

Harvey introduced Dr. Wesley M. Oler as the type of doctor we should all emulate in academic medicine, research or in practice. Oler was an impressive gentleman who caught my immediate attention. He was, physically and in demeanor, the spitting image of Dr. Paul Benet, the person who was so instrumental in saving our lives in the south of France during the dark days of WWII. Oler spoke about *Caritas Medicini,* the art of being a complete and compassionate physician. He was witty, entertaining and a gifted communicator. Oler's talk dispensed with the usual cliches and cleverly concentrated on his message:

*Anger is not a scientific state of mind. If, while taking care of a patient, you find yourself becoming angry, for whatever reason, get off the case. Also being heavy-handed with a patient reflects a similar state of mind. We can all take care of the easy patient. The physician must be at peace with himself and make his patients feel good about themselves. It is not only what you say to a patient but the way you say it.*

He closed his talk by recounting a personal experience which I have never forgotten:

*A while ago, one of my more sophisticated older patients called me. She was very upset. She asked to see me immediately with an urgent problem. I brought her in the same afternoon. She was visibly distraught and said to me: "Dr. Oler, you will not believe what is happening to our young people nowadays. I sublet my basement to a Ph.D. candidate from George Washington University. She came to me with excellent references. Everything was fine. But now, she enter-*

*tains a man on weekends in my house! I am mortified. What should I do, Dr.*
*Oler?"*

*I looked her straight in the eyes while holding her hands and told her that in*
*my professional opinion, 'a little bit of fornication never hurt anyone.' She left*
*with a broad smile on her face.*

We all laughed enthusiastically. Dr. Oler received a standing ovation. Everyone was inspired, especially the interns. This was my first, but not my last exposure to Dr. Oler; later I would join him in practice. But I mark that lecture as a turning point in my attitude.

On returning to 2-East, I was determined to emulate this great practitioner, pay heed to my internal dialogue and take care in the way I expressed myself. Internship was an opportunity, not just something to be endured, but rather a stepping stone to a great profession, a meaningful life. I felt the change of my attitude deep within me. Others noticed it as well.

Mortality conferences took place every Thursday at noon. The case presentation, made by the intern who had cared the longest for the deceased patient, was intended to be a powerful learning exercise, and it usually was. The conference, also called the *CPC* (clinico-pathological conference) was in keeping with the best tradition of medical teaching. All the physicians who had consulted on the deceased patient attended the conference and expressed their viewpoints. The pathologists presented their findings and voiced their opinion of the cause of death. The case was then open for general discussion under the direction of Dr. Kyle.

Usually, the ambience was civilized but occasionally the involved intern was taken to task. One Thursday, as I was finishing my first tour of duty on 2-East, I presented two cases. This particular day, Kyle had a visitor, a doctor with whom he had trained in Boston. During the discussion, Kyle attacked me in front of his friend but I was not rattled in the least. Later that day, the visitor came by on 2-East to seek me out. He was eager to talk to me in private, and we went to the cafeteria for a cup of coffee. He said he had known Kyle for a long time as a friend and colleague, but "I had never seen this side of him. He really was rough on you, and you took it so well." I told him about my discovery of the real Kyle, and he seemed relieved.

Talk of mortality conferences brings back additional memories. I became accustomed to seeing dead people, and over time that was not a problem for me. What was a problem for me was pronouncing people dead. Many times in the early days of my internship, I could not be completely certain whether a patient had passed on or not. Other interns experienced the same qualms. How sad it was to tell the family that their loved one had died; to say nothing of wondering if there was anything more that anyone could have done. That's why the *posts* (autopsies) and CPCs were so important.[6] The other thing I remember about death and mortality at Georgetown is that often one cared for a VIP patient and had to "hide" the fact the patient had died until meeting and telling his or her family. Otherwise, the possibility existed that some orderly or other staff member would be paid to release the news to the media. Certainly we did not wish the family to be notified in that manner. I had personally experienced this problem and understood it only too well.

We no longer have the "posts" to the extent we did then, probably because of two factors. First, new technology makes a correct pre-death diagnosis more likely and second, medico-legal issues have become of paramount importance. The CPC, so long a powerful teaching tool, has been relegated to a much lesser place in American medical education.

Mortality conferences were not a difficult experience, but preparing the cases for presentation was time consuming and cut into what little free time was available. Failure to obtain permission for an autopsy was considered a serious shortcoming and a breach of duty on the part of the intern. The chief resident maintained a scoring record. Dr. Kyle frequently looked at this record, using it as an index of the rapport the intern had established with the patient's family.

I completed my first rotation on 2-East on September 1, 1962. I had survived and felt good about myself. Mary, the head nurse, had a little celebration featuring a few delicacies and aromatic coffee she had personally brewed. I thanked her and her staff for facilitating my metamorphosis from medical student to R.D. i.e., real doctor. I actually looked forward to another stint on 2-East.[7]

Up to this point in my internship, I had a perfect "post" record. One day, however, a DC cab driver of French extraction was admitted to my service with a puzzling clinical picture. The case was dominated by multiple endocrine (glandular) manifestations, and he died within three weeks of a widespread cancer of an unknown origin. We were anxious to get permission for a post-mortem examination to establish some etiological clarity in this case, but his only living relative was his younger sister, a nun in a French convent near Paris. I tracked her down but to my dismay, she could not come to the phone as she belonged to an order that did not allow its members to have any contact whatever with "the secular world." Nevertheless, I persevered and obtained permission for the post-mortem examination from the DC medical examiner on the basis of using the cadaver for scientific educational purposes. My record remained unblemished.

My next two months, October-November 1962, were spent on the 7th floor. The pace was less hectic, and the patient responsibilities were lighter than on 2-East. Every patient had a private, outside physician. And the challenge on this rotation was to get along with the private attending physician, while at the same time benefitting from his experience. I made the most of my relations with the private physicians, learning much from them. It is amazing how well these doctors responded to courtesy and good manners. They gladly shared with me their knowledge, experience and expertise. They welcomed my calling in consultants and gave me leeway in managing their patients. I discussed the cases with the consultant, usually one of the specialists at Georgetown, reporting their opinions and recommendations to the involved private physician. It was the best of both worlds, and I absorbed a great deal in the process. Some interns in contrast, felt otherwise and overtly resented the intrusion of the "LMD." Seemingly they were unaware that one day many of them would become local medical doctors.

There was more leisure time on this rotation. The medical students helped the interns, shared some of their burden and more of the responsibilities than on 2-East. Perhaps my new attitude encouraged them in that direction. I even found time to look at medical journals despite the adage that if you read anything while interning, you were not doing justice to your assignment.

One Sunday evening, before calling it a day, I decided to look in on a patient located on the 6th floor. To my surprise, I ran into John, who was in the room. He was working a double shift as a private nurse. Though the job was humbling, it allowed John to do some studying, which for him went a long way. It also allowed him to earn $90.00, the equivalent of a week's wages at the liquor store. I told John I would take his place so that he could go to the cafeteria for dinner and a change of scenery. I made myself comfortable. The room was spacious, well-appointed, and the patient was asleep. I reflected about where John and I had come from and where we were now. When John returned, I said spontaneously, "Only in America!"

Aware of chest X-ray fundamentals, thanks to Dr. Katz, I decided now to master the basics of ECG (*electrocardiogram*) reading. The interpretation of the ECG is a separate and additional skill unrelated to clinical competence and must be learned independently. Some medical professionals quail at attempting to grasp this skill. Luckily a one-month elective was available to medical interns at Georgetown. I took mine with Dr. Recep Ari, who was the director of the heart station (where ECG's were read) and who, Dr. Harvey said, knew and taught ECG reading better than anyone in the world. Dr. Harvey was always right, it seemed, and under the tutelage of Dr. Ari, and with collateral reading, I became a proficient ECG reader.

This elective also gave me time to become interested in a disease which at the time had attracted some attention at Georgetown. The name itself, *hyperparathyroidism*, gave the disease a certain mystique. The *thyroid gland*, located in the neck below the Adam's apple and over the voice box, controls the metabolic rate of the body. This gland, involved in goiters (sluggish or overactive metabolic states), is composed of two lobes, the right and the left, joined together by a narrow band of tissue called the isthmus. Most people are likely to be familiar with this gland, since it is routinely examined during a physical exam. The thyroid moves up and down during swallowing and, usually, the patient is given water to help the examiner feel the gland. Embedded within the thyroid are four tiny structures barely visible to the naked eye, known as the parathyroid glands. Occasionally, one of the parathyroid glands is aberrant; that is, it is located outside the thyroid gland.

The parathyroid glands control the metabolism of the minerals, calcium and phosphorus, through the secretion of *parathyroid hormone*, known as PTH. This hormone causes the calcium level to go up and the phosphorus level to go down in the blood. Hyperparathyroidism is the disease state that occurs with an overproduction of PTH which is normally turned off by an increased level of blood calcium. The excess calcium causes multiple confusing symptoms, including mental changes. The role of the lower phosphorus is not clear. Eventually, the surfeit of blood calcium is deposited in the tissues of organs. The end-result is progressive organ dysfunction, renal failure and death from a cardiac arrhythmia, i.e., disturbance of the electrical activity of the heart. The usual etiology of this disease is a benign, autonomous growth of one or more of the parathyroid glands.

Kyle and his able associate, John J. Canary, active in clinical endocrine investigations, were considered leading authorities on this disease, having developed special tests to confirm the diagnosis of the disease. These tests could usually, but not always, distinguish primary hyperparathyroidism, the disease, from secondary hyperparathyroidism, conditions mimicking the disease. The only definitive treatment was surgical neck exploration with removal of the offending parathyroid gland or glands. Dr. Coffey, the hospital's Surgeon-in-Chief, was the master of this operation.

To me, hyperparathyroidism appeared to be a neat disease which was diagnosable, physiologically captivating, usually benign and totally treatable. As stated before, the chairmen of medicine and surgery at Georgetown had major interests in this disease. I began to read all that I could about this ailment and attend conferences where the disease was discussed and cases presented. Such conferences were frequent at Georgetown. I, however, had not personally treated a case of hyperparathyroidism, and I became obsessed with finding a case.

Today, we take things for granted in many areas of medicine and so it is with hyperparathyroidism. Serum calciums and phosphorus tests have been part of routine, automated profiles for years now. The diagnosis comes to you; you no longer need to look for it. The confirmatory tests have become refined and precise with PTH levels easily determined. An elevated level of this hormone is the telltale sign of the disease with the parathyroid adenoma identified by preoperative imaging. After surgical removal of the adenoma, a much simpler procedure than it used to be, a parathormone level is done intraoperatively (during the operation). The result is immediately available, and normalization of the secretion of this hormone confirms the success of the operation. The diagnosis and management of hyperparathyroidism is no longer the big deal it used to be. The patient goes home the day of the operation. The disease is not endemic by any means, but it is also not uncommon.

During my internship days, only a few tests were routinely done, serum calcium and phosphorus testing not usually among them. These two tests had to be ordered individually. If you suspected this particular disease, three serial blood tests were recommended. I quickly determined there was a gap here and began to order the three serial blood calcium and phosphorus levels on all patients. Because of my insistence on these tests, it was said,"Oscar is ordering too many blood tests." Initially, the diagnosis of cases of hyperparathyroidism evaded my best efforts, but I did not give up. There must be a stubborn streak in me, but I was convinced it would pay off. And it did!

During May and June 1963, my second rotation on the private floors was clear sailing. My internship was coming to an end, and so were my days at Kober-Cogan. Georgetown made no dormitory provisions beyond the level of intern. I would return to the Doreen. Mother was pleased. A car became necessary. Uncle Nat, who still owned the Sparkle Car Wash at Florida Avenue and U Street, where John and I had worked sporadically, facilitated the purchase of a new Chevy II from a friend of his in the automobile business. The car was purchased for $2,000; Nathan Gildenhorn cosigned with me and placed me on his insurance policy for the next two years. I was most grateful.

The Chevy II opened new horizons for John and me. However, even though we had buried the hatchet as rival siblings long before and were getting along well, the new Chevy II almost drove a wedge between us. It was to be John's car as much as mine. John was soon away at Hopkins for his internship and on occasion John would come to Washington and take the car to Baltimore for his free weekends. Then I would need a neighbor or friend to drive me to and from the Georgetown Medical Center. Sometimes I was irritated by this. Nothing else of significance, however, has ever come between us. Uncle Isor watched and nurtured the relationship between John and me, telling us that nothing in life was more important than close family ties. He was very wise!

I officially became a first year medical or junior resident at Georgetown on July 1, 1963. The mission of a junior resident is delicate leadership, a function that becomes rewarding and fulfilling. His first obligation as the "platoon leader" or the "team leader," is to exercise a meaningful but subtle supervision over the intern. Ideally, the intern should be given latitude but not be aware of close oversight. He must be allowed to "sweat," but should never be abandoned. The junior resident is also responsible for the teaching and guidance of the students assigned to his team. A good junior resident establishes *esprit de corps* ("team spirit"), doing all his duties seemingly with ease, but with enough leisure time to read medical journals, analyze things, as well as relate to everyone.

I had developed a good rapport with Dr. Thomas Keliher during my medical clerkship days.[8] Keliher was crippled by poliomyelitis at a young age. He walked with a significant limp, using a heavy cane and orthopedic appliances. He had put all of his life energy into becoming an extraordinary clinical teacher and an excellent diagnostician. He had certainly succeeded. This quiet clinical giant was unassuming, friendly and always available to others. My association with Keliher was rewarding. It was also a privilege. His office was on 5-East, and I visited him informally in my spare time, seeking his advice on how to be a good junior resident. He helped me considerably by suggesting ways of dealing with my collagues; in the process of taking his advice we became friends.

Thomas Keliher lived on O Street with a sister in their late father's home. He had attended Trinity School, Gonzaga High School, Georgetown College and Georgetown Medical School. He was a protege of Yater and he prospered in the Jeghers era. His idea of a vacation was to go to Baltimore by train for dinner with a friend. Clifton R. Gruver, M.D., a prominent retired Washington internist, recently reminded me: "Someone once said of Dr. Keliher that no one could see how he made a living—all of his patients were either doctors, doctors' families, or priests and nuns! No charges."[9]

My first rotation as a junior resident was between 2-East and 2-South. The system had changed somewhat since my intern days. The two units were combined as one service since a great deal of overlapping had always prevailed between 2-East and 2-South. Two teams were assigned to the newly combined service. I was the leader of one team while the other resident was Patrick, a delightful fellow.[10] Both interns were solid chaps and our students were qualified and hard-working. We were a happy family.

Exciting new changes were occurring in the Department of Medicine at Georgetown at that time. Kyle, in his own way, was a progressive chairman. He had recently worked out a rapprochement with the Johns Hopkins Medical

Center. Georgetown medical graduates were now being accepted as interns by Hopkins; my brother, John, was one of the first involved in this program. John went on to do his graduate medical work there before splitting his sub-specialty training in infectious diseases between the National Institutes of Health and Hopkins.[11] Further, Kyle had announced a new educational strategy at the last Grand Rounds: Georgetown and NIH had entered into a mutually complementary agreement. As part of this program, there would be a regular exchange of physicians for teaching purposes, with Georgetown fellows rotating at NIH. This appeared wise and innovative to me. The residents were asked to cooperate with this plan. For years, residents had traditionally decided on the cases to be presented to a *teaching attending physician*.[12] An old, dirty trick involved sticking the latter with a case out of his specialty. Kyle asked that this not be done. I remember his exact words: "Pump the attending for all that he has to offer, but don't embarrass him by presenting cases totally out of his field."

Under this policy, our first teaching attending on 2-East/2-South was Baruch S. Blumberg, M.D., Ph.D. Dr. Blumberg was a noted hematologist (specialist in blood diseases) who was engaged in hepatitis research at NIH. He was a fine, unassuming man who combined a brilliant intellect with a pleasant demeanor and a low-key bearing. He had a constant smile and projected openness and enthusiasm. He told us immediately that he was bringing a colleague with him because he felt a little rusty in clinical medicine. I liked Blumberg from the beginning for his candor, but the two interns, and especially Patrick, the other resident, to my dismay, felt otherwise. Their position was "Our time should not be wasted by a non-clinician," and they were barely polite to Dr. Blumberg and his associate. Patrick, usually agreeable, led the charge and insisted that we present only cases out of Dr. Blumberg's field of expertise. I adamantly disagreed. It was the closest I ever came to a fist fight. Somehow I prevailed and we presented only hematology and liver cases. Blumberg ignored the bad manners and taught us much about hepatitis and its blood factors. However, the experience was wasted on the others, who could not, in their ignorance, maintain a scientific state of mind, as Dr. Oler had urged that we do. They even contaminated the virginal minds of the medical students. At the end of his tour, Dr. Blumberg invited Patrick, me and the two interns for a Friday family dinner. They declined the invitation. I went.

Blumberg lived in a modest house, near NIH, but it was a warm home, with children running around and his wife busy fixing a traditional Jewish Sabbath dinner and lighting candles. I enjoyed the evening, all the while thinking to myself, "I am the guest of good people. "

In 1976, Dr. Blumberg won the Nobel Prize in Medicine for his discovery of the hepatitis B virus.

*Dr. Blumberg has been at the forefront . . . . His discovery of the hepatitis B virus*
*is considered one of the greatest medical achievements of the twentieth century*
*. . . . He and his colleagues discovered the virus in 1967, developed the blood*
*test that is used to detect the virus and invented the first hepatitis B vaccine in*
*1969. These outstanding accomplishments have contributed significantly toward*
*making the world a much healthier place to live . . . .* [13]

I was in private practice in 1976 when his prize was announced and called
him to offer congratulations. He took my call and was as gracious as when I
first met him.

Medical school does not teach good character, charm or good manners. The
*schmatta* business and my army training did give me some experience working with others, getting along with higher and lower ranked persons and attracting and keeping good relationships with co-workers and customers in
business. I believe that the way my mother brought us up in the dark days of
the war formed John and me and gave us both interpersonal skills and early
emotional maturity. That is where it all began for me.

When I became the junior resident on the private floors, I was there with
an entirely new team. Things were going well. We had a wealthy Middle East
patient with an FUO (fever of undetermined origin). The patient had been
seen by many of the full-time consultants, but the case continued to defy classification. "LMD" Frank G. MacMurray, called in by the patient's family, arrived on the scene. My team mates were bitter that an "LMD" had been consulted on this difficult case "in a teaching hospital, of all places," as they put
it. The animosity was palpable, and again I became the pacifier.

MacMurray, tall, fit, and relaxed, ignored the cold reception. He spent a lot
of time discussing the case with us, and took us downstairs to review with a
radiologist all the x-rays on this patient. I was most impressed. Then came
MacMurray's question: "Did you guys put on a PPD?"[14] We had not, so the
intern did; and it was positive, big time positive. It all led to a liver biopsy and
the diagnosis of *miliary tuberculosis*.[15] The chest x-ray never did turn positive, which I learned was not unusual in this form of tuberculosis. So much
for "dumb LMDs."[16]

Caro Luhrs, M.D., a Harvard Medical School graduate, was two years
ahead of me. She had been a hematology fellow under Dr. Charles Rath, Director of Hematology, who was brought from Boston by Dr. Jeghers. Rath, an
accomplished clinician and an excellent teacher, taught a popular course,
Laboratory Diagnosis, in the second year of medical school. He had a dry
sense of humor and was somewhat detached, but he was shrewd. He made the
well-liked Caro Luhrs, a member of the faculty, his main assistant, the man-

ager of lab services and the director of the blood bank. She was young, friendly, bright, beautiful and always helpful. She stood out among the then all-male, full-time clinical faculty in the department of medicine. Dr. Kyle liked to talk to Caro at medical-staff meetings, toying with her name tag, and pretending to have forgotten her name.[17]

At that time, I was thinking of cardiology as my specialty, but I felt it could not hurt to take a detour under the tutelage of the attractive Caro Luhrs, so I took a two-month elective in hematology. The elective began on a pleasant, sunny November day and ended on a note which was anticlimactic, compared to my romantic expectations. Caro Luhrs challenged my male chauvinism and dashed the hopes of my male ego by immediately assigning me a hefty project. An in-depth review of two new agents, Vincristine and Vinblastine, to be presented to the entire division of hematology at the Friday conference, two weeks hence, was now mine and mine alone, courtesy of the rising young star of hematology.

Vincristine and Vinblastine are two chemicals found in the Madagascar periwinkle. The natives of Madagascar used this plant, *Vinca rosea*, to treat diabetes and all kinds of ailments. In the 1950s, the two compounds were found to lower the number of white cells in blood and became new chemotherapeutic agents. They were used for treating leukemia, Hodgkin's disease and other lymphomas. Preparing my review turned out to be interesting and exciting, and the presentation went well. I eventually forgave Caro for the two weeks of incarceration in the medical library as the project enhanced my knowledge of chemotherapy.

While on the hematology service, I came in contact with a new Georgetown intern, Henry Safrit. Henry was from Beaufort, North Carolina, had graduated from Duke Medical School and had decided to intern in Washington. Despite very different backgrounds, we became and have remained close friends.

It was Friday, November 22, 1963, an ordinary day, my clinic day. After the weekly hematology conference, I grabbed a quick bite at the Macke machine vending room and walked over to the out-patient department where I arrived at 12:45. My first patient was due at 1:00 P.M. Something was amiss. Everything was chaotic. Nurses, patients, orderlies were crying, visibly agitated and running around, while doctors with grave facial expressions, looked worried and were mostly silent. For a minute, I thought that I was back in the surreal exodus from Paris of June 1940.[18]

President Kennedy had been shot and mortally wounded in Dallas. At 2:38 (EST), Walter Cronkite, wiping tears from his eyes, announced "The President is dead." Catholic Georgetown University was particularly affected.

There had been such festivity at Georgetown from November 1961 to January 1962 to "toast in" the first Catholic president in the history of the country. I had gone to parties to celebrate this momentous occasion. Suddenly, I relived the death of President Franklin Delano Roosevelt.[19] Again, the world stopped. The event was overwhelming, and everything was canceled. I attended mass for the late president that afternoon in the hospital chapel, overflowing with people. Early in the morning, the day of the burial, Caro Luhrs, her friend, Barbara Bostock, Henry Safrit and I walked over to Memorial Bridge, which carries Memorial Drive over the Potomac. After clearing security, we stood for hours near the statue of the golden equine guarding the entrance to the bridge, looking west. The Lincoln Memorial was to our left and Arlington Cemetery straight ahead across the Potomac—we had an unobstructed view of the proceedings. We wanted so much to pay our personal respects to the president.

We saw the cortege go by at close range. The sight of the riderless horse, saddled but with boots reversed in the stirrups, followed by the carriage with the coffin and the many bereaved family members and dignitaries on foot was so sad in its quiet grandeur. For the only time in my life, I saw the imposing Charles de Gaulle, who looked so tall, marching alongside the diminutive Emperor Selassie from Ethiopia.

Caro, Barbara, Henry and I forged a bond right then and there. Caro was personally distressed by the death of President Kennedy: "Only a few weeks before, I had spent 15 minutes talking to him when he sneaked up the stairs to the 6th floor of the hospital to see a close friend who was one of my patients."[20] Caro was giving the patient a platelet transfusion, and the president remained there with them.

During a similar visit by the president, the 6th floor head nurse was in the room with the patient. She fainted on seeing President Jack Kennedy, and was caught by him just in time to prevent a fall. That story was all over Georgetown.

In late December 1963, I received a call from Bess Gildenhorn, the gracious wife of Nathan Gildenhorn, Isor's youngest brother. She wanted me to take out a nice Jewish girl, Amy C. Schwartz. I had not dated a Jewish girl since my clinical years of medical school, but I could not deny Bess. Reluctantly I called the unknown Amy.

First surprise! Her father was Anthony Schwartz, my old friend and client from Circle Liquors.

Second surprise! Amy was a cut above the other girls I had known. She was bright, attractive, congenial, well-spoken and a good listener.

Surprise again! Amy was without any pretense.

Things clicked from the beginning. On our first date, we saw the film *Move Over, Darling,* with Doris Day, and had a bite at the Hot Shoppes on Georgia Avenue, near East-West Highway. It was an evening to remember.

We soon had another date. We saw *Around the World in 80 Days*, with David Niven and Shirley Maclaine at the Uptown Theater, and then crossed Connecticut Avenue to the Roma Restaurant where we had a nice salad and delicious spaghetti. A week later we dined in style at *Chez François* on Connecticut Avenue near the White House. Those were different days. The total bill, including the tip, was $15.00.

At her door, we kissed passionately; Amy then said to me, and I quote: "Please give me a ring soon."

She has always claimed that she meant phone me again. Be that as it may, the fine nuances of the English language were still being lost on me at times but what a fortunate misunderstanding! I began looking for a ring, calling my old boss, Myer, who referred me to a friend, Rose V., who owned and operated a pawn shop across Key Bridge in Arlington. Amy accompanied me.

Ms. Rose V., who was a bit solicitous, showed us rings which I understood ranged in price from $6.95 to $12.95. Not able to tell the difference between rings, I gamely said that although I could not afford anything expensive, I was willing to go for something a little higher. Amy focused on one particular ring, and she seemed to be very happy with it. It was $19.95, still well within my price range. I took out a twenty dollar bill and gave it to Ms. Rose V. She broke out in loud laughter, and while still laughing, called Myer in our presence: "Your cousin may be a nice guy, a good doctor and he may have been an excellent liquor clerk, but certainly he has no street smarts " By 19.95, she had meant $1,995.00. Again, the idiomatic intricacies of my adopted language had played a trick on me.

Myer's booming voice came back, loud and clear, as if through a microphone. It was heard distinctly by all: "Lay off my cousin, Rose, if you know what's good for you. Hand him over the $1,995 one with no delay and leave the street smarts to me. I'll bargain the hell out of you and settle with you later. You're not going to fool me, Sister. I wasn't born yesterday"

This was vintage Myer Gildenhorn. Ms. Rose V. removed the ring guard, so that the ring would fit, and it did, perfectly. Over time, I paid Myer $500. The mark-up apparently was not unusual for pawn shops but Myer, a smart business man, was not easily duped. On February 7, 1964, Amy and I were officially engaged.

Life on the other track continued. Hematology had been an elective chosen for ulterior personal reasons. The junior residency year offered me another two-month elective. This time, my elective, chosen with serious career consideration, was in clinical cardiology and began in early January 1964.[21]

The W. Proctor Harvey clinical cardiac fellowship was one of the most sought-after specialty programs anywhere and it was right under my nose at Georgetown.[22] I secretly hoped to be accepted into this select postgraduate program in 1965 at the completion of my graduate training in internal medicine. The competition was intense. Only six spots were open, and people were applying in droves from all over the country. In due time, I would apply. In the meantime, I would not talk about it. It would be my secret aspiration. Even a one time *schmatta* boy of the Old World could cherish his dreams in America.

The division of cardiology consisted of the great clinician and teacher, W. Proctor Harvey, M.D., the brilliant Joseph K. Perloff, M.D., and the talented Modestino Criscitiello, M.D. They were ably assisted by rising young stars in the division, James Ronan, M.D., Anthony de Leon, M.D. and the accomplished Frank Marcus, M.D., chief of cardiology on the Georgetown service at DC General Hospital. These full-time people were backed up by the likes of Recep Ari, M.D., Jack P. Segal, M.D., Alan Weintraub, M.D. and other exceptional clinical cardiologists of the volunteer faculty. I would work well with each one and would give this elective my best.

An amusing incident occurred at the beginning of the elective. Dr. Harvey, who loved to conduct "walk rounds", would take a small group of house officers and medical students to the bedside of patients with interesting heart murmurs. We would bring along the auscultation apparatus from which we could listen simultaneously with Dr. Harvey through multiple electronic stethoscopes connected through a central amplifying device. On the second day of my elective, I was privileged to be invited to Dr. Harvey's walk rounds. There were 12 of us and the patient. Dr. Harvey had just about finished demonstrating the systolic (active phase of the cardiac cycle) murmur of *mitral regurgitation* (leakage of blood between the upper and lower chambers on the left side of the heart), a murmur easy to recognize because of its high frequency. The patient had listened with us to his own murmur, something that Dr. Harvey was fond of letting the patient do. He suddenly asked how many were hearing the faint diastolic (passive phase of the cardiac cycle) murmur of *aortic insufficiency* (blood swirling back into the main chamber of the heart because of an incompetent valve at the outflow tract of the heart). Ten hands went up. Somehow, I could not hear that murmur, a murmur which had never been a problem for me before, but that day it eluded me even after switching stethoscopes. I kept my hand down. So did the patient and Dr. Harvey. The master clinician-teacher then casually remarked that there was no such murmur in this particular patient, adding: "Be careful not to be misled by preconceived notions."

Later that afternoon, Dr. Harvey winked at me, with a wide smile on his face.

I could not get enough of this clinical cardiac elective. I stayed long hours, boned up on my auscultation and ECG reading skills, and became captivated by phonocardiography, the graphic recording of heart sounds and cardiac murmurs. These were the days before echocardiograms, and a phonocardiogram was the only way to display graphically for the record what one heard on auscultation.

It was exciting to me to do phono-cardiograms. I did many, and I volunteered constantly to do more. What I liked best about it was the development of the large negative film roll. Alone in the dark room with the precious cannister, I felt creative in making the recorded heart auscultation come alive on special photographic paper. Somewhere in me there must be a frustrated amateur photographer. Especially, I liked to measure, label, discuss and present phonocardiograms. I also developed an instant interest in the mysterious vectorcardiogram. This novel modality was appealing to me but seemed difficult to learn. I would make it a personal challenge. A highlight of the cardiology elective was the Thursday evening cardiology conference. While on the elective, I offered my services in the preparation and presentation of this conference, usually, in the audio-visual realm, gathering the slides or acting as a projectionist. The cardiology elective was so enjoyable that time simply flew by.

Enter Arlington Hospital. Ever since 1948, there had been an association between this active community hospital and the Georgetown University School of Medicine and Medical Center. Georgetown covered Arlington Hospital, providing senior students, residents, academic consultants and clinical teachers. In turn, Arlington Hospital supplied a wealth of patient material for Georgetown. Community hospitals on their own cannot get such sophisticated backup, and teaching hospitals always need more patients for their students.

*Georgetown assigned residents and senior students to Arlington, but no interns. The absence of interns allowed senior students more direct responsibilities for patients under resident supervision: the army sergeant/private model that Harold Jeghers had described.*[23]

This symbiotic arrangement was greatly enhanced and constantly nurtured by pathologist William Dolan, M.D. Dr. Dolan, a Georgetown medical school graduate and a member of the Georgetown clinical faculty, was in name the director of the clinical laboratories of Arlington Hospital. In actuality, he was the *de facto* head of Arlington Hospital. He ran the place, exerting a magical power and reigning supreme on his turf. All the private physicians admitting their patients to Arlington Hospital, and there were many, seemed awed by him. Dolan, a superb person and an astute entrepreneur, was totally dedicated to the Georgetown-Arlington relationship.

In a brilliant move, he had attracted William F. Enos, M.D., as the director of pathology at Arlington Hospital. Dr. Enos had shocked the medical world with a landmark article he authored in 1953. At the time, he was an U.S. Army Major and he and associate medical officers had published what was to become a classic study about coronary artery disease in the *Journal of the American Medical Association* (JAMA).[24]

As a result of this milestone study, there were those who said that Arlington Hospital was now on the map.

I have good memories of my student days at Arlington Hospital. The ambience was always pleasant and friendly, and the hospital ran smoothly. Our quarters were relatively comfortable and the cafeteria was excellent and free of charge to Georgetown medical personnel. We always felt welcomed at Arlington Hospital. Georgetown's clinical "luminaries" came over to Arlington frequently as consultants and teachers. We were instantly promoted at Arlington Hospital. The senior students became acting interns and the residents became "kings." The emergency room was one of the best in the area.[25]

On-call private physicians were readily available. I began to feel like a doctor in the Arlington ER, where, as a student, I sewed one laceration after another.

I was sent to Arlington Hospital for a two-month rotation in January 1964, this time as a junior resident. Joseph Romeo, my old friend from internship days, was the other resident. Our students were excellent and eager to be acting interns. We were a congenial group and worked well together. Amy used to come over frequently and have dinner with me. Arlington Hospital was as pleasant as ever for me. Everyone accommodated us and I had time to devote time to my clinical obsession, *hyperparathyroidism*.

I arranged to speak to Dr. Dolan who was always available to us. Over coffee and doughnuts in his office, he advised me that I could order any test which I believed would be beneficial to patients at Arlington Hospital. He stated: "Oscar, just call the private physician of record, discuss your idea with him, and if anyone objects, ask that they call me. There will be no problem." And there was none.

Every patient I saw at Arlington Hospital during this rotation got three serum calciums and phosphorus tests. In this fashion, I uncovered three cases of the disease during those two months at Arlington. The three patients were transferred to Georgetown after consultations between Dr. Canary, Director of Endocrinology at Georgetown, their private doctors and myself. All three were confirmed medically as suffering from primary hyperparathyroidism and were referred to Dr. Coffey. All three had benign hyperparathyroid autonomous adenomas. They were all surgically cured. Everyone was happy. I had not performed an extraordinary feat but was given credit for my efforts. The myth of my diagnostic abilities grew. I did nothing to discourage this and I would spend the rest of my medical career trying to live up to my reputation. After this episode, Kyle never said anything further to criticize me. Coffey and I entered into a mutual professional admiration society. Perseverance had paid off.

One last word on this disease: *In 1971* [I was in practice and Dr. Coffey had stepped down as Chairman of Surgery] . . . *Coffey delivered Georgetown's forty-seventh annual Kober Lecture, speaking on the Management of Hyperparathyroidism—as he remarked, an appropriate subject.*[26]

At this well-attended lecture, masterfully delivered by Coffey, my thoughts drifted to my continuing interest in hyperparathyroidism: "I have come full circle in my understanding and knowledge of this disease!"

It was now early February 1964 and I was still at Arlington Hospital. Every Friday, the entire medical and surgical staff, mostly doctors in private practice in Northern Virginia, would gather in the dining room for lunch and a presentation. Once a month it was a staff meeting, and the other Fridays it was a clinical conference, with the junior resident from Georgetown, by tradition, setting up the conference. The admitting staff was excellent, consisting of many doctors well-trained in academic medical centers. The conferences usually were of good caliber. On this particular rotation, I had time to think and prepare well.

The first two were conventional conferences, with outside guest speakers. One was on *idiopathic thrombocytopenia purpura* (ITP) a serious and often fatal bleeding disorder in which the body gobbles up its own platelets.[27] I had been able to line up Dr. Edward Adelson, a clinical professor from the George Washington University Medical Center, as the guest speaker. We had a young school teacher with this disease on the floors, and she agreed to be presented in person. The conference went well, and Dr. Adelson, an expert in the disease, acquitted himself extremely well. The other conference was on *gastrointestinal (GI) bleeding*, a common problem then. Drs. Irving Brick, director of gastroenterology, and Thomas C. Lee, general surgeon and associate of Coffey, both of Georgetown, gave an excellent discussion on the topic. It was said in those days that you could judge the quality of a hospital by the mortality from acute GI bleeding, and both Brick and Lee emphasized this and the importance of a team effort in the successful management of this condition.

I had one more conference to arrange. I decided to pattern it on the Thursday evening Georgetown cardiology conference and went to great lengths to produce my last Arlington conference. First, I requested 90 minutes instead of the usual hour, and Dolan granted my request with ease. I wanted a topic of exciting interest to both medical and surgical people. I thought about it and settled on the preoperative medical evaluation of patients for general surgery. I hoped to present four live patients to an outstanding expert in front of the entire group. I was able to achieve all my objectives. Dr. Modestino Crisci-tiello, one of the three greats from Georgetown Cardiology, agreed to be the guest speaker. He was magnificent, the conference a great success and I was elated. Everybody was happy, particularly Dr. Dolan, who did not fail to express his appreciation. The conference was animated by a degree of audience participation that I have rarely witnessed. Dr. Harvey heard about the conference, and I heard from Dr. Harvey, who was complimentary of my efforts, thanking me for trying to extend the spirit of the Thursday evening cardiology conference.

I departed Arlington Hospital with a heavy heart but with pleasant memories of my days there. A few years later, while in full-time practice and clinically active on the volunteer staff at Georgetown, I learned through the Georgetown grapevine that Donald M. Knowlan, M.D., was being considered for the new full-time position of chief of medicine and director of medical education at Arlington Hospital. Knowlan, a graduate of the Harvey fellowship, a protege of Harvey and a full-timer on the Georgetown staff in the department of medicine, was born for such a position. He was a fine clinician, a terrific teacher, a happy fellow with a good sense of humor and an ardent Redskins fan who became the team physician. Don seemed to entertain no ambition in life other than being an outstanding medical educator. I called Dr. Dolan and told him that, in my humble opinion, Don and Arlington would be a marriage made in heaven. It was, and it lasted over 30 years. I do not think that my call carried any weight, but I have always felt good about my endorsement of Don.

It was now May, 1964. I was back at Georgetown on the private floors, in fine form and excellent spirits. I had been thinking about the future and began to formulate my plans. I was getting married on July 19, 1964, only a few weeks away. I would take a senior residency year and strive to get the Georgetown clinical cardiac fellowship preparatory to going into private practice. I did not consider academic medicine as a career; clinical medicine seemed to be my forte rather than research or lab investigation. I felt that my talents were best suited for private practice, with a close academic affiliation. Additionally, mother's simple and old fashioned concept of a doctor preyed on my mind. She could not understand what a full-time position in a medical center was all about. To her, one became a doctor, entered practice, saw patients, and made a nice living. There were objective reasons for doing just that: mother was still working, our finances were dwindling again, John was still in medical training and I was getting married. Further in my heart, I knew that I didn't want to spend my career doing academic medicine as I enjoyed seeing patients too much. In the end, the extent of my mother's influence on my choice was minimal. As part of my plans, I would take my year of senior residency at Georgetown. It was mine for the asking.

Enter Dan Mintz, M.D. He had been an endocrine fellow with Kyle and Canary, and had recently become director of the Georgetown medical service at DC General Hospital. After many years, the venerable Sol Katz had departed that venue to become chief of medicine at the VA Hospital. With his departure, there was a large vacuum and big shoes to fill. Dan Mintz had the "smarts," the drive, the ambition and the deep intellectual equipment for the position. He persevered in enticing Georgetown house officers to come over to DC General.

He found a receptive audience in Henry Safrit and me. Henry and I had become best friends. We both subscribed to the notion that ideal medical training was best obtained by a combination of clinical tours at both private and city hospitals. Dan Mintz played up this angle.

He was articulate, enthusiastic and convincing. He told us it was time "to sever the umbilical cord, round out your medical education, get the experience which only city hospital patients can offer and become thoroughly tested physicians." Dan Mintz promised us "a banner year."

Henry decided to spend his entire elective time with Dr. Paul McCurdy, the dynamic, first-rate hematologist at DC General, and Dan Mintz agreed forthwith. In my case, there would be no problems with leave time for my forthcoming wedding. To facilitate things on my behalf, he would have me begin an elective with him. And he would also arrange a two-month rotation with Hugh V. Pipberger, M.D., the Mount Alto Hospital pioneer in vector cardiography, something I much desired. Dan Mintz even dangled before my eyes the chief residency of the Georgetown medical service at DC General for the following year. This, I thought, would be a good fall-back position if I did not obtain the cardiology fellowship. I had not told anyone of my intention to apply for it, not even Dan. Henry and I both accepted Mintz's offer.

It was early July 1964. Henry, as a junior resident, and, I, as a senior resident, were now at DC General. Henry, who had begun his long hematology elective, was highly impressed by McCurdy's breadth of clinical knowledge and astonished by the wealth of cases. Henry was happy. I served an endocrine elective with Dan Mintz, and gradually, little things rang alarm bells in my head and caused me some concern. Dan was cordial and jovial, something that was out of character for him. It also struck me that he did not seem to have his heart in the Georgetown medical service at DC General.

On my first day on the service, his efficient secretary wished me well on my approaching marriage and told me that Mintz was giving me three weeks off, instead of the two weeks which I had requested, and added that Amy and I were invited for dinner by Dr. and Mrs Mintz at their home for the following Saturday. They were perfect hosts. The evening was pleasant and Amy, in particular, found Dan Mintz charming and congenial. Things were too good to be true.

As the senior resident on endocrine elective, I was in and out of Mintz's roomy office. I noticed that the setting of the office was changing under my very eyes. I initially thought it was my imagination. The place was developing a vacant look, more so on a daily basis, and I shared my thoughts with Amy and Henry. We could not fathom what was happening; but, something felt wrong. It was soon time for the wedding, and I forgot about my observations, Mintz and DC General.

The marriage was a traditional Jewish family affair, attended by many relatives, including those from Canada. However, it was not a big blow-out wedding, and I was grateful for that. The ceremony and the reception took place at Mount Sinai Temple on Military Road. John, my brother, was best man, and Henry Safrit was my main attendant and chief usher. Amy and I honeymooned in Florida. The wonderful three week disconnect from medicine was my first real break since the fall of 1958, when I had entered medical school. Amy and I established residence on Battery Lane in Bethesda, Maryland, not far from NIH and soon I was back at DC General, while Amy began a research job at George Washington University.

I found life on the Georgetown medical service at DC General much as when I left. It was now almost mid-August 1964, and my previous observations were, if anything, more dramatic, especially the empty-looking office of Mintz. A few days later, a special meeting was called. Mintz made the announcement: "I have just accepted an offer that I could not refuse in good conscience." The shocker was in the timing. He was leaving town in December for a new academic position in Pittsburgh, and, since the position involved sophisticated research, he would be out of DC General in two weeks to begin intensive training at NIH. A sense of betrayal for many in the audience accompanied this news. Henry Safrit was vocal and spoke up on behalf of all house officers enticed to come to DC General by Dan Mintz. He expressed anger, dismay and outrage. Not one of the full-time staff people, colleagues of Mintz, came to his defense. There was no defense. It is a well-known no/no in academic medicine for house officers or staff doctors to violate the traditional date of July 1, in the absence of overriding personal reasons, to move from one job to another.

I completed my elective with Dr. Mintz. The long Labor Day weekend was soon gone and so was Dan Mintz. My newlywed frame of mind enabled me to remain on good terms with him during those last few weeks.

We not only survived, we prospered and had a very good year at DC General. The reasons were several. The camaraderie among house officers was greater than I had seen at Georgetown. Team spirit was alive and well, not only among the medical people, but also between all the Georgetown services such as surgery, Ob-Gyn, orthopedics and others. Furthermore, there existed a healthy competitive spirit among the three schools clinically maintaining DC General, Georgetown, George Washington and Howard universities.

*This was a time when the chiefs of services of the three medical schools and their next in command would appear regularly at DC General for teaching rounds, consultations, and surgery, providing their expertise to the community, house staff, and students.*[28]

Mintz's place was taken by Robert Donohoe, M.D., chief of pulmonary service, a veteran at DC General, a protege of Sol Katz, and the nicest person in the world. This appointment immediately calmed the troops. Irving Brick, M.D., director of the Georgetown gastrointestinal division, had been named the acting chairman of medicine at Georgetown when poor health led Kyle to resign. Brick was a diamond in the rough, an excellent clinician, a supremely confident individual and a humorous character. He immediately and wisely took great interest in the Georgetown service at DC General. Of note, Dr. Brick had served his own internship at DC General years ago. Under Brick's leadership, Donohoe, Marcus, McCurdy and the other full-timers redoubled their efforts on our behalf. Prodded by Uncle Irv. (Brick's nickname), all the Georgetown greats came over to further superior clinical teaching. Brick, Harvey, Schreiner, Katz, Keliher and their associates all came. Canary, the brilliant Director of the Division of Endocrinology at Georgetown, and his fellows covered the endocrine service after Mintz's departure. The Georgetown division of rheumatology was established in 1958 and Nathan Zwaifler, M.D., joined the full-time faculty in 1959 as the director of its division. He was exciting, enthusiastic, and created a strong division. He and his associates became visiting attending physicians at DC General.

We did have a banner year at DC General as Dan Mintz had promised us, despite, or maybe because of the way he had abandoned us. In his own way, Dan Mintz probably did us a favor. Henry was so pleased at DC General that he signed up to stay there for his senior residency year.

There never will be another hospital like DC General. The midnight snack—a free dinner for all the people on call at *the General*—was a popular daily event. Social life between nurses and doctors flourished, but not for me anymore. I had become a married man and took my marriage vows seriously. One Saturday evening, a group of us on call were watching an old movie on a big TV screen in the social room, when two men in coveralls walked in with a pushcart. "We came to fix the TV and need to take it to the shop," said they. Not one of us objected. They must have been aware that doctors are not well grounded in "street smarts." They left with the TV, and it was not until a few days later that we realized that the big screen TV, a novelty in those days, had been working perfectly well. It goes without saying that the TV was never seen again. Like Dan Mintz, it had disappeared.

Although DC General is no more, it is well remembered by many medical people who received wonderful training there. Sol Katz, who spent many years there, was fond of saying: "It was home to me."

My last elective of the year was to take me to Mt. Alto Veterans Hospital with Dr. Hubert Pipberger, cardiologist and researcher in the discipline of *Vector Cardiography* (VCG). This field of study is the graphic recording of the electrical activity of the heart in spatial projections. Hubert V. Pipberger, M.D., was a pioneer and renowned expert in the field. He and his brilliant wife, who had a doctorate in Mathematical Sciences, also investigated methods of displaying and storing medical data on computers, both hard data such as ECGs and VCGs, as well as soft data such as symptoms and physical findings. Banks of large, old-fashioned computers lined room after room. These main-frame computers operated at all times, processing digital patient information. I desired to learn computerized medicine and wanted badly to learn vectorcardiography, having read and reread Grant's classical VCG textbook. Pipberger was challenging the principles advanced by Grant. Although this dispute left me somewhat confused, Pipberger tutored me one on one. I also spent hours in the library trying to digest articles on VCG, but if truth be told, vectorcardiography and I were not meant for each other. I did not fully understand it. The phonocardiogram and the vectorcardiogram never had a chance to come into their own as they were both soon supplanted by the versatile echocardiogram. The dramatic advances in the latter have transformed clinical cardiology. Only the cardiology group at Emory University Medical Center still uses VCGs to any extent.

In early May 1965, I was coasting to the finish line at DC General, when one evening, I received a personal call from Dr. Harvey at home, informing me that I had been accepted for the cardiology fellowship. I could not believe it. Because of my familiarity with Georgetown, Harvey told me that I would begin on the consult service, considered the busiest cardiac rotation of the fellowship. My spirits were high and I was looking forward to becoming a cardiac fellow with Harvey on July 1, 1965.

Out of the blue, one day in late May 1965, I was paged and directed to report to the DC General security office. I thought it probably had something to do with the TV incident. Much to my surprise, a security officer casually handed me a legal summons, but made me sign no papers or registry. At first, I was certain that the entire thing was a mistake, but on careful reading, it became clear that I was being sued for malpractice along with John Maylath, M.D., the chief urology resident. The plaintiff was a Lorton Reformatory inmate who had been a patient of mine a few months previously, when he was in the DC Jail. I remembered the patient well. We saw him daily in the jail infirmary for several weeks. He was a drug addict with bland scrotal swelling and possible tuberculosis. He had been thoroughly worked-up, and though nothing definite was found, he had been presented to our attending physician and to the appropriate consultants. It was their consensus that we needed to obtain an *epididymal biopsy*.[29] With the patient's written permission, the procedure was carried out uneventfully. The biopsy revealed only chronic nonspecific inflammation. The patient was treated with a course of cortisone and three weeks of broad-spectrum antibiotics. The scrotal swelling gradually subsided. He was transferred back to Lorton, Virginia, from whence he came. I had been particularly nice to him, as he had seemed to be a gentle soul who had gone wrong. There had been no patient-doctor relation incidents, and I had not detected any bad vibrations from him.

He sued me, as the captain of the medical ship, and also named Dr. Maylath. He was acting as his own lawyer, suing us for $40,000.00 each, and was giving us 30 days to legally respond to his contentions that we had "withheld pain medications from him and experimented on him." The security officer who handed me the official papers said to me: "Don't worry, we get a lot of these; the DC Counsel's office will take care of it."

Three weeks later, having heard nothing, I went to talk to Robert Donohoe, director of the pulmonary service and the acting chief of Georgetown medicine at DC General. He went to work on my behalf and established that my case "had fallen between the cracks" in the DC Counsel's office as there was no trace of the case, and no one knew anything about it. Dr. Donohoe, after making several calls, arranged for me to meet with Dr. Bruce Shnider, the assistant dean of the Georgetown University School of Medicine, at 8:00 A.M. the very next day. My brother, John, had experienced an unpleasant incident with Dr. Shnider, and I did not relish the idea of going to him for help.[30]

Dr. Shnider, reputed to be aloof and dour, readily came to my rescue in my moment of need. "Oscar, we won't let you down," said he as soon as I walked into his office. He talked to me over coffee and doughnuts. He was affable, gracious, businesslike, and saved the day for me.

Dr. Shnider had the famed legal firm of Edward Bennett Williams *et al*, the Georgetown defense attorneys, take my case. "A malpractice suit has to be killed before it reaches a jury; otherwise, all bets are off," said our counsel.

He promptly established that the summons had not been properly served; the suit was thus quashed on technical grounds, without prejudice.

Dr. Shnider wore another hat, that of a medical oncologist. In my early days of practice, I consulted him on my cancer patients until he moved out of the area. Bruce Shnider was a very decent man.

Things were now clear for me to begin my cardiology fellowship on July 1, 1965.

## NOTES

1. The medical center is now under the umbrella of MedStar Health.

2. See Chapter 15.

3. *Steroid* is a generic term for *cortisone*.

4. *Rhabdomyolysis* is the dissolution of muscle due to prolonged pressure.

5. A *cut-down* is the surgical exposure of a vein.

6. *Autopsies* are postmortem examinations performed by the Department of Pathology.

7. In May 1963, I returned to 2-East for a second two-month rotation. It was so much easier than my first one that I actually enjoyed it. The right state of mind was everything.

8. See chapter 15.

9. Personal communication from Dr. Clifton Gruver, October 2003.

10. "Patrick" is intentionally a fictitious name.

11. John fulfilled his military obligation in the Public Health Service. He was fortunate to be assigned to the Institute of Allergies and Infectious Diseases at the National Institutes of Health (NIH) in near-by Bethesda.

12. An *attending physician* is the physician of record who is legally responsible for the patient. A *teaching attending*, on the other hand, is presented cases for discussion only, and carries no primary legal responsibility for the patient.

13. Taken from the Hepatitis B Foundation "Founders' Award," presented to Dr. Baruch Blumberg, M.D., Ph.D. on April 21, 2001. See htpp://www.hepb.org/10th founders.html, 1 (accessed 2/24/2003).

14. Skin test for *tuberculosis.*

15. *Blood-borne tuberculosis.*

16. He was in practice with Dr. Oler. A few years later, I would become their partner.

17. In 1968, Caro Luhrs left Georgetown to become a White House Fellow and later a high official in the Department of Agriculture. She developed a rather high media profile. It was a big loss for Rath, Georgetown and me, but she became and has remained a loyal family friend. We often reminisce about those days. Hematology served me well in private practice, where *anemia* and other blood diseases are frequent findings.

18. See Chapter 4.

19. See Chapter 7.

20. Personal communication from Caro Luhrs, March 2003.

21. In medical parlance, an *elective* is a *clinical rotation* in a field of one's preference and choice. An elective is usually no longer than 4 to 8 weeks.

22. A *fellowship* is postresidency training in a sub-specialty, lasting at least a year and, nowadays, two or more years.

23. Stapleton, *Upward Journey*, 131.

24. Enos *et al*, "Coronary Disease Among United States Soldiers Killed In Korea,", *JAMA* (July18,1953): 2859–2862. Assessing Enos's work in 1986, Jack P. Strong wrote *The article appeared at a time when mortality from coronary disease was reaching a zenith in the United States and being recognized worldwide as a modern epidemic. This widely cited publication dramatically showed that atherosclerotic changes* [hardening of the arteries] *appear in the coronary arteries years and decades before the age at which coronary disease(CHD) becomes a clinically recognized problem.* See Jack P. Strong, "Coronary Atherosclerosis in Soldiers, A Clue to the Natural History of Atherosclerosis in the Young," *JAMA* 256, no. 20 (November 28, 1986): 2863–2866.

25. Before there were emergency room physicians, the E.R. was staffed by well-trained, experienced nurses, and us. Young physicians just starting out in practice often "hung around" the E.R. to pick up new patients.

26. Barry, "Surgeons," 291.

27. *Platelets* are blood cells involved in clotting.

28. Personal communication from Tom Magovern, M.D., Professor of Ob-Gyn at Georgetown, March 2003.

29. The *epididymis* is a para-testicular structure, not infrequently involved in acute or chronic infections.

30. See Chapter 14.

## Chapter Seventeen

# W. Proctor Harvey, M.D.

A desirable medical sub-specialty fellowship is composed of two players—a master clinician-teacher and an eager pupil. During my cardiac fellowship at Georgetown, I grew in the light shed by accomplished clinical diagnostician, medical innovator and teacher W. Proctor Harvey, M.D.

It was my good fortune to have Dr. Harvey, the master of the stethoscope, teach me not only sophisticated auscultation—the art of listening to the heart with a stethoscope—but also the whole spectrum of clinical heart disease. As he educated me in cardiology, he also taught me to appreciate clinical excellence and to temper science with empathy. Dr. Harvey, by his example and teaching, influenced how I conducted my life. He was the best of mentors.

Dr. Harvey was born on April 18, 1918, in Lynchburg, Virginia. He was raised there, attended Lynchburg College, and studied medicine at Duke University School of Medicine in Durham, N.C., where he soon became an avid reader of medical literature.

> *Proctor Harvey's decision to pursue cardiology began as he completed his internship at Harvard's Peter Bent Brigham Hospital in Boston, where he met the legendary cardiologist Samuel A. Levine. Indeed, it was Levine who inspired Harvey to pursue a fellowship in cardiology . . . . Harvey began his training as the 1st fellow in cardiology at Brigham Hospital, becoming as well Levine's 1st fellow . . . and perhaps [his] most beloved pupil . . . .*
>
> *While still in medical school at Duke University . . . Dr. Harvey read Dr. Levine's textbook* Clinical Heart Disease, *noting that 'it read like a story book.'*[1]

While serving with Sam Levine, Dr. Harvey co-authored a best selling textbook with him, entering a path that led to prolific medical authorship.[2]

[Harvey] *is perhaps best known for the classics,* Clinical Auscultation of the Heart *and* Cardiac Pearls, *both of which set the standard for medical education in cardiovascular diagnosis, evaluation and care.*[3]

Both of two classics were further augmented by *Classic Teachings in Clinical Cardiology*, a two volume collection of 62 essays by 50 former cardiac fellows and four associates, published in 1996 as a *Festschrift* celebrating Proctor Harvey.[4]

In parallel fashion, the W. Proctor Harvey Foundation was established in Washington, DC, by Dr. Harvey's fellows some 40 years ago. The Foundation has funded various significant programs, including an endowed Harvey Professorship of Cardiology at Georgetown.

In 1946, Dr. Harold Jeghers, the newly appointed Chairman of Georgetown's Department of Medicine, needed a physician to head a Division of Cardiology at Georgetown. Dr. Charles Rath, who had come from the Peter Bent Brigham Hospital in 1949 to become director of Georgetown hematology, recommended Dr. Harvey to Dr. Jeghers for this position.

*Jeghers offered him* [Dr. Harvey] *a free hand at Georgetown . . . . Harvey began the formidable task of building Georgetown's division of cardiology.*[5]

Dr. Rath would later say, "The rest is history. Proc [Harvey's nickname] has been running well ever since, just letting 'Proc' be 'Proc.'" To me, he has always been Dr. Harvey.

Dr. Harvey achieved fame by bringing the time-honored skill of auscultation into the modern era. His talent, passion and genius changed cardiac auscultation.

The monoaural stethoscope, an instrument made from cedar and brass, and looking much like a small telescope, was invented by René Laënnec, in 1816.[6]

Although an instrument which allowed greater precision in auscultation, acceptance of the stethoscope was not neither easy nor rapid: "Before the invention of the stethoscope . . . the physician put his ear on the patient's chest to listen to the heart and lungs. Many doctors were offended by the idea of something mechanical inserted between themselves and their patients."[7]

For his part, Laënnec credited the invention of the stethoscope to his solicitude for the modesty of women, stating:

*Chez les femmes, l'auscultation immédiate n'est pas practicable dans toute la région occupée par les mammelles . . . .*[In women, direct auscultation is not feasible in the entire area occupied by the breasts].[8]

Laëennec's shyness with women was featured in a *Harvard Medical Alumni Bulletin*: "Laënnec, embarrassed to place his ear against the chest of a well-endowed woman . . . ."[9]

In Laënnec's own words:

*I was consulted by a young woman. . . application of ear . . . inadmissible by the age and sex of the patient . . . I rolled a quire of paper into a sort of cylinder and applied one end of it to the region of the heart and the other to my ear . . . and was not a little surprised and pleased, to find that I could perceive the action of the heart in a manner more clear and distinct than . . . through the immediate application of the ear . . . .[10]*

The rudimentary device of 1816 was a predecessor to today's binaural stethoscope. Over the years, there were many clever and innovative modifications to Laënnec's design. Dr. Harvey, in the mid-1950s, ingeniously conceived and produced a most sophisticated three-head instrument, *The Harvey Stethoscope*, an important element in his approach to patients. The first Harvey stethoscope was designed by Dr. Harvey and manufactured by the Cefaly Research Corporation of Brentwood, MD. It was known as the *Harvey Cefaly Stethoscope*. Later Tyco, a well-known manufacturer of medical equipment, took over its production.

Very similar to the standard first head of a conventional stethoscope, Dr. Harvey's second stethoscope head, a corrugated diaphragm, helps to bring out faint heart activity. By varying the pressure, one may assess a wider range of frequencies than with the bell or flat diaphragm.

For me, the second piece, an exquisitely designed small bell, is the winning feature of the Harvey scope. This bell, when properly applied, creates a sealed hollow dome on the chest wall, an ideal acoustic chamber for low-frequency sounds.

The third head, of course, is a flat diaphragm.

I have only owned Harvey scopes, at first out of loyalty to be sure, but second because for me the Harvey scope has always been the best. Clifton R. Gruver, M.D., now retired and one of the most respected Washington, DC internists, adds: "I always used, and still have, my original Harvey stethoscope—I agree, none better."[11]

There are the first and second heart sounds, the so-called "*lub-dub*" sounds, easily heard by everyone and universally recognized as the sounds produced by a normally functioning heart. Dr. Harvey emphasized detecting low-frequency heart sounds. Sometimes these sounds are normal physiological findings, but often they are signs of heart disease, then called *gallops*.

*Proc made better use of gallops than anyone heretofore, distinguishing the different gallops, defining the significance of each variety and so describing the character of each type as to facilitate detection. All Harvey fellows could hear gallops.*[12]

Dr. Harvey liked the concept of "tuning in", i.e. listening specifically for low frequency sounds. To hear faint gallops, one must "tune in." Such gallops —third, (mnemonic, TENNE-ssee), and fourth, (ken-TUCKY)— are best appreciated with only a light touch of the bell on the chest wall. Gallop sounds are easily obliterated by too much pressure and this is the reason they elude uninitiated listeners who, in their eagerness, press too hard on the stethoscope.

Some physicians, unable to appreciate gallops, have resorted to humor to cover up this gap in their auscultatory skill. Our Pathology Professor, Charles Geshickter, always prone to levity, was fond of saying: "there are more gallops heard at Georgetown than at the race track."[13]

Cardiac murmurs are sustained sounds generated by turbulence in the blood flow caused by diseased heart valves or anatomical anomalies within the heart. *Bruit*, French for noise, has been adopted by cardiologists to signify the murmur heard over partially obstructed vessels.

Back in the early 1960s, we were seeing many women with *mitral stenosis* (obstruction of the mitral valve, the valve between the upper and lower chambers of the left heart), a sequel of rheumatic fever, once a prevalent condition, and causing progressive clinical disability in these patients. Closed-heart surgery was available to relieve the symptoms of severe mitral stenosis; Georgetown's Charles Hufnagel, M.D., an early pioneer of cardiovascular surgery, was a master of this operation. In those days before sophisticated diagnostic studies, the severity of mitral stenosis was determined clinically. Cardiac surgery at Georgetown antedated *cardiac catheterization* and Proctor Harvey referred many patients for cardiac surgery solely based on clinical findings. The surgeon was rarely misled by Harvey's evaluation.

*Proc also made much use of the mitral opening snap. Proc revived our understanding of this sign and, as with gallops, made better use of it than anyone else.*[14]

Harvey also elucidated the detection and significance of systolic (the contraction phase of the heart) clicks, common extraneous heart sounds.

In the summer of 1950, Dr. Harvey arrived at Georgetown together with the medical class of 1954. Its yearbook would be dedicated to W. Proctor Harvey.

*Four years ago we came to Georgetown with college cap and gown so freshly set aside. To learn of medicine was our goal . . . W. Proctor Harvey came to Georgetown as we, four years ago. Year by year our admiration and respect for him have grown. Whether in the classroom, conference, or at the hospital*

*bedside, he strove to give individual attention, never tiring of repetition and the*
*difficulties of the less gifted. His teaching aids and personal enthusiasm are*
*well-known to all of us and 'Proc' has become a symbol of quiet leadership by*
*his zeal, selflessness and gentle ways . . . . It is with the deepest gratitude and*
*appreciation that the class of 1954 dedicates this* Grand Rounds *to you, W. Proc-*
*tor Harvey.*[15]


Dr. Harvey had introduced me, as he did all Georgetown medical students,
to his *five finger approach to cardiovascular diagnosis*: the fingers being medical *history, physical exam, ECG, chest x-ray* and *lab tests*. This analytic
method stressed using the head, the eyes, the ears, and the hands, with Dr. Harvey assigning the greatest significance to the history and the physical exam. Dr.
Harvey likened the history to the thumb because the thumb is the most important finger. In parallel fashion, doctors and occupational therapists specializing
in disabilities of the hand focus on the thumb as the "brain" of the hand.

Every day of cardiac fellowship reaffirmed his principles as Dr. Harvey animated his teachings in his own inimitable way; precepts became living and
memorable teaching pearls. Under Dr. Harvey, assimilating the fine points of
extra-heart sounds such as gallops, opening snaps and clicks and the intricacies of heart murmurs was a labor of love, passed on with joy and humor.

J. Willis Hurst, a clinical cardiology giant who became Chairman of Medicine at Emory University School of Medicine, recognized in the late 1940s
the potential of young Harvey: "'I was across town at the Massachusetts General Hospital when he was at the Brigham. The messages were already clear.
He was going to be a leader.'"[16]

Harvey is still a leader, influencing by example, teaching by example and
leading an exemplary life. He possesses the rare gift of making others feel at
ease with themselves—the orderly, the janitor, the senator, the businessman,
the intern, the medical student, the ambassador—and always, the patient. He
has a miraculous way with patients.

Dr. Harvey's bedside manner is that exquisite courtesy so characteristic of
a true Virginia gentleman, a southern version of the Boston gentleman. He
never fails to win over the patient as he readjusts the head pillow to be certain that the patient's neck is well supported while sometimes rolling a towel
under the patient's neck. Next Harvey, sitting rather than standing by the patient, touches him by gently taking his pulse and gains the full confidence, co-
operation and approval of the patient being evaluated before a group. The
silent attention to the patient goes on while the house officer presents the patient's history and general physical findings.

Then and only then will Dr. Harvey proceed with the actual examination of
the heart by inspection, palpation, percussion and last of all auscultation. Dr.

Harvey has always favored this systematic approach. The patient, already relaxed and comfortable, is reassured by expressions such as, *You would be the rare patient if we could not help you . . . regular, strong pulse . . . I have fibrillated myself. . . . your doctor can take care of my family . . . benign innocent murmur . . . it does not mean anything . . .* I smiled at the sense of *déjà vu* when I came across these familiar gestures and words in the erudite and touching history-of-medicine article by Kimara March already cited.[17]

As for me, an ex-*schmatta* boy of the old country, I always felt at ease with Dr. Harvey. He was always amiable with me. Remarkably, Dr. Harvey achieved his reputation with a good-natured disposition, an easy going demeanor and unique personal attributes, disproving the old adage that nice guys finish last.

In his quiet way, Dr. Harvey made his personal concern and regard for me evident one Tuesday evening in the city of Baltimore. Our family was gathered for a birthday at *Tio Pepe,* a much frequented restaurant. As we were taking our seats, I spotted Dr. Harvey in an adjacent large private dining room. Iintrigued, I walked over, peeked into the room and discreetly contemplated the scene. He was receiving an award from the Johns Hopkins University School of Medicine. Not wanting to disturb the proceedings, I backed away and rejoined my party, making myself a mental note to send Dr. Harvey a congratulatory letter.

Later, the evening over, I walked out of the restaurant with my sister-in-law, Risa, not only a professor of pathology at Hopkins but also an extremely attractive woman. The rest of my family was still in the restaurant. Dr. Harvey was outside on the sidewalk talking to friends, and I went over to introduce Risa and to congratulate him. But I noted the hint of a frown on his face.

He hesitated a moment, then asked, "Where is Amy?"

"Inside Tio Pepe," I replied.

He said nothing, but his expression spoke volumes. It was asking,"What are you doing in Baltimore with another woman?"

A few minutes later, when Amy walked out, Dr. Harvey's usual amiability returned.

Professor Emeritus of Medicine and Cardiology at Georgetown, John F. Stapleton, M.D., Harvey's first cardiology fellow, and an exemplary and decent person, was Medical Director of the University Hospital and Associate Dean of the Georgetown University School of Medicine. He served as Dean for one year during an interregnum. Dr. Stapleton, who has always impressed me as inherently practicing the art of fairness to its ultimate dimension, recounts his own "Harvey" story:

*The Professor pro Tempore* [visiting distinguished professor] *concept, introduced by Harvey, was used by the department of medicine for many years thereafter. The Harvey manner reminds me of Sam Levine's visit to Georgetown as*

*Professor pro Tempore in 1951. As chief resident at the time, I had to guide Dr.*
*Levine around during the day. I thanked him for taking the time out of his busy*
*life to visit Georgetown. He said* Well, Proc Harvey asked me. I couldn't say no
to Proc. He never said no to anyone at the Peter Bent Brigham Hospital during
the years he was there, including teachers, colleagues, maids and janitors.
*Levine told Proc that it was a good thing he was not born a woman because he*
*didn't know how to say no.*[18]

Rotating through the cardiac consultation service at Georgetown Hospital
was a very busy experience for fellows since all consultation requests were
originally handled by the cardiac fellow. Everyone seemed to get a cardiac
consultation. Thus, during July and August 1965, all these requests were fil-
tered through me. We also took pediatric cardiac consultations, since an independent pediatric cardiology service did not yet exist at Georgetown. As a
fellow responsible in part for teaching, when the nature of the case permitted,
I sometimes let a student, an intern or a resident do the initial work-up. I was
accountable, however, for going over every consultation before the presentation to the attending cardiologist of the day.

During the consultation service, every fellow thought he ran the Thursday
night conferences. Dr. Harvey, in his gentle, generous and courteous southern
Virginia manner, allowed this idea to germinate in each fellow. The conferences always went well because of their detailed preparation at a preliminary
planning session late Tuesday afternoon in Dr. Harvey's office. Meticulous
implementation of the arrangements was the responsibility of the fellow on
the cardiac consultation service. The fellow also made the introductions and
presented the history of the patient, who was then interviewed, and examined.
Next, the case was discussed by one of the Georgetown cardiology department's clinical faculty members. Dr. Harvey discouraged "a single clinical
star" conference, preferring "a different star for each case."

In 1966, Colonel Jules L. Bedynek Jr. was chief of cardiology at the Walter Reed Army Medical Center. Dr. Harvey, being at Walter Reed one morning to make teaching rounds, subsequently invited the colonel to begin presenting cases at Georgetown's weekly conferences. A new tradition was born
with physicians from the National Institutes of Health, Bethesda Naval and
Walter Reed medical centers, as well as other distinguished guests from far
and wide, now participating regularly in the conferences.

The event took place every Thursday from 8:00 to 10:00 P.M., with four
cases being presented and discussed each week. Electronic stethoscopes and
sophisticated audiovisual equipment allowed audience participation to the
fullest extent in the spacious, then very modern Gorman Auditorium. A pleasant and collegial ambience prevailed with all attendees being invited to an informal pre-conference dinner held at 6:30 P.M.

*One evening, Dr. Eugene Braunwald* [Head of the National Heart Institute & later Chief of Medicine at the Peter Bent Brigham & Women's Hospital in Boston] *attended a Thursday night conference and had dinner with the staff and fellows. He made a few comments, including the observation that Harvey ran the best fellowship program in the United States.*[19]

The Thursday evening conferences grew in popularity and attendance, attracting numerous physicians from far and wide, Harvey directing the conference with a firm hand. The genius of Dr. Harvey was that no one, including Dr. Harvey, seemed to appreciate this fact. "The conference runs itself," people said.

Dr. Harvey nurtured this weekly event, his brain child, with constant attention to details, periodic refinements and new improvements. We soon had closed-circuit TV and electronic and teaching videos. The *palpator,* an ingenious device developed by Jim Waters, M.D., one of Dr. Harvey's acolytes, came into use in the mid-1960s. This new gadget, an electronic small box-pad, transmitted the motions of the patient's chest wall as the audience members put their own hands on the pad and felt everything the demonstrator experienced. Likewise, the *Cardiology Patient Simulator*, a computerized mannequin, named "Harvey" and brilliantly conceived and developed by Dr. Michael S. Gordon, one of the six fellows in my class, mimicked classic cardiac conditions and became a popular teaching aid.

The effectiveness of Dr. Harvey's teachings was exemplified for me on the cardiac surgical service where I was rotating as the cardiology fellow. Mrs B., a middle-aged married woman with teenage children, had been referred directly to Dr. Charles Hufnagel, and she had been admitted with the diagnosis of *mitral regurgitation, class IV*, for consideration of *mitral valve replacement.*[20] This was a tall order in those early days of mitral valve replacement, as the danger of the operation made it somewhat prohibitive. Wisely, the referring physician had requested a pre-operative consultation with Dr. Harvey who saw her immediately on the evening of admission. I presented the patient to Dr. Harvey in front of a small group, with the diagnosis seemingly not in question.

Normally one feels a gentle, localized tap under the left breast, and this is the *point of maximal impulse (P.M.I.)* of the heart against the chest wall, due to *early left ventricular contraction* (main chamber of the heart). As the heart becomes affected by disease, the P.M.I. gets displaced and presents a more vigorous and prolonged impulse, readily palpated by any astute physician. At times the right ventricle, usually not palpable, can be appreciated along the lower left sternal border. One can usually distinguish right from left ventricular movements.

Dr. Harvey immediately became suspicious of the admitting diagnosis as he felt that the history was more compatible with an *obstructed valve* than with a *regurgitating valve*. Further, on palpation, he felt that the entire chest was occupied by the right ventricle and that the left ventricle was "under-represented." And on auscultation, Harvey determined that the loud murmur represented tricuspid insufficiency, a right heart event, stating that "the bedside findings just don't fit with *mitral regurg*. Let's look for *silent mitral stenosis*."

He then turned the patient into the *left lateral decubitus position* (halfway on the left side) and for a long time looked for a sign of a left ventricle, saying to the patient, "please, turn a little more to your left side." He finally exclaimed, "I can feel a *diminished left ventricular impulse*," and asked us to all listen over it. To our utter amazement, the classic acoustic events of mitral stenosis were there for all to hear. Indeed, this patient had *severe mitral stenosis* with *secondary right ventricular failure* and a murmur of *tricuspid insufficiency*. Replacing the mitral valve would have been the wrong operation. Instead, she underwent closed heart surgery by Dr. Hufnagel who performed a successful finger opening of her mitral valve. This operation resulted in an impressive decrease in the debility which Mrs. B. had been experiencing and she could now await in relative comfort the maturing of mitral valve replacement into a technically more refined and safer operation. Dr. Harvey, in his low-profile manner, had performed a clinical *tour de force*. In the days of *mitral commissurotomy* (opening of the mitral valve without replacing it), a *loud apical systolic murmur of mitral regurgitation* was considered a contra-indication to surgery. This case exemplifies a patient with tricuspid regurgitation masquerading as mitral regurgitation and—but for Dr. Harvey's acumen—a near miss of valuable surgery.

Dr. Harvey's teaching postulates were never dull dogma but always rather logical and fun to learn. He taught bedside medicine with passion, enthusiasm and facility. This case made the truth and wisdom of Dr. Harvey's clinical competence abundantly clear to me. Dr. Harvey's clinical skills rubbed off on me to some extent, and for this I will always be indebted to him. I learned a big lesson. The two big fingers of the *five-finger Harvey approach*, history and physical, have stood the test of time, and they are a cardiologist's—and any doctor's—best diagnostic tools. I was to discover that these tools, optimally sharpened by Dr. Harvey, would serve me well in practice.

The fellowship was skillfully devised by Dr. Harvey to provide six rotations; the cardiology consultation service; the pulmonary service; the cardiac lab and cardiac surgery, all at Georgetown where Dr. Recep Ari was always available for advanced ECG teaching, a big ticket item in those days. National Institutes of Health and DC General Hospital cardiology rotations were extramural. But the imprint of Dr. Harvey was on each rotation of this well-rounded and diversified program.

We came in close contact with the cardiac stars of Georgetown, excellent young instructors of the full-time faculty and prime members of the volunteer faculty. On the pulmonary service, we trained under the brilliant Kenneth Moser, M.D., a fine authority in lung diseases, and at DC General Hospital, we were fortunate to receive the attentive tutoring of Dr. Frank Marcus, a quiet, dedicated and affable clinical cardiac great, who became Chief of Cardiology at the University of Arizona.

At the National Heart Institute, we performed phono-cardiograms and presented them to "Mr. Cardiology," Dr. Eugene Braunwald. The wealth of cases on Braunwald's service was breathtaking; recording phonocardiograms on these patients taught me much. There was an added feature at the NIH. Joseph Perloff, M.D., came every Wednesday for a conference, attended by the NIH cardiology staff, and it was the job of the fellow to prepare two "tough cases" for presentation and "attempt to stump Joe."

Those were the days when *intracardiac catheterization* was beginning to come into its own in America. Catheterization involves inserting a catheter into a peripheral blood vessel and guiding it into the heart. Dye is then injected through the catheter to highlight the actual heart valves, vessels and chambers in motion. As opposed to other modalities, it is invasive and can result in complications such as bleeding, infections, vessel laceration and even death. At Georgetown, Dr. Perloff was the director of the catheterization lab. At the NIH, however, catheterization was already being done on every patient, so we had the diagnosis on the cases we presented to Dr. Perloff.

Dr. Perloff, in his careful, systematic and brilliant manner, usually arrived at the diagnosis through the Harvey five finger approach and seldom allowed himself to be stymied. With Joe, one had to stay on his wavelength or be lost. However, if one remained intellectually in tune with Dr. Perloff, one absorbed his genius at arriving with clinical cardiology points for the final diagnosis.

Now, for a patient's eye view of Harvey, enters David F. Jackson, then a receptionist at Georgetown University Hospital:

*I met Dr. Proctor Harvey in 1982 when serving as a volunteer, back-up and ECG technician in the heart station at Georgetown University Hospital. I was immediately and tremendously impressed with Dr. Harvey as a very congenial individual who I could see was highly respected as a medical professional and who was a 'diehard Redskins' fan.' Periodically I would see Dr. Harvey in the hospital, usually with several other physicians, as he went about demonstrating his expertise . . . .*

*In 1983 I had an experience with hardening of the arteries of the heart, for which I received a new treatment, angioplasty. Dr. Harvey knew about my case. I was somewhat of a* pioneer patient *with this procedure. Dr. Harvey felt that having me as a subject for an upcoming cardiology conference would be a*

*welcome addition to his program before an assembly of medical doctors in a
packed Gorman auditorium. Dr. Harvey and I engaged in a bit of humorous ban-
ter on stage as he made his presentation regarding the popularity and effectiveness of the angioplasty procedure . . .*[21]

*Angioplasty* is a non-surgical dilation of a narrowed heart vessel. A *balloon
catheter* is inflated and deflated against the obstruction, thereby compressing
it. The procedure was first carried out successfully in 1977 by Andreas Gruentzig, M.D., in Zurich, Switzerland. The procedure restores blood supply to
the vessels of the heart obstructed by hardening of the arteries, and it has become a common procedure, more frequently performed than bypass surgery.
Angioplasty led to new dawn in cardiology, and with it was born the modern
age of *interventional cardiology*, also called *transcatheter therapeutics*.

In 1985, with the premature tragic death of Dr. Gruentzig, who was by then
at Emory University Medical Center, Kenneth M. Kent, M.D., Ph.D., took
over the mantle of championing angioplasty in this country from his central
vantage point at the NIH Heart Institute, and he became one of the leaders in
this field. Dr. Harvey had the foresight to lure Dr. Kent to the full-time staff
of Georgetown University Hospital, where he performed the successful angioplasty on patient Jackson. Dr. Kent remains one of the major players at the
cutting edge of interventional cardiology.

Leave it to Dr. Harvey to be at the forefront of cardiology and to continually educate people in the medical community about advances in the realm of
heart disease. He does it in his own way, Harvey's way, a way "always built
around a patient," as David Jackson has observed.

W. Proctor Harvey, M.D., was Director of the Georgetown University
Medical Center Division of Cardiology from 1950 to the mid-1980s. Dean
Ray Mitchell comments:

*Dr. W. Proctor Harvey has recently celebrated his 51st anniversary at Georgetown
University—concurrent with the graduation of the 150th class from the School of
Medicine. In the early 1950s, Dr. Harvey was instrumental in developing innovative techniques to take bedside teaching to a full auditorium of learners; he has also
maintained that teaching throughout the subsequent fifty years.*

*He continues to teach the entire first year class and physiology graduate students
auscultation annually, and he has delivered a school and house staff-wide course
during a "Senior Colloquium" for all senior students, interns, residents and fellows. Dr. Harvey has moved his office to the front lobby of the School of Medicine,
where he actively meets and mentors students. Last year, Dr. Harvey and Laënnec
Publishing donated 1000 sets of the Harvey teaching tapes to all students at the
school and each incoming class, a kindly contribution worth $150,000.*[22]

Concurrently with his teaching activities, Dr. Harvey is working on his
*magnum opus*, the definitive cataloguing, editing and digital recording of the

prodigious collection of Harvey's tapes of heart sounds and murmurs on DVD. The message is unambiguous as Harvey, not believing in retirement, has yet to slow down.

Dr. Harvey was President of the American Heart Association from 1969 to 1970, having served previously as President of Washington Heart.[23] In 1978, the American Heart Association conferred on Dr. W. Proctor Harvey the James B. Herrick Award:

*He has exerted an extraordinary influence on modern cardiological teaching, nurturing generations of medical students and developing and conducting postgraduate training for physicians in practice throughout the United States.*

*His achievements in research into auscultation and physical assessment of the heart patient and improvements in teaching methods are measurable. Not measurable is the magnitude of his contribution in terms of those whom he has inspired to reach just a bit higher.*[24]

Deep down, nearing the end of my fellowship, I knew that I was a "thinking" doc, not a "cutting" one or an "invasive" one. In my mind, I had found my professional niche, the practice of internal medicine and cardiology. And I knew that *invasive* cardiology would not lure me. Harvey took an inordinate personal interest in his fellows and told me to follow my instincts. He wished his fellows to be competent, principled and happy physicians. In the latter part of my fellowship, several tentative offers to practice in Washington came up, but nothing definite materialized. In late May, 1966, Dr. Harvey called me in to discuss my plans for practice. He asked me what I thought of Drs. Frank MacMurray and Wesley Oler. I had been favorably impressed, to say the least, by both, but I never dreamed that these two prominent WASP Washington physicians had noticed the Jewish immigrant house officer at Georgetown.

There were two incidents which may have led to this fortuitous development. The first was the Colonel Graling episode which had occurred early during my rotation on the consultation service. At a Tuesday pre-conference session, Dr. Harvey had decided that he wanted to present Colonel Graling, a patient of Dr. Oler's. Following established Harvey routine, I called Dr. Oler to get his permission to present Colonel Graling and to invite him to the conference and to the pre-conference dinner. Those were the days of misunderstanding between "town" and "gown" doctors in Washington. Some were pushing for the European system, a *coupure* (split) between the two groups, while Drs. Kyle and Harvey fostered a rapprochement between "town" and "gown." Dr. Oler seemed genuinely surprised and touched by my call. It apparently was the first time that anyone from Georgetown had called him to ask his permission for anything. He accepted the invitations and came to both the dinner and conference. We had a chance to chat and I told him how much everyone enjoyed his yearly August talk to new house officers.

Dr. MacMurray's comportment with the miliary tuberculosis case was still fresh in my mind.[25] I related my views to Dr. Harvey, who told me emphatically "I would put Frank and Wes up against anyone in American medicine, be it academic, practice, research or whatever. They are looking for a young pup and they are talking of two or three years. You do for them what you did for us; they won't let you go, I guarantee. Oscar, this is a natural for you."

And so was forged the association of MacMurray, Oler and Mann, to begin on August 1, 1966, allowing time to fix up an office for me.[26] I asked few questions about specifics and they seemed satisfied with what they had learned from Dr. Harvey. To me, just being with them was a golden opportunity. The contract was a hand-shake over lunch at a nearby Sholl's cafeteria. Little did I know that we would still be together several decades later.

Dr. Harvey has had an impressive impact on American medicine. And American medicine has contributed enormously to our world. New invasive and noninvasive diagnostic techniques and therapeutic modalities, not to mention wonder drugs, have revolutionized the care of patients. Mankind has been the great beneficiary of these advances. People live longer and better, but something has happened on the way to the forum:

*Medicine has become driven by research and technology, both of which have yielded indisputable benefits. Yet we are now so dependent upon such advancements that many practitioners have lost the basic clinical skills that enable bedside diagnosis.*[27]

The art and science of medicine, not mutually exclusive, are complementary to each other. The pendulum of American medicine, however, has swung far in favor of technology. It is sad but true that hands-on skills and competent auscultation are neglected and falling out of favor in the grand scheme of medical education. I hope that the pendulum will swing back, as well it should, toward clinical medicine. Surely we need more bedside clinical giants. We need more old-time clinicians. We need more W. Proctor Harveys.

## NOTES

1. March,"W. Proctor Harvey,"183,188.

2. See Samuel Levine and W. Proctor Harvey, *Clinical Auscultation of the Heart* (Philadelphia: WB Saunders, 1949).

3. March, "W. Proctor Harvey," 188. March's second reference is to W. Proctor Harvey, *et al*, *Cardiac Pearls* (Newton, New Jersey: Laënnec Publishing; 1993).

4. Michael A. Chizner (ed.), *Classic Teachings in Cardiology: A Tribute to W. Proctor Harvey, M.D.* (Newton, New Jersey: Laënnec Publishing, 1996).

5. March, "W. Proctor Harvey," 183.

6. See, for example, R.T.H. Laënnec, "Stéthescope: Son origine, Description de la découverte," in his *Traité de l'auscultation médiate et des maladies des poumons et du coeur* (Paris: Brosson, 1819).

7. From the original text of a lecture given by Lucy Candib, M.D., of the Family Health Center of Worcester, Massachusetts. Reproduced by permission of Dr. Candib.

8. Laënnec, "Stéthoscope," 20.

9. Paula Byron, "The Art of Touch in Healing," *Harvard Medical Alumni Bulletin* 76, no 3 (Winter, 2003), 14. Cited with permission of Lucy Candib.

10. See Haragopal Thadepalli, "Women Gave Birth to the Stethoscope: Laënnec's Introduction of the Art of Auscultation of the Lung," *Clin Infect Dis*, 2002 Sep 1; 35: 587 (http://www.journals.uchicago.edu/cid/journal/issues/v35n5/020389/020389 .html). Epub July 31, 2002. Accessed March 8, 2005.

11. Personal communication from Dr. Clifton R. Gruver, August 2003.

12. Personal communication from Dr. John F. Stapleton, April 2003.

13. See chapter 14.

14. Personal communication from Stapleton, April 2003.

15. *Grand Rounds*, Joseph S. Costa, M.D. (Ed), Georgetown University School of Medicine: Class of 1954.

16. March, "W. Proctor Harvey," 183.

17. March, "W. Proctor Harvey," 184–185.

18. Personal communication from Stapleton, April 2003.

19. Personal communication from Stapleton, April 2003.

20. In the scale devised by the New York Heart Association to describe *symptomatic status,* class IV is the most advanced category, meaning that the patient experiences cardiac symptoms even at rest.

21. Personal communication from David P. Jackson, March 2003.

22. Personal communication from Dean Ray Mitchell, M.D., May 2003.

23. At the time Dr. Harvey presided over it, Washington Heart was the Washington, DC, Heart Society. Since then the name has also come to represent cardiology services at the Washington Hospital Center.

24. The 1978 American Heart Association James B. Herrick Award, as quoted by March, "W. Proctor Harvey," 190. This award is named for James Bryan Herrick, M.D., a clinical pioneer in the early 20th century.

25. See chapter 16.

26. See Chapter 18.

27. March, "W. Proctor Harvey," 183.

# Chapter Eighteen

# The Early Days of Practice

John and Oscar, the *schmatta* boys, have always been there for each other, especially in times of need or illness. In fact, John's appendicitis episode was my inaugural medical foray into the outside world, my first house call.

On the first Tuesday of August 1965, I had been a cardiology fellow for a little over a month. Dr. Harvey holidayed during August at Nag's Head, North Carolina, trusting that the incoming fellows were sufficiently oriented for him to be away.

Not withstanding vacations, the Thursday Evening Cardiology Conference was always convened on schedule. In Dr. Harvey's absence, the pre-conference meeting was chaired by Dr. Modestino Criscitiello, who had come to Arlington Hospital at my request.[1] The meeting was about finished when I received a message from Amy about John. Apparently, John had been ill for two days.

Amy was concerned about how he sounded over the telephone. I turned over my duties at the hospital to another cardiology fellow, Joe Le Bauer. I left to visit John at his apartment on Democracy Boulevard near the National Institutes of Health, taking along my friend Jim Waters, who was reputed to be a savvy clinician.

John had been complaining of a stomach ache for 36 hours. This he had self-treated with the traditional remedy of our ancestors, a hot water bottle. He had no appetite, was experiencing nausea without vomiting or diarrhea, and complained of pain localizing to the middle of the belly. It was growing in intensity.

John was febrile, had a fast pulse with a moderately elevated blood pressure, and looked sick. His abdomen was soft to palpation with no soreness and no rebound tenderness at the midpoint between his navel and his right hip.[2] The rest of the exam was normal. The lack of diarrhea and vomiting, the admission of constipation, the soft abdomen to the examination and the absence of shaking chills argued against a viral infection or acute pancreatitis.[3]

Jim Waters taught me a trick in his examination. He showed me the *obturator sign*.[4] John gave an immediate positive response to the maneuver, indicating to us localized inflammation deep in the right abdomen.

We called Dr. Jack E. Bennett, an authority in the field of infectious diseases and John's mentor at the NIH. He felt secure that we were not dealing with a viral or bacterial infection, and assured us that John was entitled to medical care at the Bethesda Naval Medical Center as a Public Health officer. John was relieved that he was not going to NIH, saying, "They wouldn't know what to do with a routine case." I rode with John in the ambulance and heard him moan, "My belly feels every bump in the road." The diagnosis was thought to be *retrocecal appendicitis*, a condition where the inflamed appendix is located behind the cecum, a pouch at the point where the small and large intestines join. In this setting, the classical findings of acute appendicitis are camouflaged and an exact diagnosis difficult.

As we reached Bethesda Naval, John overheard a nurse ask the ambulance attendant"What kind of package are you bringing us today?" John was upset with this comment, likely said in jest.

A rectal exam and the laboratory tests in the emergency room gave more weight to the diagnosis of *retrocecal appendicitis*. John had surgery without delay, and his surgeon found a *gangrenous (necrotic) atypical retro-cecal appendicitis* with an *early localized perforation of the appendix.*[5]

John made a quick and uneventful recovery, but has never forgotten our mother's reaction. She did not see him until he awakened in the recovery room, where she confronted him by asking loudly "What did you do wrong?" Jewish people of my mother's generation did not acquire a sense of guilt; they were born with one and thought their children shared this view of everything bad that happened to them.

Jim Waters and I had been indoctrinated, along with generations of young doctors, that appendicitis can be the easiest diagnosis to make or the most difficult one. The situation is facilitated today with ultrasonography and/or CAT scan imaging of the abdomen.[6] Yet, even in this day and age, older people and small children, where the diagnosis remains elusive and treacherous, and where immunity is impaired by age or disease, still die of complications of a ruptured appendix.

The second lesson I took from this episode is the question of appropriate access to medical care. In John's case, the august National Institutes of Health would not have been the right place because NIH has little experience in day-to-day, garden-variety medical problems. If one has a serious rare condition beyond the capabilities of local or academic hospitals, NIH should then come into the picture. The choice of the right doctor and/or the right facility remains a critical issue in modern medicine.

In July, 1966, I had completed my cardiology fellowship and was eager and ready to enter practice with Drs. MacMurray and Oler on August 1, 1966. Jim Waters, aware of my open month of July, arranged a two-week *locum tenens* for me[7]. A busy and successful doctor, "Dr. R.," desired to take some time off. I was acquainted remotely with Dr. R. from my years of training at Georgetown Hospital. He was an old-time general practitioner. He was affable and well-liked by house officers who usually managed his hospitalized patients. In solo practices, these practitioners carried a heavy load of patients, made social rounds late at night and appreciated the help of the house staff. We admired their clinical intuition, as they seemed to sense and know when a patient was really sick. They frequently admitted their patients and called for help. One of these general physicians, whom we shall call Dr. S. L., "could smell appendicitis a mile away." Dr. Coffey would often add, "when Dr. S. L. admits a patient with the diagnosis of acute appendicitis, I operate first and ask questions later."

Dr. R.'s office was located on upper Massachusetts Avenue, N.W., in the fashionable Spring Valley section of Washington, DC. His patients came from all over the area. The place had been a home/office arrangement, but the entire house had been converted to a large office in 1961 when Dr. R. moved to a smaller house after his children left home. The office was efficiently run by a registered nurse, and she was assisted by three medical aides. These women were dedicated to Dr. R. and the welfare of his patients, many of whom came in droves as soon as the doors to the office opened.

The office contained multiple examining rooms, various cubicles and the private consulting room of Dr. R. Each area was dedicated to a specific problem, such as sore throats, workplace injuries, mild trauma, injection rooms and one room, just off the entrance, with several beds for non-ambulatory patients. The atmosphere was pleasant and friendly, and the patient flow was smoothly controlled. The patients all appeared content that they were getting good medical care. They worshiped Dr. R. and kept asking me when the good doctor would be coming back.

The triage was masterfully carried out by the nurse who confidently displayed an exceptional clinical sense, born of many years with Dr. R. The hours were suited to the needs of the patients, from 9:00 A.M. to noon and again from 5:00 P.M. to 8:00 P.M. Between these office hours came the many house calls which Dr. R. did. During the afternoon, the office staff took over, with patients coming in for blood drawing, lab work, immunization injections and lesser procedures, such as heat treatment, ultrasound and, yes, countless shots of vitamin B12. The staff also did simple diagnostic tests such as vision checks, lung function evaluations, blood pressure checks and electrocardiograms. The time after office hours in the evening was reserved for hospital rounds at Georgetown Hospital, so as "not to interfere with the hospital system."

Dr. R. had explained all of this to me. He had told me in jest, or possibly not, that what the staff did in the office was more lucrative than what he did. There were no office appointments. Every patient was a walk-in and usually left with a prescription. The R.N. ran the office and the Georgetown University Medical Center doctors cared for his hospital patients. He was fond of saying: "I know my limitations." He also said," I have a sixth sense and so does my staff." It soon became clear to me that I was no Dr. R. and did not possess his clinical acumen.

I had expected a rather easy routine time at Dr. R.'s office but, instead, I experienced another clinical baptism. Little did I realize that I was still too academic for this down-to-earth medical practice. My clinical skills needed honing and polishing. During the two weeks I spent in that office, the witty words spoken by Bob Hope at my graduation from medical school played back in my mind, "You are about to leave the inside world and enter the outside one. My advice is, don't go."

Alone with my thoughts in the evening I was reminded of what Father O'Donnell used to emphasize in his course on medical ethics during medical school; something to the effect that "every time you see a patient and commit yourself to a working diagnosis, you will be conducting an experiment in the laboratory of life."

My time in Dr. R.'s office, however, did wonders for the intangibles of my clinical dexterity. I suffered, without knowing it, from having always been in a protected medical environment where someone else always made the basic decision that a patient was sick. My brother John's appendicitis episode had given me a sense of this problem but not full insight. One had to master it.

Most patients had garden-variety problems, but among them were some patients whose problems were not routine and some were really sick. It was essential to sharpen my clinical acumen, to weed out abnormal from normal, routine from serious and chronic from acute. I needed to let my five senses separate the grave cases from everyday ones. I saw three acute appendicitis cases masquerading as tummy bugs, a teenager "with the flu" which was concealing an advanced lymphoma, a sore throat patient" with a *purulent abscess* of a tonsil, and a heart attack patient complaining of only fatigue and a rapid pulse.

Then there was the memorable elderly lady with a head injury. She complained of a mild headache and, according to her daughter, had been exhibiting some mental dullness, quite out of character, following a fall in her bedroom. I had been taught that a bruise around the mastoid, the bone behind the ear and blood in the ear canal could be signs of an "*occult* (hidden) *basilar* (base of the brain, near the first neck vertebra) *skull fracture*." I encountered these findings, for the first and only time in my medical career, on this nice, matriarchal lady, who was sitting patiently, waiting for me in Dr. R.'s office. However, I was given a "leg up," once again, by a nurse. She whispered into my ear: "Take a good look at Mrs. Hastings; she is not herself today."

I was on call 24 hours a day, seven days a week, for two full weeks and I was ceaselessly on my guard, aware that I could easily miss something significant with the number of patients I was seeing. I felt lonely and promised myself that I would never again be in a solo practice.

About that time, my dear friend Henry Safrit called saying that he had some news to share with Amy and me. We invited him that same evening, over to our apartment in Bethesda for dinner. He told us his news. He had known since early December 1965 that he was slated to serve in Vietnam as a medical officer, adding: "It really dampened my parents' Christmas spirit this past year." However, Henry continued to exhibit his usual good natured demeanor.

Dr. R. came back one day early. I was relieved. The nurse told him in my presence, before he even sat down: "Dr. Mann did a yeoman job in your absence, but he knows nothing about immunization shots or running an office. They must not teach them these things in medical school."

I thanked the good Lord that I had survived my experience in the real world of general medical practice without a clinical disaster. Dr. R. sat down with me, thanked me, consulted the books, and without delay began to figure out my financial remuneration, saying "I owe you for all the work you did directly in my absence. What my office people did on their own is excluded. Remember, that was our deal. I will pay you right now, collection notwithstanding. Incidentally, my collection rate is excellent."

Before leaving, I shook hands with Dr. R., said goodbye to the staff and told both I now understood better the expression, "General practitioners are the backbone of American medicine." I walked away with respect for this experienced physician, his staff and his practice while thinking to myself, "My hat is off to you, Dr. R. and to others like you." High patient volume offices, with solo general physicians under constant time pressure rushing off "somewhere," were the norm of the day. This is how most of medicine was practiced for many years.

Dr. R. had presented me with a check for $2,750.00. This was then big money for me. I was not scheduled to begin with Drs. MacMurray and Oler until two weeks hence. On the spur of the moment, Amy and I decided to take a ten day vacation to Florida. Dr. R. and several other colleagues had mentioned a new resort, Hilton Head Island, South Carolina, which was then one of many little-known islands off the Southern Atlantic Coast, some of which were undeveloped and unspoiled. Hilton Head, however, was reputed to have all the charm of Robinson Crusoe's island and none of its hardships. Comfortable places to stay were available, but not many as yet. The entire island was a "subtropical" resort, still in its infancy, and we thought it would be a perfect halfway stop on our way to Florida.

We started out very early in the morning and drove all day, making the stops necessary. Route 95 had not yet been completed. The route South was 301. We had the opportunity to see much of the South, rolling farm land, lots of shanty towns, plenty of poverty and many wonderful people. At one gas station, a bedraggled-looking man was holding out a tin plate and a sign which read, "I am collecting for President Johnson's Poverty Program." We gave him a dollar.

Most details of that trip are now sketchy at best. We remember miles of backwoods, towering pine trees, pecan pralines at roadside stops and the fun-but-tacky "South of the Border" motel and amusement park complex which straddled the border between the Carolinas. Above all, we recall the friendliness of the people along the way.

It was dark by the time we reached the long causeway from the mainland to Hilton Head. One more bridge to cross and finally we were there.[8] The island did seem to be tropical. In the darkness, we could make out palm trees and other plants reminiscent of the jungle. The live oaks, dripping Spanish moss, reminded Amy of a landscape from a Faulkner novel. We later learned that the climate was only subtropical. The palm trees were really palmettos. The environment seemed more like that of a rainforest that had not yet been tampered with, unlike Florida's, which had been altered to please tourists from up North.

We stayed at the Sea Crest Motel. There were only two other establishments for vacationers. Hilton Head in 1966 was an island of second homes and long-time natives. We should have invested in an ocean front lot. A $15,000 investment in 1966 would now be worth $1,500,000.

At the motel, we were greeted cordially by a pleasant, Southern gentleman who introduced himself as Wilton Graves—he did have a vacancy. We learned that he was Hilton Head's state senator and a leader in the South Carolina Senate. He was a highly respected citizen of the area. The crucial bridge now bears his name to memorialize this respect.

The room was comfortable and adequate for Amy and me. The next day we got a good look at the island. The big establishment on the island was the Sea Pines Plantation, which at that time consisted of a fine resort hotel and a tournament-quality golf course. The Sea Pines Development contained acre upon acre of lots plotted out for second homes. In 1966, very few houses had been built. It was possible to see, unobstructed, an exquisite view of land and sea, the low country of South Carolina.

It was a pleasure to be on the beach and to go into the tepid water. The gulf stream is sixty miles out to sea. An East-West shoreline, with corresponding shallow, gentle waves assured that it was safe to swim. On the beach, we met a young doctor, his wife and two small boys. They, too, were vacationing. She was expecting her third child in two months, and we were pleased to become acquainted with this couple from the upcountry of South Carolina. They confided to us that they were building their own summer home on another island, but they had vacationed at Hilton Head for years, regularly staying with Wilton Graves, who had become their good friend. We realized that we were in paradise and quickly gave up on Florida. We stayed at Hilton Head for our entire vacation.

Our holiday was totally relaxing. The area was underpopulated and at times we felt remote from the stress at home. One day, I decided to rent a motor scooter and see the island like the Europeans, most of whom enjoyed this mode of transportation (motor scooters had become a way of life in Italy). Amy sat on the back, and for an hour we were imaginary Harley bikers.

Early, the next morning before Amy was out of bed, I started up the scooter again. I was enjoying this unique journey along the shore when suddenly a huge black dog (probably a Rottweiler) ran after me. I prayed I could accelerate fast enough to lose him, which I finally did, and that experience ended my biker fantasies.

One thing upset Amy. After the daily shower, thousands of tree frogs covered the ground. These were not one-inch amphibians, but substantial frogs, about three inches long. They may have existed back home, but they were not a visible part of the landscape there.

One night, we were in the motel dining room, having dinner with our new friends. Amy had started the evening with a strong double whiskey sour. Suddenly, a heavy rain poured down. After it passed, Amy hurried onto the terrace.

" Baaah, frogs!" we heard her say. "Go! I'm not afraid of you!"

When she returned, our friend, the doctor, said "You must be very drunk, Amy," and we all had a good laugh.

Another evening, we all drove down the coast to Savannah, Georgia. At that time, Savannah was in the process of a great restoration. Stately antebellum homes surrounded the city squares. Many were getting facelifts, and these historic sites were taking on new life. We had a wonderful meal at a restaurant by the old waterfront. We added Georgia to the list of states we had visited.

On our last night there, Wilton Graves's wife made a Tidewater dinner for all of us—country ham, biscuits and a shrimp boil with sausage in it. The next morning it was difficult to say goodbye. We were leaving paradise, with its friendly people. We promised to be back. Alas, this has never happened. For some reason, fortune has not led us down to Hilton Head again. Perhaps one day we shall return.

The trip back to Washington lay ahead of us. We would take it step by step, allowing two days for travel. Our immediate objective was an afternoon stop at Beaufort, North Carolina (not to be confused with Beaufort, South Carolina). This attractive seaside town was where our friend Henry Safrit was born and raised. He was in Vietnam, but his parents lived in Beaufort. They had said that they would welcome a visit from us.

We passed rather quickly through South Carolina, then crossed the border into North Carolina and rode through more countryside and traversed what seemed to be endless outskirts of Camp Lejeune. Finally, we crossed bridges into Morehead City and Beaufort, and followed the directions the Safrits had given us to find their home.

I don't know why—perhaps it was because of stereotyped ideas—we were expecting a plantation. That is not what we saw. The house was a large cottage on less than one acre. It was a nicely furnished, shore-type dwelling, informal in character. Henry's parents were the only ones at home.

They were extremely hospitable. They showed us the entire house. We soon sat down in the library. On one wall was a large map of Vietnam with a dart on it which they changed whenever they learned that Henry had been moved. The dart was on Danang. "That's where Henry is now," his mother said. "We worry about him all the time. I don't know why they had to do this. There were already enough doctors over there."

We discussed the Vietnam situation at some length. Since Henry's father had to attend to some business, Mrs. Safrit took us to eat lunch at a famous old restaurant across the bridge in Morehead City, known as Tony's Sanitary Fish Market. After lunch, Mrs. Safrit drove us around the area. We saw the most picturesque shore communities and now well understand Henry's affection for his birthplace and home. As we said farewell to these special people, all four of us silently hoped that Henry would be able to make many visits back to Beaufort. Fortunately, Henry came back safe and sound from Vietnam. He and his lovely wife, Karin, settled in San Francisco but return to Beaufort frequently. We have remained in close touch with them.

The trip home was otherwise uneventful. We stayed overnight in Emporia, Virginia, where we obtained a clean and comfortable room at a Holiday Inn for $12.00. The next day, we were home.

This southern trip was only my second ever actual vacation and provided a good break between the local medical doctor and the MacMurray-Oler practices. As a child, I hid from the Nazis, later rendered military service in the United States Army, worked and studied for the next 12 years and experienced only one real vacation—my honeymoon! Now, after this Hilton Head trip, I was ready to be a big city doctor.

The first Monday in August 1966, "spruced up and looking in me prime," I joined the well-established practice of Drs. MacMurray and Oler at 1150 Connecticut Avenue in downtown Washington, DC.[9] Beginning with day one, at their request, they were Frank and Wes to me. I immediately felt at ease with them and their staff and sensed that the chemistry was right.

The building at 1150 Connecticut was the most prestigious medical address in Washington. It was at the top of the medical ladder. The building featured an old-fashioned Otis cage elevator with uniformed operators who wore white gloves. This sixty year old building was imposing and elegant. Its halls were wide. Its suites were spacious with a high ceiling. There was a feeling of understated Old World splendor. Frank and Wes had taken over a vacant suite adjacent to their office. The recent death of Michael McInerney, M.D., a Georgetown favorite and an associate clinical professor of medicine at Georgetown, had made these rooms available. Frank and Wes renovated and furnished the office and presented the new quarters to me as my private medical den in the heart of Washington medicine. To say the least, I was thrilled. From peddling clothes for years in the suburbs of Paris, I had now reached "the promised land." Such things only happen in boyhood dreams.

Worth Daniels, M.D., the father of modern medicine in Washington, was the mentor of many well-regarded physicians, two in particular—MacMurray and Oler. As John F. Stapleton has noted:

*Worth Daniels* [from a well-known publishing family in North Carolina] *was a distinguished internist who published many papers, usually on infectious diseases. While serving in the army, he produced a landmark paper describing a* leptospiral [a type of organism related to the bacteria causing syphilis] *disease known as* Fort Bragg Fever. *As a civilian after the war, he submitted a significant paper in 1952 entitled* Cat Scratch Disease: a Non-Bacterial Regional Lymphadenitis, *which he coauthored with Frank MacMurray, also a member of Georgetown's volunteer faculty. This disease was a previously undescribed syndrome. Besides teaching and writing, Daniels provided important counsel to* [Dr. Harold] *Jeghers and to subsequent chairmen* [of medicine at Georgetown]. *He founded a group practice whose members provided excellent teaching services to the university hospital for many years. In June 1962—33 years after he joined the Department of Medicine—Georgetown University awarded Daniels an honorary Doctorate of Science.*[10]

In 1951, Frank MacMurray, a graduate of Harvard Medical School, who trained at Johns Hopkins Hospital, "had achieved enough practice" so that he could set up his own shop. Wisely, Frank stayed at 1150 Connecticut Avenue, the hallmark Washington location for physicians, where he had been a young assistant to Dr. Worth Daniels. About a year later, Frank persuaded Wesley Oler, a graduate of Columbia University School of Medicine, who trained at Bellevue Hospital in New York City, to first be an understudy to Dr. Daniels and then to join him. The practice became a new group, MacMurray & Oler.

There was magic in the association of Frank and Wes, two superb physicians and wonderful people. Great individuals that they were, they became even greater as a medical team. By the mid-1960s, Frank and Wes were preeminent in Washington. Active at the Washington Hospital Center, Georgetown University Medical Center and the DC Medical Society, in addition to an increasingly busy practice, they were much in demand as consultants. Stapleton writes:

> *MacMurray later served as governor of Washington, DC and suburban Maryland for the American College of Physicians. Wesley Oler . . . taught and admitted patients to Georgetown University Hospital. He also served as governor of Washington, DC, and suburban Maryland for the American College of Physicians* [the DC metropolitan area for the College of Physicians includes not only DC and nearby suburban Maryland, but also Northern Virginia].[11]

Frank and Wes, once pups themselves to Dr. Worth Daniels, now needed a pup of their own. Enter Oscar Mann. They had been frank with me early on and and told me in no uncertain words:

> *You are a pup and will remain a pup to us, and once no longer useful to us as a pup, in a couple of years or so, you will be expected to move on to set up your own shop, as we have done when we left Dr. Daniels. In the meantime, to the outside world, you will be one of us. This is 'the Daniels system'.*

I smiled and did not say anything. I had decided I would never leave. I would be the best medical "pup" in the world if that was what it took. Sooner or later, they would invite me to remain aboard. Together, we would create the premiere internal medicine group practice in Washington.

I had read somewhere that keeping a burning secret all to oneself is a good way to bring it to fruition. It had worked for me with the cardiac fellowship. So I did not share this sentiment, or my ardent determination, with them or anyone, my wife Amy excepted. Instead, I laced my intimate thoughts with a bit of humor and subliminally broadcast them to Frank and Wes, under cover of a pleasant shield.

*Frank and Wes, you are decent people, principled physicians and non-greedy fellows, but your business sense needs a little guidance. You have acquired for your pup a highly-trained young physician. What you don't know, at least not yet, is that Oscar is an ex-schmatta boy!*

*On my arrival, you generously extended me the Daniels formula, emphasizing personal incentive rather than a 9:00 A.M. to 5:00 P.M. mentality. Frank and Wes, you would never take financial advantage of anyone under the cover of an 'adequate stipend or a set salary'; to the contrary, you are straight-shooters. For those patients you directly refer to me, 50% of the fees collected belong to the office. That is all well and good. So if Wes, for example, refers a patient to me, the office is entitled to 50% of whatever I collect from that patient. On the other hand, if I "originate" the patient (patient initially referred to me), I get to keep 100% of the collected billings. I pay not another penny toward office expenses. From these collections, I pay no rent, no fees, nothing.*

*You should know that Dr. Harvey and other Georgetown physicians are feeding me patients. One of Harvey's referrals was the Pakistani Deputy Chief of Mission. After a while, he brought me his entire embassy. I mean, I am developing a large practice of my own. You sincerely want me to succeed. I know I have a good deal. I have no intention of ever leaving you. That would make no sense to me. I came a long way to reach the mountain top. You two Wasp elite Washington physicians are not going to send me back away. I am staying. What say you?*

At any rate, for Wes and Frank, I was still a pup albeit a good one. For myself, I was caring for many of my own patients and keeping 100% of the income such patients entitled me to. In November, 1966, I went to Wes and Frank and told them:

*Guys, you're overlooking something important in the financial framework of your office; I am an ex-schmatta boy with a business head, and thus I'm offering you, in the name of good economics, 50% of all my income. Further, I discussed this matter with Uncle Isor, a savvy businessman, as you know; he says you are cheating yourselves and that he would be glad to advise you from an economic perspective.*

But they would not hear of it. "We are bound by the Daniels formula," they said. And no amount of talking on my part seemed to sway them from the "sacred formula." For a while longer, I continued to enjoy an almost free financial ride, but to my utter relief, just as I was beginning to wonder about their street-smart judgment, they saw the light. Frank and Wes accepted my formula, henceforth known as the "50% across-the-board formula," and the formula has stood the test of time in our practice as it is today, even with the three of us no longer part of the office.

Be that as it may, things were going well for Frank, Wes and me. The practice was lucrative, the staff and I were working smoothly. Mary Wilson, the office manager and her assistants, clearly liked me, and I them.

These were civilized times in medicine. The office would close from noon until two P.M. every day so we could catch up on paperwork and go to lunch. Sure, it was only Scholl's Cafeteria down the street, but there was nothing better in terms of well-prepared food and ambience and the price was always right. We had Saturday hours until one P.M. Then came the highlight of the week; a luncheon at Scholl's with Dr. Zigmond Lebensohn, the dean of Washington psychiatrists. As the youngest present, I listened. Everything was fair game for discussion, especially current events. It would be a better world if the wisdom expressed by Zig, Frank and Wes, were allowed to influence governmental decisions, or at least we thought so.

It was the golden age of fee-for-service medicine. Patients received good, personal medical care, physicians enjoyed their profession and doctors made a decent living. A better system has yet to be devised.

In those days, insurance companies were generous and often asleep at the switch, thus allowing us to bill without having to itemize or code every item. The general rubric of "Services Rendered" sufficed. Typical examples of such laxity included "three hours in attendance with patient in the emergency room and admission to the hospital;" "complete initial check-up," "comprehensive consultation," " initial home visit of one hour," "initial nursing visit with history and physical of one-and-a-half hours," etc.

In the mid-1960s, few of our older citizens had reliable insurance. This meant that many senior patients were reluctant to be hospitalized, even if it was medically indicated. The Medicare program was signed into law on July 30, 1965, and the early years were good. However Charles P. Duvall, M.D., a retired member of our group with a very active role in Washington medicine and in the AMA, and a former President of the American Society of Internal Medicine, saw the light from the beginning:

> *Some doctors and the AMA were clairvoyant about Medicare: they warned that the cost estimates, particularly over time, were egregiously low; that government control and intervention would become inordinate; and that such would critically intrude on the practice of medicine and its professionalism. That is why they opposed the final language of the legislation, though supporting the intent of the program.*[12]

I had no insight then and with many others saw only the short-term gains. Medicare paid well, most particularly in hospital confinements, now allowing the people covered to be freely hospitalized. Medicare reimbursed office care,

house calls, and nursing home visits equally as well, if not better, than good
private insurance. Medicare was a boon for physicians, and initially, our
billings survived intact. What has happened to Medicare, the private insurance network and, as a result to the entire business of medicine, is a national
disaster and beyond the scope and competence of this author. While the science of medicine has made giant strides and continues to improve at a rapid
pace, our medical care delivery system is broken and begs to be fixed. Dr.
Clifton R. Gruver, among my favorite colleagues, comments:

> *We had it best in those years. Fee-for-service was the dominant system in med-*
> *ical economics when I started practice. I couldn't agree more with your disser-*
> *tation on what has become of our profession, with the gradual and continual*
> *erosion of our leadership, and the inroads of third party carriers and Medicare*
> *and other government regulations. We have made wonderful scientific advances*
> *but have lost our way as a profession. Amen to your words on this subject!*
> *Where do we go from here?*[13]

It was the summer of 1968. Having witnessed the events surrounding the
tragic assassinations of Martin Luther King and Robert Kennedy, America,
and Washington, DC, were slowly returning to normal. Dr. Harvey had pre-
dicted that Frank and Wes would not take too long to make me a partner in
their practice. They did just that, even earlier than I had hoped. Yes, me, the
*schmatta* boy! They joked that I pushed them "kicking and screaming into the
20th century".

Sadly, that fall, the smart Washington money zeroed in on 1150 Connecticut Avenue, and the venerable old building soon was demolished for a new
edifice. The wrecking ball removed every physical trace of 1150, closing a
gentler medical era and relegating it to history.

In November, 1968, we moved to 2141 K Street, a modern and compact
building with none of the grace of 1150 Connecticut Avenue. The inside of
our office lacked the spaciousness and classic form to which we had become
accustomed. We dubbed it the "ugly building."

The building, however, soon became the site of many leading Washington
medical practices. There was also a thriving psychiatric in-patient facility located on the top two floors of the building and run by the Psychiatric Institute
of Washington, which owned the whole building.

Shortly after we moved to the K Street location, Dr. Oler stopped me in the
hall one Thursday afternoon and casually said: "Oscar, you had a light afternoon tomorrow; I just filled it up for you. I have this good friend, Congress-
man George Bush, who called me a little while ago. His teen-age children are
overdue for their school physicals. So I put them all in your schedule for tomorrow afternoon."

Doing school physicals in those days was considered "scut work." Usually, school physicals were assigned to the most junior person, in this case, me.[14]

My Friday afternoon had been free and I really didn't mind meeting the Bush family. I spent most of the afternoon doing school physicals on George W., Jeb, Neal and Dorothy "Doro" Bush. They were accompanied by their mother, Barbara Bush. What a nice family, I thought. They were all pleasant and down-to-earth, especially Mrs. Bush, who graciously helped me fill out the many school forms. She was clearly in command of her brood. Little did I realize at that time that I had just helped a future First Lady of the United States, while examining a future Governor of Florida and a future President of the United States. Only in America!

MacMurray, Oler & Mann were an elite and very busy practice. We began to look for a young associate. Dr. Harvey recommended Mary Restifo, M.D., who had just completed her second year as a Harvey Fellow. She received her M.D. degree in 1967 from Western Reserve University in Cleveland, Ohio and did her internship and residency in internal medicine at the University of North Carolina at Chapel Hill (1967–1970). Her cardiology training was at Brompton Hospital, London, England (1970–1971) and at Georgetown University Medical Center (1971–1973). Dr. Harvey told us "she can hold her own with anyone and will be a wonderful asset to your group."

We interviewed Mary Restifo, and she expressed a strong desire to join us in the practice of internal medicine rather than pursuing a career exclusively in cardiology. Fully qualified in both, Mary became our new "pup" in July 1973. Before long, Mary had garnered a large practice and was made a partner.

It was now time for a new name for the group. We became known as "Macomar." The name was a compression of MacMurray, Oler, Mann and Restifo. Today, few people remember Macomar. In its day, however, Macomar represented a milestone in Washington medicine. In the late 1960s, Washington medicine was still in a very provincial mode, and when partnerships were offered to a Jewish immigrant and a woman, these were landmark decisions that caught Washington by surprise.

In today's Washington, established practices of medicine are open to all who are qualified, but this was not always so. Practices were divided along religious and ethnic lines. Women were not welcome as full partners. When Mary and I were made full partners, we thought that a powerful message was going out to the Washington medical establishment. I think that message is in part what made our group unique. Established medical practices in Washington began to open up and have continued to do so.

Four people acted boldly in the late 1960s, when others in Washington medicine were still closed-minded. In deciding to make Mary and me full

partners, although they probably didn't see themselves that way, Frank Mac-
Murray and his wife, Rose, and Wesley Oler and his wife, Ginny, were in a
very real sense pioneers.

I learned a great deal from Frank and Wes. They were both great physicians. I initially met Frank when I was a first-year medical resident on the 7th
floor at Georgetown University Hospital. He stunned me with his brilliant diagnosis in a difficult case.[15] However, there was an even more important side
to Frank, as I will now relate.

Frank admitted a lovely young patient to the hospital. Tragically, she died
shortly after of overwhelming sepsis (infection) induced by acute aplastic
anemia (failure of blood production by the body). Frank received a letter
from the girl's out-of-town family, saying that they were in shock and
disbelief and asking for a detailed explanation. Frank replied with a long
letter enclosing a copy of the entire hospital record. I well remember his
concluding paragraph:

> *But these medical facts are cold comfort for you. I have a daughter the same
> age, and if she had died as yours did, I would be full of anger and unable ever
> to forget. I sympathize with you as only a father with a daughter can. My heart
> goes out to you.*

Frank showed the draft of the letter to Wes and me. The shadow of litiga-
tion was changing the climate of the practice of medicine in the late 1960s
and early 1970s. Wes and I looked carefully at the letter and advised Frank
against sending such a letter without first obtaining legal counsel. Frank, feeling strongly that "human considerations overruled legal ones," sent the letter.
The family responded to Frank and their letter expressed gratitude to him for
his candor and compassion. That is vintage Frank MacMurray.

I was with Frank and Wes now, in a high-grade, well-paced and ideally
structured practice. I was well-trained, confident of my clinical skills and
even a little smug about my clinical acumen. My ego soon was to be taken
down a peg or two by a humbling medical situation, reaffirming my conviction that there is no substitute for clinical experience.

I saw a patient of Wes's in the Georgetown emergency room on a Tuesday
evening in late August 1966. Things were slow and I was not pressed for time.
A few days earlier, she had fallen in a wooded area and injured her left leg. I
did not like the appearance of the leg. It just didn't look right to me, and I considered admitting her to the hospital. These were the days of "house staff"
versus "attending physicians," "appropriate admissions" versus "inappropriate "admissions, and lack of hospital beds, all in the context of a persisting
coolness between "town" doctors and "gown" doctors. I let myself be talked
into "working her up in the E.R."

The working diagnosis was severe cellulitis (infection of the soft tissues) secondary to leg trauma. The x-rays failed to show anything of significance — specifically, there were no fractures and no foreign bodies. The surgical resident felt it was not a surgical situation, and the orthopedic resident did not see it as an orthopedic case. I stood on ceremony and did not promptly call an attending consultant. That was my mistake.

My friend, Dr. Coffey, chairman of surgery, would have easily admitted her over the telephone with no questions asked. Although I was new in practice and did not want to ruffle any feathers, I would also have been within my rights to admit her to the medical service under my name. The medical resident dangled the sign of inappropriate admission in front of me, "She just ain't a medical admission."

After phone consultation with the infectious diseases fellow, I loaded the patient up with intravenous penicillin and placed her on two broad-spectrum antibiotics to be taken by mouth for ten days. She went home. I could not forget her. Two days later, she reported to me by phone that she was not improving and had decided in "her wisdom to see the old master himself," that is, Wes.

Later, Wes called me in. The leg looked bad. I was mortified. I began to have visions of amputation, malpractice, and of being run out of town. Wes examined the leg with great care and said to the patient "Dr. Mann saved the day when he gave you powerful antibiotics, allowing the process to mature, and now comes the easy part."

And, then he casually and with great ease removed a very long thin twig embedded in the leg. All the while, Wes was explaining to the patient the difference between opaque and nonopaque material. He said that a negative x-ray did not exclude a non-opaque foreign body. Then Wes told the patient "see Dr. Mann for follow-up in two days. He has done a great job on you."

To say the least, I was touched, but still I did not feel particularly satisfied. The patient came back to see me two days later. There was near-complete resolution. Was I amazed? You bet. On a subsequent visit, the patient, a lovely lady but no fool herself, rubbed it in a little: "I am glad that I was able to see the master himself last week." Taking a cue from Wes's wit, I replied, "So am I." Wes always looked out for the other guy. Here, I was the other guy, and Wes had bailed me out gracefully. And, he did it in a distinctive way, "Wes's way."

I bought myself a whole lot of personal annoyance by not standing my ground, but at least I learned a profound lesson — the learning curve never stops. Never again did I fail to admit a patient when my inner voice so dictated. Being flagged for an "inappropriate" admission was far better than taking the case to bed with one's worries.

Wes was an unique individual. A superb professional, he was blessed with a winning personality, a wonderful disposition, and was so likeable that he was often asked to serve on committees. Among the most important was the Board of Trustees of the Washington Hospital Center, to which he devoted many years of service. Dr. Clifton Gruver, former President of the Medical Society of the District of Columbia, MSDC, adds:

*The year I was president of the medical society (1974), Wes was Chairman of the Utilization Committee, a position he had held for a number of years. This was a very important committee in those times, acting as agent for the membership in arbitration with third-party carriers. He chaired many committees of the medical society and was one of its most important and effective leaders.*[16]

Wes had several pet campaigns for the seriously ill, and he waged these constantly with nurses and house officers. One was for adequate control of pain. Another was for genuine sympathy in understanding the emotional stages of coming to terms with death and dying. For these patients and their families, Wes advocated a time-honored medical tincture—the old-fashioned caring physician—in big doses.

In dealing with people, Wes was the master. One day at 2141 K Street, the office wasn't busy after a big rainstorm. Patients were simply not coming in. Wes invited Frank and me for lunch at Sholl's but Frank decided to stay in the office to catch up on paperwork. I went with Wes, who parked in front of Sholl's on Connecticut Avenue, near M Street, where there was a "No Parking or Standing" sign.

"We'll be O.K., it's raining," said Wes with his customary confidence.

When we came out, it was no longer raining—and wouldn't you know it— a motorcycle policeman was writing up a ticket.

Wes: "Pleasant afternoon, officer."

Cop: "What were you doing inside? Saving a life?" [the car had MD tags]

Wes: "Officer, I was breaking the law and I fully deserve the ticket you're giving me."

Cop: "You're sure you weren't acting as a doctor?"

Wes: "Officer, I was feeding my face and breaking the law. I deserve the ticket."

The cop was clearly puzzled and he looked at Wes for a while before saying, "You know, I gave you a ticket yesterday– same time, same place."

Wes: "I was breaking the law yesterday as well."

The cop clearly didn't believe his ears, so he asked again: "Are you sure you were not acting as a doctor?"

Wes: "Absolutely."

Cop: "I have never met anyone like you– let's forget about the ticket."

As the policeman was tearing up the ticket, Wes thanked him and we started to leave. The cop leaned our way and said: "Tell you what—I still have my copy of your ticket from yesterday."

And sure enough, he pulled the copy of the ticket out and tore it up. Wes thanked the officer again. Afterwards, Wes said to me "Most doctors would have been indignant, claimed to be on professional business, would have ended up with two tickets and would have stewed over the incident for days." That was vintage Wes Oler.

It was a bright, sunny day, the Tuesday before Memorial Day 1971. The office was in a relaxed mode, eagerly anticipating the long weekend heralding another summer season. My patient, Norman Silberman,[17] had been worked into my schedule, his father having called early that morning to say he would like to bring Norman to see me because of a "heavy throat." I said yes, not even suspecting that I was about to see someone with a life-threatening medical emergency.

Let me tell you a little about Mr. Silberman. He and his parents were family friends who had become patients of mine soon after I entered practice. Now in his twenties, Norman had been plagued since his early years at various times by attacks of pain in the abdomen, episodes of transient localized swelling of his hands and feet, and severe constipation. There was no family history of genetic diseases. He had never experienced swelling of the voice box or swelling in the subcutaneous tissues of the face, lips, mouth or around the eyes. Over the years, he had been examined at George Washington University, Georgetown University, and the Johns Hopkins University Medical Centers. The diagnosis of *irritable bowel syndrome* on a functional basis was consistently determined. This diagnosis in retrospect was correct, but there was much more to the case. Somehow the patient's intermittent swelling of the extremities had not been accorded any significance and a clinical interpretation of this fact had never been placed on this recurring and troublesome problem.

His mother was convinced that Norman was afflicted by some rare disease. She pursued a search for etiological clarity and took him to several well-known consultants in Boston, New York and Los Angeles. Each new consultation was followed by further disenchantment. I was to learn the hard way that conventional medical wisdom is no match against a strong and determined maternal instinct. By diagnosing Norman as having "irritable bowel on a functional basis," the prior diagnosticians from around the country were declaring his illness to be a non-serious condition, something which turned out to be incorrect.

When I saw Norman that morning, he stated that about two days earlier, after receiving penicillin for dental work, he began to experience a sense of fullness in his throat and noted that his voice was noticeably higher. He looked fine and showed no signs of distress and appeared to be in good spirits. His general physical exam was normal except for the presence of a pale swelling on the roof of his mouth, which extended back to the posterior upper palate on the right side. There was some swelling of his lips as well as a distinct change in the quality of his voice. There appeared to be no clinical evidence of inflammation or infection. A blood count was totally normal, which ruled against an infection. I thought he was having an allergic reaction to penicillin without realizing the enormity or gravity of the immediate clinical situation. However, I did ask my friend and colleague, Robert Pumphrey, M.D., an excellent ear, nose, and throat specialist in our building, to look at Norman. I called for my next patient, with Norman having gone to see Bob Pumphrey.

Soon Bob Pumphrey called me back, stating that he agreed with my diagnosis but that he was puzzled by the blandness of the swelling, which was atypical for an allergic reaction. He said that he had asked James MacFarland, M.D., his senior partner, a well-known and experienced otolaryngologist, to look at Norman. Dr. MacFarland also thought that Norman was experiencing an allergic reaction with no evidence of compromise of the airway. They treated Norman with epinephrine, antihistamines and corticosteroids. In addition, to err on the conservative side, they were admitting Norman to the E.N.T. service at the Washington Hospital Center for close clinical observation and possible tracheotomy, a surgical procedure often referred to in medical parlance as "trach."[18] " Norman and his father are on their way to the hospital," added Bob.

Everything seemed to be under control, and yet I sensed unexplained alarm bells in my subconscious. I was uncomfortable, sweating the case of Norman; I had difficulty concentrating on the patient in front of me at the time. Somehow, I felt relieved when my secretary buzzed me to announce, "They are back and wish to talk to you before going to the hospital." I excused myself, stepped into the hallway, and met again with Norman and his father, who said to me "Norman is complaining of some difficulty breathing; I think it is his nerves but I want to be sure he is O.K. before I drive him to the Washington Hospital Center."

Norman seemed to be in no distress. Suddenly, I bolted into my office, quickly got Bob on the phone and blurted out, " Set up for a 'trach,' we'll be right up." This was not an intellectual decision on my part but a foreboding that something awful was about to happen to Norman. Trying to act calmly, I led Norman and his father back to the E.N.T. office, where the "Trach Tray" had already been readied and opened up.

Norman had some qualms about the proposed procedure, and his father also was uneasy about our recommendation. I began to think that perhaps I had overreacted to the situation. Norman, after a few minutes, however agreed to a prophylactic "trach," but asked to go to the men's room first. The nurse accompanied him. As Norman came back, he suddenly turned blue and collapsed in the nurse's arms. MacFarland, a big man, picked him up and placed him on the procedure table. Dr. Pumphrey successfully established immediate venous access while orchestrating matters in a loud, firm voice:

To his senior partner, "Neck, cut, cut, cut. . . ."

To me, "Epinephrine, inject, inject, inject. . . ."

To the nurse, "Vital signs, monitor, monitor, monitor. . . ."

Despite the precarious situation, all went smoothly, the tracheotomy was accomplished with lightening speed, or so it seemed, and we, the doctors and nurses, somehow survived. I was utterly amazed and relieved.

Norman soon regained color, showed stable vital signs and displayed normal breathing. Bob Pumphrey and I went in an ambulance with Norman and delivered him with no further incident to the E.N.T. floor of the Washington Hospital Center. I then went to talk to James Curtin, M.D., the chairman of medicine and a person for whom I have had enormous respect since medical school at Georgetown. Dr. Curtin rendered a thorough consultation, connected the dots and soon put us on the right track.

*Angioedema* is usually associated with allergic reactions to foods, medications, insect bites and exposure to various factors. The level of serum complement, a non-specific blood protein reflective of body process activity, is usually normal or elevated, and should have been high in Norman's clinical setting. However, his serum complement was on the low side, hinting at the diagnosis of a rare disease. This disease, *Hereditary Angioneurotic Edema*, a totally different disease from generic angioedema, is also referred to as Quincke's disease.[19] It is a genetic disease caused by a lack of a protein called *C1 esterase inhibitor.* This protein normally prevents activation of a cascade of proteins leading to the kind of swelling characteristic of this disease. The name itself is a misnomer since emotional stress is only one contributory cause of this phenomenon. Dr. Curtin advised me to get in touch with Michael Frank, M.D., the director of the National Institute of Allergic and Infectious Diseases. Michael Frank was wonderful to Norman and me.

Norman was admitted to NIH and was found to have an abnormally low level of *C1 esterase inhibitor* in his blood. Specific testing for this protein was not commercially available then but was conducted at NIH, where the genetic basis of Norman's condition was thus established. In the absence of a positive family history, Michael Frank attributed Norman's situation to a spontaneous single gene mutation. Norman was formally diagnosed as a case of *Sporadic Hereditary Angioneurotic Edema*—a rare medical occurrence. After the definitive diagnosis was established, he was tested cautiously at NIH and found not to be allergic to penicillin. In retrospect, it was felt that the tooth extraction was the mild trauma which precipitated the acute attack of facial and throat angioedema in Norman, not an uncommon occurrence in *Hereditary Angioneurotic Edema*. Airway obstruction due to swelling of the voice box can then develop suddenly and dramatically as it did to him. During a subsequent admission to NIH for an attack of severe abdominal pain, Norman was found by X-ray to have considerable swelling in the wall of his small intestine, establishing the cause of his recurrent "irritable bowel syndrome."

Norman was followed for many years at NIH, until the protocol for this disease was discontinued. He was treated with an androgen, Danazol, a medication Norman still takes, to minimize the frequency of recurrent attacks, and with fresh frozen plasma (FFP) at the beginning of an acute attack to try to abort it.[20] Norman, having survived with this life-threatening disease, is now retired. He lives in Silver Spring with his wife.

I still dread to think of what would have happened if he had not stopped by our office on his way to the hospital that morning. And now for Norman's perspective, in his own words:

*Since childhood I suffered from swollen hands and swollen feet. Occasionally, I would have severe stomach attacks that would debilitate me for about 24 to 36 hours. I was taken to numerous doctors and they didn't have a diagnosis. We even tried allergists. I was taken to John Hopkins and one of the doctors thought I should see a therapist.*

*At age 24, a dentist prescribed penicillin for having a tooth removed. Several hours later my voice became higher and I had swelling in my lips. I went to Dr. Mann's office and was examined. We went to Dr. Pumphrey's office and he examined me. My throat was still open at that time. A short time later, I had gone to the men's room; when I started walking back to Dr. Pumphrey's office, I could not breathe. I managed to get back to his office and was turning blue. I remembered being carried back to another room, and being put through some procedure. The last thing I remember was hearing the words, 'cut, cut, cut.' I was taken to Washington Hospital in an ambulance with Dr. Mann. Dr. Mann thought that this might be* hereditary angioedema, *and he recommended me to be a patient at NIH. At that time, Dr. Frank was head of Allergy and Infectious Diseases. He followed me for years at NIH. After numerous tests, I was placed on an amino caproic acid. When I had a stomach attack or any swelling, they gave me fresh frozen plasma to try to stop the new episode.*

*At some point they changed my medicine to Danazol 100 mg once a day, which I am presently on. At age 57, my episodes are rare . . . .*

The longer I practiced, the more I realized the scientific impact of good history-taking in clinical medicine and the importance of listening to what a patient says in practicing the art of healing. Norman certainly taught me these facts dramatically.

In 1972, Bob Pumprey, Michael Frank and I gave conferences on the topic of *angioneurotic edema* both at the Washington Hospital Center and at Georgetown Hospital. These sessions were well-received, with Bob Pumphrey concluding his part each time by declaring "From now on, any patient Oscar refers to me with a history of intermittent abdominal pain, funny swelling and any throat complaint will get a 'trach' first and a consultation second."

This statement caused laughter and applause. But the implied clinical adage—"if you think 'trach' don't delay"—remains a profound medical truth.

My memory of 1970–1971 at 2141 K Street is indelibly connected to the story of Richard Aaron, M.D. Richard had once trained under me at Georgetown. There are several reasons why Richard's story has stayed with me: He had been a model student when I tutored him in physical diagnosis; his last name, Aaron, was the same as my father's first name; my wife, Amy, had known him at Cornell University as an undergraduate and had nothing but good things to say about him. His mother, Molly Aaron, was the business manager for the prominent ophthalmology practice of Drs. Melvin Alper & David Berler in our building.

I had coffee on many mornings with Molly Aaron in the little coffee shop at 2141 K Street. Our talks inevitably turned to Richard. Molly was justifiably proud of her fine son and she kept me posted on Richard's activities, especially after he entered the Army as a medical officer and was sent to Vietnam. I noticed that a few months passed without my seeing Molly. I asked David Berler about her, and he told me the sad news: Richard had been killed in Vietnam. I was deeply saddened and troubled. Molly Aaron eventually came back to work. However, she was never quite the same again; at least, this has been my perception.

Years later, on a sunny day in June, 1996, I went to the Vietnam Veterans Memorial Wall to pay my respects to Richard's memory by making a traditional wall rubbing and, then, tracing his name. At the memorial office, I asked for guidance in locating the appropriate panel bearing the name of Captain Richard A. Aaron, M.D., from Washington, DC I was surprised when the guard, without consulting a list, handed me a small piece of paper upon which he had just scribbled Richard's name and panel number. He said, "That's an easy request. We have few doctors on the wall."

After rubbing his name against the black granite, I felt that I had established my closure with Richard. This, however, proved not to be the case. When I began to write this book, Richard Aaron came to my mind often, and I wanted to know more about his life and death.

I received a communication on March 10, 2003, about him from John C. Rose, M.D. who is the former dean and now a professor emeritus of physiology and medicine at Georgetown: "Oscar, I can verify the story about Richard but about no other physicians killed in Vietnam. You might check Vietnam casualties with the American Medical Association archives in Chicago. He was an excellent student and a great boy. He did some research in physiology with me.[21] Years ago, we made a little memorial to him in the Department of Physiology Library, but I doubt that it is still there now."

The memorial still exists, with a photo and a plaque located in room 239, Basic Science Building, Department of Physiology and Biophysics Library. The plaque reads:

*Richard Alan Aaron, M.D., Georgetown 1968, B. January 2, 1943, D. February 6, 1971. True scholar, inquisitive scientist, concerned physician. Closely associated with the Department of Physiology and Biophysics throughout his student years. Killed while serving as a medical officer with the U.S. Army in South Vietnam. His memory lives in the hearts and minds of all those who knew him.*[22]

Officially, 58,202 American soldiers died in the Vietnam War, and among them was my friend, Captain Richard Alan Aaron, M.D.:

*Army Medical Officer Captain Aaron, killed in Vietnam on February 6, 1971, was coded as an internist. There was one additional Army medical officer, coded as an internist, who was killed in Vietnam. He was Captain Howard Martin Gerstel, killed in action on 10/4/1967.* [23]

Were there other medical officers of the U.S. Armed Forces killed during the Vietnam War? The answer to this question was not readily available. I became determined to find it. Richard Aaron had walked the same grounds at Georgetown as John and I. It could so easily have been one of us. Perhaps, because of my early history, I felt it was important for me to pay special recognition to him and to the other members of my profession who had given their lives in Vietnam.

During my search, I contacted two former patients, Linda Winslow and Annette Miller, both from *The News Hour with Jim Lehrer*. They graciously helped me with my inquiry. I received my answer in September 2003:

> *Dear Oscar, We are enclosing the results of Sandi Fox's efforts to determine the number of doctors on the Vietnam Memoria . . . . Sandi is our research librarian . . . .She talked to many people. It was a challenge she enjoyed, but it took much longer than Annette and I thought it would . . . Sandi was her usual tenacious self . . . . Whenever she had a free minute during the past month, she searched for the answer . . . . In typical Sandi form, she is a little dissatisfied with the results since she cannot state definitively that she has the exact number, but she believes she has gone as far as she can.*
>
> *Her answer is 'at least 26.' She can document 26 names with the 'virtual wall' website . . . . Sandi was amazed to find that her sources did not readily have the information available, and even thanked Sandi for helping them arrive at a number!"*[24]

I still think of Richard's untimely death.

It was now 1972. Our practice was thriving. Problems with 2141 K Street, however, became a recurring agenda item at our regular monthly business meetings. Parking facilities were expensive, user-unfriendly and nearly nonexistent. This location, situated near George Washington University Hospital but in the middle of intense downtown traffic, was becoming wrong for us and for most of our patients. Also we had outgrown our facilities. Soon, we began looking for a new and better location.

Our permanent, now well-established address does justice to the famous old adage, "The three most important questions in real estate are location, location, location." Out of the hustle and bustle of downtown, easily accessible, close to Georgetown University Hospital and Sibley Memorial Hospital, only a couple of blocks from prestigious Foxhall Road, the Foxhall Square building, 3301 New Mexico Avenue, N.W., Washington, DC, 20016, was discovered by my wife, Amy, who recounts:

> *Construction of the Metro along the K Street corridor was the final reason for the decision to move to another location. Traffic wasn't just heavy—passage was sometimes impossible.*
>
> *Oscar and I were driving up Massachusetts Avenue one evening, and on the west side of the street, just before Ward Circle, we noticed a large building under construction. '4200 Massachusetts Avenue—Luxury Condominium Homes,' the sign announced. Magazine Brothers were the developers. A phone number was posted.*

*'I wonder if that building will have any space for doctors' offices?' Oscar asked me. 'Amy, please, could you call them tomorrow and find out.'*
 *The next day, I called the number, and a nice, polite woman took my call.*
 *'We won't have offices in the Condominium,' she said. 'But right behind it on New Mexico Avenue, we are constructing a medical building.'*
 *'Oh, when will it be finished?' I asked.*
 *'About this August,' she replied, ' if everything goes on schedule.'*
 *I thanked her heartily and called Oscar immediately. The rest is history.*

May I remind the reader as to why the permanent location of our office has always been so close to my heart? It was in Washington, in 1948, that I had daydreamed: " . . . I suddenly experienced a vision. In my mind's eye, I fantasized about practicing medicine on the Glover Estate. I vividly saw myself being a well-established physician and working out of an office in that prime location . . . . "[25]

Few people know that it was Amy who found the place on the old Glover Estate. As soon as she told me it would possible to have a medical office on the Glover Estate, I responded with enthusiasm. To practice medicine in this particular place would be for me a dream come true. I went immediately to Frank, Wes and Mary and convinced them that this location "was meant to be for us."

We moved in mid-September, 1973, and Foxhall Square has been our home ever since. As new doctors joined the group, "Macomar" became *"Foxhall Internists."*

## NOTES

 1. See chapter 16.
 2. Halfway between the navel and the right hip is the spot surgeons call *McBurney's Point*. It is usually but not always the location of the appendix *Rebound tenderness* describes any increase in pain noted during a medical examination after a pressing hand is removed quickly from the abdomen. It typically suggests intra-abdominal irritation/inflammation in the area of concern.
 3. Which was being more and more frequently reported in the medical literature after cycles of fast-feast dieting, an eating pattern which John had adopted.
 4. The *obturator sign* is a medical term which describes the phenomenon of lower abdominal pain amplification upon inward twisting of the bent right hip
 5. Advanced stage in the evolution of *appendicitis*, right before frank rupture of the appendix.
 6. CAT (Computer-Assisted Tomography) scan and ultrasonography are state-of-the-art radiological methods.
 7. *Locum tenens* is the temporary take-over of one's practice, during one's absence usually because of vacation or illness.

8. That bridge was established by the state government of South Carolina after much lobbying by interested local people. Connecting the island to the mainland, the bridge played a big and vital role in the meteoric development of the island of Hilton Head.

9. The quote is from the musical *My Fair Lady*, by Alan Jay Lerner and Frederick Loewe.

10. Stapleton, *Upward Journey*, 179–180.

11. Stapleton, *Upward Journey*, 180.

12. Personal communication from Dr. Charles P. Duvall, May 2003.

13. Personal communication from Dr. Clifton R. Gruver, August 2003.

14. School physicals were never covered by insurance and were always self-paid. They usually involved much paperwork. Today, doctors, already conditioned to paperwork, but preferring to avoid the hassle of third party payers, welcome them. How things have changed!

15. See chapter 16.

16. Personal communication from Dr. Clifton R. Gruver, August 2003.

17. He has given express consent to tell this story including the citing of his name.

18. When a doctor performs a *trach* or *tracheotomy*, he is performing an emergency procedure whereby a small tube is inserted through the anterior surface of the neck into the trachea (the portion of the upper airway leading down into the bronchi and lungs). This provides an alternative pathway for the air to get down into the lungs, bypassing the blockage higher up in the airway.

19. Dr. Heinrich Quincke (1842–1922) included a classic description of the disease of *hereditary angioneurotic edema* among his other significant contributions to the literature of medicine.

20. *Fresh Frozen Plasma* (FFP) is produced from donated blood by removing the red and white cells and freezing the liquid material which remains.

21. W. H. Straub, D.F. Flanagan, R. Aaron, and J.C. Rose, "Fate of injected radiodinated 4-iodoantipyrine in the dog and rat," *Proceedings of the Society of Experimental Biology and Medicine*, 116 (August, 1964) 1119–1122.

22. Personal communication from Ellen Martin, executive secretary, Department of Physiology and Biophysics, Georgetown University School of Medicine, March 2003.

23. Personal communications from Mariah French, assistant director of communications, Vietnam Veterans Memorial Fund, and Tom Campbell, program analyst with the Directorate for Information and Reports at the Department of Defense, April and May, 2003.

24. My friend, Richard Aaron, was one of these 26 physicians killed in Vietnam. Interested readers can find details on the other casualties in *Appendix 3, Physicians on the Vietnam Veterans Memorial Wall*. This information was obtained through the courtesy of Linda Winslow, Deputy Executive Producer; Annette Miller, Director, Research & Information Services; and Sandi Fox, Research Librarian; all at *The News Hour with Jim Lehrer.*

25. See Chapter 9.

*Chapter Nineteen*

# The Foxhall Years

As Oscar Mann, M.D., a senior partner at Foxhall Internists, my dream was finally realized.[1] I was a physician, well-established in my favorite city. These thoughts gave me great satisfaction. I was now enjoying the happy life.

The Foxhall years were very good years. I enjoyed my family, my profession, my partners, my patients, my colleagues, my staff, and my friends. These were *golden years* in American medicine and more especially, they were my golden years.

I remained active at the Georgetown University Medical Center, admitting almost all my patients there, and I participated in teaching and training programs there. I helped with mending fences between "town and gown," served on committees and became active in the Georgetown Alumni Association. In time, I was promoted to the rank of clinical professor. I continued to pursue national professional recognition by becoming a Fellow of the American College of Physicians, the American College of Cardiology and the American College of Chest Physicians.

The move from K Street to New Mexico Avenue occurred during the financial recession of 1973. As revenues sagged and cash flow turned sluggish, we became concerned that "we had bitten off more than we could chew," as Dr. MacMurray was prone to say. His worry proved unnecessary as many of our patients — downtown lawyers, business executives, politicians and civil servants — found our new location convenient and accessible. Our downtown clientele held firm — for the most part they made the transition — while our uptown and suburban patients were delighted with our close-by location. Parking was excellent with a large three-floor attached garage. The efficiency of the office had been greatly enhanced by a congestion-free location, modern and spacious quarters, and the proximity to our hospitals. Soon we began looking for a new associate.

Enter Alexander (Alec) C. Chester, a 1973 graduate of the Columbia University College of Physicians and Surgeons with postgraduate training at Georgetown where he was a second-year nephrology fellow working with Dr. George Schreiner.[2] He caught my attention while helping to care for a patient with end-stage kidney disease. I was enormously impressed by his comportment, clinical skills and prolific publishing record. Rumor had it that Alec was headed for an academic career. One summer day in 1977, I ran into him at a Baskin-Robbins ice cream parlor in suburban Bethesda and, much to my surprise, learned he was looking for an opportunity to practice internal medicine in the Washington, DC area. I wasted little time in bringing him to the attention of my partners.

Frank, Wes, Mary and I met to share our impressions. All signs were favorable:

Frank: "He's a young Wes Oler."

Wes: "He's a young Frank MacMurray."

Mary: "He's both a young Frank MacMurray and a young Wes Oler."

Oscar: "It does not get any better than that."

We made him an offer he couldn't refuse, and he came aboard in July 1978.

Solo practice is no longer realistic, except for a hardy few, because of the complexities required for the delivery of present-day medical care. On the other hand, I do not know the optimum number or ideal mix of physicians for a medical practice. We subscribed to the premise, as many corporate chief executive officers do, that if an organization does not grow, it will get smaller with age and eventually disappear.

Charles P. Duvall was a 1962 graduate of the University of Rochester School of Medicine. He trained in internal medicine at Yale and Rochester, and he sub-specialized in hematology-oncology at the National Cancer Institute and then at Georgetown. Chuck went into private practice in 1968 with Drs. Charles Ordman and John Hughes, who were two prominent physicians in downtown Washington. He acquired a reputation of being an outstanding clinician during 11 years in that practice. Chuck brought his established practice into our group in 1979. As a full partner, he enhanced Foxhall's prestige and appeal. As a result, we gained patient patronage, especially from downtown Washington. Chuck remained active in organized medicine on the local and national level. His activities included the presidency of the American Society of Internal Medicine, service as a delegate to, and then Legislative Council Chair of, the American Medical Association and later the chairmanship of the Board of Blue Cross-Blue Shield of the District of Columbia.

Charles Duvall was elected a Master of the American College of Physicians. The honor was officially conferred in April, 2004.

Larry E. Klein, M.D., was referred to us by my brother, John, who had worked with him at the Johns Hopkins Hospital. As Klein himself told us, his "background was not completely Hopkins, though it was mostly so." He had served two years of medical residence at Strong Memorial Hospital in Rochester, New York. Prior to joining our group, he had been on the Hopkins faculty full time in the Division of General Internal Medicine. He enjoyed an excellent reputation. Larry specialized in geriatrics and was one of the first U.S. physicians to become certified in this then-new specialty. A former president of the District of Columbia component of the American Society of Internal Medicine, he is now governor of the American College of Physicians for the District of Columbia and related areas.

Next came West Coaster Saulius Naujokaitis, M.D. He went to medical school and trained at the University of California, Los Angeles, from 1970 to 1977. He then worked at the National Cancer Institute from 1977 to 1982. Saulius joined us in 1986, after having been on the full-time staff in internal medicine at Georgetown.

On July 1, 1989, Andrew Umhau joined our group. A 1985 graduate of the Duke University School of Medicine, he had completed a three-year medical residency at Georgetown before becoming chief medical resident there.

He recounts: "I happened to run into Alec Chester before Grand Rounds at Georgetown one morning and he asked me what I was going to do after my chief year. When he heard I was interested in practicing, he called me a short time later to have me meet with him and introduce me to Foxhall. . . . I count myself very fortunate to have run into Alec that morning—I might have ended up in some dead-end, now bankrupt, internal medicine practice elsewhere in the city which would have left me disillusioned and bitter, working as a managed-care wage slave. Instead I have the best practice imaginable."[3]

Our practice continued to expand. Richard D. Schubert was a *summa cum laude* graduate of the State University of New York Medical School at Brooklyn. He did his postgraduate medical training at a prestigious Boston medical establishment. Richard was a highly regarded internist-rheumatologist at the old Worth Daniels group in downtown Washington when he joined us as a full partner in July, 1993. He later commented: "Smartest move I ever made . . . after marrying Geane, of course."

In May, 2003, Dr. Schubert published a novel, *Chickering & Sons*, which is a story that gives, unlike current T.V. medical sitcoms, a most realistic picture of what it's like to be a doctor. The role is seen through the eyes of a middle-aged female medical student.

Beth L. P. Ungar, M.D., was a 1977 graduate of Georgetown University School of Medicine. She joined Foxhall in 1994. She took her postgraduate medical training at Georgetown (1977–1980) and specialized in infectious diseases at Hopkins (1981–1983) before spending two years as a Medical Staff Fellow at the National Institute of Allergy and Infectious Diseases, in Bethesda, MD, from 1984 to 1986. She then spent several years in academic positions.

Theodore C. M. Li, M.D., a graduate of Cornell University Medical College, received his postgraduate training at the New York-Cornell Medical Center (1977–1980). He was a Fellow at the Division of Internal Medicine of Cornell University Medical College (1980) as well as a Henry J. Kaiser Fellow in General Internal Medicine at Harvard Medical School. Ted served as Director of the American Board of Internal Medicine (1996–2000). He was also a busy, well-regarded practicing internist in Washington. As did his predecessors, Dr. Duvall and Dr. Schubert, Ted joined our group with an established practice and as a full partner.

Linda L. Yau, M.D., a 1994 honors graduate of Johns Hopkins University School of Medicine, did her postgraduate medical training at the Johns Hopkins Hospital (1994–97). She worked at the Johns Hopkins Medical Services Corporation from 1997 to 1999. Linda came to us in March 1999 and quickly became a bright light in our office. She has taken over much of my practice.

Kristin E. Thomas, a 1994 graduate of the University of Michigan School of Medicine, did her internal medicine postgraduate training at Hopkins, including a year as assistant chief of service, more commonly known as chief resident. She joined the practice in December 1999, after serving as a Hopkins Fellow in rheumatology.

Patti Allen Colevas, a 1989 graduate of Duke University School of Medicine, received her postgraduate medical training at the Johns Hopkins Hospital (1989 to 1992), and she joined our office in January, 2001, after being on the staff of Harvard Medical School and working as an attending physician at Brigham and Women's Hospital in Boston.[4]

David M. Hansen, a Johns Hopkins Medical School classmate of Linda Yau's, received his postgraduate medical training at Stanford University Medical Center. He had worked at the Menlo Medical Clinic for five years after residency before joining our group in the summer of 2002.[5]

Thomas L. Sacks, a Tufts graduate, obtained his postgraduate medical training at Boston City Hospital (1972 to 1975) before moving on to do hematology at the University of Minnesota (1975–1977) and oncology at the National Cancer Institute from 1977 to 1980. He was in the well-established practice of Washington Internal Medicine & Oncology from 1980 to 2002, joining Foxhall in 2003 as a full partner.

Foxhall has expertise, talent, quality as well as a close relationship with the Johns Hopkins Medical Center. Some in the Washington medical community have said we have developed critical mass. Today, Foxhall is a 13-member group practice considered by both doctors and laymen to be the finest practice of internal medicine in Washington, another of my dreams come true. These physicians have taken Foxhall into the 21st century. They are carrying our flag in difficult times for medicine and doing a magnificent job.

To date, no one has turned out to be a *prima donna*, but as more doctors joined the group, multiple viewpoints had to be accommodated, and, from time to time, some personalities needed to have their egos massaged. Foxhall was fortunate to benefit for many years from the leadership of Frank Mac-Murray, assisted by Wes Oler and myself, and subsequently from the guidance of Alec Chester who carried on Frank's enlightened role, assisted by Larry Klein. Our steady expansion was made possible and greatly facilitated by Avis Strader, our office manager, as well as by Corky Vance and Maria Difranscesco, our business officers. Often affectionately referred as A/C/M, they were, and still are our three musketeers, the backbone of our administrative infrastructure and computerized business organization. All three women are not only adept technically but have great people skills in dealing with the staff and the doctors. Given the wise and competent direction of our managing physicians and the effective administration of A/C/M, Foxhall became the thriving force in the Washington medical community.

I was blessed to have Beth Bell as my private secretary and clinical medical assistant for many years. She attended Radford University in Southern Virginia from 1974 to 1975, and, in 1978, obtained a B.S. with a major in English and a minor in Biology at San Antonio College, while her father, a colonel in the U.S. Air Force Medical Corps, was stationed in San Antonio, Texas. She was proud to have been concurrently nationally certified as a clinical medical assistant, having taken two years of study to qualify for certification. Beth, who came to Foxhall in 1978, has been a major part of my professional life, and I cannot write enough nice things on her behalf. The easiest way to tell you how I feel about Beth is to tell you what happened when Beth was thinking about moving out of town, after marrying a wonderful fellow, Chris Bogusky, in October 1999. She asked me for a generic letter of reference. I gave her a recommendation letter with which the entire office agreed, especially the fact that patients loved her and depended on her. The highlight of my letter was: "If Beth comes to you for a position, I would suggest you lock the door until she signs on the dotted line, and then be sure to contact me."

Beth comments: "I am still with Foxhall; this November will mark my 25th year here. I still get to 'take care' of a lot of Dr. Mann's patients while working for Dr. Linda Yau now. Dr. Mann, thanks for sharing your manuscript with me. It brought back many memories and how much I miss you."[6]

There were other major advantages to Foxhall. Frank MacMurray was our founder and remained at the helm for close to 50 years. Dr. Albert Schweitzer once observed: "Example is not the main thing in influencing others. It is the only thing."

A typical scene at Foxhall illustrates this aphorism. In the face of a snow forecast, Washington had panicked and everyone in the office was gone by late morning or early afternoon, but not Frank G. MacMurray. He not only stayed behind; he actually slept in the office. In the morning, there he was, the senior partner, manning the phones and accommodating patients. Although most patients canceled their appointments, some struggled in, regardless of how bad the weather was. Frank's predictable behavior—he always led by example—tells us why he was so loved and respected by our group and by the patients we served. Frank MacMurray embodied Dr. Schweitzer's definition of leadership.

Practicing medicine in our nation's capital was not without its unique features. Alec Chester and I played a role in a noted Washington incident, each of us initially unaware of the other's participation.

In early July 1993, I was called by the wife of a patient. She was concerned about a family friend on the White House staff. She mentioned the name, Vincent Foster. At the time, the name meant nothing to me. The caller said that the person in question was depressed and needed help. She asked me to recommend a psychiatrist in Washington and to help with the referral. As it was vacation time, I gave her the names of two psychiatrists, and, to close the loop, I informed these two colleagues of the referral. Accommodating requests of this nature was part of my daily routine, and I quickly went on about my day and days.

On July 20, 1993, the body of Vincent Foster, an apparent suicide, was discovered at Fort Marcy Park, along the Potomac, in nearby Northern Virginia. A note was found on the deceased, and its contents were immediately publicized. Scribbled on a crumpled piece of paper were the names of Drs. Stefan Pasternack and Marty Allen, with their telephone numbers. These were the names of the two psychiatrists that I had provided, albeit indirectly, to Mr. Foster, now identified as the Counselor to the President of the United States. I never saw Mr. Foster and neither did Drs. Pasternack or Allen.

On the very evening of the day that the body of Mr. Foster was discovered, Dr. Chester was awakened about 11:30 P.M. by a telephone call from a patient, a Washington psychiatrist, who said: "I need your help on a grave matter. As soon as possible, meet me at the corner of 36th and P Streets and be sure to bring your medical black bag with you."

Dr. Chester complied with the request. Just before midnight, he and the psychiatrist were picked up by a sedan and taken to a Georgetown townhouse. The door to the Foster home was opened and Dr. Chester was invited in by no less than President Bill Clinton to minister to the widow.

Drs. Pasternack and Allen were interviewed immediately by the authorities. The referral was easily traced to me; however, I was never contacted by the investigators.

A couple of months later, an ABC News White House reporter, whose name I no longer recall, called my office and left a message for me to get in touch with him. Ann Compton, White House ABC News correspondent, answered the phone when I returned the reporter's call. Ann, the wife of Dr. William Hughes, knew me, and she vouched for my credibility. The reporter demanded to know the name of the person who initially had contacted me about Mr. Foster. He was informed that this was privileged medical information, but I let it slip that I had been approached by a woman. He became very insistent. Ultimately I said: "I am not at liberty to give you the name of the person who called me, but I can tell you it was definitely not Hillary Clinton."

That answer did it. I was never again contacted by the media or anyone else, for that matter, about the late Mr. Foster.

Larry Klein recently refreshed my memory about his own Washington medical story, which I sheepishly admit to having initiated:

*When you talk about Alex meeting President Clinton, it reminded me of the time I walked into work one morning and had several people tell me they enjoyed seeing my name on the front page of* The Wall Street Journal. *I thought this was a joke, but after several people commented, I went down to the drug store in the building and bought a* Wall Street Journal. *Indeed, there I was, quoted as an expert in geriatrics ('Professor of Medicine at Johns Hopkins and Georgetown') discussing what I thought about President Reagan's mental capacity in an article discussing his weak performance in the first debate of his second campaign.*

*The next thing I knew, there were reporters from various TV stations. Various members of my family and my wife Gayle's family saw me on a short segment of Dan Rather's 6 P.M. news (including Gayle's relatives in Canada). I then got a call from Ted Koppel's* Nightline *to appear on that show. Georgetown encouraged me to go on the show (they thought it would be good publicity for Georgetown) but Frank and Wes then suggested to me that perhaps this was all getting out-of-hand and that I would probably be best off turning down offers such as* Nightline, *as well as a request for an interview from* Time Magazine.

*Considering all of Frank's and Wes's experience over the years, I decided they were right, and I followed their advice . . . You, Oscar, had a role in all this, as you may remember. The reason I was interviewed by a reporter from* The Wall Street Journal *is that you gave him my name as a geriatrics specialist. Without that 'referral,' I would not have had that 'opportunity' to be on the front page of* The Wall Street Journal *or seen on Dan Rather's news show.*[7]

Washington, DC, is certainly an interesting place to practice medicine!

When I finished my training, we were living in a modest apartment on Battery Lane in Bethesda, MD. Amy worked at George Washington University on a research project on driver behavior, from August 1964 to early autumn 1966. She later worked for the Washington Performing Arts Society until the fall of 1968. Once I began private practice in downtown Washington, Amy and I felt it was time to upgrade our living quarters and to be closer to the center of action. We found the perfect place, a brand new high-rise apartment building in Chevy Chase in Maryland just past the DC line, the Irene, just finished by Abe Pollin and named after his wife.[8] A deluxe edifice, the Irene featured many desirable conveniences, such as a large, handsomely decorated lobby, a 24 hour desk service, a nice size party room, a big swimming pool and a tennis court on the roof, as well as a sauna room off the lobby, the latter a totally new amenity for most of us in 1966. Coming home from work, taking a dip in the pool and a sauna bath became a very pleasant and relaxing routine for me.

However, after two enjoyable years at the *Irene*, we felt that instead of continuing to pay rent, we ought to begin building equity. We bought our first home, an attractive moderate size house on Ridgefield Road in Chevy Chase, MD. We were ideally situated, close to Washington, and were living there when our twin daughters were born at Georgetown University Hospital. Our lives suddenly experienced the true joy and bliss of parenthood, especially as we watched the girls grow. As the twins became older, we outgrew our house. Amy had always dreamed of living in upper Northwest Washington and I wished to be even closer to the epicenter of my professional activities. Our house had appreciated significantly. However, the catalyst for our next move was a newly passed District of Columbia law: namely, a significant tax would now be levied on professional people living in the suburbs and practicing in DC.

In October 1977, we moved to Weaver Terrace in the Kent section of Washington, where we purchased an elegant, large and almost new townhouse from Sam Pardoe. Now I was less than a mile from my office, and we were only a few minutes away from the Kennedy Center and downtown Washington. It was country living within the city. We loved our new neighborhood and enjoyed its wonderful features of privacy, beauty, location.

Our neighbors included my eminent former teachers and now patients, Drs. Coffey and Holden. We soon became good friends with many neighbors, notably Dr. Francis Fowler and his extended family. We felt secure in our new environment, but in 1980 our tranquil neighborhood was shattered by the murder of Dr. Michael Halberstam during a burglary. This incident hit home in a big way as Dr. Halberstam, a well-known Washington internist, from a prominent DC family, lived just around the corner from us.

Our daughters went to private schools from kindergarten through high school: St Patrick's Episcopal Day School, St Andrews School, and to private colleges, Bates and Davidson. When I grew up in France, public schools were considered superior to private schools. I never understood why the opposite is for the most part true in the U.S.A. This dilemma continues to this day and defies solution.

Our summer vacations were spent in Longport, New Jersey, where Amy's parents maintained a summer home. These were joyous days. We explored the New Jersey coast from Ocean City to Cape May, including Strathmere, Sea Isle, Avalon, Stone Harbor, etc. The New Jersey beaches are among the best sandy beaches in my experience. We loved to ride the scenic route from Atlantic City to Cape May, take the ferry to Lewes, Delaware, and then turn around and return to Longport. We enjoyed the big boardwalk of Ocean City, New Jersey. The girls particularly liked the amusement park and merry-go-round. Life was simple, enjoyable and almost carefree, compared with the current century. In the words of cousin Oscar Rozansky, "Life was good, I had arrived." The issues were different and so much more pleasant back then.

Along with everyone else, I experienced the change of pace and the new complexity of life during the ensuing years. Advancing science, new technology and the information explosion all played a role. However, we human beings, doctors included, are not making things simpler. A little incident remains dear to my heart, and still causes me to chuckle. It illustrates our changing way of life.

I was active at the Washington Hospital Center in my early days of practice. I was assigned to their outpatient committee which passed a rule expelling clinic patients who missed three consecutive clinic appointments. One recipient of such a notice answered with a letter:

> *I have been going to various clinics for several years. I am followed in medical, surgical and orthopedic clinics. But I never have had an appointment in the consecutive clinic.*

The wisdom of this letter brought much needed laughter to our committee. It led to the reinstatement of this common sense lady to the clinic system, and a complete reconsideration of the rule.

It was the winter of 1979. I had been in the practice of internal medicine and cardiology since July 1966. Anna and Karen, our twin girls, who were then seven years old, came down with the flu. They woke up one night, coughing and calling, "Mommy." Amy, a deep sleeper, did not respond. Anna and Karen wanted to know if they could take more medicine, namely Robitussin-DM. My answer was, yes.

They responded: "We want Mommy."

I replied, a little annoyed: "She is asleep; nothing will wake her up. I am a doctor. I know best."

Karen came back: "You are an adult's doctor, not a kid's doctor."

Anna chimed in: "You don't know anything about medicine for us."

Finally, Amy went into their room half-asleep, and told them that it was fine and dandy to take more cough medicine. They took their medicine and were promptly in slumber land. Amy went back to sleep as well. I stayed awake. Kids don't lie. They knew that I was not comfortable taking care of children. Fortunately, my practice did not include children.

Foxhall accommodated a diverse clientele, including a significant international referral base, the largest being from Central and South America. I quickly became aware that Spanish was becoming the second most spoken language, at least in the United States. Several of our doctors, Dr. MacMurray in particular, were able to communicate in limited Spanish, while some members of our staff were fluent. We easily welcomed this important patient segment.

The core strength of our practice was the many Joes and Janes, the American people, individuals from every walk of life and many ethnic backgrounds, all of whom make this such a great country!

We also took care of VIPs and their families. Drs. MacMurray and Oler were totally at ease with VIP patients. Initially, I was not. A little demon seemed to be hovering over me and causing me some kind of insecurity in their presence: "Why should I, Oscar, an immigrant who came from very humble roots, be asked to care for some of the nation's high and mighty?"

I did not understand how a person with such a giant ego as mine could possibly be shy. I don't think this insecurity ever interfered with my performance, but I found the feeling annoying to the point that I visited a therapist for help. I learned not to dwell on this trait. The new Oscar finally appeared, but truth be told, my little "hang-up" has never left me completely, even to this day. I once had a conversation with a VIP patient of mine, to whom I confided my inhibition. This is what he said to me: "Oscar, when I prick myself with a pin, I bleed, believe it or not, just like you do. And I have my quirks. Lighten up."

What my patient told me made sense. I did lighten up.

Some of my memorable medical school teachers included Robert J. Coffey, Andrew A. Marchetti, Raymond T. Holden, George E. Stevens, Alexander M. Burnett and Thomas F. Magovern.

Each of these teachers was to reappear in my life during my years at Foxhall. As I reflect on the reason, the answer is simple. Despite the fact that Washington, DC, is the capital of the most powerful country in the world, it has remained a small city, with distinct communities. All of these men were from the Georgetown University Medical Center. We each tend to live and function within our own community.

The first of these people to reappear was Robert J. Coffey. Born in Elmira, N.Y., on November 14, 1908, he entered the Georgetown University School of Medicine in September 1928. Dr. Coffey was the Chairman of Surgery at the Georgetown University Medical Center 22 years, from 1947 to 1969. He remained active until his retirement from surgical practice and teaching in 1982. He was 73 years old when he stepped down. He died at the age of 86 in 1995.[9] I developed a long-term professional and personal relationship with Dr. Coffey. This included a life-long friendship with his family. In his senior years, I had the privilege of caring for him. He was a model patient.

Obstetrician-gynecologist Andrew Marchetti was a patient at Georgetown shortly after I went into private practice. His doctor, Dr. James Fitzgerald, who had taken a few days off, asked me to cover his practice and to look in on Dr. Marchetti. As a patient, he was the same wonderful gentleman who graciously picked up a junior medical student (that student being me) at a bus stop and gave him a ride in his big black auto. Dr. Marchetti was also a man of the arts and loved classical music, especially opera. He could be heard humming and whistling *Aida* on the wards, in the delivery suite or in the operating room. Dr. Marchetti has since passed on. He was truly a clinical giant and a rare human being.

Dr. Raymond Holden was also a prominent Ob-Gyn specialist in private practice and held the title of Clinical Professor at Georgetown. He attended the Georgetown University School of Medicine and graduated in 1928. His father, also a well known Washington physician, had completed his medical studies at Georgetown in 1881. During World War II, Raymond Holden served with distinction in the U.S. Navy. He was the commanding officer of a military hospital in the south of England during and after D-Day. Dr. Holden ultimately reached the rank of rear admiral. While in private practice, he admitted his patients to Georgetown Hospital and actively participated in the teaching program of students and residents. He joined the full-time Ob-Gyn staff at Georgetown after leaving private practice at the age of 73, and had yet another distinguished career. He became the director of the training program and a senior consultant in his field at the medical school. Dr. Holden rose to the chairmanship of the American Medical Association's Board of Trustees in his "spare time." While I was in practice, we treated several patients together. It was also my privilege and honor to serve with him on an important Georgetown committee, reviewing the last ten-year performance of the Department of Surgery. At 85, Dr. Holden became my patient. I found him a marvel of good health. He was a man "ten feet tall" in every way when I first met him. Today, as he nears 100, he is still a man of great stature. Dr. Magovern adds

*Ray . . . is the oldest living alumnus of the school, is in command of all his faculties, continues to be an avid reader, does not need a hearing aid and is happy to render a reasoned opinion on anything one wants to talk about.*[10]

Lastly, as I joined Frank and Wes at Foxhall, Drs. Stevens, Burnett and Magovern also went into private practice. I interacted professionally with them throughout the years.

When John and I were still in our basic years of medical school, our mother required a moderately complex surgical intervention. After careful research, we selected Dr. Stevens to be her surgeon. The operation went well. Thankfully, there was no bad news. We never received a bill from Georgetown or from Dr. Stevens. We were grateful.

John and I remember best Dr. Stevens's bedside manner. Mother had never had surgery. She was frightened. Dr. Stevens was superb in managing her anxieties. The evening of discharge, Dr. Stevens met John and me in the GYN conference room and spoke to us with directness, openness, kindness and professionalism. This meeting became etched in our memories and influenced the way John and I later related to patients and their relatives. I was one of the few non Ob-Gyn physicians invited to his retirement party. Amy and I were honored. Dr. Stevens is now gone. Mother worshiped him until her dying day.

Dr. Alexander Burnett, now retired, delivered my twin daughters. He was one of the most caring physicians I have known. I was once told by a colleague, whose wife had a delivery by Dr. Burnett, that "Alex must have been psychoanalyzed by God himself."

A few special words about Dr. Thomas F. Magovern. Tom remains a close friend to this day. We spent many hours together on the Medical Board of the Georgetown University Alumni Association. We served in various capacities and each of us was nominated to the position of chair of the medical alumni board. We each received the John Carroll Award, the highest recognition of alumni service given by the Board of Governors of the Georgetown University Alumni Association. I often exchange nostalgic reminiscences about Georgetown with Tom, now a full professor of Ob-Gyn at Georgetown.

I continue to enjoy the closeness of long-established friendships, especially with my medical school sidekick Charles Tartaglia and his lovely wife Ann. My esteemed and prominent colleague, Clif Gruver (now retired), observes:

> *Charles Tartaglia became an outstanding psychiatrist on the staff at George-town, and a person to whom I often referred patients with utmost confidence. I recall a very impressive video interview he taped with a woman who had end-stage kidney disease and decided to come off hemodialysis (artificial kidney ma-chine), fully knowing the consequences. I've never forgotten.*[11]

Washington is, in some ways, indeed a small town for those of us who are its permanent residents. We live in our own little circle. We mingle—usually professionally and only occasionally socially— with members of "official Washington." But one never knows who one might run into in D.C.

For example, it was a delightful early spring Saturday in Washington, and I was on weekend call for the office. Foxhall had few patients in the hospital. Things were quiet, so quiet, that I kept calling the Medical Bureau answering service to be certain my beeper was functioning properly. I was told not to worry and to take it easy as they would not fail to contact me. I went to my office to do some paperwork. About noon, I decided to visit my cousin, Vivian, who was recuperating from surgery at the old Doctors' Hospital downtown on K Street. I was in a light mood, with not a care on my mind, content that the rest of the weekend would be uneventful.

I parked in the mostly empty doctors' lot, visited with my cousin for about an hour and decided to get a bite of lunch. The eating places near Doctors' Hospital were closed. I was hungry. I left my car at the hospital and walked a few blocks with the intention of lunching at Sholl's cafeteria on Connecticut Avenue. Sholl's never closed. I passed the classy Duke Zeibert's Restaurant on M Street and thought: "Oscar, why don't you take advantage of the circumstances and treat yourself to a nice lunch at Duke's "

I walked into the restaurant and was greeted by the maitre d', Mel Krupin, who expressed surprise at seeing me alone for lunch. He understood my explanation, and he led me to a separate, small and private dining room. I ordered lunch. While waiting to be served, I began to feel a bit guilty and scrupulous: "What am I doing here? Am I not on call for the office? Dr. Harvey, Frank and Wes would not approve. Neither would Uncle Isor."

I heard a clear, loud voice from the main dining room yelling: "Is there a doctor in the house?"

Just then my beeper went off for the first time that day. But there was no question—I had to respond to the urgency of the cry from the main dining room. When I got there, I saw a crowd of people around a center table. As I approached, I identified myself and the people immediately stood aside.

I recognized a patient of Dr. Oler, the famous lady of jewelry, Madame Wellington. She was choking and speechless, pointing a finger at her throat. She was blue. Seated next to her was one of my own patients, a leading Washington businessman, Mr. P.R. He greeted me effusively: "Dr. Mann, am I glad to see you! Your sense of timing is incredible."

I immediately moved into position behind Madame Wellington, who was obviously choking on a piece of food in her windpipe, experiencing what is often called a *café coronary*.[12] I performed a *Heimlich Maneuver*.[13] No results. I tried again. Still no results. I had been trained in the *Heimlich Maneuver*, but I had never performed it in a real emergency situation. I was sweating and scared. I tried again, double checked the position of my joined fists on the patient's *epigastrium* (center of the stomach) and applied a vigorous localized compression to that area. This time, to my enormous relief, a pink chunk of lobster came flying out of Madame Wellington's mouth and across the table. She instantly regained her color, and in a raspy voice, said: "Thanks for the hug. You saved my life. I will tell Dr. Oler that you were a good boy."

People applauded and someone called out, "You are a hero."

Mel Krupin thanked me. He added, "on behalf of Duke Zeibert and all of us here, lunch is on the house."

He offered me a cocktail which I declined. I remained a bit shaky, but I was happy that she was alive. Only then did I return the Medical Bureau answering service's call which turned out to be a routine prescription refill. I was able to finish my lunch in a leisurely manner, but I still felt a bit shaky. As I was leaving Duke's, I bumped into Michael Petite, M.D., a psychiatrist, a friend and a colleague, who with his wife, Jeannette, and children, was going to a nearby Brooks Brothers store. Michael asked what I was doing there, pointing to the restaurant. My nerves still on edge, I replied: "Mike, if I told you the story, you would not believe it, so I will save it for another time. I don't feel like being analyzed by a psychiatrist just now; nothing personal. Have a nice day."

On Monday, during our early morning conference call, I reported my adventure to our group.[14]

Living and practicing in Washington, DC, was rewarding in many respects. Amy's love and companionship, the twins' birth, our superb family life, our children's activities, my excellent relationship with my brother, John, and my sister-in-law, Risa, as well as my other relatives — all these things brought joy to my life. I was also grateful for the close personal and professional relationships that I had formed.

At the risk of sounding self-serving, let me share with you, the reader, a little something else about myself, something of which I am proud. In all my years of practice, no desk ever came between me and my patients. I communicated with them face to face on their side of the desk.

One day in 1995, I received a report from an aging senior psychiatrist about a patient. The letter was fine in every respect but one. It was addressed, *"Dear F.D.R."*

I decided not to call this "obvious blooper" to the attention of my consultant, rationalizing that "The poor guy is beginning to lose it." However, a few days later, a patient, a prominent Washington lawyer, presented me with a small gift-wrapped package. Inside, was a framed Xeroxed copy of a page from a book that had recently been published. The title had been added in bold and elegant font at the top center of this page. The inscription read *No Ordinary Time: Franklin and Eleanor Roosevelt: The Home Front in World War II*, by Doris Kearns Goodwin.

The contents of the page, reproduced in part below, described a grueling fact-finding journey to the Pacific theater that had been undertaken by First Lady Eleanor Roosevelt at the urging of President Franklin Roosevelt:

> *As Eleanor settled into her seat for the flight to San Francisco, she thought of all the things she wanted to tell Franklin. Bone-tired but unable to sleep, obsessed with the thought that somehow there must be a way, through fundamental change in the postwar era, to make sense out of all the carnage she had witnessed, she took out her pad and scribbled a series of notes . . . .*
>
> *Yet, when she called him from the airport in San Francisco, he could not resist teasing her 'as if she had been on a pleasure jaunt which he* [President Roosevelt] *had been big-hearted enough to fix up for her.' Eleanor was devastated.*
>
> *The only thing that had kept her going through the long and tiring days was the thought that she . . . was accomplishing what the president had asked her to do. And now he seemed uninterested and unconcerned. As soon as she hung up the phone, she called Anna* [her daughter] *in Seattle and poured out her disappointment, remarking that 'she had never worked harder in her life.' Eleanor said she was going to ask her Pacific escort, Major George Durno, to report to the "OM" on the trip, in the hope that he'd tell him* [President Roosevelt] *how successful it was. "Poor LL," Anna commented to John* [her brother].[15] *('OM,' 'Old Man,' 'Oscar Mann,' 'LL' and ' Lovely Lady' were the codes Anna and John used for the president and the first lady).*[16]

It is easy to understand the appellations, "LL" and "Lovely Lady." The code names, "OM" and "Old Man," are standard military terms for a commander. It is the "Oscar Mann" that's strange! I have no explanation for the inclusion of "Oscar Mann," as a code name in the context of the World War II White House. Perhaps someone in the Secret Service knew of my unbounded admiration for President Franklin Delano Roosevelt, though it is something I seriously doubt.[17]

My rush to judgment of an older colleague, a psychiatrist, had obviously been erroneous. The framed page still hangs in my study, and reminds me of some of the lighter moments side of my days of medical practice.

Alas! Nothing is forever. The years go by. Life changes. Frank MacMurray and Wes Oler retired at 75, Wes died at 80, our mother died at 91, and this chapter ends with the fact that I selected another path—or rather that life chose one for me.

## NOTES

1. Our practice had become bigger than any of its parts. So, hereafter, I refer to it as *Foxhall*.

2. As previously noted in chapter 14 *nephrology* denotes the medical specialty of kidney diseases. Dr. Schreiner was then the Director of Nephrology at Georgetown University Medical Center.

3. Personal communication from Dr. Andrew Umhau, August, 2003.

4. Brigham and Women's Hospital (BWH) is a major teaching hospital of Harvard Medical School, resulting from a merger of three hospitals: the Peter Bent Brigham Hospital, the Robert Breck Brigham Hospital and the Boston Hospital for Women.

5. The Menlo Medical Clinic is a Stanford-affiliated group located in Menlo Park, a small town adjacent to Palo Alto.

6. Personal communication from Beth C. Bogusky, October, 2003.

7. Personal communication from Larry Klein, September, 2003.

8. Abe Pollin, the well-known Washington, DC entrepreneur, owner of the Washington Wizards basketball franchise.

9. This chronological information was obtained from personal communications with his family.

10. Personal communication from Tom Magovern, M.D., October, 2003.

11. Personal communication from Dr. Clifton Gruver, September, 2003.

12. *Café coronary* is a popular term for acute airway obstruction occurring while eating and caused by a chunk of food. It is a critical, sometimes deadly problem.

13. A series of under-the-diaphragm abdominal thrusts applied to a choking individual. This lifesaving maneuver was developed in 1974 by Henry J. Heimlich, M.D., the noted American thoracic surgeon. The maneuver forces enough air from the lungs out through the mouth to expel a foreign object blocking the airway. In 1984, Dr. Heimlich received the Lasker Award for his discovery, which is credited with saving many thousands of lives.

14. We had a regular conference call every Monday (Tuesday on long weekends), very early in the morning, so that the person on call could inform the other doctors about the weekend activities.

15. Two of the children of Franklin and Eleanor Roosevelt.

16. Doris Kearns Goodwin, *No Ordinary Time: Franklin and Eleanor Roosevelt: The Home Front in World War II* (New York: Simon & Schuster, 1995), 466.

17. See chapter 7.

## Chapter Twenty

# Opening a New Chapter

In July 1999, as I approached the age of 65, I began to think about retirement. My hope was to continue my practice until the age of 70, working at a slower pace and taking advantage of our office policy of no night or weekend coverage after one's 65th birthday. Nature, however, decided otherwise. On July 9, 1999, I suffered a cerebrovascular accident, better known as a stroke. I was stricken with left-sided weakness. Fortunately, I retained my mental faculties. I was forced, however, to retire from the daily practice of medicine and began a new chapter in my life.

Reality had to be faced. On January 15, 2000, I sent out my retirement letter:

*Dear patients, colleagues and friends:*

*It has been said, Life is an adventure . . . we close a chapter . . . we open a new chapter. After a great deal of reflection, I have decided to retire from medicine and hope I will be able to pursue retirement successfully. For many years, I have truly enjoyed taking care of my wonderful patients, and I have also enjoyed my relations with my many colleagues and friends.*

*I leave with many misgivings and regrets, but I am fully aware that part-time practice in the current changing climate of medicine is not an acceptable option for me.*

*I am proud of all the doctors at Foxhall and I am confident that the doctors in our group will continue to deliver the very best of sophisticated internal medicine.*

*Beth, my devoted and very able assistant for many years, will be pleased to help you select another doctor in our group. Also, we will be more than happy to make your records available to any doctor of your choosing. My very best wishes and best personal regards to each and every one of you.*

*God bless,*
*Oscar Mann, M.D.*

A difficult period of reorientation concerning my new life followed. For the next year, I had little interest in pursuing any intellectual activities. Weak and unable to spend much time on my feet, I had little stamina. And to add to these physical issues, my attention span was almost nonexistent. I also became extremely depressed. To my chagrin, I had even given up reading medical journals.

My strength slowly returned. My depression gradually lifted. I became increasingly aware that I was still Oscar. I began to think about reinventing myself and about rewiring myself for a new beginning in life. And this is the choice I made, and the course that I embarked on.

Amy was there for me day in, day out, every day and every night. Without Amy's love, constant attention and complete devotion, my recovery would not have been possible, and my rehabilitation would not have taken place.

Luck was with me, because I had a support system of people who cared about what happened to me and worked with Amy. They would not let me quit.

I felt that my bubble had burst when I was transferred from Sibley Memorial Hospital to the Washington Hospital Center. Later, after my situation stabilized, rehabilitation became the critical issue, and I was moved to the National Rehabilitation Hospital (NRH), a facility adjacent to the Washington Hospital Center. The low point probably came a few days after my arrival at the NRH. I was ready to give up on life. "My wife and daughters will be well taken care of," I said to my brother John, refusing to believe that money would mean very little to them if I were not around.

"Well," he replied, "you can stop everything. You can stop eating and drinking. You can cease to take an interest in anything going on around you. But there are two things you may not stop. One is *occupational therapy* and the other is *physical therapy*. I won't let you"[1]

With those simple sentences, my brother defined my future. I had to learn to live each day, one day at a time. The expertise and dedication of the staff at NRH encouraged me and gave me hope that my motor skills would return.

John continued to act as my advocate all the way through my hospitalization at the NRH, during my convalescence at home and again when I was admitted to Johns Hopkins Hospital in March of 2000 for triple-bypass surgery. He remains my advocate to this very day. In addition, Risa, my sister-in-law, a physician, professor of pathology at Johns Hopkins University School of Medicine, understood the physical and psychological aspects of my condition. Perhaps more importantly, a caring person, she was right by my side the whole time, and her encouragement and advice were welcome and well received. I am at a loss for words to adequately express my appreciation to Risa and John.

Many people tended to my needs and helped the healing process which has allowed me to recover from the stroke and from open-heart surgery. I'm grateful to each one of them. Some are still helping me today. Delphis Miller is a nursing assistant, and she is always pleasant to be with, as well as being extremely helpful. Beverly Etter, who facilitated my return to being myself, deserves extra special mention.

Beverly has been with us since 1979. She has helped us as a gardener *extraordinaire*, as a driver and as a helpful assistant. I had no idea that she had taken primary care of several elderly and disabled people, including her grandmother, who lived to the age of 103. Beverly, who was a pillar of strength, was able to lift, move and support me. Her steadfastness and her good cheer have been instrumental in my recovery. I would not have progressed as far and as fast as I have without her care and support.

My twin daughters, Adriana, whom we usually call Anna, and Karen, were also there for me, despite the fact that they had full-time jobs and lives of their own. Karen, who lived in Washington, DC, made sure she was with me daily. Anna, who lived and worked in Boston at the time, made numerous trips to Washington to be with me and to help with my care. Karen's behavior during a hospital episode remains dear to my heart. I was scheduled for a "swallowing test," as a nurse had seen me one evening gag on some food which had gone down the wrong way with a resulting episode of coughing. I was disturbed by the idea of the test. Karen offered to accompany me to the Radiology Department at the Washington Hospital Center, where I was kept waiting for the longest time in a cold hall. Finally a speech therapist came down to administer the study with the x-ray team. My spirits were low and I was very anxious. Karen stayed with me, comforting and supporting me through the entire ordeal. To my great relief, the test turned out to be normal. I will never forget what Karen's devoted attention meant to me that day.

The three years which followed the stroke and subsequent heart surgery have been a period of readjustment and of learning hard lessons such as "life goes on" and *c'est la vie*. Many friends called and visited me. Some didn't. I was disappointed and even felt at first that some people proved to be only fair-weather friends. But, I reminded myself that some people are not comfortable being with friends who are experiencing acute illness. Conceivably, they identify with the ill person, and thus, delay their visits or calls until the sick person is well into his or her recovery. As I was trying to lift myself off the mat before the 15th round, my thinking was not always clear. Some contacts seemed uneven, now and then on the perfunctory side, while others were marked by a high degree of concern, care and friendship. On the whole, however, my contacts with old friends, colleagues and former patients have been wonderful and provided good therapy.

Tom Yau, now my ophthalmologist, walked the extra mile for me from the beginning. Tom, the husband of Linda Yau, a physician in our office, came to visit me frequently in the hospital and at NRH. In parallel fashion, Linda Yau was attentive to Amy's and my needs from the outset of my illness. In addition, she became my physician. The doctors of my office were all there for Amy and me. Charles Duvall, who had just retired from our group and moved to Hilton Head, kept in close touch with me. So did the members of the staff, especially the three musketeers, Avis, Corky, Maria, and my former private assistant, Beth.[2]

Fay Fletcher, the widow of James Fletcher, twice administrator of NASA, Frank Fowler, retired orthopedist, long-time neighbor and friend, and his wife, Bernadine, did not give us flowers. Rather they gave Amy and me guidance and their time. Amy reminded me recently "I could not have done without them. They also gave you excellent advice on your book. Many times."

Frank MacMurray, my retired senior partner, and Mrs. Edmund H. Feldman (Fran Feldman), a former patient and family friend, were admirable and so important to my recovery; Former colleagues Ian Spence and Caro Luhrs, and patients Ronald Osnos, Richard Rivers, John Dobrin and his late wife, Maryse Pailla, proved to be true friends. So were my former colleagues Raymond Holden, Tom Magovern, Stefan Pasternack, Marty Allen, and Charles Tartaglia. They all kept in close touch with Amy and me. John and Saundra Bouchard, financial advisers and former patients, telephoned us almost daily and are devoted to this very day. Mary Catherine Coffey, the widow of Dr. Robert J. Coffey, Julie and Urban Lester, former patients and neighbors, were among some of my regular pillars of support. Bob Menegaz, my dear classmate from medical school, and Donna Santarsiero, our good friends from New York, were frequent callers. Our next door neighbors, Joseph and Shakun Drew as well as Walter and Marianne Threadgill were attentive to my needs.

On the advice of my brother, my advocate and counselor, I decided not to dwell on my expectations from people. I stopped keeping a mental scorecard aimed at figuring out who was faithful and who was a fair-weather friend. Instead, I welcomed every contact, and tried to meet everyone more than halfway. As my attitude improved, so did the frequency and quality of my relationships with people. My brother, John, was indeed correct.

In particular, I was pleased to revive a connection with Frank Weiner, my old friend from premedical studies and medical school days. He and his wife live in Chapel Hill, North Carolina. Frank and Barbara were gracious to me in medical school and have kept in touch during my illness. Frank still "gives me hell" to be sure that procrastination does not derail my motivation and momentum. Frank has not changed; he is still a diamond in the rough. Good old Frank!

I knew very little about computers before my illness. However, my interest in these machines was kindled by Richard Rivers who gave me a leisurely, guided tour of his sophisticated, powerful personal computer. Walter S. Mossberg, a guru in that field and a former patient, who had kindly cited my name in the *The Wall Street Journal*, installed a personal computer in my home office on Weaver Terrace.³ He warned me to expect frustration from time to time, since computers are more complicated to operate than TV or radio. Nevertheless, I became computer-literate and proficient in the language and ways of the Internet with the help of two special friends, former patient John Dobrin, retired distinguished Foreign Service Officer and technical genius, and Corky Vance, computer programmer at Foxhall. With their help and problem-solving, I began to communicate far and wide via e-mail. At the urging of former patients in the high-tech field, I briefly flirted with the idea of creating an Internet advisory medical service, to be called *Ask Oscar*.

I also thought seriously about doing medicolegal work. Fortunately, thanks to the counsel of brother John, I soon realized that anything of a clinical nature in medicine was no longer right for me. One's clinical touch is a talent that requires constant nurturing, and I had not cared for a patient since July, 1999. Stefan Pasternack and Frank Weiner, among other close colleagues, strongly advised me against medicolegal endeavors in my new life. The venerable Dr. Raymond Holden, my wise senior colleague and former medical school teacher, gave me the same admonition. Notwithstanding, former patients continue to call me. I am glad to give them simple general advice, or merely talk with them. I enjoy their calls.

Former patients and family friends, Fay Fletcher and Fran Feldman, deserve special mention. Fay Fletcher had talked to me for several years about writing my story, and I always put her off with a polite, diplomatic "Maybe some day." After a decent interval following my illness, she revived the idea, repeating, "You have a story to tell—now is the time."

When I was not sure I could finish the project, Fay Fletcher and Fran Feldman urged me to complete *A Journey of Hope*.

*Fay: Oscar, this is a book that must be written, a story that must be told.*

*Fran: Oscar, it's very important to do it. Those who were lost deserve to be remembered and those who survived have a legacy of wisdom and strength to pass on to us who face today's challenges.*

I hasten to add that "This should be said over and over again, while praying and hoping, NEVER AGAIN."

Psychiatrist Stefan Pasternack reinforced Fay's and Fran's exhortation, telling me "Oscar, I like the idea of this book. Writing your story is an ideal project for you."

The book began slowly for me and, I admit, without great conviction. Gradually, however, it became a labor of love. It was the right decision for me and resulted in numerous and frequent contacts with many old friends, teachers, patients and literary and technical advisors.

At the same time, along with writing, I continue my rehabilitation and enjoyment of my retirement. Three days a week I do "water-walking" at the Tenley Sport and Health Club, followed by a session in the steam room, jacuzzi and sauna baths. I engage in regular exercise, periods of relaxation, meditation and reading at home.

I attended a special driving program at NRH, regained my driver's license, and drive with ease, using a handicapped-outfitted minivan and avoiding only the Washington Beltway and long trips. Driving has been a big boost to my morale. Amy and I take frequent day trips to explore the many scenic places of interest near Washington, such as Annapolis and St. Michael's, MD, and Middleburg, Virginia.

I also enjoy meeting friends, colleagues and former patients, usually for lunch, occasionally for dinner. I also manage my finances and personal affairs daily.

In time, I became aware that our elegant home in Kent was not handicapped-friendly and could not easily accommodate an elevator. Additionally, in truth, I craved a new beginning. Amy and I found the perfect house in a new section of Spring Valley where we were able to have a state-of-the-art elevator installed to service all three floors. We moved there, admittedly with trepidation, on January 23, 2001, but are now pleased and happy with our new home.

Since retirement, I no longer attend medical conferences or pursue activities related to medicine, feeling for better or worse that I paid my dues and served my time in my profession. Reading medical journals, staying up-to-date with the medical literature and keeping up with postgraduate medical education are, in the absence of clinical patient contact, abstract exercises to me nowadays. I am now out and retired.

Every rule has its exceptions. Recently, at the urging of Dr. Frank Weiner, I talked to Dr. Jules Bedynek, Dr. Harvey's long-time associate, about renewing some ties with my former cardiology colleagues. Soon afterwards, I received an invitation from Dr. Harvey that Amy and I accepted with pleasure.

On April 10–12, 2003, we attended a premiere cardiac event, the annual Georgetown University School of Medicine Auscultation Course, as guests of Dr. Proctor Harvey. Dr. Harvey has presented this landmark symposium on auscultation to several thousand physicians since the 1960s when I was a part of it as a cardiology fellow at Georgetown. It was initially sponsored by the American College of Physicians and now, by the American College of Cardiology. Ray Mitchell, M.D., Dean of Georgetown University School of

Medicine notes "this is by far the most popular postgraduate course given by the college."

Dr. Proctor Harvey has not changed. At age 85, he looks well and has not lost neither cognitive capacity nor intellectual curiosity. His is a positive outlook on life. His eyes twinkle with good humor as he expounds on auscultation and clinical cardiology. In short, the Harvey manner and the Harvey enthusiasm are alive and well. The course is better than ever. Dr. Harvey received highly positive feedback on his 2003 "Auscultation Fest," just as he has every year since the inception of this postgraduate training program. Physician J.J. Alva, M.D., from Durham, North Carolina, took this year's course, and offers these comments in a letter to Dr. Harvey:

*I cannot find words to express my sincere thanks for the wonderful course you and your associates put out on clinical heart disease with focus on auscultation . . . . You are the role model that is badly needed in today's medical world . . . .*[4]

I enjoyed the conference, was pleased to see that Dr. Harvey has not changed and that his course, which I had attended on several occasions in the past, has only improved with time.

The dinner concluding the conference took place at Dante's Restaurant in McLean, Virginia. The usual Harvey ambience prevailed. A private room, a cozy group, pleasant conversation; no one-upmanship or showmanship—in short, it was a time of retreat with fellow soldiers in the cardiac wars. Although I enjoyed the occasion and the opportunity to see old friends and colleagues, I was fully aware that the dinner was my last hurrah in medicine. This was no longer my world. I realized, without bitterness, that I had no neither regrets or negative thoughts.

I promised myself I would look to the future and savor each day to its fullest, determined not to flunk my retirement. Life is now entirely different from the one I was privileged to lead as an active Foxhall internist. I am happy to spend more time with my family and to enjoy the pleasures of new, unhurried, creative, fulfilling days.

In Washington, DC, as in so many places in today's world, what you do as a profession often seems to be the same as who you are. Therefore, if you like what you do, if you're proud of it, you are most fortunate. To love one's work is a joy, a privilege, and a gift. I was in that category.

But what happens when such a person can no longer participate in his or her world of work? The transition is unlike that of moving from one job to another, one career to another. It can be devastating. It can be liberating.

My original focus in writing this book was to say that here in America, in this land of hope, dreams can come true, and that we must cherish and protect this great country and its ideals.

I wanted to tell you about the young Oscar who survived threats to his very being, who struggled in the garment trade, and dared to dream of a different life in a distant land. I wanted to share with you the joys of his achievements as a young scholar, medical student and physician. I also wanted to share the gratitude he feels to those who helped him along the way not just to survive but to succeed.

Now I realize that this is also a love story, the love of a mother for her children, the love of brothers, of wife for husband and husband for wife, father for children and children for parents . . . in sickness and in health, for richer or for poorer.

This is also the story of what happens when the realized dream of a young man comes to an end. And the young man, now a senior, albeit a young senior, must find meaningful activity to provide quality of life for the days and years ahead. That, indeed, is another journey of hope.

## NOTES

1. *Occupational Therapy* (usually called OT) and *Physical Therapy* (PT) are ancillary medical services used in the rehabilitation of patients' physical and mental conditions.

2. See Chapter 19.

3. " . . . finally, I want to thank the four doctors who saved my life: Oscar Mann, Albert Pfister, Ramin Oskoui, and Jerold Share. They reinforced my view that, while technology is crucial in every aspect of our lives—including medicine—no computer chip or laser can replace human skills, judgment and compassion." *Wall Street Journal*, February 12, 1998.

4. Citation of a May, 2003 letter from Dr. Alva to Dr. Harvey. used with the consent of Dr. Alva.

# Reflections

My journey began in a world vastly different from the one in which we live today. Along the way, I learned one truth which is as valid now as it was then: A single decision can have a profound effect on one's life.

Similarly, during my career, I have often observed the impact of a single medical decision on a patient's outcome. That complex and awe-inspiring fact has never ceased to impress me. There are many factors, conscious and unconscious, that are involved in the decision-making process. Let me share with you a case in point.

The enormous difficulties that people faced in Europe in 1939 are not dissimilar from those we are facing in contemporary America today. The parallels between then and now offer pause for reflection.

Why have politicians and intelligence experts, then and now, failed to appreciate the significant danger signals so clearly evident in hindsight? The potential for major bioterrorism or a nuclear holocaust, even here in fortified Washington, DC, makes it legitimate to ask whether every Washingtonian should now be planning to resettle in a safer place. At what point does a rational person conclude that danger is imminent? At what point does one dismiss one's fears and choose to stay? I certainly do not have the answer to these questions.

This relevant analogy evokes great empathy for the dilemma my parents faced. While they were aware of the social and economic problems in Europe, they never anticipated the Holocaust. We, in America, never anticipated anything like the events of September 11, 2001. I believe none of us today would abandon our homes and our daily activities any more than my parents did in the late 1930s in France.

I would like to share with you some of my private thoughts, perceptions and impressions of people who made a difference in my journey. Therefore, I shall ask the indulgence of the reader while I recall certain previous lines from *A Journey of Hope*.

## FATHER

In the turbulent and dangerous times of the 1930s, our father devoted his life to his family. His undaunted, dynamic and courageous spirit lives on in our hearts and minds. Now, in a different time and place, his name carries on anew in our family (see *Epilogue*).

## MOTHER

John and I were fortunate to be blessed with a farsighted and brave mother. She engineered and managed our escape from Europe. As I said in her graveside eulogy:

> *A woman of valor, mother assured our survival. She gave us roots and stability in the difficult and dangerous days of the war. To John, age 16, and to me, age 18, she gave wings to leave the nest. She would not hold us back. Tough-minded and selfless, she made the decision resolutely and without reservation. She ignored the advice of her well-meaning friends, when they warned her that she would be saying goodbye to her two sons, who would be an ocean away.*

My maternal grandfather, Asher Biegun, would never know that one of his daughters, my mother, would guide two of his grandchildren, John and me, to realize in full his unconsummated American dream. I am certain he would have been happy and proud had he known that she, born and raised in Dombrowitz, had the foresight to see to it that her grandchildren, Gilda, Anna, Karen and Stacie, would all be born in America.

*A Journey of Hope* is written, from beginning to end, in homage to our mother's singularly strong character and my brother John's unwavering optimism.

## BROTHER JOHN

My brother, John, with his gentle disposition, great sense of humor and deep intellect, has always been there for me. John found his way to Johns Hopkins University in Baltimore and would exclaim in wonder "I am the only Hopkins physician who spent his teenage years selling clothes on the streets near Paris."

At Hopkins John thrived, becoming a doctor's doctor, as many in Baltimore, Washington, and beyond know. I can attest personally to his diagnostic acumen. In July, 1999, he diagnosed my cerebrovascular accident at a critical time in its evolution, and if not for John, who knows what the outcome might have been?

His natural intellectual endowment led him to follow a distinguished academic career. The jewel in John's crown, however, was not academic but a lovely young Vassar-educated Johns Hopkins medical student, Risa Berman. Risa was from a respected Jewish professional family in Washington. Marrying Risa was John's finest hour. That marriage brought great joy to John, and our families have shared the pains and triumphs that have come with the years.

## AMY

Amy plays a tremendous role in my life. She has helped me grow in so many ways that it is not within the realm of my abilities to express adequately the impact of her influence on my life.

She is a permanent "Americanization School" tutor, a steadfast companion and my private joy. I'm so glad Amy told me to give her a ring. And "once in love with Amy, always in love with Amy . . . . "[1]

## UNCLE ISOR AND AUNT BELLA

My mother was a first cousin to Isor Gildenhorn. Technically speaking, John and I were first cousins of Isor, once removed. However, Isor Gildenhorn would become the proverbial American uncle, and naturally enough, we called him "Uncle Isor." He became to us an anchor of hope after the stormy days in the old country and a tower of strength during the subsequent early challenging years in America. Uncle Isor, with his love, generosity and constant encouragement, became a surrogate father to John and me.

Isor was born March 26, 1903, in Dombrowitz, Poland. By the time Isor was a young man Dombrowitz, once a thriving small town, had become a village of little consequence. He saw no future there, but he stayed while four of his brothers left for the "New World."

Then on August 28, 1939, not even a month before Warsaw and Poland fell to the Nazis, Isor, then 36 years old, set out from Dombrowitz on his way to America.

Isor was born at the turn of the 20th century. He lived to see the dawn of the 21st century. In turbulent times, Isor overcame adversity, adapted quickly, persevered and prospered, living a life of wisdom and compassion. He loved people, and people loved him. Old age was kind to Isor. He retained his mind throughout his 98 years and his death came peacefully and swiftly.

Let me share with the reader some of Isor's defining moments:

- Isor's papers to emigrate to America came in the late summer of 1939; however, because of a capricious immigration system, there were no visas for his wife, Rosa, or his son, Joseph. Under the circumstances, Rosa insisted that Isor should go alone to America and pave the way for her and Joseph to come later.
- In the late 1930s, no one envisioned what the Nazis had in store for European Jews. Isor left Poland confident that Rosa and Joseph would soon follow. However World War II cut off all communications between them, and it was not until 1945 that Isor found out the horrible truth. In 1941, after Germany's invasion of Russia left Poland in Hitler's hands, Isor's wife and child, Rosa and Joseph, along with the entire Jewish population of Dombrowitz, were shot by the Nazis and their bodies were thrown into a mass grave in the cemetery of Dombrowitz.
- Coming to America alone and later sending for other family members was not an unusual practice for the heads of European families prior to WW II. Having lost his wife and child forever, Isor would spend the rest of his life helping people in need.

  Understandably, Isor rarely spoke of his lost wife and child, and of that experience, he once told me: "Life had ended for me." Subsequently, Isor met Bella: "She gave me a reason to live; she turned my life around."
- With his marriage to Bella, Isor's life blossomed anew. The two of them made a new life for themselves. They could have turned their backs on those left behind, or the painful memories. But they didn't. Instead, they stood strong for us — my mother, a widow, in a Europe ravaged by World War II, and her two small children, my brother John and me. Our best hope was to come to America, and Isor made it possible. Assisted by Oscar Rozansky, of blessed memory, Isor sponsored us to a new beginning.

  Isor promised he would be there for us once we came, and he was. Owing in large part to Uncle Isor and Aunt Bella, John and I became doctors. What he did on our behalf, with his constant encouragement, we will remember forever.
- Sadly, after 40 years of a blissful marriage, Bella died. Isor grieved deeply, lamenting that "life has ended for me a second time." Isor became despondent. Normally an active, engaged person, for a time he vegetated only to later improve.

He decided to move from his home of many years to the Classic Residence in Chevy Chase, a Washington suburb in Maryland. On the morning of the move, he called me, saying, "I am comfortable at the Colonnade. Why move? What for? Who am I kidding? I am approaching 90."

After an early lunch at the nearby Westchester Apartments, Isor stood up and told me, "I am ready to move. You better take me home. The movers are coming at 2:30."

In his new setting, Isor's life blossomed once again. There he met Bertha, a spry, elderly resident whose friendship Isor treasured. Their ten-year relationship was rejuvenating for both of them.

Allow me to quote some words I spoke at Isor's graveside:

*Isor used to tell me,* In my little way, I did fairly well.
*Isor, in your own way, Isor's way, you, indeed, did very well.*

It has been said: "All good things come to an end, as all things must and all things will."[2]

So it was that Isor's life came to an end, but not until almost a century after his birth. The lives of Uncle Isor and Aunt Bella were a continuum of *menschlichkeit*,[3] and recapitulated the sad yet triumphant story of the Jewish people of the 20th century.

## OSCAR ROZANSKY

Oscar Rozansky bore the same limited relationship to us as Isor did. However, along with Isor, he acted admirably on our behalf. Cousin Oscar was a charismatic man, with an infectious smile and a cheerful word for everyone. His difficult early life of trials, suffering and lessons learned through rugged adventures were very much in evidence in his persona. He had a unique ability to adapt. He always remembered and loved his extended family and never lost touch with his friends in Israel.

In his own way, he helped mother, John and me fulfill our dreams. Oscar, his family, the house at 3917 Massachusetts Avenue, the 1948 Cadillac and the Horace Mann School playground—these things stayed in my mind following our return from North America to France in the fall of 1948. These memories gave me comfort and hope as we impatiently waited in Paris for an answer concerning Oscar's assistance in cosponsoring us to America.[4]

## MYER GILDENHORN

Our lives during the premedical and medical years were eased greatly by Myer Gildenhorn, Isor's nephew, who enabled us to be gainfully employed while pursuing our academic goals. He was a benevolent boss, an easy-going, affable human being, who constantly looked out for John and me. He adapted his business needs to our scholastic requirements. John and I are truly indebted to Myer and often speak of him with fondness.

## DR. HARVEY, FRANK AND WES

John and I were privileged to attend medical school in America and to have the opportunity to become part of this profession. Dedicated educators, talented clinicians and model physicians enlightened our paths. We remember with fondness, gratitude and honor all those who taught us. John is proud to have had the great Hopkins clinician, Dr. Phillip Tumulty, as his life-long mentor. I am proud to claim Dr. Proctor Harvey as my mentor and Drs. Frank MacMurray and Wes Oler as my senior partners over many years. All three played great roles in my career.

Dr. Proctor Harvey, the first cardiology fellow of the legendary Boston cardiologist, Dr. Samuel Levine, has become an American medical icon in his own right. I was a Harvey fellow. He influenced the way I saw my role as a physician and the way I related to colleagues and patients. That he had confidence in me meant a great deal to me personally. As a result of his endorsement, Frank and Wes invited me to associate with them. And because of Harvey's conviction that ours would be a fine professional match, I recognized this outstanding opportunity from the onset. I have often replayed Harvey's words in my mind: "I would put up Frank and Wes against any one in American medicine."

My partnership with Frank and Wes enabled me to enjoy many years of a rewarding professional life.

## THE FRENCH VILLAGERS AND PÈRE JEAN BAPTISTE

*. . . Everybody in Le Bosc knew that there was a Jewish family of seven people living among them, but no one said a thing. No one turned us in . . . It was common knowledge that French people were being shot for harboring or hiding Jews . . . .*

*. . . we were Jewish. [Curé] Père Jean Baptiste . . . became obsessed with our welfare. Our blending in with Le Bosc's other villagers was his prime concern.*

*We attended Mass, took communion and went to Sunday school along with the children of the village.*[4]

Frank Weiner has suggested an interesting correlation: "I was struck by the role of the Christian clergy in helping you. First there was Père Jean Baptiste, and, later, Father O'Donnell. You end up playing an important role at a Catholic medical school. Is there an unconscious connection there?"[5]

Perhaps the answer to Frank's question can be found in the verse, "Light Shining out of Darkness", composed by the English poet William Cowper (1731–1800). This poem, now a traditional hymn, begins with these familiar lines:

> *God moves in a mysterious way,*
> *His wonders to perform;*
> *He plants his footsteps in the sea,*
> *and rides upon the storm.* [6]

For us, French country people proved to possess a far nobler character than did French residents of the big cities, especially Paris, during the dark days of France.

## DR. BENET AND FARMER MERCADIER

*. . . Dr. Benet himself called the owner of the grocery store in Le Bosc on the only existing telephone to alert us that a Gestapo squad car was making its way to us. The grocery owner immediately dispatched his teenage son to the farm by bike to deliver the message. Farmer Mercadier gathered all seven of us together . . . ."*

*. . . He took us to an old family cabin well-hidden in the forest . . . After five days, Mercadier himself came to give us the all-clear signal and take us back to the farm. Doctor Paul Benet and farmer Pierre Mercadier saved our lives.*[7]

May God bless the souls of these two, who represented the finest human attributes.

## ANONYMOUS VICHY OFFICIAL AND DR. BENET

We were being detained in a "Vichy France" Gendarmerie.

*. . . When the questioning by the uniformed gendarmes was finished, we were turned over to an authoritarian older senior civilian, the local Vichy administrator,*

*who was to dispose of our case . . . . He then told us that he had decided to give mother a safe conduct permit to take John and me to our uncle in southern France . . . . Then in a hushed tone of voice, he bent over and whispered to my mother, 'listen to me, do not return here.'*

*He planted the seed. His advice would save mother's life.*[8]

Enter Dr. Paul Benet, the mayor of the town and, unknown to the Vichy authorities and the general public, the leader of the regional underground: . . . *Dr. Benet listened with great empathy, stating that mother was in no condition to go back to the Gendarmerie. He signed a medical certificate to that effect . . . .*[9]

This was a watershed point in the journey. Without the courageous and decisive actions of the anonymous Vichy official and Dr. Benet, mother would have been deported to a concentration camp and no doubt would have met the same fate as our father. That was the plan that the enemies of human decency had for millions like our parents and, by extension, John and me.

## THE RODITIS AND HUCHON FAMILIES

*. . . despite a clear danger to people harboring Jews, the Roditis welcomed us graciously. . . Truly brave and decent folks, they gave us room, board and shelter for a few days. . . We had to get away. . . Guy Huchon and his parents were our long-time friends. With peril to themselves, they offered to hide us in Le Corubert—about 200 miles to the west . . . .*[10]

Thus it was that various French individuals—ordinary citizens, villagers, a priest, a doctor-mayor, a farmer and a Vichy official—all risked their lives so that mother, John and I would survive. Yes, there were French folks—*righteous Gentiles*—who protected and saved Jews. Nowadays, many Americans tar all French people with the brush of racism and anti-Semitism. John and I wish to counter this view. We, together with mother, were saved by French people who rose, without hesitation to the level of compassion that the Bible says is within reach of all who grasp for it.

## THE SCHOOL DIRECTOR AND THE TEACHER

*We were forced to wear the yellow star to school and we expected our classmates to humiliate us. My teacher . . . shielded us from the impact of wearing a yellow star in her class. Furthermore, the director of the school . . . said that . . . he would tolerate no harassment nor taunting throughout the Place des Vosges school. There were almost no such incidents in the school.*[11]

The director and teacher of the *Place des Vosges* School acted boldly during those perilous times. I no longer remember their names. But I shall honor their memories always. Their graciousness and kindness will live as long as I and the other beneficiaries have breath to tell of their good deeds.

François Durelle, a French family friend living in retirement on the French Riviera, offers his perception — not his personal experience, he hastens to add — of the French people who assisted persecuted Jews:

> *Born in 1940, I was of course too young during the war to be able to comment directly on your reflections concerning French citizens sheltering Jews, but they sound right to me. I have heard several stories of similar events (Jews being informed, forewarned, helped, protected or hidden) told by Jewish friends or customers of my mother's pharmacy. In fact, I think this attitude was that of French people protecting their fellow countrymen against the Germans, and of course, those who helped knew that Jews were more at risk to be deported—don't forget that during the war very little information existed about the concentration camps—and that they themselves were risking more by helping the Jews.*
>
> *I believe from what I heard that it was not unusual, except for some pro-Germans and people whose job/freedom was at stake or people scared of reprisals (possibly like your 'concierge'). This is not at all to diminish the merits of those who helped; on the contrary, it is to say that this commendable and courageous attitude may have been rather widespread. Again, I was too young to know; I am giving you the feeling I have from having heard people talk about this. And this is corroborated by the comments of my friend Jacques Borek* [Jewish psychiatrist who lived and hid in France during World War II] *that I sent you.*

## THE SHEINBAUM CONNECTION

In 1946, Oscar Rozansky contacted mother by letter from Washington, DC. Could we offer room and board to their immigrant relatives, the Sheinbaums, on their way to America from Poland?

> *Mother immediately sent a letter to Oscar Rozansky stating that she would be glad to help. This prompt action would turn out to be a wise and fruitful move. Mother's answer to that letter marked the beginning of our link to America and a new era in our life . . . .* [12]

What appeared, at the time, to be an incidental interlude in our lives became an important milepost in our journey. Viewing the Sheinbaum episode with perspective, I now clearly see it as the catalyst for our detour to Washington in the summer of 1948. This event played a pivotal role in my journey to the apotheosis that is being an American citizen.

Mother offered her hospitality to the Sheinbaums as an act of kindness out of the goodness of her heart. She never guessed, nor did we, that it would lead to a life in America for herself and us. But the wisdom of King Solomon came true: "Cast thy bread upon the waters; for thou shalt find it after many days."[13] She even experienced the variant which I once heard from a colleague: "Cast your bread upon the waters, and it will come back cake!"

The idea of paying attention to the people who pack one's parachute is well-treated by former Vietnam prisoner Charles Plumb in a powerful essay, *Packing Parachutes*.[14] Plumb's message aptly applies to my story.

Fortunately, good people packed my parachute during my journey, assuring me of a safe landing despite dangers, obstacles and challenges — to them and to me. My journey has thus evolved into a journey of hope.

It was the early 1950s. I was bogged down in the Old World and, as I described previously, going to America was constantly on my mind:

> *The contrast beween life in the open-air* schmatta *business and what I perceived our lives might become in America began to consume me . . .*
> *I came to think of America as the opposite of the open-market life of France. I pictured the American dream as freedom and opportunity to realize one's potential. Although I did not know what my potential might be, I knew in my mind that I would not find it in the* schmatta *trade. The kind of personal fulfillment I sought could be found only in America.*[15]

It was the fall of 1962; I was serving my internship year at Georgetown University Hospital, while my brother, John, was in the midst of his senior year at Georgetown University School of Medicine.

> *One Sunday evening, before calling it a day, I decided to look in on a patient located on the 6th floor. To my surprise, I ran into John, who was in the room. He was working a double shift as a private nurse. Though the job was humbling, it allowed John to do some studying, which for him went a long way. It also allowed him to earn $90.00. This was the equivalent of a week's wages at the liquor store. I told John I would take his place so that he could go to the cafeteria for dinner and a change of scenery. I made myself comfortable. The room was spacious, well-appointed, and the patient was asleep. I reflected about where John and I had come from and where we were now. When John returned, I said spontaneously:* Only in America![16]

This expression "Only in America" harmonizes well with my favorite verses from the poem "America for Me", by Henry van Dyke:

*. . . So it's home again, and home again, America for me!*
*My heart is turning home again, and there I long to be,*
*In the land of youth and freedom beyond the ocean bars,*
*Where the air is full of sunlight and the flag is full of stars.*
*Oh, London is a man's town, there's power in the air,*
*And Paris is a woman's town, with flowers in her hair;*
*And it's sweet to dream in Venice, and it's great to study Rome;*
*But when it comes to living, there is no place like home . . .*
*I know that Europe's wonderful, yet something seems to lack:*
*The Past is too much with her, and the people looking back.*
*But the glory of the Present is to make the Future free,*
*We love our land for what she is and what she is to be.*
*Oh, it's home again, and home again, America for me!*[17]

In these simple, elegant words, Van Dyke captures the essence of America for me.

Nearly two thousand years ago, the Sermon on the Mount touched on my vision of America: *. . . You are the light of the world. A city that is set on a hill cannot be hid . . .* [18]

Nearly four hundred years ago, Governor John Winthop borrowed the simile in voicing his hopes for the Pilgrims aboard their ship, the *Arbella*, as it approached the New World: *For we must consider that we shall be a city upon a hill.*[19]

And just a few decades ago, Ronald Reagan, our 40th President, centered his administration on his assertion that *America is . . . for all mankind, a shining city on a hill . . . and a beacon of light for the rest of the world.*[20]

I can attest to the truth of these words from my personal experience, and I add an "Amen" of thanks to this land of freedom and opportunity. My family followed the beacon of light. We found the shining city on a hill and felt welcome. We will be eternally grateful.

## NOTES

1. "Once in love with Amy," (Words and Music by Frank Loesser), as sung by Ray Bolger, in the film *Where's Charley?*, 1952.

2. I once heard Rabbi Stanley Rabinowitz, former chief rabbi of Adas Israel Congregation, Washington, DC, use this expression.

3. *Menschlichkeit* is an old Yiddish word, expressing the aggregate of compassion, wisdom and doing for others. It contains the notion of knowing one's duty and performing it without shirking.

4. Reproduced from Chapter 8.

5. Personal Communication from Frank Weiner, M.D., October, 2003. Father O'Donnell is featured in chapters 14 and 15.

6. William Cowper (1731–1800), "Light Shining out of Darkness," *The New Oxford Book of English Verse*, ed Helen Gardner, (London: Oxford University Press, 1972), 466–467.

7. Reproduced from chapter 7.

8. Reproduced from chapter 7.

9. Reproduced from chapter 7.

10. Reproduced from chapter 7.

11. Reproduced from chapter 7.

12. Reproduced from chapter 8.

13. Ecclesiastes 11.1

14. http://homeport.usnaweb.org/parachute.html (accessed December 27, 2004).

15. Reproduced from chapter 12.

16. Reproduced from chapter 16.

17. Henry van Dyke, "America for Me," in *Poetry for a Lifetime*, ed. Samuel N. Ethridge (California: Mira Vista Press, 1999, 372). The poem, which can be found in its entirety in Appendix 1 below, is now in the public domain (Library of Congress, Copyright Office, Reference:2003300724, (September 23, 2003)).

18. Matthew 5:14.

19. Governor John Winthrop, 1630. See, for example, http://worldpolicy.org/chace2 .html (accessed February 21, 2005).

20. President Ronald Reagan, 1980. See, *inter alia*, http://www.presidentreagan .info/speeches/city_upon_a_hill.cfm (accessed February 21, 2005).

# Epilogue

Mother, John and I experienced first-hand all the hope that America holds for newcomers. We were not disappointed; we found our destiny in this golden land.

John and I were privileged to enjoy fulfilling medical careers. Our families continue to be blessed with the privileges of life here in America. All of our children live nearby, in the greater Washington and Baltimore area.

More than 50 years ago, May 1, 1953, with *un brin de muguet* (a sprig of lily-of-the-valley) in my lapel, I departed Europe, full of hope, bound for America.

On Mother's Day, May 11, 2003, I celebrated the 50th anniversary of my arrival in America with a gathering of family and friends. Just about a year later, on April 22nd, 2004, a blessed family event took place, cause for yet another celebration! Our cup was full. It now "runneth" over.

In legend, the Phoenix, a bird of ancient mythology, rose from the ashes and began a new cycle of life. Similarly, in the New World, our family has come full circle and a fledgling rises from the ashes of the old.

Our father, Aaron Mankowski, was murdered on June 19th, 1942, in the infamous Auschwitz concentration camp. He was only 40 years old. Now, 60 years later, his name lives again in the first male baby to be born into our family since our father's death. The baby is Aaron Lev Zimmet, the son of my niece Gilda and her husband Brian. He is the grandson of my brother John and his wife Risa.

Giving the name of Aaron to our father's first great grandson has deep meaning for us. We hope and pray that the deathless spirit of Aaron, our father, will blossom anew in his namesake, little Aaron. Our father will still be "alive" in 60 or 70 years when Aaron Zimmet tells his grandchildren that he is named after his paternal great-grandfather.

Little Aaron is now heir to the promise that America offers. America was right for me yesterday it is right for me today, and it will be right for me to-morrow. I am certain that it will be the same for little Aaron.

And may his life voyage be a new journey of hope!


Dear Reader,

Thanks for reading the book! Now, I cordially invite you to visit the website of *A Journey of Hope* >www.journeyofhope.info< where over a hundred pic-tures and documents, keyed to the events in the book, are displayed.

# Appendix One

# Eclectic Bits and Pieces

### *America for Me*
### Henry van Dyke

*"Tis fine to see the Old World, and travel up and down*
*Among the famous palaces and cities of renown,*
*To admire the crumbly castles and the statues of the kings,—*
*But now I think I've had enough of antiquated things.*

*So it's home again, and home again, America for me!*
*My heart is turning home again, and there I long to be,*
*In the land of youth and freedom beyond the ocean bars,*
*Where the air is full of sunlight and the flag is full of stars.*

*Oh, London is a man's town, there's power in the air,*
*And Paris is a woman's town, with flowers in her hair;*
*And it's sweet to dream in Venice, and it's great to study Rome;*
*But when it comes to living, there is no place like home.*

*I like the German fir-woods, in green battalions drilled;*
*I like the gardens of Versailles with flashing fountains filled;*
*But, oh, to take your hand, my dear, and ramble for a day*
*In the friendly western woodland where Nature has her way!*

*I know that Europe's wonderful, yet something seems to lack:*
*The Past is too much with her, and the people looking back.*
*But the glory of the Present is to make the Future free,*
*We love our land for what she is and what she is to be.*

*Oh, it's home again, and home again, America for me!*
*I want a ship that's westward bound to plough the rolling sea,*
*To the blessed Land of Room Enough beyond the ocean bars,*
*Where the air is full of sunlight and the flag is full of stars.*[1]

267

Henry van Dyke (1852–1933), the author of this poem, was a Presbyterian minister, a professor of English literature and held several government posts, including that of American ambassador to the Netherlands and Luxembourg.

Song of allegiance to Maréchal Pétain:

**Maréchal, nous voilà**
**(Montagnard et Courtioux)**
**Crée en 1941 par André Dassary**

*Une flamme sacrée monte du sol natal*
*Et notre France enivrée te salue Maréchal*
*Tous tes enfants qui t'aiment et honorent tes ans*
*à ton appel suprême ont répondu présent*

Refrain:
*Maréchal nous voilà*
*Devant toi le sauveur de la France*
*Nous jurons nous tes gars*
*De servir et de suivre tes pas*

*Maréchal nous voilà*
*Tu nous as redonné l'espérance*
*La patrie renaîtra*
*Maréchal nous voilà*

*Tu as lutté sans cesse pour le salut commun*
*On parle avec tendresse du héros de Verdun*
*En nous donnant ta vie ton génie et ta foi*

*Tu sauves la patrie une seconde fois.*[2]

# DRS. GESHICKTER AND COPELAND

Dr. Geshickter would occasionally visit Dr. Copeland during his surgical clinic. Murray Copeland referred to his office practice as "my surgical clinic." This terminology was the tradition and custom at the old Hopkins Hospital. It was then that Georgetown medical students witnessed the genuine respect and affection of these two men for each other: *Copeland was the brilliant organizer and Geshickter was the brilliant idea man in their relationship.*[3]

The yearbook of the class of 1954 accords a fine appreciation to Copeland:

*Dr. Murray M. Copeland has succeeded in giving us the most thorough and interesting kind of training in Oncology. Through his efforts we probably know more facts about cancer than we do about any other disease we have studied.*[4]

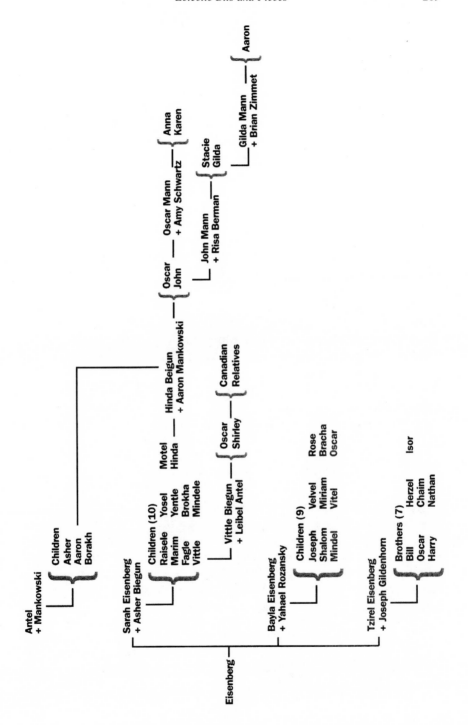

## MOTHER IN DOMBROWITZ

Mother told me that her family once owned some cattle in Dombrowitz and that the children became very fond of and attached to a particular young calf that they raised from birth. The calf became a member of the family. This pet died suddenly without reason and the whole family became quite upset. Mother remembered this little calf and told us the story as she tended cattle in *Le Bosc*, the French village which sheltered us from 1942 to 1944.

## GILDENHORN BROTHERS IN AMERICA

Those of the Gildenhorn brothers fortunate enough to come to America well before the war had prospered. Oscar Gildenhorn, in particular, thrived and became known as "Rich Oscar," an appellation he enjoyed. I recall that he smiled or laughed at being called that. He was fond of repeating that the day he left Dombrowitz was the best day of his life. He often said he would never visit his native village, and true to his word, he never did.

Oscar Gildenhorn was proud of his bright and attractive daughter-in-law, Alma, and his enterprising lawyer son, Joseph. They became well known to the Washington community as prominent figures in the Republican Party, leaders of charitable causes and active supporters of Israel. Joseph was named U.S. Ambassador to Switzerland by President George H.W. Bush, and served from August 1989 to March 1993.

## OTHER GILDENHORN BROTHERS

Two of the Gildenhorn brothers, Chaim and Herzel, never came to America. At the time Isor left for America, his brother Chaim became an affluent man as the result of the recent sale of his business, and therefore chose to remain in Dombrowitz where he and his family perished. Chaim had hoped to survive the war there by bribing local residents. He, his wife Etel, and two young children, Musa and Joseph, hid for two years in Dombrowitz cellars. They were discovered and killed by the Nazis in 1943.

Isor's brother, Herzel, died of a heart attack in Kiev on February 18,1953, eight years after the end of World War II.

Perlya, later known as Beba, Herzel's daughter, did come to America, but not until well after World War II. Her tale is closely linked to Dombrowitz and the people who lived there.

Born in Dombrowitz in 1922, Perlya was nicknamed Beba. She attended elementary school in Dombrowitz and later went to a gymnasium (high school) in Rovno. Her mother had died of pneumonia in 1932. On graduation, she returned to Dombrowitz, which was under Russian domination by then, where she worked in the post office and fell in love with the postmaster Mikhail Leshchiner, a Russian Jew.

Perlya, her father, and her boyfriend Mikhail escaped to Siberia in August 1941, when the Germans were only twenty miles from Dombrowitz. In Siberia, Perlya lived in the village of Chasha, about 30 kilometers from Cosobrobsk, a small train station. She and Mikhail were married in Chasha in 1941, just before Mikhail was called to active military service in the Red Army. She spent the war years in Siberia with her father under difficult conditions. After the war, reunited with Mikhail, they lived in Kiev where her son Boris was born in 1947. Beba never went back to Dombrowitz as she and her family, sponsored by Isor and his brothers, emigrated to the U.S. in 1978, making Silver Spring, Maryland their home.

## MILITARY SERVICE

There is one interesting footnote to the story of my visit to Paris in 1954. Years after John "terrified me," I was told at the French Embassy in Washington, DC, that it was perfectly safe for me to visit France. Service in any NATO country was being considered by the NATO members to be the equivalent of serving in the country of one's birth. John fulfilled his U.S. military obligation by serving in the U.S. Public Health Service during the years of 1966 to 1967. We both have been back to France on visits with no problems whatever.

## MOUNT ALTO HOSPITAL

Of interest, Mount Alto Hospital was located on one of the highest ground elevations in the District of Columbia. Prior to becoming a VA Hospital, it had been a private girls' academy. Today, Mount Alto is the site of a large Russian compound. Stories have circulated about the possibility of Russians using electronic devices to spy on the Nation's Capital; the C.I.A.—usurping one near-by apartment building—is said to listen in on what is happening in the Russian complex and is said to have tunneled under the compound .

A congressional investigation into why this high terrain in Washington, DC had been sold to the Russians was later considered by the U.S. Senate.

Apparently, a favored location in Moscow for a new U.S. embassy had been bartered for Mount Alto. Somehow, it appeared, the State Department had overlooked Mount Alto's height factor.

## DR. LEBENSOHN'S PAPERS

Dr. Lebensohn's 1962 Kober Lecture, entitled "American Psychiatry: Retrospect and Prospect" has been preserved. This paper, together with his collected reprints from 1938 to 1991, was presented to the Dahlgren Library, the new Georgetown medical library, in 2001.[5]

## NOTES

1. Henry van Dyke, "America for Me," in *Poetry for a Lifetime*, ed. Samuel N. Ethridge (California: Mira Vista Press, 1999), 372. The poem is now in the public domain (Library of Congress, Copyright Office, Reference:2003300724, (September 23, 2003)).
2. See chapter 4.
3. Personal communication from Dr. Fowler (see chapter 14) in October 2002.
4. *Grand Rounds 1954*, Joseph S. Costa, editor. The Georgetown University School of Medicine, Washington, DC, 73.
5. Personal communication from Dr. Lebensohn, February 1, 2003.

*Appendix Two*

# My Professional Resumé

**Oscar Mann, M.D., F.A.C.P., F.A.C.C., F.C.C.P.**
**Clinical Professor Emeritus of Medicine**
**Georgetown University School of Medicine**
**Retired from Practice, January 2000**
**(Medical Disability)**

**Birth:**
October 13, 1934—Paris, France

**Personal:**
Married July 19, 1964—wife Amy, née Schwartz
Twin daughters: Adriana Margaret and Karen Jeanette—
    Born December 2, 1972.

**Address:**
5137 Yuma Street, N.W.
Washington, DC 20016
Phone: (202) 244-1125

**Military:**
United States Army, (Infantry, Staff Sergeant—
    October 1953–October 1955)

**Nationality:**
Naturalized U.S. citizen (February 26, 1954—Columbia, South Carolina)

**Education:**
George Washington University, Associate in Arts Degree
    (With Distinction), June 1958

Georgetown University School of Medicine, M.D. (Cum Laude),
June 1962

Internship in Medicine, Georgetown University Medical Center,
Washington, DC, 1962–1963

Junior Assistant Medical Resident, Georgetown University Medical
Center, Washington, DC, 1963–1964

Senior Assistant Medical Resident, Georgetown Service, District of
Columbia General Hospital, Washington, DC, 1964–1965.

W. Proctor Harvey Cardiology Fellow, Georgetown University Medical
Center, Washington, DC, 1965–1966.

## Appointments:

Clinical Professor of Medicine, Georgetown University School of
Medicine (October 1985–July 1999)

Clinical Professor Emeritus of Medicine, Georgetown University School
of Medicine (February 10, 2000)

Attending Physician, Department of Medicine, Georgetown University
Medical Center. (July 1966–1999)

Attending Physician, Department of Medicine, Washington Hospital
Center (July 1966–1976)

Courtesy Privileges in Medicine, Sibley Memorial Hospital
(July 1966–1999)

## Fellowships:

Fellow, American College of Physicians, elected 1972

Fellow, American College of Cardiology, elected 1980

Fellow, College of Chest Physicians, elected 1984.

## Professional Society Memberships:

Alpha Omega Alpha Honor Medical Society.

Phi Delta Epsilon Fraternity.

Medical Society of the District of Columbia

American Medical Association

American Society of Internal Medicine

American Heart Association

Academy of Medicine of Washington.

## Boards:

National Board of Medical Examiners of the United States
(Certified March 1964)

American Board of Internal Medicine
(Certified March 1969—Re-certified October 1977)

American Board of Internal Medicine, Sub-specialty in Cardiovascular
Disease, (Certified June 1979)

American Board of Internal Medicine, Advanced Achievement in Internal Medicine (Certified May 1987)

**Awards, Honors And Offices Held:**
Mead Johnson Postgraduate Scholar of the American College of Physicians (July 1964 to June 1965)

Alpha Omega Alpha Honor Medical Society (elected 1962)

Georgetown University School of Medicine, Appointed to Council to the Dean (1977)

Physicians Recognition Award, American Medical Association for Continuing Medical Education (1969–1999)

Vicennial Medal, Georgetown University School of Medicine (1986)

Listed as one of the "Top Washington Physicians" in *The Washingtonian* November 1993 and on previous similar and subsequent surveys

Chairman of the Warwick Evans Society Committee, Georgetown University School of Medicine (June 1992–June 1995)

Elected to Membership into the Cosmos Club (October 1992)

The Founders Award, Georgetown University (1996)

John Carroll Award, Georgetown University Alumni Association (April, 1999)

Elected, Member, Board of Regents, Georgetown University (May 1999; resigned August 1999)

Regional Chairman Medical Alumni Fund, Georgetown University School of Medicine ( July 1, 1991 to June 30, 1992)

National Chairman of the Medical Alumni Annual Fund (July 1993–June 1995)

Elected to Board of Governors, Georgetown University Alumni Association (July,1993)

Elected, Chair Medical Alumni Board, Georgetown University Alumni Association (May 1995)

**Publications:**
O'Rourke, Robert, Oscar Mann, W. Proctor Harvey: "Control of Coronary Pain by Prevention of Tachycardia." *JAMA,* 1964, 188:1005–1007.

Mann, Oscar, A.C. DeLeon, Jr., J.K. Perloff, J. Simanis, F.D. Horrigan: "Duchenne's Muscular Dystrophy: The Electrocardiogram in Female Relatives," *Am. J. Med. Sci.,* 1968, 255:276–281.

Mann, Oscar: "Hyponatremia in Congestive Heart Failure," *G.P.* 1968, 37:108–114.

Ronan, James A. Jr., Joseph K. Perloff, Patrick J. Bowen, Oscar Mann: "The Vectorcardiogram in Duchenne's Progressive Muscular Dystrophy," *Am Heart J.,* 1972, 84:588–596.

Rios, Jorge C., Ross M. Fletcher, Gordon A. Ewy, Oscar Mann: "Electrocardiogram Precursors of Complete Heart Block," *Arizona Medicine*, 1973, 30:164–171.

Garagusi, V.F., L.I. Neefe, Oscar Mann: "Acute Meningo-Encephalitis", *JAMA*, 1976, 235:1141–1142.

Waller, Bruce F., Patrick J. Dean, Oscar Mann, Jeffrey Rosen, William Roberts: "Right Ventricular Outflow Obstruction from Thrombus with Small Peripheral Pulmonary Emboli". *Chest*, 1981. 79:224–225.

Danovitch, Stuart H., Robert Paley, Oscar Mann, Robert Choisser, Theodore Bayless: "Vanishing Pancreas", *JAMA*, 1985. 253:1442–1443 (also published in the Japanese JAMA edition, 1985).

Chester, Alexander C., Frank G. MacMurray, Mary Restifo, Oscar Mann: "Giardiasis as a Chronic Disease". *Digestive Diseases and Sciences*, 1985, 30:215–218.

## Appendix Three

# Physicians Named on the
# Vietnam Veterans Memorial Wall

I. U.S. Army Medical Corps Officers—Battle Casualties (Killed in Action / Died of Wounds)—8
- Delgado, Jose A., Captain, 4th Infantry Division, 25 July 1969, KIA— mine explosion, Binh Dinh, RVN [Republic of Vietnam]
- Gerstel, Howard Martin, Captain, 1st Infantry Division, 4 October 1967, KIA—small arms fire, Binh Duong, RVN
- Lewis, Arthur E., Captain, 25th Infantry Division, 17 May 1966, KIA— mine/grenade, battalion aid station surgeon
- Lokken, Gary Dan, Captain, 14th Engineer Battalion (Combat), 10 April 1968, KIA—mine battalion surgeon (?)
- Shenep, Karl E. Captain, 1st Cavalry Division (Airmobile), 16 April 1967, KIA, small arms fire while passenger in helicopter, ?, RVN
- Singer, Norman Paul, Captain, 18 May 1969, KIA—mortar attack, Long Khanh, RVN
- Sosnoswki, James Francis, Captain, 45th Surgical Hospital (MUST), 16 February 1968, died of wounds—mortar attack, Tay Ninh, RVN
- Wratten, Gary P., Major, Commander, 45th Surgical Hospital (MUST), 4 November 1966, KIA—mortar attack, Tay Ninh, RVN

Disease and Nonbattle Injury Casualties—8
- *Aaron, Richard Alan, Captain, 6 February 1971, American Division, passenger, helicopter crash, Quang Tin, RVN*[1]
- Drewes, Richard Charles, Captain, 17 December 1968, passenger, fixed-wing aircraft crash, Quang Tin, RVN
- Fox, Howard T., Captain, 25 February 1969, died of illness—hepatitis, Pleiku, RVN

- Livingston, Peter Bernard, Captain, 19 November 1968, passenger, helicopter crash
- Philipson, Joseph B., Jr., Captain, 9th Infantry Division, 28 February 1968, died while missing in action (helicopter crash), Long An, RVN
- Quinones-Borras, Nicholas, Major, Special Forces, 16 June 1972, passenger, fixed-wing aircraft crash, Pleiku, RVN
- Stasko, Thomas William, Captain, 3d Field Hospital, 18 February 1966, passenger helicopter crash, near Saigon, RVN (first Medical Corps officer to die in Vietnam)
- Whiteman, William Earl, II, Captain, 299th Engineer Combat Battalion, 19 October 1971, passenger, fixed-wing aircraft crash, Ninh Thuan, RVN

2. U.S. Navy Medical Corps Officers
   - Farrell, Bruce Charles Lieutenant, /03
   - Hyde, Lloyd Patterson Lieutenant, /03
   - Lewis, Stanley Lieutenant /03
   - Saunders, John Lieutenant /03
   - Baker, Curtis Richard Lieutenant /03
   - Griffin, Gerald Charles Lieutenant /03

3. U.S. Air Force Medical Corps Officers
   - Simmons, William Prestwood, Captain, 12 USAF Hospital, South Vietnam, 3 September 1966, near Khanh Hoa, South Vietnam
   - Trickey, Jr., Joe H., Captain, 388 Tactical Dispensary, South Vietnam, 26 November 1966. Lost in crash after takeoff from Tan Son Nhut AB, South Vietnam
   - Fields, Robert Wayne, Captain, 14 USAF Dispensary, Nha Trang Airbase, South Vietnam, 26 March 1969, near Duc My, South Vietnam
   - Jones, Bobby Marvin, Major, 432 USAF Hospital, Udorn Airfield, Thailand, 28 November 1972. Aircraft lost near Danang AB, South Vietnam

The finalized information on the physicians who died in Vietnam represents the fruit of the labor of Sandi Fox, Research Librarian, at *The NewsHour With Jim Lehrer*. She used these sources in her research:

**Websites:**
- Virtual Wall Search: http://www.thevirtualwall.org/search/search_index.htm
- Office of History, Army Surgeon General: see http://history.amedd.army.mil/default_index2.html
- National Archives Record Group 407: Records of the Adjutant General's Office; Series; Data File from the Casualty Information System, 1/1961— 12/1981. http://aad.archives.gov/aad/search.jsp?file_id=534&coll_id-null

- 1st Battalion 50th Infantry Assoc. Vietnam Era Army Military Occupational Specialties http://www.ichibanl.org/htlm/history_mos.ht

**People:**
- Dr. John T. Greenwood, Ph.D. Chief, Office of Medical History, Office of the Surgeon General. 703-681-4598
- Mr. Tom Campbell. Department of Defense, Directorate of Information Operations and Reports (DIOR). 703-604-4576
- Mr. Andre B. Sobocinski. Office of the Historian and Navy Medicine Magazine, Bureau of Medicine and Surgery. 202-762-3244
- Mr. Cliff Snyder, National Archives. Modern Military Records Unit. 301-837-3010
- Dr. James Nanney, Air Force Medical Historian. 202-767-4185

**NOTE**

1. Richard Alan Aaron was my friend—his story appears in chapter 18.

## Appendix Four

# *Leaving Poland* by Oscar Antel[1]

I don't recall all the events leading to my parents' decision to leave their home. I do recall that I was only five years of age in the late 1920s when I began to hear and see unfamiliar whispering and movements about a change in our family life. I recall there was grumbling about ill treatment by the authorities, about Jews being arrested for minor infractions of the law and about a Jewish *macher* who had been paid to go to the police to get someone out of trouble or even to avoid a flogging.[2]

I recall my mother, who ran a store in the market area, letting a Polish peasant into her store on a Sunday and locking the door behind her since it was now forbidden to do business on Sunday. Someone then tipped off the police who padlocked the store for a future arrest or payoff. Talk was that for Jews, the new laws and practices for doing business were deliberately designed to ensure so that Jews could barely eke out a living. Jewish store owners were subject to all kinds of new penalties. In general, conditions for Jewish citizens in our town had become so difficult that my parents, who were part of a large and loving family and actually liked their home, felt forced to think the unthinkable, that is, to consider leaving their home.

Leaving home meant decisions had to be made, including leaving an aging mother (my grandmother), whose whole life revolved around her son's family and her grandchildren. It also meant making plans for her to follow in the future, if at all possible.

Leaving Poland was not easy. It was in a way a Catch 22. Poland neither wanted its Jews, nor did it want the Jews to leave. There was a price to be paid and there were officials ready to make it difficult and to see that they were included on the receiving end of the price. The chosen country for the new home, in this case Canada, would not easily receive Jewish immigrants in

1929, and immigration had to be very carefully arranged. Other members of the family were consulted on how they would explain your absence, and plans had to be made for how those who would follow and to which countries they would go. My father explained to me, much later in life, that they already had the feeling of impending doom, but they did not know exactly who the worst enemy would be. They did, however, have no doubt about who would be the first victims.

My father slipped out of the *shtetl* of Dombrovitz quietly (people thought he went to Rovno to purchase merchandise for his dry goods store).[3] My mother and her two children, Shirley and I, were to follow a year later, and my grandmother, who lived with us, would do so at the same time, if possible or as soon thereafter as could be arranged. My aunt, Hinda, and her husband to be, Aaron, were to leave for France to join my younger uncle, Motel, who had already left for Paris.[4] This was all done so that all of us could eventually reunite in Canada, but all agreed that it was crucial to leave Poland while leaving was still possible.

My father arrived in Canada in 1929, not a good time for newcomers. The economy was bad, and getting work was not easy. The priority was a job of any kind, to earn enough to send tickets home for wife and children.

My dad worked as a presser. Canadians must have set a record for wearing pants pressed by those who starved themselves to save enough from their below-minimum wage to bring their families and settle them in the new country. This became a matter of even greater urgency, since the immigration laws were closing Canada's borders to newcomers, more particularly those from Eastern Europe, and most especially Jews.

My mother, my sister, and I came in 1930; my grandmother, as well as my aunt and uncle, who were to follow from France, did not make the immigration deadline. Since efforts to bring them were delayed, they suffered the same fate as the rest of our large family and the Jews of Europe during the *Shoah*.

The year before we arrived, my father wrote my mother to keep me in a *cheder* for the year because once we arrived in Canada, we would be receiving secular Yiddish education, as was his choice, and he wanted me to have a memory of the *Shtetl cheder*[5].

After a year, we said our goodbyes. This included very emotional trips to surrounding towns where my mother said goodbyes to her brothers and sisters and to my grandmother. The clouds of impending things, not too difficult for some to guess, were still vague enough so that not everyone cut the cord and left, even had it been possible for everyone to do so.

We left Dombrowitz by train and were joined by my uncle in Rovna. He would accompany us to a ship in Gdansk.[6] During our stopover in Rovna, we were inspected by an eye doctor who recommended expensive treatment for a few weeks. My father had warned us in advance to disregard any such suggestions along the way. Immigrants, since they proceeded with fear along the entire route, were being taken advantage of everywhere.

In Danzig, we made our way from one emigration office to another. There were so many procedures involving papers for leaving. In Danzig, we saw airplanes doing military maneuvers over the city. This was 1930, and already the fear of things to come was in the air. Also in Danzig, immigrant children and young people suffered humiliating procedures such as delousing and head-shaving. We discovered later that much of this harassment was unnecessary but, at the time, that was the treatment administered especially to people from eastern Europe. We finally went through another emotional experience of saying goodbye to my uncle ignoring the feeling that we might be the last survivors of the family.[7]

Once aboard ship, life settled down for the long trip. The food was comparatively good, if one could keep it down. We did not travel in first class, but the experience was not bad. Everyone, except for the children, suffered from seasickness during the whole voyage. But the passengers were relieved that they were on their way to a new land, and we, of course, were pleased to be joining our father.

We traveled from Halifax to Winnipeg by train. The trains were crowded. We did not travel in luxury. The seats faced each other, however, and we quite comfortably could sleep by putting our luggage between the seats and covering our suitcases with pillows and blankets. We purchased food from the "newsies" on the trains and from stores at the station stopovers.[8] At the larger cities and towns, Jewish immigrant-aid people would board and explain things and provide comfort. By now, all the other immigrant passengers were *shifbridder,* one family, which would remain so forever in Winnipeg.[9] We entertained and encouraged each other; everyone was lonely for those left behind, but we looked forward to seeing those who had gone before.

We finally arrived. This was to be our home. I doubt if anyone could think of it as home right away. It would take years. My father and some of his friends and *landsleit* met us.[10] It was very emotional. Then, we took our first streetcar ride from the station to our new home.

My father lived with a family who became lifelong friends. Our first week was spent with them as renters, and then we looked for larger quarters.

There followed a series of moves for our family of four—mother, father, myself (then 7) and my sister (then 4). The first was a move into the house of a nice family on Magnus Avenue; they were certainly pleased to have the rent. They gave up two upstairs rooms for us. This was a crowded arrangement, but we were made welcome and felt comfortable. At this time we enrolled at the

*Peretz School*, a day school. Learning English took a few months. The teachers understood our needs, but it took a little while longer to be accepted by fellow students, some of whom considered us "greenhorns." My closest friends today are people who shared that first year of school with me. I can still remember those who gave me a rough time because I was different. Throughout the ensuing years, I remained connected to the school, the teachers and the families who were active in the school.

My father became a partner in the fruit business with an immigrant friend from Dombrowitz, which prompted a move to quarters above the business on Selkirk Avenue and then to King Street. All these places were far from the school, but we walked back and forth in all kinds of weather, including some very wintry cold days. We moved several more times to Manitoba Avenue, Flora Avenue, and back to Manitoba. During that period, I entered Aberdeen School since Peretz School went only to the end of grade five.

Enrollment in public school was a big change. I now confronted a new culture, new teachers and new friends. They saw the country and the home I lived in differently than I did. My approach to history, literature and social awareness was also different from theirs. I believe that my experiences in a Jewish day school made my adjustment easier, rather than harder, since I had an understanding of my own culture with a pride that understood and matched theirs. I attended Aberdeen School and Isaac Newton High School, while going to evening classes in the higher grades at the Peretz School.

Differences between ethnic groups were very marked. Anti-Semitism existed on different levels from various ethnic groups. Pluralism was a fact, but it was not yet a factor in better relationships among Canadians. But friendships between us and our neighbors and fellow students were being made, and when we look back today on our neighbors, business associates and colleagues, we see some things that could not be understood in our early years.

## NOTES

1. My cousin from Winnipeg, Canada.

2. As defined earlier (Chapter 7), a *macher* is a "maker" or "doer." The Yiddish term denotes a broker, facilitator or middleman.

3. *Shtetl* is a Yiddish word typically describing a small Jewish rural village.

4. Hinda and her husband, Aaron, were the future parents of Oscar and John Mann. Also see the story of Maurice Biegun in Chapter 3 and 7.

5. *Cheder* is a Yiddish word for an early school where Hebrew, Yiddish and religion were taught.

6. "The port city of *Danzig* (now *Gdansk*) was designated a "free city" following the First World War. The city's status was addressed in one of Woodrow Wilson's

Fourteen Points. The Germans always regarded it as properly belonging to Germany. By 1933, there was a large and active Nazi party in *Danzig*, agitating for Germany's interests. This was the pretext for Hitler's demands against Poland. When WW II began, there was some fighting in other parts of Poland, but *Danzig* "fell" on September 1, 1939, the very first day of the war. It was simply taken over without any significant resistance." Personal communication from Richard Rivers, November, 2003.

 7. He and his immediate family perished in the Holocaust.

 8. "Newsies" were men who held concessions from the railroad companies to ride with the train and go up and down the passenger cars, selling newspapers, drinks, chocolates, sandwiches, and whatever else they thought could be sold to the passengers.

 9. Yiddish word for fellow travelers on a ship.

 10. Yiddish word for countrymen who came from the same area.

# Bibliography

Ambrose, Stephen E. *The Supreme Commander: The War Years of General Dwight D. Eisenhower.* New York: Doubleday,1955.

Barry, Patricia. *Surgeons at Georgetown.* Franklin, Tennessee: Hillsboro Press, 2001.

Braudel, Fernand. *The Wheels of Commerce.* Paris: Librairie Armand Colin, 1979.

Brody, Jeanne. *Rue des Rosiers: une manière d'être juif.* Paris: Editions Autrement, 1995.

Byron, Paula (ed.). "The Art of Touch in Healing", *Harvard Medical Alumni Bulletin* 76, no 3 (Winter, 2003).

Chizner, Michael A. (ed.). *Classic Teachings in Cardiology: A Tribute to W. Proctor Harvey, M.D.* Newton, New Jersey: Laënnec Publishing, 1996.

Costa, Bernadette. *Je me souviens du Marais.* Paris: Parigramme, 1995.

Eban, Abba. *Heritage: Civilization and the Jews.* New York: Summit Books,1984.

*Grand Rounds, 1954.* Joseph S. Costa, M.D. (Ed), Washington: Georgetown University School of Medicine: Class of 1954.

*Grand Rounds,1962.* Washington: The Georgetown University School of Medicine, 1962.

W. Proctor Harvey, *et al. Cardiac Pearls.* Newton, New Jersey: Laënnec Publishing; 1993.

Harvey, W. Proctor and Samuel Levine. *Clinical Auscultation of the Heart.* Philadelphia: WB Saunders, 1959.

Kaplan, Alice. *The Collaborator: The Trial and Execution of Robert Brasillach.* Chicago: University of Chicago, 2000.

Klarsfeld, Serge. *French Children of the Holocaust—A Memorial.* New York: New York University Press, 1996.

———. *Memorial to the Jews Deported from France, 1942–1944.* New York: The Beate Klarsfeld Foundation, 1983.

Laënnec, R.T.H. "Stéthescope: Son origine, Description de la découverte," *Traité de l'auscultation médiate et des maladies des poumons et du coeur.* Paris: Brosson, 1819.

March, S. Kimara "W. Proctor Harvey, Master Clinician-Teacher," *Texas Heart Institute Journal* 2002; 29:182–92.

Marrus, Michael R. and Robert O. Paxton. *Vichy France and the Jews.* New York: Basic Books, 1981.

Schoettler, Carl. "A Voyage of the Heart". *Baltimore Sun,* August 6, 1998.

Shirer, William L. *The Rise and Fall of the Third Reich: A History of Nazi Germany.* New York: Simon and Schuster, 1959.

Stapleton, John. "Oscar Mann, M.D.—Blending Science with Empathy". *Georgetown Medical Bulletin*, Vol. 45, Issue 1, Winter/Spring, 1993.

Stapleton, John F. *Upward Journey.* Washington: Georgetown University, 1996.

Todorov, Tzvetan. *A French Tragedy, Scenes of Civil War, Summer 1944.* Hanover, New Hampshire: Dartmouth College, 1996.

Tyrrell, Jr., R. Emmett. "Faithless France". *The American Prowler.* Http://TheAmericanProwler.org, April 5, 2002.